LIVES OF
THE POPES

LIVES OF THE POPES

ILLUSTRATED BIOGRAPHIES OF EVERY POPE FROM
St PETER TO THE PRESENT

CONSULTANT EDITOR: MICHAEL J. WALSH

BARNES
&NOBLE
BOOKS
NEW YORK

This edition published by Barnes & Noble, Inc.,
by arrangement with Salamander Books Ltd.

9 8 7 6 5 4 3 2 1

© 1998 Salamander Books Ltd

ISBN 0-7607-0802-9

All correspondence concerning the content of this book should be addressed to Salamander Books Ltd., 8 Blenheim Court, Brewery Road, London N7 9NT, United Kingdom

Credits

Editors: Dennis Cove, Richard and Amanda O'Neill
Designers: John Heritage, Graham Mitchener and Vicky Zentner
Indexer: Richard O'Neill
Color and monochrome reproductions: Dah Hua Printing Press Co. Ltd, China
Filmset: SX Composing DTP, England

Printed in China

Consultant Editor

Michael J. Walsh is a distinguished Roman Catholic historian and writer. His numerous books include *Vatican City State*, *Roots in Christianity* and *Pope John Paul II: A Biography.* In addition he has edited several journals and contributed to both the Catholic and the mainstream press. A former Jesuit, he is currently Librarian at Heythrop College, University of London.

Contributors

Dr Peter Clarke is a Fellow of the British Academy, specializing in Religious History.

Peter Duskin is Head of the Department of History, St Joseph's College, London.

Dr G. R. Evans is Senior Lecturer in the Faculty of History, University of Cambridge.

Anthony Levi is Professor of French at the University of St Andrews, specializing in Religious History.

Andrew Louth is Professor of Theology at the University of Durham.

Dr Richard Price is Head of the Department of Church History at Heythrop College, University of London, specializing in the Early Church.

Dr Oliver Rafferty is Lecturer in Modern History, University of Oxford.

Dr Diana Wood is a former Lecturer in History at the University of East Anglia.

Prelim Captions
Page 1: St Francis and Honorius III
Pages 3-4: Entrance to the Sistine Chapel
Page 5: Gregory the Great

CONTENTS

INTRODUCTION

THERE IS A PASSAGE FROM Thomas Babington Macaulay's essay on Leopold von Ranke's *The Ecclesiastical and Political History of the Popes of Rome* which is known to almost every British or Irish – and possibly American – Roman Catholic of a certain age. The essay appeared in the October 1840 edition of *The Edinburgh Review*, but it is known to Catholics because it was quoted in *Apologetics and Catholic Doctrine* by Monsignor M. Sheehan, a book once much used in the religious instruction classes of Catholic schools. "The proudest royal houses are but of yesterday", wrote Lord Macaulay, "when compared with the line of Supreme Pontiffs. That line we trace back in an unbroken series, from the Pope who crowned Napoleon in the nineteenth century to the Pope who crowned Pepin in the eighth; and far beyond the time of Pepin the August dynasty extends, till it is lost in the twilight of fable." Macaulay goes on to reflect that the Catholic Church "may still exist in undiminished vigour when some traveller from New Zealand shall, in the midst of a vast solitude, take his stand on a broken arch of London Bridge to sketch the ruins of St Pauls." Now, well over a century and a half since

Left: Baldacchino altar canopy *by Bernini. Built of bronze, it was begun in 1624 and inaugurated by Urban VIII in 1633. The altar below is by Maderno.*
Below: The Pope at work, *with Swiss Guards. The Swiss Guards are the only remaining section of the papal armed corps, which was disbanded by Paul VI.*

those words were written, the papacy not only still survives but, in the pontificate of John Paul II, has probably achieved greater prominence in world affairs than ever before.

There are many histories of the papacy. This is not another one. At least, not exactly. Instead it is a biographical dictionary of the Popes arranged in chronological, rather than in alphabetical, order. It can be read consecutively, but it is designed for readers to consult Pope by Pope rather than for them to read it through from cover to cover. It is also about Popes, rather than about the men who became Popes. Although individuals who were elected to the office of Pope may have had an interesting career before they were chosen, little will be found about the earlier part of their lives. It also says very little about antipopes, except for the period when it was not always clear who was the rightful claimant to the throne of Peter. However, because it is not a history book in the

usual sense, there are some facts about the papacy which may not emerge, or be obvious, from the story as it unfolds in these pages.

The first of these is the title itself. The term "Pope" comes from a Greek word meaning "father". It was, and still is, used in the Eastern part of the Christian Church as an honorific title for a parish priest, rather as, in the Western tradition, many clergy are called "father". It was, and again still is, used also of the Patriarch of Alexandria. In the Western Church, however, from the sixth century it came increasingly to be used solely of the Bishop of Rome, and in the *Dictatus Papae* Pope Gregory VII, who reigned from 1073 to 1085, seems to have insisted that the title be used of the Bishop of Rome and of no-one else, though by that time he was only laying down in law what had in any case become the custom throughout the Western Church – "Western" because by then the Western, or Latin-using, Church had separated definitively from the Eastern, or generally Greek-speaking, Church.

The story of this gradual separation, and then of occasional vain attempts at reunion, is one of the themes of the history of the papacy. Yet to understand it one has to begin with the earliest structures of the Church as it developed from New Testament times onward.

I said above that the Pope is the Bishop of Rome. That is to say, when someone is elected to that office, technically his task is to run the diocese of the city of Rome, and the person holding that office was recognized, certainly until the Reformation, as having a form of "primacy" over the whole of Christendom. What precisely that primacy meant has long been debated, but it was formally accepted at the first general gathering of bishops of the Church, the Council of Nicaea held in 325, that the three most important bishoprics, or Sees (from the Latin *sedes* or seat, meaning the place where the bishop resided), had an undefined authority over the others in their territory. These were Alexandria, Antioch, and Rome. Of these three, the bishopric of Rome had precedence.

But then, in 330, Constantine, the first Christian Emperor, moved the capital of the Roman Empire from Rome to the Greek city of Byzantium. It was renamed Constantinople and is now called Istanbul. Obviously, this altered the political balance of power within the Empire as the focus shifted eastward, but it also altered the ecclesiastical balance of power as well, though not quite as dramatically as might have been expected. When a council met at Constantinople in 381 honorary precedence was granted to the Empire's new capital over all other Sees except that of Rome itself. Roman legates did not attend, nor did any Western bishop, but Rome was not happy at this rise in status of its rival. However, the decision was confirmed at the Council of Chalcedon in 451, when it was asserted that Constantinople deserved its prominence after Rome due to its political importance within the Empire.

That was precisely the principle which the Bishops of Rome did not like. They based their claim to their See's primacy over all the other churches because the Church of Rome had been founded by Peter, the

Left: Chapel at the Tomb of St Peter. *The papal altar is situated exactly above the Tomb, where St Peter was buried after he suffered martyrdom under Nero.*
Right: Michelangelo's Pieta, *St Peter's. Completed in 1500 when Michelangelo was only twenty-five years old, it is the only work to bear his signature.*

Left: Crowds gather in St Peter's Square *to join with Pope John Paul II in celebrating in the Day of the Family, 8th October, 1994.*
Above: Pope Paul VI *addresses the world from the balcony of St Peter's. St Peter's Square below holds 300,000 people and covers 70,000 square yards.*

leader of the Apostles, and co-founded by the Apostle Paul. Around the time of the Council of Constantinople the theory began circulating that Alexandria and Antioch deserved their leading status because they, too, had in some way been founded by Peter.

But was it true that Peter had founded the Christian Church in Rome? It is not now much disputed that St Peter went to Rome and died there, probably in the persecution of Christians by the Emperor Nero. Nero made them the scapegoats for the fire which destroyed much of the city in 64 AD, though he had probably started the fire himself so he could rebuild Rome in accordance with his own tastes. It even seems likely that the present basilica of St Peter – the first was built by Constantine, and survived, much modified, until the sixteenth century – stands over the grave on the Vatican hill which had once held the bones of the Apostle to whom, according to St Matthew's Gospel, Christ had said, "You are Peter, and upon this rock I will build my Church" (the name "Peter" means "rock"). These words are inscribed around the cupola which stands over Peter's tomb. The confessio before the papal altar in the basilica leads down to the place where Peter was buried.

It is clear from the New Testament, however, that before Peter arrived at the capital of the Empire a Christian community must already have existed. He did not found it. And although the Vatican's yearbook, and most other Catholic reference books, includes Peter as the first "Bishop of Rome", he was certainly not a bishop as that term has come to be understood. The "single bishop" system of Church government did not emerge until the very end of the first Christian century, and then in Asia Minor. It did not become the norm at Rome, it seems, until around the middle of the second century. It nonetheless fairly soon became evident that the Bishop of Rome was regarded as having a special authority, though an authority which was in no way defined, with regards to the other Christian churches. Indeed, there is evidence from about 96 AD, contained in what is known as the *First Letter of Clement*, that the Church in Rome thought it had some kind of oversight of other churches even before the "monarchical episcopacy" came into being.

That is the background to the contest for "primacy" between the major Churches of the early Christian world. From the sixth century onward the heads of these Churches – Rome, Constantinople,

Alexandria, Antioch and Jerusalem – have been called "patriarchs": the Bishop of Rome is the Patriarch of the West, though it is a title which is rarely used. Largely as a result of the rise of Islam, the significance of the Patriarchs of Alexandria, Antioch and Jerusalem diminished from the seventh century onward, though the titles themselves survived, and are in use to this day. The use of the term "Patriarch" has more recently been extended to the heads of other independent Churches within the Orthodox tradition, most particularly perhaps of the Patriarch of Moscow, a title granted to that See by the Patriarch of Constantinople toward the end of the sixteenth century. Moscow is sometimes referred to as "the third Rome", third after Rome and Constantinople. But the Patriarch of Constantinople remained as titular head of the Churches of the East (the "Orthodox" Churches) and the Bishop of Rome as head of the Church in the West. Relations between them are a recurring theme in this book.

Even this brief history of the early origins of the notion of papal primacy shows that the Roman pontiffs did not exercize the same degree of authority in the Church from one century to the next. Some apologists for Roman Catholicism tend to present papal authority as something that developed steadily, winning ever greater recognition in the West while it was contested in the – in their eyes less important – East. This book will demonstrate that papal authority, papal control over the Churches in the West, quite apart from authority over those in what was the Eastern half of the Roman Empire, waxed and waned. Pope Innocent III, who died in 1216, undoubtedly exercized more authority over the Church, and even over kings and emperors, than did his successors two centuries later. Then, during the "Great Schism" (1378–1417) there were first two rival Popes, and later three, competing for recognition.

C.S. Lewis once wrote that "the unhistorical, without knowing it, are usually enslaved to a fairly recent past", and many people's image of the papacy is one which has been formed in the nineteenth century. Yet even then the development of doctrine about the papacy did not proceed smoothly. In a small book entitled *Controversial Catechism: or, Protestantism Refuted*, the author, Father Stephen Keenan, wrote:

Q. Must not Catholics believe the Pope in himself to be infallible?
A. That is a Protestant invention; it is no article of the Catholic faith.

Fr Keenan's book was published in its third edition in Dublin in 1854, only just over a quarter of a century, in other words, before the doctrine of papal infallibility was defined at the first Vatican Council as a truth to be held as an article of faith by all Catholics.

With the late nineteenth and twentieth-century model of the papacy in one's mind, it is difficult to imagine what it would have been like in the seventeenth century, let alone the seventh. The office of the papacy tended to mirror the form of secular government at any particular era, so Popes were in turn Italian dukes, feudal monarchs, renaissance

Left: Interior of St Peter's basilica. *The dome was designed by Michelangelo but when he died in 1564, work was taken over by Fontana. It was completed in 1590.*
Right: The grand spiral stairway *at the entrance to the Vatican Museums. Millions of visitors come to the Vatican each year to admire the incomparable works of art.*

princes. Though today the Pope rules over only the Vatican City State, the world's smallest independent country by far. At one time he ruled with secular authority over great tracts of Italy, and even over part of what is now France: the vineyards which produce Châteauneuf-du-pape are not named after the "Pope's new castle" by chance. It is impossible to understand much of the history of the papacy unless it is remembered that the Popes had territorial interests to defend, as well as – or in some cases even more than – spiritual ones. Pope Alexander VI, the Borgia Pope at the end of the fifteenth century (he died in 1503), was unabashedly more concerned with advancing the interests of his family than he was with advancing the spiritual agenda of the Church over which he ruled.

As will be seen from the biographies which follow this introduction, the election of the Bishop of Rome has frequently been vigorously disputed, sometimes even to the shedding of blood. The election of Pope Damasus in 366, for instance, was reported to have left 137 dead in the Liberian basilica, now Sta Maria Maggiore, where supporters of his rival had taken refuge. At this time the choice of a bishop still lay in the power of the local community, though quite possibly the clergy played a prominent part in the process of decision-making, and, too, the laity who were involved belonged to the upper classes of society, rather than being representative of the community in general.

One thing that will be noticed in many of the entries in this book is that there was, especially in the first millennium of Christianity, quite a long gap between the election of a Pope and his consecration. Until the sixteenth century it was held that whoever had been chosen became the Bishop of Rome through the exercize of that choice. In other words, he did not have to wait until his consecration as bishop, or, if already a bishop, his installation, to take over his office. This was quite important, because, often, the newly-elected bishop needed the approval of the Emperor in Constantinople before he could be consecrated. And that approval could be a long time in coming – though sometimes it was given by the imperial representative in Italy, the Exarch, based in Ravenna. Later on approval was needed of an Emperor who might very well be in Germany or elsewhere.

The notion that the election of a new Bishop of Rome lies in the hands of the cardinals, as it does today, was a long time developing. To understand how it came about, one needs to know who "cardinals" are. The name undoubtedly comes from the Latin *cardo*, meaning a hinge, but its precise significance in this instance, why the term was used, has been lost. The cardinals were the priests in charge of Rome's major churches (these were "cardinal priests"), or were cardinal bishops in charge of the dioceses around the city (the "subicarian" Sees), of which the most important by far is that of Ostia. As well as bishops and priests there were also cardinal deacons, people who were the Bishop of Rome's representatives in administrative matters, especially in welfare. It was very common in the early middle ages to elect as bishop one of the deacons, rather than a priest, possibly as the deacons were better known, and perhaps because they were more powerful figures in the politics of the city. Later on, it was often a former "apocrisarius"(the Pope's ambassador in Constantinople) who was selected.

Left: Ordination of new priests *in St Peter's. The photograph gives an indication of the immense scale of the basilica, which rises to 430 feet at the dome's zenith.*
Below: Concert for the 200th anniversary of Mozart's death, *in the Audience Hall. Built by Pier Luigi Nervi, the Hall can seat seven thousand people.*

In the first millennium of the papacy there were no "conclaves" as these are now known. *"Con clave"* means "with a key", and implies that those who gather to elect a Pope are locked up in a confined space. This first happened in 1241, on the death of Pope Gregory IX. Gregory, it was reported, was afraid that the cardinals were so divided that it would take too long to elect a successor. He therefore summoned to his deathbed the leading layman in Rome, and instructed him to lock up all the cardinals until they had reached a decision – this was advice that an English professor of canon law had once given him. This suggestion was carried out with enthusiasm. The cardinals were promptly arrested after Gregory had died, and immured within a crumbling palace called the Septzonium, together with the coffin of the late Pontiff. There they were subjected to all kinds of discomforts: one cardinal died during his incarceration. They still, however, took two months to make their choice, and even then it was a compromise: they chose someone so old and ill that he died within a month of being elected. But this ruse had freed the electors to carry out their subsequent deliberations in greater comfort.

This implies that the electors were, by this time, only the cardinals. The significance of the laity in choosing Rome's bishop rose, fell and rose again, but a decree by Pope Nicholas II in 1059 gave the task of drawing up a list of candidates to the cardinal bishops, and of election to all

the cardinals, yet the assent of the lower clergy, and of the laity, was still to be sought. A Lateran synod in 1130 gave entire authority to the cardinals, and in 1179 a Lateran Council laid down that the majority in favor of a candidate had to be two-thirds – which is still the case today.

Nowadays the cardinals who choose a new Pope – cardinals under eighty years old – are all bishops. But though they may have a diocese over which they rule in some part of the world, they still have a "title" to a Church in Rome, or to one of the subicarian bishoprics, so that the Pope is still, by a fiction, elected by the clergy of the city. They are very unlikely to choose anyone but one of their number. This has not always been the case, and occasionally they have even chosen a man who was not even yet a priest, let alone a bishop, to become Bishop of Rome.

Elections now are always held in the Sistine Chapel within the Vatican palace, but again, it has not always been the case that elections were held in Rome. Sometimes the political situation in the city was too volatile for the cardinals to gather there, or, frequently, the papal court was elsewhere – in Avignon, for instance, during most of the fourteenth century. In any case, the Vatican has been the usual papal residence only since the return from Avignon. Before that when the Pope was in Rome he normally lived in the Lateran, the palace-cum-basilica, which had once, in imperial Roman times, belonged to the Laterani family and had been given to the Pope by Constantine. It is the basilica of St John Lateran, and not St Peter's, that is the cathedral of the city of Rome.

What else Constantine gave to the Popes of his day, and in particular to Pope St Sylvester (314-335) was one of the great topics of debate in the middle ages. The "donation of Constantine" was a document of uncertain age and provenance, though it probably came from the Frankish Empire in the 8th or 9th centuries. It became embodied in the Church's law, and was regarded as authoritative. It justified the papal primacy over the other major Sees, and gave him civil authority over most of Italy. The real donor to the Roman Church of the lands it controlled, more or less, until the coming of Napoleon (and which were largely, with the exception of those in France, restored to it at the Congress of Vienna in 1815) was Pepin, who became King of the Franks in 751. In the aftermath of the Congress of Vienna the Papal States in

Above left: The Osservatore Romano, *founded in 1861, is the Holy See's daily newspaper, published every day except Sunday and carrying official news.*
Above: The Vatican State Post Office. *The Vatican City has its own postal service and issues its own stamps. It also has its own coinage.*
Right: The Vatican Gardens *are situated northwest of the building complex, within walls built by Paul III, Pius IV and Urban VIII between 1550 and 1640.*

the Italian peninsular were gradually lost to the new Kingdom of Italy: Rome itself fell in 1870, and Pope Pius IX became "the prisoner of the Vatican". This situation was resolved in 1929 with the establishment of the Vatican City State, which now serves as the Pope's headquarters.

The status of the Vatican City State is much misunderstood. It is not because the Pope is at its head that he receives and sends ambassadors (or nuncios). Rather oddly, it is the Holy See itself, the administrative structure of the Church, with the Pope at its apex, which is the important sovereign entity, and is recognized as such in international law. It is a kind of juridical persona, which has its seat in the Vatican City State, but is independent of it. It could be anywhere.

However, the Pope is Pope because he is Bishop of Rome. He may be an Italian, and for some five hundred years before the election of the Polish Pope John Paul II, always was. But before that there had been Germans, Spaniards, even a solitary Englishman. They may not always have lived in Rome, but that city was the basis of their authority. The way that authority functioned tended to reflect, without being identical with, the type of secular government in vogue at the time.

Recently, the international community has seen the emergence of world leaders, people whose authority, if not their political base, has reached around the world. Politics, like the market, has been "globalized". And so, under Pope John Paul II, has the papacy. Not all Roman Catholics are happy about this. Certainly, there is as yet no developed theory of the Church which supports such a role. Rome, it has been said, needs a bishop, and there are some who would like to encourage any future Pope to give more time to that aspect of his post. The papacy is an office which has changed vastly over two millennia. One can be sure that it will go on doing so for generations to come.

CHRONOLOGICAL BIOGRAPHIES OF THE POPES

❖

Left: Christ and the Keys
The keys to the kingdom of heaven were symbolic of the power vested in Peter as the first "Pope", and keys remain an important part of papal imagery.

St PETER
Papacy: 33 to c.64 AD

All three Synoptic Gospels tell of how Peter, originally called Simon, dramatically forsook his nets and boat to follow Jesus, who promised to make him "a fisher of men" (Mk 1:16–18). Peter is recorded as saying to Jesus, "Lord, we have left everything and followed you" (Mk 10:28), but in other texts he appears as the head of a household, with a house and wife, who accompanied him later on his missionary journeys. He is placed first in the Gospel lists of the twelve disciples. He was indeed the first of the disciples to recognize Jesus as the Christ, in return for which Jesus gave him the name of "Cephas" (in Greek "Peter", meaning the "Rock"), adding, "On this rock I will build my Church" (Mt 16:18) – a saying which has been interpreted in the Catholic Church since the third century to provide Scripture warrant for the primacy of the Pope as the successor of Peter. Peter's threefold denial of Christ during Christ's trial is balanced in the Gospel of John by a threefold commission from Christ to feed his sheep (21:17). The picture in the Gospels of an impulsive Peter, whose failings were made up for by the intensity of his love for Christ, makes him one of the most vivid and attractive personalities in the New Testament.

In the early chapters of the Acts of the Apostles Peter is represented as the leader of the original Christian community in Jerusalem, but later on he was eclipsed by James: it was James who took the lead at the Council of Jerusalem (Acts 15), and it was out of fear of James that, on a visit to Antioch, Peter ceased eating with Gentiles, despite the keen indignation of St Paul (Gal 2:11–14). But whatever his standing in Jerusalem, Peter obtained a wider glory as an outstanding missionary, active in Antioch (Gal 2:11), Asia Minor (1 Pet 1:1), Corinth (1 Cor 1:12), and Rome (1 Pet 5:13). His death as a martyr, referred to in John's Gospel (21:19), is unanimously located in Rome by reliable tradition, as is likewise the martyrdom of St Paul. Literary sources from c.200 locate the tomb of St Peter on the Vatican Hill. Excavations in the 1940s confirm that there was a shrine to St Peter from the middle of the second century immediately under the great high altar of the present-day St Peter's. The contrast between the extremely modest second-century shrine and the magnificent architecture of Michelangelo is the most telling visual symbol of

Above: Christ Delivers the Keys to Peter. *Peter was the first of the disciples to recognize Jesus as the Christ and it was Peter who was chosen as the "Rock" on which Christ would build his Church on earth.*

Left: Peter's Denial of Christ. *During Christ's trial Peter denied knowing Christ three times, as foretold by Christ. This act, and his subsequent repentance, shows Peter as an impulsive person with human failings counterbalanced by his intense love for Christ.*

the growth over the centuries of the power and prestige of the Holy See.

The apocryphal Acts of Peter tell how he was persuaded to flee from Rome to escape martyrdom, but was shamed into returning by a vision of Christ, who said to him, "I am going to Rome to be crucified again." The Acts narrate how he insisted on being crucified head downward, as being unworthy of too close an imitation of Our Lord's Passion, and that he died praying to Christ as his "father, mother, brother, friend, servant and steward." These legends are true to the Peter of the Gospels and, although not proven conclusively, these traditions would seem to be supported by modern scholarship.

Can Peter be called the first Pope? Already at the beginning of the second century it was presumed that Peter and Paul had exerted authority together in Rome (*Ignatius*, Rom. 4.2). But the earliest lists of Bishops of Rome (notably Irenaeus 3.3.3, from the end of the second century) do not attribute the title of bishop to either Peter or Paul. It was the fact that these, the greatest of the apostles, consecrated Rome with their blood, rather than guesswork as to their precise role among the Roman Christians, that was the foundation of the unique standing of the Roman See throughout later centuries.

Above: The Crucifixion of St Peter. *Peter insisted on being crucified head downward as he felt unworthy of being martyred in the same fashion as Jesus Christ. Traditionally throughout Christian history Peter has been venerated as the first Pope of the Catholic Church, although it is unlikely that such a title was introduced until later.*

Above: **St Linus** *followed St Peter as leader of the early Christian church. However, early records of dates for his "papacy" must be seen as unreliable.*

Below: **St Paul** *was probably the most influential figure after Christ in the early church. His epistles formed the basis of Christian thought for every succeeding generation.*

St LINUS
(Elected c.64; died c.76)

St Linus' first appearance in history is as one of the companions of St Paul during his first captivity in Rome (2 Tim 4:21). By the end of the second century Linus was recognized as the first Bishop of Rome, appointed by Saints Peter and Paul; lists that go back to early in the third century, and are our source for the dates of the early Popes, assign him an episcopacy of twelve years. The *Liber Pontificalis* (a sixth-century dictionary of Popes) attributes to him particular concern that women in church should have their heads covered.

The "episcopacy" of Linus is open to some doubt. Modern scholarship agrees, however, that the system of having a single Bishop (so-called "monarchical episcopacy") did not become established in Rome till at least the middle of the second century. Before then, there were a number of officials called indifferently Bishops or presbyters, each (we may presume) in charge of a house church serving one group of Christian immigrants in the city; it was the large number of such immigrant communities, and their tendency to look for leadership to their home churches rather than to bishops in Rome, that delayed the development of monarchical episcopacy. This does not mean, however, that the lists of early bishops are to be dismissed as fiction. There is evidence for regular meetings of the presbyter-bishops, and such meetings are inconceivable without a chairman. It would be anachronistic to refer to Linus and his immediate successors as "Popes", but they may genuinely have enjoyed preeminence above the other presbyter-bishops in Rome.

St CLETUS
(Elected c.76; died c.88)

The early episcopal lists name Cletus (or Anacletus, or Anencletus) as Linus' successor with a twelve-year term of office. The variety in the forms of his name led some early papal lists to name Cletus and Anacletus as two distinct Popes.

St CLEMENT
(Elected c.88; died c.97)

Clement is referred to by the Roman prophet Hermas as the official who wrote letters on behalf of the Roman Church to other Churches. One of these letters survives: the (First) *Letter of Clement to the Corinthians*. It is written in the name of "the Church of God which sojourns in Rome", not of Clement personally; but early and reliable tradition names Clement as the author. This letter rebukes the Corinthians for deposing some of their presbyters (or bishops), and appeals to principles of hierarchy and orderly government revealed both in the natural order of the universe and in revelation. One of the great texts of early Christianity, this letter, a masterpiece both of homiletics and of practical diplomacy, was accorded in the early Church an authority only inferior to Scripture itself. It is the first known case of the Roman Church exercising a pastoral responsibility over other churches.

Clement's reputation is confirmed by the development from the middle of the second century of a mass of apocryphal literature, largely of Syrian origin, claiming his authorship. A legend developed that he was exiled to the Crimea and there died a martyr. His supposed relics were returned to Rome by Saints Cyril and Methodius eight centuries later, and buried in the Church of San Clemente, which still contains ninth-century frescoes depicting the legend of the saint.

St EVARISTUS
(Elected c.97; died c.105)

Apart from his appearance in the oldest lists of the Bishops of Rome, nothing certain is known about him. His name suggests Greek origin, which is scarcely surprising, since most of the early Christians in Rome were of Greek or near-Eastern origin, and Greek remained the chief language of the Roman see till the middle of the third century.

St ALEXANDER I
(Elected c.105; died c.115)

As in the case of Evaristus, the inclusion of this utterly obscure figure in the oldest lists of Roman bishops argues for the lists' authenticity. The *Liber Pontificalis* attributes to him the inclusion of reference to the Passion in the canon of the mass.

St SIXTUS I
(Elected c.115; died c.125)

The appearance of Sixtus (which means "sixth" in vulgar Latin) as the sixth name in the early lists of Popes, which omitted St Peter, seems to some critics too great a coincidence to be credible. But the early sources give his name in the form "Xystus", which has no numerical significance. The *Liber Pontificalis* attributes to him the insertion of the Sanctus into the mass.

St TELESPHORUS
(Elected c.125; died c.136)

He is the only second-century Pope whose martyrdom is directly attested in early sources, though no record is preserved of the details. The *Liber Pontificalis* (in another of its agreeable fictions)

Above: The Death of St Clement. *Sentenced by the Emperor Trajan to labor in the Crimea, St Clement is said to have preached extensively amongst his fellow miners and founded 75 new churches amongst the Christian community there. His punishment for this activity was to be tied to an anchor and drowned.*

Above: St Hyginus *was a somewhat obscure figure in the early Church but is thought to have been a Greek philosopher who preached Christianity in Rome before being martyred.*

Above: St Pius *was once a slave who became Pope. His brother, Hermas, wrote the masterpiece of early Christian literature* The Shepherd *which was the forerunner of all subsequent Church writings in its symbolism and allegorical meaning.*

Right: The Martyrdom of St Victor. *Victor was mainly concerned throughout his papacy to assert the growing authority of Rome over matters of Church doctrine and discipline. It was he who inaugurated the system of synods or councils which have played such a significant part in the develop-ment of the Christian Church.*

attributes to him the insertion of the Gloria into the mass and the introduction of midnight mass at Christmas.

St HYGINUS
(Elected c.136; died c.140)

According to later tradition, Hyginus was a philosopher from Athens who devoted himself to Christian teaching in Rome until his work was crowned by martyrdom.

St PIUS
(Elected c.140; died c.155)

According to the *Muratorian Canon* (a list of Scriptural books normally dated to the end of the second century) Pius was the brother of the prophet Hermas, whose surviving writings give us a clear picture of the pastoral problems of the Roman Church, arising from the tendency of the more wealthy Christians to develop social links with pagans that pulled against their active membership of the Church.

Pius may be the bishop who, because of his standing as a confessor (one who had suffered for the faith), was elected bishop in preference to Valentinus, the great Gnostic teacher from Egypt, according to the African writer Tertullian (*c.*200). That Valentinus was not excluded because of heresy is a startling indication of the toleration of theological pluralism at this early date. However, it was under Pius that the teacher Marcion was excommunicated by the Roman Church. Marcion's heresy was less extreme than Valentinus', but constituted a greater threat to Church unity, because of his wish to exclude from baptism and communion those who did not renounce sexual relations even within marriage. The presence of Justin Martyr as a teacher in Rome in this period is further evidence for the status of the Roman Church as the center of Christian intellectual life.

St ANICETUS
(Elected c.155; died c.166)

In the time of Anicetus the Roman Church still consisted of a number of immigrant communities who followed the customs of their home churches (*see above under* Linus). A particular difficulty arose over the celebration of Easter, the exact nature of

which cannot be determined from our fragmentary evidence, which consists of extracts in Eusebius' *Church History* from a letter written at the end of the century by Bishop Irenaeus of Lyons to Pope Victor I of Rome. Possibly the dispute concerned no more than the length of the fast that preceded Easter, but on a more natural reading of the text the question was more momentous: should the Church have an Easter festival at all? After all, every Sunday is a commemoration of the Resurrection. What at least is clear is that Anicetus forbade Christians in Rome from following the Easter observance of the Churches of Asia Minor. Those Christians in Rome who had come from Asia Minor and remained loyal to the traditions of their fatherland turned for support to their home churches. St Polycarp, Bishop of Smyrna, the most revered bishop of his day, came all the way to Rome to try and browbeat Anicetus into adopting the Asian observance. The two eventually agreed to differ, and divergent practice continued at Rome. The story illustrates both the development in Rome towards "monepiscopacy" (centralized government under a single bishop) and the forces that resisted it.

St SOTER
(Elected c.166; died c.174)

We know little of Soter beyond a letter he received from Bishop Dionysius of Corinth, which praises him for "exhorting with blessed words the brethren who come up [to Rome]" and for "continuing and even increasing" the Roman custom of sending contributions to needy Christians "in every city." The presence in the Roman Church both of immigrants and of visiting teachers from the whole Christian world, though the source of divisions in both doctrine and practice (*see above under* Pius *and* Anicetus), had the advantage of strengthening the links between Rome and the other Churches, and contributing to the central position Rome had already won for herself in the Christian world.

St ELEUTHERIUS
(Elected c.174; died c.189)

Eleutherius (or Eleutherus) had been deacon (or chief administrative assistant) to Anicetus. It long remained the custom to elect as Pope one of the deacons of his predecessor – the deacons being the administrative assistants of the Pope and therefore

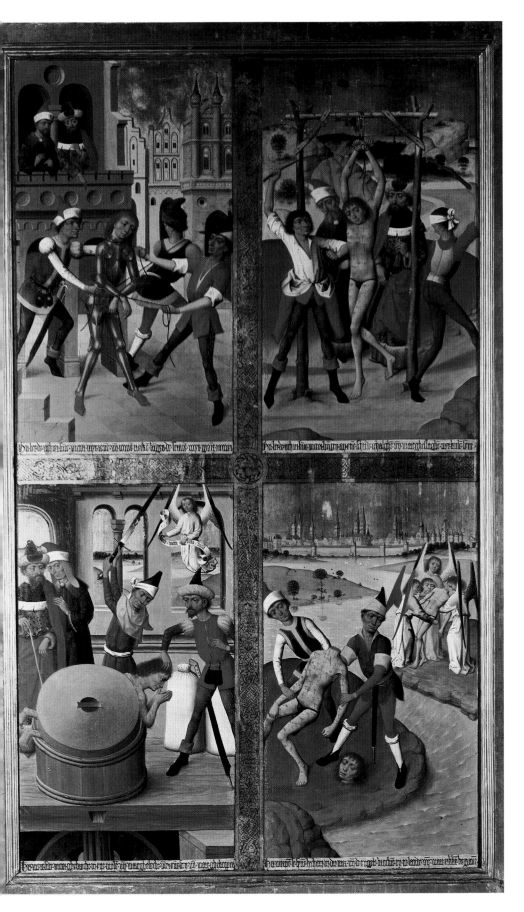

Duerde uchec hur vram mvrucne wu mue rethe laups-le lenue wrt-mane-mm

Duerde uchec hic mandroduz-u-apvnc lepue rnalghe mp weezehellaghe-weckhe lere

Hu merceter nam quebachem enu mole vm marzghelc-lee de ewelep-m-mme-uhchouper

Demeuce le pue lphem m acc un vu de erugle bauhe trp- nu lanu vm waur ebbe bzp-auc

more important than the priests who canonically ranked above them. Soon after his accession he became involved in controversy over the orthodoxy of a new prophetic movement, called Montanism, that had started in Asia Minor. Bishop Irenaeus of Lyons journeyed specially to Rome to win support for his own position on the issue. Whether he was pleading for toleration or for condemnation of the Montanists, and what side Eleutherius adopted, are questions to which the fragmentary evidence does not provide a clear answer. Rome itself remained at this time a microcosm of the Christian world in which a whole variety of opposing views on doctrine and practice were represented, and where the bishop had to tolerate what he could not suppress.

St VICTOR
(Elected c.189; died c.199)

A curious incident that illustrates the influence a Roman Bishop could wield at this early date was the intervention of Marcia, the Christian concubine of the Emperor Commodus: she obtained from Victor a list of the Christian confessors imprisoned in the mines of Sardinia and procured their release. But the episode in Victor's pontificate of which we are best informed is a new and painful chapter in the long history of dispute over Easter. This problem, which had already led to conflict both within Rome and between Rome and other parts of the Christian world (*see above under* Anicetus), now erupted again. At Victor's instigation synods (councils) were held throughout the Christian world, which largely supported Victor's insistence that Easter should always be celebrated, and the Lenten fast end, on a Sunday – in contrary to the older Quartodeciman ("14th") practice of celebrating Easter on the fourteenth day of the Jewish month Nisan, in other words on the day of the Passover, irrespective of what day this was in the Christian week. The Churches of Asia Minor, however, remained loyal to their Quartodeciman tradition. Victor retaliated by breaking off communion with them, and demanding that the other Churches should do the same. At this Bishop Irenaeus of Lyons and other bishops, who were not themselves Quartodecimans, protested at such severe treatment of Churches which were simply keeping to ancestral custom. The immediate upshot is unknown, but the Quartodeciman position continued to lose ground.

While sometimes criticizing Victor for high-handedness, historians have been impressed by this example of Rome's increasing power and self-confidence; and it has been suggested that Victor was the first of the Roman Bishops to wield full episcopal authority. If, however, we remember the history of varied Easter practice in Rome itself, with communities of immigrants following the customs of their home dioceses, however various (*see above under* Anicetus), we may surmise that Victor attempted to dictate to the Churches of Asia simply because this was the only way to secure uniformity within his own diocese. In this case we shall read the episode as evidence not for a new imperialism in the Roman See but for increasing desperation in the face of the fragmentation of the Christian community in Rome itself. Indeed, according to a different interpretation of the text of Eusebius on which we rely, Victor excommunicated not the Asian Churches but simply the Asian parishes in Rome itself, in which case the significance of the episode in terms of the power of the Roman See diminishes still further.

St ZEPHYRINUS
(Elected c.199; died 217)

Rome remained at this date the intellectual center of the Christian world (*see above under* Pius), attracting teachers widely varying in their degree of orthodoxy. The Montanist movement was still one source of division (*see above under* Eleutherius), while a whole series of doubtful speculations about the nature of God and the precise status of Christ were now at their height. Zephyrinus was criticized by some of his contemporaries for inexperience and misjudgment in dealing with the problem of false teaching; to some extent this simply means that he

Above: St Zephyrinus *has been seen as indecisive in his government of the Roman Church and during his quite lengthy pontificate, persecution of Christians was renewed under the Emperor Septimus Severus.*

antagonized those he declined to back, but the evidence does suggest that his rulings were at times inconsistent and open to misinterpretation. It was during his pontificate that Origen, the greatest of the Eastern Fathers of the Church, visited Rome, which is further evidence of the high status of the Roman See throughout the Christian world.

St CALLISTUS
(Elected 217; died 222)

Little was known of this Pope until the discovery in 1841 of a unique manuscript of the *Refutation of All Heresies* by St Hippolytus, who was revealed as a bitter opponent and as a rival claimant to the Roman See – we may call him the first "antipope." Hippolytus gives a full, and naturally uncomplimentary, account of his rival's past life and episcopal acts. The story he tells is at least amusing.

Callistus, according to this account, started life as a slave who embezzled large sums of money entrusted to him both by his Christian master and by other fellow-Christians, which won him a spell on a treadmill. For making a hostile demonstration in a synagogue (with the intention of solving his problems by provoking martyrdom) he was sent to the mines of Sardinia. On returning to Rome, his reputation restored by the glory of suffering for Christ, he became a deacon and the chief advizer of Pope Zephyrinus, who entrusted him, among other responsibilities, with the Christian cemetery on the Appian way – now known as the Catacomb of St Callistus.

On the death of Zephyrinus there was a disputed election that left Rome divided between the supporters of Callistus and those of Hippolytus. Callistus evolved, to his rival's scorn, a compromise position on the still raging controversies on the

Below: The Catacombs. *Situated outside the walls of Rome, the catacombs were sacred as burial grounds and therefore were useful hiding places during the persecutions of the early Christians. This painting shows the niches in which bodies were arranged for burial. In later times, once the persecutions were past, the catacombs became places of pilgrimage and the settings for ceremonials.*

nature of Christ (*see above under* Zephyrinus). He was likewise ingenious and diplomatic in meeting the pastoral needs of the time. Hippolytus accuses him of offering an easy forgiveness for grave sin to all who were ready to recognize him as bishop, in particular permitting the clergy to marry even after ordination and allowing women of good birth, who could not find a husband of the status required by Roman law for legal marriage, to cohabit with slaves or freedmen. Callistus declared that, just as the master in the parable insisted on the weeds being left to grow with the wheat (Mt 13:30), so sinners must be tolerated in the Church. Such realism, bordering on opportunism, came as a shock to those who liked to think of the Church as a holy sect, set apart from the world; but it won Callistus the support of most of the laity, who flooded into his Church (in the words of the indignant Hippolytus) "for the sake of pleasures which Christ did not permit." The African writer Tertullian (*fl.* 195-215) denounced an edict issued by the "bishop of bishops" that "forgave the sins of adultery and fornication to those who have performed penance," and suggested that it should be hung up on the doors of brothels to encourage those who went in; although some scholars still identify this bishop with Callistus, it is more likely that it was a slightly earlier Bishop of Carthage. Modern historians accept most of Hippolytus' facts and endeavor to give them a more charitable interpretation; some have gone so far as to recognize in Callistus a brilliant and original thinker on problems of Christian life and Church discipline. We may at least say that he showed flexibility and common sense in dealing with the pastoral problems of a community that increasingly reflected the full social make-up of the population of Rome and that faced problems in maintaining Christian solidarity and traditional moral standards.

Later tradition attributed to Callistus a martyr's death, and this finds support in the recent discovery of his tomb, which from the first was provided with a double staircase to facilitate access for pilgrims. This was the earliest martyr cult of any of the Popes since St Peter.

St URBAN I
(Elected 222; died 230)

After the dazzling but distorting light of Hippolytus' account, the Popes recede for a time

into obscurity. Almost nothing is known of Urban's pontificate beyond his burial in the Catacomb of Callistus, as confirmed by an extant gravestone in Greek, still at this date the official language of the Roman Church – which is evidence that the Roman Church still looked to the Eastern Mediterranean more than to the new Churches of the Latin West (*see below under* Cornelius).

St PONTIAN
(Elected 230; resigned September 28, 235; died 235–6)

Emperor Alexander Severus (222–35) had tolerated Christianity, but his successor Maximin made up for lost time by promptly arresting both Pontian and Hippolytus (presumably still antipope); Pontian resigned his See on his arrest, so that a successor could immediately take up the reins of government. Pontian and Hippolytus were both deported to the mines of Sardinia, where they soon died of harsh treatment. Their bodies were taken back to Rome a year or two later for honorable burial, Pontian being buried in the papal crypt of the Catacomb of St Callistus (*see below under* Fabian); the implication of their joint translation is that Hippolytus had been reconciled to Pontian and ended his schism before he died. The date of Pontian's abdication was formally recorded and is the first precise date in the history of the Popes. From now we are provided with exact dates for the election and death of almost every Pope.

St ANTERUS
(Elected November 235; died January 3, 236)

Anterus was the first of several Popes to die shortly after election. He died after a reign of only a month (probably from natural causes and not as a martyr) and was the first Pope to be buried in the newly constructed papal crypt in the Catacomb of St Callistus.

St FABIAN
(Elected January 236; died January 20, 250)

According to the Church historian Eusebius (died *c.* 340), Fabian was elected bishop because at the papal election a dove flew down and settled on his

Above: St Urban I. *Very little is known about St Urban I except that he was buried in the Catacomb of Callistus, where a number of other Popes were laid to rest.*

Above: St Pontian *was the victim of persecution by Maximin who had taken over from the murdered Emperor Severus in 235. Both Pontian and Hippolytus were sent to the mines of Sardinia where they died.*

Right: St Fabian (*left*) **and St Sebastian.** *Fabian was a sound administrator who united the early Church at a difficult time in its history. The Emperor Decius' purge saw Fabian martyred. Fabian's feast day, shared with St Sebastian, has meant they are often depicted together, although the latter's legend has come to eclipse that of Fabian himself.*

head. He had sufficient standing with the secular authorities to secure the return to Rome of the bodies of the martyrs Pontian and Hippolytus (*see above under* Pontian). He is said to have divided the diocese of Rome into seven districts, each under the control of a deacon; since deacons were directly subordinate to the bishop, this strengthened the Pope's control of the Christian life of Rome. This (if true) and the end of the Hippolytan schism (*see above under* Callistus *and* Pontian) mark the decisive stage in the centralization of ecclesiastical power in the city, for so long fragmented between virtually autonomous house churches serving different immigrant groups (*see above under* Linus) and between rival theological factions (*see above under* Pius I *and* Eleutherius).

At the beginning of the year 250 Emperor Decius unleashed the first empire-wide persecution in the history of the Church; Fabian was one of the first to be arrested and martyred. His body was recovered and buried in the papal crypt in the Catacomb of St Callistus, and later transferred to the Church of St Sebastian – a somewhat later Roman martyr who came to share a feast day (20 January) with St Fabian. The cult of St Sebastian, assisted by a colorful legend, came to eclipse that of Fabian himself.

St CORNELIUS
(Elected March 251; died June 253)

After an extraordinary interregnum of over a year, due to the Decian persecution, Cornelius, a quiet and moderate man, was elected Pope in preference to the obvious candidate, Novatian, a fiery spirit and brilliant theologian, who had been the *locum tenens* during the interregnum. Novatian refused to accept this and set himself up as antipope. The split took on theological dimensions through the opposing policy of the two rivals on the treatment of the "lapsed", that is, those who had apostatized during persecution. Cornelius favored their readmission to communion after a period of penance, while Novatian insisted on their permanent exclusion. Cornelius won the recognition of the other bishops of the Christian world, who, whatever their views on the treatment of the lapsed, could not deny the validity of his election; these included Bishop Cyprian of Carthage, whose reluctance to recognize Cornelius won his lasting distrust. Novatian and his followers set up a schismatic

church, that spread throughout the Christian world and lasted for many centuries, respected for its high moral standards.

A surviving fragment of a letter of Cornelius boasts of the presence in the Roman Church of "46 presbyters, 7 deacons, 7 sub-deacons, 42 acolytes, 52 exorcists, readers and door-keepers, and more than 1,500 widows and persons in distress, all of whom are supported by the grace and loving-kindness of the Lord" (i.e. the Roman Church). These statistics, unique for the third century, are particularly interesting for the stress laid on widows and the destitute, who were to be described in the legend of St Lawrence as the true wealth of the Church (*see below under* Sixtus II).

In June 252 Cornelius was banished by the Emperor Gallus to Civitavecchia (near Rome), where he died a year later. His body was taken back to Rome and buried in the crypt of Lucina in the Catacomb of St Callistus, where his tomb can still be seen with the inscription "Cornelius Martyr". This was the only papal epitaph of the third century to be written in Latin. Rome remained a bilingual Church, that used Greek and Latin equally, but continued to respect Greek as the first language of Christendom; Rome had no wish to be marginalized as a western See on the outskirts of the Christian world, with authority only in the Latin West. St Cornelius shares a feast day with St Cyprian (16 September), which is ironic in view of the difficult relations between the two men.

St LUCIUS I
(Elected June 253; died March 5, 254)

Like his predecessor, Lucius I was exiled by the Emperor Gallus, but on the death of the latter shortly afterward returned to Rome. He imitated Cornelius in opposing the rigorism of Novatian. He died after a brief pontificate and was buried in the papal crypt of the Catacomb of St Callistus.

St STEPHEN I
(Elected May 254; died August 2, 257)

The sixth-century *Liber Pontificalis* provides the quaint but unreliable detail that Stephen forbade priests and deacons from wearing their eucharistic vestments outside Church. But reliable knowledge of him depends on the correspondence of Cyprian of Carthage, with whom he had a whole series of

Above: St Lucius I. *Exiled by the Emperor Gallus, Lucius returned to Rome after the Emperor's death. Lucius was short-lived and he was buried in the Catacomb of St Callistus.*

bruising confrontations. One concerned Bishop Marcian of Arles (in Gaul) who in the wake of the Decian persecution and the resulting problems this caused over the lapsed (*see above under* Fabian) insisted on the rigorist position that Cyprian himself had abandoned under pressure. Cyprian saw this as an opportunity to prove the sincerity of his newfound principles, and urged a clearly reluctant Stephen to use his influence to secure Marcian's deposition. A similar dispute arose over two Spanish bishops who had been deposed for apostasy (or, more precisely, for pretending to pagan officials that they had apostatized) during the Decian persecution. They appealed to Stephen, who declared them restored on the grounds of their own unreliable testimony. Their opponents appealed to Cyprian and the other bishops of the Roman province of Africa, who fiercely attacked Stephen's stand.

The most interesting of these disputes concerned the question of the validity of baptism outside the Church. Cyprian, and many Eastern bishops, insisted that such baptism was invalid and had to be repeated when someone who had been baptized in a schismatic sect became a member of the true Church; Stephen insisted on the contrary that baptism is always valid, even outside the true Church, and should never be repeated. He admitted that the Holy Spirit cannot be received outside the Church, but argued, quaintly, that the rite of baptism forgives sins but does not communicate the Spirit. (It has been suggested that his ruling reflects a previous "gentlemen's agreement" in Rome, whereby the rival Christian communities accepted each other's baptisms, in order to discourage sinners from transferring from one sect to another in order to seek a rebaptism that would wash away their previous sins

Above: Scenes from the Life of St Stephen. *It was from the first Christian martyr, St Stephen, who was martyred in Jerusalem in c.35 that Pope Stephen I took his name. This painting shows St Stephen debating with the elders of the synagogue (left) and also before the Sanhedrin, the Jewish council. The power and authority of his eloquence on Jesus's role as the promised Messiah meant that his legend inspired numerous Popes to take his name as their own on being elected to the papacy.*

Above: St Sixtus II *was martyred during the persecution of Christians by the Emperor Valerian.*

Above: Emperor Valerian
initiated the renewed persecution of the Christians but he was himself captured and enslaved by the Persians.

without any need for the rigors of penance.) Stephen's ruling is the basis of the later western practice of accepting the validity of baptism conferred by schismatic groups outside the Church; it has the great merit of enabling Christians of different denominations to accept each other's baptism. It is ironic that it was based on the wholly unacceptable premise (subsequently abandoned) that baptism does not communicate the Holy Spirit. Bad theology is sometimes providentially useful.

St SIXTUS II
(Elected August 30, 257; died August 6, 258)

Sixtus (or Xystus) upheld against Cyprian of Carthage the position of Stephen opposing the rebaptism of schismatics, but since Pontius, the author of the *Life of Cyprian*, describes Sixtus as "a good and peace-loving priest", we may suppose that he was moderate enough to accept the principle (denied by Pope Stephen) that each local church had the right to determine its own custom; generally, the early churches were intolerant of divergences in doctrine but agreed that each church was autonomous in matters of practice and discipline.

Sixtus' pontificate was overshadowed by the renewed persecution of Christians initiated by the Emperor Valerian. As Bishop of Rome he was a prime target, and it can have been no surprise to him when he was arrested with most of his deacons when preaching in a Christian cemetery and instantly put to death. Four days afterward his one remaining deacon, Lawrence, likewise met a martyr's death. Later legend related how Lawrence promised his persecutors to produce the Church's funds and then appeared with a band of beggars, claiming that it is the poor who are the true treasure of the Church; punished for his cheek by being roasted on a gridiron, he mocked his torturers by telling them to turn him over, since one side of his body was already well cooked. The body of Sixtus found burial in the papal crypt in the Catacomb of St Callistus, where the bloodstained chair on which he had been sitting at the time of his arrest was also displayed. The subsequent cult of Sixtus as a martyr was sufficient to win his name inclusion in the canon of Roman Mass.

St DIONYSIUS
(Elected July 22, 260; died December 26, 268)

An interregnum (or *sede vacante*) of almost two years followed the martyrdom of Sixtus II and all his deacons, which complicated the succession since it

Left: St Dionysius of Paris *was an Italian by birth but was sent to Gaul as a missionary from Rome in the middle of the third century. There he established a center for Christianinty but his success aroused the wrath of the Emperor Valerian. Dionysius was beheaded along with two companions. Pope Dionysius took his name as a mark of respect and esteem.*

was the normal practice to elect as Pope one of the deacons. But in the summer of 260 the persecuting Emperor Valerian met his just deserts when he was captured and enslaved by the Persians; his successor Gallienus inaugurated a toleration of the Church that lasted till the Great Persecution of 303. The Roman Church could now assemble and elect a bishop. The choice fell on Dionysius, a prominent priest who had already corresponded with his namesake Bishop Dionysius of Alexandria on the subject of the baptismal controversy; the bishop persuaded him to shift from the uncompromising position of Stephen to the more accommodating one of Sixtus, and rewarded him by describing him as "learned and wonderful."

As Pope, Dionysius received an appeal from the Bishop of Ptolemais (the First See of Libya) against his immediate ecclesiastical superior, the same Dionysius of Alexandria, who had condemned him for heresy on the vexed and intricate question of the precise relation of the divine Son to the Father. Dionysius of Rome promptly condemned the language which the Bishop of Alexandria had used, and wrote to him asking for an explanation. Dionysius of Alexandria replied with a lengthy treatise in which with subtlety and tact he explained away the unfortunate expressions he had used. The episode is remarkable as evidence for the acceptance in the East of the authority of the Roman See – not in the sense that Rome was regarded as a sacred oracle whose teaching was infallible, or as a supreme court whose rulings were definitive, but in the sense that Rome was generally recognized as having a right to exercize a pastoral responsibility for the good of all the churches, and in disputes between churches Rome was often appealed to and could not be simply ignored. Dionysius of Rome was also active in Asia Minor, where he was remembered with gratitude a century later by the great St Basil of Caesarea for sending money to pay the ransoms of Christians captured by the barbarians.

St FELIX I
(Elected January 269; died December 30, 274)

Further evidence of the international standing of the Roman see at this time is given by the episode of the deposition of Paul of Samosata, Bishop of Antioch. A council of unprecedented size assembled in Antioch in 268, attended by bishops from Asia Minor, Syria and Palestine, to condemn and replace the Bishop of Antioch for a long list of offences ranging from grave heresy to "training women to sing hymns to himself in the middle of the Church which would make one shudder to hear." Paul, who

Above: Emperor Gallienus *brought to an end the persecutions of his predecessor Valerian, and inaugurated a toleration of Christianity which lasted until the Great Persecution of 303, which was instigated by one of his successors, Diocletian.*

Above: **St Gaius** *was said to be a relative of Emperor Diocletian but little is really known about his pontificate.*

Above: **Emperor Diocletian**
inagurated the great persecution of 303 which broke with forty years of toleration. It proved less effective than previous persecutions.

Above: **St Marcellinus** *was tested by the Great Persecution and his resulting apostasy damaged the standing of the Christian Church.*

enjoyed the support of the Palmyrenes, at this stage in control of Syria, ignored the council and continued to occupy the cathedral and episcopal palace, despite the ineffective protests of the bishop elected to succeed him. But on the defeat of the Palmyrenes by the new Emperor, Aurelian, in 272, Paul's days were numbered. Aurelian ruled that the lawful bishop was the one recognized by the Bishops of Rome and Italy. This implies that Felix of Rome had held a council in Italy to condemn Paul yet again, and that the Christians of Antioch referred to that council as settling the issue. Again (*see above under* Dionysius) the episode should not be read as evidence for some universal jurisdiction enjoyed by the Popes; but it does show that the standard criterion for a valid bishop was recognition by the Bishop of Rome (*see below under* Damasus for the obscuring of this principle in the following century). Apart from this striking episode nothing is known of Felix's pontificate.

St EUTYCHIAN
(Elected January 275; died December 7, 283)

Eusebius, the great Church historian, was already a young man when Eutychian died, but heard so little about him that in his *Ecclesiastical History* he makes the curious mistake of reducing his nine-year pontificate to a mere ten months. This was one of the quietest periods in the history of the third-century Church. Eutychian was the ninth and last of the Popes to be buried in the papal crypt in the Catacomb of St Callistus.

St GAIUS
(Elected December 17, 283; died April 22, 296)

No other source compensates for the continued silence of Eusebius. The *Liber Pontificalis* makes Gaius a relative of the Emperor Diocletian, and claims that during Diocletian's persecution he hid in the catacombs for eight years. In fact the persecution only began some years after his death.

St MARCELLINUS
(Elected June 30, 296; died 304)

Marcellinus was enjoying as quiet a pontificate as his predecessor when suddenly in 303 the aging

Emperor Diocletian broke with the policy of toleration that had lasted for forty years and inaugurated the "Great Persecution". It proved less effective than the Decian persecution of 250 (*see above under* Fabian and Cornelius), since it enjoyed little popular support, and most of those martyred had to draw attention to themselves by provocative behavior; but prominent Christians, such as bishops and public servants, were certainly put to the test. Among those most tested and most found wanting was the unfortunate Pope Marcellinus. Choosing the path of discretion rather than valor, he meekly obeyed the imperial authorities by handing over copies of the Scriptures and burning incense to the pagan gods. The *Liberian Catalogue* of 354 indicates that he ceased exercising episcopal functions exactly nine months before he died, which may imply a formal meeting of the Roman clergy on that date to strip him of his office. His apostasy seriously damaged the standing of the Roman See, at a time when a clear voice from Rome would have helped the Churches considerably in coping with the many problems that followed in the wake of persecution. Later legend piously surmised that Marcellinus repented of his apostasy and died a martyr. On the strength of this he was later listed among the saints of the Roman See. It is a curious fact that an inscription of 298 which refers to him as "papa" is the first example we have of Bishops of Rome being addressed as "Pope".

St MARCELLUS I
(Elected March 308; died October 7, 309)

Not only are the dates of Marcellus' pontificate uncertain – an alternative date for his death is January 16, 308 – but his very existence has been questioned, on the less than adequate grounds of the similarity of his name to that of his predecessor Marcellinus and confusion between them in some of the sources. Elected after the long interregnum that followed the apostasy of Marcellinus, Marcellus attempted to distance himself from his infamous predecessor, on whose presbyteral council he had sat, by taking a rigorist line toward the lapsed. This led to divisions among his flock, and even rioting and loss of life. Emperor Maxentius thought it prudent to send Marcellus into exile, where he died not long afterward. On the strength of this experience he was later counted a "confessor" – someone who had suffered for the faith.

St EUSEBIUS
(Elected April 18, 309 or 310; died September 26, 309 or 310)

Strife over the treatment of those who had compromised themselves during the Great Persecution continued to divide the Christians of Rome. Eusebius adopted a moderate line, offering forgiveness to those who did penance. His opponents, led by one Heraclius, possibly an antipope, caused such disturbances that Emperor Maxentius sent both him and Eusebius himself into exile. There Eusebius soon died, like his predecessor in similar circumstances. This enabled the later Pope and poet Damasus (died 384) to hail him as a martyr.

St MILTIADES
(elected July 2, 311; died January 10, 314)

After an interregnum of nine or twenty-one months (depending on the uncertain dates of Pope Eusebius) the Roman Christians were able to assemble and elect a new Pope, Miltiades. He soon won the trust of Emperor Maxentius, who ordered a restoration of all the Church property confiscated during the Great Persecution. Maxentius himself lost his throne and his life at the battle of the Milvian Bridge (October 28, 312), which left the young Constantine master of Rome. Constantine had entrusted his fortunes to the God of the Christians, and now rewarded the Roman Church with lavish gifts, including the Lateran palace on Monte Celio. This now became the residence of the Popes, a dignity it maintained until the Avignon papacy of the fourteenth century and the subsequent move to the Vatican.

Miltiades demonstrated his political sagacity at a synod held in Rome in 313 in an attempt to solve the Donatist schism. This had arisen in Africa a year earlier over a disputed election to the See of Carthage. An unpopular presbyter, Caecilian, had been chosen in a rushed election, and one of his consecrators, Felix of Aptunga, was of doubtful standing because of a charge that he had compromised himself by handing over copies of the Scriptures at the time of the Great Persecution. A large number of African bishops refused to accept Caecilian and appointed as rival Bishop of Carthage one Majorinus; he was succeeded at his death soon afterwards by Donatus, after whom the resultant schism became named. Both sides appealed to Emperor Constantine, who entrusted the matter to a meeting of bishops chaired by Miltiades. Miltiades evaded the embarrassing task of investigating the charges against Felix by insisting that, even if true, they did not invalidate Caecilian's consecration. By condemning Donatus, while offering generous terms to other Donatist bishops, he tried to divide the schismatics. The Donatists refused to accept the

Above: The Battle of Milvian Bridge (312) *saw Emperor Maxentius lose his throne and his life, leaving the young Constantine as the master of Rome.*

Above: Constantine *lavished the Roman Church with gifts on his accession to the throne.*

Above: Maxentius *exiled St Eusebius and restored Church property before losing his life in 312*

35

verdict and appealed again to the Emperor, who reluctantly agreed to a further and larger council to meet at Arles in 314. Before it met, Miltiades himself had died, after a brief but momentous pontificate which, after the scandals and divisions of the previous decade, had fully restored the standing and morale of the Roman See.

St SYLVESTER I
(Elected January 31, 314; died December 31, 335)

The Emperor Constantine spent only brief periods in Rome; at the same time he poured endowments on the Roman Church. Quite apart from his gift of the Lateran Palace, he built and richly endowed a whole series of fine Churches, including St John Lateran's, St Peter's, St Paul's, and the Sessorian Basilica (now Santa Croce in Gerusalemme). It is true that these lay outside the center of the city, which was still dominated by the historic pagan shrines and still housed a largely pagan population. But we may now speak of the beginnings of papal

Rome. At the same time the role of bishops throughout the Empire was greatly expanded by state subsidies which enabled the bishops to take on the role of the benefactors of all the urban poor, not just Christians, and by such judicial privileges as the authority to settle civil cases without the parties having any right of appeal. Add to this Constantine's appointment of a whole series of Christians as Prefects (or imperial governors) of Rome, and it will be clear that Sylvester's power and influence in the city must have far outstripped that of all his predecessors.

In the broader sphere, however, of the Church politics of Constantine's reign Sylvester played little part. He did not take on a central role in the developing stages of the Donatist controversy (*see above under* Miltiades), nor did he or the representatives he sent exert influence on the proceedings of the First Ecumenical Council held at Nicaea (in north-west Asia Minor) in 325, which issued the Nicene Creed (in its original form); indeed he was less active in the affairs of the Eastern Churches than many of his predecessors. It would in any case

Above: View of St John Lateran, *which was one of a number of Churches built and richly endowed by Emperor Constantine, marking the beginnings of papal Rome.*

Below: Constantine, the first Christian Emperor. *In addition to building new Churches, Constantine appointed a series of Christians as Prefects (or governors) of Rome.*

have been difficult for the Roman See to maintain its position as the center of the Christian world at a time when theological debate was concentrated in the East and when Rome, no longer the home of the imperial administration, was becoming in secular terms a political backwater; but Sylvester's inaction made it too easy for politically astute bishops of lesser Sees to upstage him.

Later legend was dissatisfied with the sparse historical record of the relations between the first Christian Emperor, who transformed the future of the Church, and the Pope of his day, and so it filled up the gap with a narrative which, although fictitious, was more worthy of the occasion. This related that Constantine, at first a persecutor of the Church, was struck with leprosy and received a miraculous cure from Pope Sylvester, at which he adopted the Christian faith and was baptized by Sylvester himself; it was then Pope and Emperor acting in consort who summoned the Council of Nicaea. Soon, throughout Christendom, this colorful fiction replaced the genuine history recorded in Eusebius' reliable but turgid *Life of Constantine*. To it was added in the eighth century the legend of the Donation of Constantine, which supposedly gave the Popes not only supreme authority in the Church but political authority over all Italy and the West generally. Sylvester was elevated into the founder of the medieval papacy in all its glory.

St MARK
(Elected January 18, 336; died October 7, 336)

Little is known of his short pontificate, though he continued his predecessor's policy of founding new Churches, to advance the Christianization of Rome and show the Pope as benefactor of the city.

St JULIUS I
(Elected February 6, 337; died April 12, 352)

If Sylvester had steered clear of the disputes associated with the Council of Nicaea of 325, the new Pope Julius, a far more forceful personality, leapt in with relish. Bishop Athanasius of Alexandria had been deposed by the Council of Tyre (335) for his use of violence to frustrate the reconciliation of two warring factions in Egypt in accordance with the decisions of the Council of Nicaea (325); his ally

Bishop Marcellus of Ancyra (modern Ankara) was widely accused of heresy and deposed at the order of the Emperor Constantine in 336. In 339 both bishops fled from the East and arrived in Rome. Julius, flattered by their appeal to his jurisdiction, was happy to summon and preside at a council at Rome which declared the deposition of the two bishops null and void. Julius argued in particular that Bishops of Alexandria should be judged by the Roman See, not by Eastern councils – a claim based on the special relationship between the two Sees that we can trace back to the middle of the third century (*see above under* Dionysius). His skill in using the dispute to advance the claims of his own See, and undo the ill effects of Sylvester's inaction, can only be admired, though his defense of Athanasius and Marcellus was grossly partisan.

In 343 the Emperors Constans and Constantius (the two remaining sons of Constantine, who had died in 337) summoned a great council at Sardica (modern Sofia in Bulgaria), which soon split up into rival Western and Eastern assemblies which condemned each other. The Western assembly, in its eagerness to refute the opponents of Marcellus, virtually adopted Marcellus' own defective understanding of the relationship between the Father and the Son. It also affirmed the right of any convicted bishop to have recourse to the Roman See as the highest court of appeal; later Roman bishops laid stress on this ruling and ascribed it erroneously to the Council of Nicaea. Julius enjoyed the support of Constans the Western Emperor, and achieved partial success in the East when in 346 Athanasius was allowed to return to Alexandria.

In Rome itself Julius built a number of Churches, including S. Maria in Trastevere and SS. Apostoli, and is credited with reorganizing the Roman chancery on the lines of the central administration of the empire; this is the first indication of the tendency of the fourth-century Popes to appropriate the style of the Emperors, a tendency seen in the papal decretals (*see below under* Siricius).

LIBERIUS
(Elected May 17, 352; died September 24, 366) and **ST FELIX II** *(Elected late 355; died November 22, 365)*

Liberius tried to maintain the stand of his strong-willed predecessor, in exceptionally difficult circumstances, since from 353 Constantius II was sole

Above: St Mark *was instrumental in continuing his predecessor Sylvester's Christianization of Rome by founding several new Churches.*

Above: Emperor Constantius II *was the son of Constantine and ruled with his brother Constans, from the year 337 when their father died. From 353 Constantius was sole Emperor.*

Above: Liberius. *Liberius and Felix II "shared" the papacy at the instigation of the Roman Emperor, Constantius II and the two bishops divided the Roman See between them until Felix's death in 365.*

Emperor and supported the enemies of Athanasius. Councils of western bishops at Arles (353) and Milan (355) condemned Athanasius, and Liberius was exiled to Thrace, while the Roman clergy yielded to imperial pressure and elected in his place Felix II, a firm opponent of Athanasius and of the Creed of Nicaea. Finally, Liberius himself acceded to the condemnation of Athanasius (for which, after all, there were good canonical grounds) and was allowed to return to Rome in 358, not to replace Felix but as joint bishop with Felix – the Emperor's quaint solution to a problem he had himself created. The Christian population largely rallied to Liberius, and Felix was forced to abandon the Lateran palace and the main basilicas to Liberius, while setting up his own court in the suburbs, in a villa on the Via Aurelia. Thus, the two bishops, Liberius and Felix, divided the Roman See between them, until Felix's death in 365.

Felix was subsequently included together with Liberius in the official lists of Bishops of Rome. Through confusion with martyrs of the same name, he even came to be venerated as a martyr himself. Through a quaint reversal of the historical facts, he was thought to have met his death through upholding the faith of Nicaea, while Liberius was misrepresented as a persecutor of Nicene orthodoxy. This made Liberius the first Pope to be denied recognition as a saint. There were to be many more who were denied canonization thereafter.

St DAMASUS I
(Elected October 1, 366; died December 11, 384)

The uneasy peace between the supporters of Felix and those of Liberius broke down at the latter's death. On the very day of his death his most loyal supporters met together in the Julian basilica (S. Maria in Trastevere) and elected as Pope the deacon Ursinus, who had always remained loyal to Liberius; he was there and then consecrated by the Bishop of Tibur. But on the same day the supporters of Felix elected as bishop the deacon Damasus, who had started as one of Liberius' deacons but had then become a partisan of Felix II. Damasus' supporters, strengthened by armed thugs hired for the purpose, stormed the Julian basilica and massacred whatever supporters of Ursinus they could lay hands on. On 1 October they seized the Lateran basilica, and there Damasus was consecrated by the Bishop of Ostia.

The prefect of the city (the pagan Viventius) tried to dampen down the conflict by sending Ursinus into exile. Fighting, however, continued in the city, and Viventius prudently withdrew to the suburbs, leaving the Christians to fight it out. The supporters of Ursinus had as their last redoubt the Basilica of Sicininus (built by Liberius); this was stormed on 24 October, in an attack which left 137 corpses on the Church floor. There were supporters of Ursinus in Rome during the rest of Damasus' pontificate, but the Emperor, Valentinian, excluded Ursinus himself from Rome, and by Damasus' death the

Above: St Damasus I *was an influential figure on the early Church, bringing it more power and authority. He also contributed greatly to the ongoing process of Christianizing Rome, by building several Churches and restoring the catacombs as places of pilgrimage. Damasus is often seen as the architect of the medieval papacy.*

Ursinians had dwindled to a small remnant.

Despite this unsavory inauguration of his pontificate, Damasus was arguably the most effective of the fourth-century Popes, and may even be called the creator of the medieval papacy. He promoted the expression "the Apostolic See", which implied authority to rule, in preference to the older expression "the Chair of Peter", which referred simply to authority to teach. He secured imperial legislation that made the Roman See throughout the West the judge of metropolitan bishops and the court of appeal for bishops condemned by local synods. His attempt to promote papal authority in the East was less successful. The Emperor, Theodosius the Great, in reimposing Nicene orthodoxy on the East in 380, defined true belief as that transmitted by St Peter to the Roman Church; but in the schism of Antioch, where there were two rival Nicene bishops, Paulinus and Meletius, Damasus' support for Paulinus was not considered to settle the matter (as had Felix I's support back in 272 for one of the rivals in an earlier Antiochene schism), and Damasus' refusal to accept Meletius and his successor Flavian weakened his influence in the East.

The Christianization of Rome continued apace during his pontificate. In 382 the Emperor Gratian removed the symbolic Altar of Victory from the senate house and confiscated the remaining endowments of the pagan temples of Rome; an embassy of pagan senators appealed against the order, but was frustrated by the skillful diplomacy of Damasus and Bishop Ambrose of Milan.

Damasus made a major contribution to the development of the Christian shrines of the city. He built several Churches, including the Church of Saints Mark and Marcellian on the Via Ardeatina, where he was buried, and another (almost on the site of the present S. Lorenzo in Damaso) which he endowed out of his own patrimony and whither his body was later translated. Most notably, he restored the catacombs as places of pilgrimage, including the papal crypt in the Catacomb of St Callistus which housed remains of nine third-century Popes; he decorated them with highly elegant engravings of his own less than elegant verses in honor of the martyrs. He also patronized St Jerome, and encouraged him to embark on what became the Vulgate, the Latin Bible of the Western Church. In all, Damasus set a new stamp on the papacy: Rome was to be simultaneously the city sanctified by the martyrs, from Saints Peter and Paul onward, and the author-

itative teacher and legislator of the Christian world. Although the acceptance of papal authority by the other Churches fell far short of the Roman theory, at least this theory was now fully developed, and Damasus' successors were able to speak with weight and self-assurance.

St SIRICIUS
(Elected December 384; died November 26, 399)

A Roman by birth, he had been one of Damasus' deacons, and continued his policies. It is with Siricius that begins the long series of papal decretals – directives on matters of Church practice and discipline, issued by Popes in the style of imperial edicts. Addressed to Churches in the West, they represent an attempt to develop what we may call a patriarchate of the West, where the local Churches were to follow Roman canon law and accept Rome as the final court of appeal for all Church lawsuits. In various ways Siricius showed himself under the influence of the ascetic movement, now at its height: in 392–3 he excommunicated Jovinian, who denied the superiority of virginity to marriage, and he was the first Pope to champion the rule that priests, to preserve the purity required for cultic acts, must at all times abstain from their wives – a rule which was gradually to develop into the requirement of clerical celibacy.

In Rome Siricius applied lavish funds provided by Emperor Valentinian II to rebuild St Paul's basilica, making it the largest Church in Rome. The usurper Eugenius (392–4) presided over a pagan revival in Rome, and the more fanatical pagans declared their intention of turning the Churches into stables, but on Eugenius' defeat by Theodosius the Great the process of Christianization took on new momentum, led by the Christian aristocracy of the city. Siricius himself showed an admirable spirit of moderation: he did nothing to encourage reprisals, and allowed his Churches to be used as places of asylum by members of the defeated pagan party. He was, however, more severe toward the Manichaean heretics who were active at this time in Rome: worried that they might feign repentance in order to avoid persecution, he ruled that converts from Manichaeism should be immured in monasteries and only be allowed to receive communion when on their deathbeds.

Siricius achieved the not very difficult feat of

Above: St Siricius *was the first of the Popes to issue papal decreteals which gave direction on matters of Church practice and discipline.*

Above: **Emperor Gratian,** *who continued apace the Christianization of Rome with St Damasus I.*

Above: **Theodosius the Great** *was another Emperor who embraced the Christian faith.*

Above: **Emperor Honorius** *confirmed Boniface as Pope over the rival claims of Eulalius, who had seized the Lateran.*

Right: St Jerome *was the outstanding scholar of the early Church. In 382 he went to Rome to act as an interpreter. He went on to become secretary to Pope Damasus I and was encouraged by the Pope to begin revizing the Latin version of the Bible, the aim being to produce a standard text. It was this document which became known as the Vulgate, the Latin Bible of the Western Church.*

alienating the cantankerous St Jerome, who left Rome under a cloud in 385. Jerome's criticisms of him, though mild by Jerome's standards, led to Siricius' exclusion from the official calendar of the saints of the Church in 1584, though the learned Pope Benedict XIV restored his name in 1748.

St ANASTASIUS I
(Elected November 27, 399; died December 19, 401)

A Roman by birth, Anastasius continued his predecessor's attempts to check the heresy of Manichaeism by taking steps to detect Manichaean missionaries from overseas who pretended to be clerics in good standing. He is attributed with the liturgical details of forbidding priests to sit during the reading of the Gospel.

The most significant event of his brief pontificate was his involvement in the controversy over the writings of Origen (died c.251), the greatest but most controversial of the Greek Fathers. The western clergy were divided, since Rufinus of Aquileia was a keen disseminator of the works of Origen while Jerome (now living in Bethlehem) was their fiercest critic. When Bishop Theophilus of Alexandria formally condemned Origen and pressed Anastasius to do likewise, Anastasius had to adopt a position on an issue in which he took no personal interest and which, indeed, he little understood. Because he prudently embraced the stronger party and urged other western Churches to do the same, he won the plaudits of St Jerome. When he died a year later, Jerome saw this as an act of God, since Rome (which had failed to appreciate St Jerome's many gifts) did not deserve so worthy a bishop.

St INNOCENT I
(Elected 21 December 401; died 12 March 417)

He is unique among Popes for having been the son of his predecessor; the rule of clerical continence (*see above under* Siricius) did not prevent bishops from having children before they were elevated to major orders. Innocent was Pope at the time of the sack of Rome by the Goths in 410. The sack was interpreted by pagans as evidence that the Christianization of Rome and the Empire was offensive to the gods, and it stimulated a short-lived pagan revival – which may be described as the last gasp of the traditional public paganism of Rome. Christian apologists responded that this sack had been less destructive than an earlier sack in pagan times, back in 387BC; they pointed out that the Goths showed some respect for Christians shrines and only raped a few virgins. Innocent's absence at the time at the court of the Western Emperor at Ravenna was interpreted as providential: just as Lot had been rescued from Sodom, so Innocent had been spared from sharing in the punishment of sinful Rome.

Innocent completed the provision of parish Churches in Rome by dedicating a Church in honor of the Milanese martyrs Gervasius and Protasius (now S. Vitale). He was also active in issuing papal decretals (*see above under* Siricius), insisting that the traditional toleration of varieties in Church practice did not extend to the Western Churches since they had received the faith from Rome. When the African Church appealed to him over the heretic Pelagius, who had been condemned in Africa but acquitted by the Palestinian Council of Diospolis in 415, he took the opportunity to enunciate the general principle that all doctrinal problems should be referred to the Pope as the successor of Peter. At the same time he advanced papal interests in the East by promoting the Bishop of Thessalonica to be his vicar (or representative) in the Balkans, where the Church remained under papal jurisdiction until the ninth century.

In 404 he broke off communion with the Eastern Churches over the deposition of the saintly John Chrysostom from the See of Constantinople; the Western Emperor, Honorius, wrote to the court of Constantinople insisting that the matter should have been referred to the Roman See, which is proof of Innocent's high standing at the imperial court of the West. The schism between Rome and the Eastern Churches continued until after Innocent's death, but he had the gratification of restoring communion with a repentant Church of Antioch in c.415.

St ZOSIMUS
(Elected March 18, 417; died December 26, 418)

A Greek who had been recommended to Innocent I by John Chrysostom, he attempted to further the policy of his predecessors with a notable lack of political sense. In the hope of promoting Roman authority in Gaul he made common cause with Patroclus the unscrupulous Bishop of Arles, elevat-

Above: St Anatstasius I *was embroiled in controversy over the writings of Origen, which he eventually chose to oppose.*

Above: St Innocent I *broke off with the Eastern Churches in 404 and caused a schism which lasted until after his death in 417.*

Above: St Zosimus. *His pontificate was characterized by a series of errors which diminshed support for Rome.*

Above: **St Boniface I.** *The Emperor Honorius took Boniface's side in the papal dispute with Eulalius, who had been elected by a rival clerical group.*

Below: **St Augustine of Hippo,** *who was one of St Boniface I's most ardent admirers.*

ing him above the Gallic metropolitans, on the dubious ground of the eminence of St Trophimus, the supposed founder of his See. This attempt to set up a Gallic vicariate, comparable to that of Thessalonica in the Balkans (*see above under* Innocent) backfired, since it united the other Gallic bishops in opposition, and Zosimus' successors abandoned his plan.

In a similar attempt to assert Roman authority in Africa, Zosimus took up the case of Pelagius (condemned by a series of African councils) and declared him innocent. Since Pelagius had been condemned by Zosimus' own predecessor, the African Church responded by appealing from Rome drunk to Rome sober. Behind the scenes they appealed to the imperial court at Ravenna, which issued a rescript condemning the Pelagians, and Zosimus was forced to eat his words. Failing to learn from experience, he promptly took up the case of an even less worthy candidate for his favor, a priest called Apiarius, who had been deposed and

excommunicated by his own Bishop of Sicca (in modern Tunisia); on the exact nature of his offences the sources preserve a prudish silence. Apiarius appealed to Zosimus, in the hope of hoodwinking a Pope who had no independent knowledge of the case. Zosimus not only declared Apiarius innocent, but demanded that the African bishops accept the right of any African cleric to appeal to Rome, basing his claim on the canons of the Council of Sardica (343) which he wrongly attributed to the more authoritative Council of Nicaea (*see above under* Julius I). Meanwhile, Zosimus had lost support even in Rome, and some of his clergy appealed against him to the court of Ravenna, which was now sympathetic to charges against him. Before the situation could become even more embarrassing, Zosimus died. His pontificate, which has been called an anomaly, showed that Roman authority had to be used with discretion if it was to be respected.

St BONIFACE I
(Elected December 28 or 29, 418; died September 4, 422)

As papal nuncio in Constantinople in 418 he was able to secure the rehabilitation of John Chrysostom and thereby end a fourteen-year schism between East and West (*see above under* Innocent I). He was back in Rome at the time of Zosimus' death. Zosimus' divisive influence continued from the grave, and the Roman clergy split into two factions, each of which elected a Pope and had him consecrated. One group chose Eulalius, and another Boniface. The matter had to be referred to the Emperor Honorius, who arranged for a council of bishops from all over the West to meet in the following summer to adjudicate the matter, and in the meantime excluded both rival candidates from the city; he had no wish to see a repetition of the disgraceful scenes that had attended the disputed election in 366 (*see above under* Damasus). But before the council could meet, Eulalius had blotted his copybook: he returned to Rome without permission and seized the Lateran. At this the Emperor forbade his candidature and confirmed Boniface as Pope; Eulalius accepted this and received as compensation a provincial bishopric.

Boniface abandoned the ill-judged initiatives of Zosimus, though in taking up the case of a deposed Bishop of Fussala in Africa he showed that Rome had not abandoned any of its claims. His hostility

one of the most magnificent fifth-century buildings still surviving in Rome. To protect Rome from false teaching, he procured in 425 from the new Emperor, Valentinian III, an edict banning all heretics, schismatics, Manichees and astrologers from the city.

Taking up the running battle with the African bishops, he abandoned the case of the Bishop of Fussala, but resurrected that of Apiarius. At a council at Carthage the papal legate firmly advanced the Roman claim that Apiarius, having been acquitted at Rome, must be reinstated; but his argument lost all credibility when Apiarius publicly confessed the justice of the charges against him. The African bishops then issued a declaration denying Rome any appellate jurisdiction. Rome's attempt to break the traditional autonomy of the African Church had failed. Elsewhere Celestine was more successful. Both the Gallic and the British bishops respected his firm stand against the pullulating varieties of Pelagianism, and in 431 he sent Palladius to be the first bishop in Ireland.

At the same time Rome's standing in the East was enhanced by a dramatic series of events arising from debate over the finer points of the Christian understanding of the divinity and humanity of Christ. The controversy was provoked in 429 by Bishop Nestorius of Constantinople, who attacked the traditional ascription to Our Lady of the title "Mother of God". Both Nestorius and his main enemy Bishop Cyril of Alexandria appealed to Rome. Partly because of Rome's traditional alliance with Alexandria, and partly because Celestine was persuaded that Nestorianism implied Pelagianism, Celestine demanded that Nestorius recant, and entrusted Cyril with the task of securing his recantation. Seeing an opportunity to crush Nestorius and humiliate the upstart See of Constantinople, Cyril wrote to Nestorius in terms that made reconciliation impossible.

At the Council of Ephesus of 431, called by the Eastern Emperor, Theodosius II, to adjudicate the matter, Cyril opened proceedings without waiting for the arrival either of his opponents or of the lay official appointed by the Emperor to chair the council, and made use of his papal mandate to justify his high-handedness. Despite this, the sessions chaired by Cyril soon came to be regarded as the sessions of an ecumenical council, and the linking of Celestine's name to the council enhanced the standing of council and Pope alike.

Above: St Cyril of Alexandria *was a central figure at the Council of Ephesus in 431 at which he presided. He denounced the absent Nestorius and influenced the others present to do likewise by his eloquence and the logic of his theological argument. Cyril's writings on such issues as the Incarnation and the Trinity proved valuable to the Church as a way of countering heresy. He was declared a Doctor of the Church by Pope Leo XIII in 1882.*

to the Pelagians preserved for him, however, the goodwill of the African bishops, and the great St Augustine of Hippo dedicated one of his writings to him in terms that express affection and esteem.

St CELESTINE I
(Elected September 10, 422; died July 27, 432)

Keen not to repeat the scandal of the dual election of 418 the Roman clergy elected unanimously the most senior of the deacons, Celestine. He began the task of restoring the Roman Churches that had suffered from the Gothic sack of 410, and an extant inscription reveals him as the founder of S Sabina,

St SIXTUS III
(Elected July 31, 432; died August 19, 440)

A senior Roman priest, who had shared in and perhaps contributed to Pope Zosimus' tergiversations over Pelagianism, he had learned courage and consistency by the time of his election. The Council of Ephesus had split into two rival assemblies which anathematized each other. It took two years after the council for patient diplomacy to restore peace to the Church. Although the chief architect of this was the court of Constantinople, Pope Sixtus (or Xystus) also played an active part, and was able to impress on the Eastern bishops the valuable role that Rome could play, even in the circumstances of a doctrinal dispute restricted to the Greek East.

Sixtus initiated an extensive building program in Rome, and used it to celebrate the victories that Rome had secured in the field of dogma. He reconstructed the baptistery in the Lateran (which still survives) in celebration of the centrality of divine grace bestowed through baptism, which the Pelagians were deemed to have denied, while he built the great basilica of St Mary Major's to mark the Council of Ephesus (431), which, under the chairmanship of Cyril of Alexandria acting as the Pope's representative in the East, had condemned Nestorius of Constantinople for denying that the Virgin Mary is the Mother of God. These and Sixtus' other building works have been described in modern times, a little floridly, as the "Xystine renaissance". They served to express a sense of pride in the Christianization of Rome, now largely complete, and its recovery from the sack of 410.

St LEO I THE GREAT
(Elected August 440; died November 10, 461)

He was elected during an absence in Gaul, as uniquely qualified by ability and experience, having been one of the chief advizers of both Celestine and Sixtus III. He became the most forceful exponent ever of the Roman claim to supreme teaching and legislative authority. Like his predecessors, he had to use diplomatic skills to encourage the various local churches to recognize Roman primacy in fact as well as in theory. In Gaul he adopted a policy of divide and rule, by playing the various rival metropolitan Sees against each other; in African affairs he was aided by the Vandal invasion, which destroyed the confidence and self-sufficiency of the African Church. When Dioscorus became Bishop of Alexandria in

444, Leo wrote to remind him that St Mark (the supposed founder of the Alexandrian See) had been the obedient disciple of St Peter, and pressed on him that Roman directives should be obeyed in Alexandria as they were (largely) in the West.

The uneasy peace of 433 between the rival factions in the East lasted beyond the death of St Cyril in 444. It was broken in 448 when some zealous heresy-hunters arraigned an elderly and revered monk, Eutyches, before a meeting of bishops at Constantinople. It soon became apparent that Eutyches was no theologian and could be condemned out of his own mouth, but his accusers went too far when they demanded that he accept the presence in Christ of two "natures" (or realities) – the divine and the human. Cyril of Alexandria had avoided using this expression without signifi-

Above: St Leo I and Attila the Hun. *In 452 Leo was sent by Emperor Valentinian III to negotiate with Attila the Hun who had invaded Italy. Leo was successful in turning back Attila's hordes and is still celebrated for his great courage in saving Italy from invasion.*

Right: St Leo *issued his famous* Tome *which was a pivotal text in asserting Christ's humanity yet it caused a rift between Rome and Alexandria and weakened western influence in the East.*

Tome, a highly rhetorical assertion of the fullness of Christ's humanity, which contained a number of expressions which an unsympathetic Eastern reader could interpret as a rejection of St Cyril and a revival of the heresy of Nestorius. The *Tome* was not even read out at the Council of Ephesus, but its day came soon afterward when Emperor Theodosius II's sudden death in 450 led to a new regime determined to reverse the decisions of the Second Council of Ephesus. In 451 a new general council was summoned to Chalcedon, across the Bosporus from Constantinople; Leo himself did not attend, but sent representatives, who played an active part. The council soon developed into a tug-of-war between the bishops, who were largely loyal to the memory of Cyril, and the imperial representatives, who gave priority to Leo's *Tome*. After a few sessions a compromise definition of faith was approved on the basis of a supposed consensus between Cyril and Leo. The council's approval of the "two natures" Christology of Leo made it suspect in much of the East, while its deposition of Dioscorus of Alexandria made it unacceptable in Egypt; this led in time to a permanent schism between the Churches of Rome and Constantinople on the one hand and the Coptic Church, and other Ancient Oriental Churches, on the other.

The council also issued a canon which ascribed primacy in the East to the See of Constantinople. This was firmly rejected by Leo, who feared that it would encourage the ancient Sees of the East, notably Antioch and Alexandria, to look in future to Constantinople, not Rome, for leadership and for arbitration in their disputes. But his *Tome* and the role it had played at Chalcedon had shattered the traditional alliance between Rome and Alexandria, and there was no possibility of a renewal of the special relationship between the two Sees. The Council of Chalcedon, despite the effusive compliments that in its sessions were heaped on the head of Pope Leo, in this way hastened rather than retarded the decline of Roman influence in the East.

Leo's memory was particularly cherished in Italy because of his courage during the barbarian invasions. In 452 he was sent by Emperor Valentinian III to negotiate with Attila the Hun, who had invaded Italy and already razed Aquileia to the ground; Leo was successful in persuading him to leave Italy forthwith. In 455 he negotiated with the Vandals as they prepared to take Rome; although he could not deter them from pillage his intervention did at least save the city from massacre and arson.

cant qualification, since it could suggest that Christ is made up of two independent elements, the Second Person of the Trinity and the man Jesus Christ, weakly bonded together. Since Cyril was by this date generally accepted as the supreme exponent of the doctrine of Christ, it was highly provocative to insist as essential for orthodoxy on a formula that Cyril himself had avoided. The strong reaction of the Eastern Churches crystallized in 449 at the Second Council of Ephesus which rehabilitated Eutyches.

Meanwhile, however, his condemnation had been communicated to Pope Leo. Ignorant of the terminology of Eastern Christology, he misunderstood the points at issue, and thought that Eutyches had committed the enormity of denying that Christ has a human nature. He therefore issued his famous

Above: St Hilarus, *diligent in the erection and enrichment of churches, dissuaded Emperor Anthemius from promoting an edict of general toleration of heretics.*

Right: The Fall of the Roman Empire *in the West. Emperor Romulus Augustulus is deposed by Odoacer, leader of the Goths, in 476*

St HILARUS
(Elected 19 November 461; died 29 February 468)

Hilarus was a Sardinian, and by the time of his election Archdeacon of Rome. He attended the so-called "Robber synod" of Ephesus in 449 as one of Leo's legates. There he witnessed the violent ill-treatment of Flavian, Archbishop of Constantinople. Since, like him, he rejected the decisions of the synod, he feared similar ill-treatment, and fled in disguise by night from Ephesus, making his way back to Italy. As Pope, he continued Leo's struggle for Christological orthodoxy and respect for the prerogatives of the Roman See. Gaul saw a continuation of the quarrel over jurisdiction between the Sees of Vienne and Arles: Hilarus continued Leo's policy of support for Arles, as an expression of the jurisdictional oversight of the Roman See. In Spain he exercized a similar jurisdiction, in response to

appeals from Spanish bishops. When on a visit to Rome, after his accession to the imperial throne in 467, the Emperor Anthemius was dissuaded by Hilarus from his intention of promoting an edict of general toleration of heretics. Hilarus was diligent in building churches, and even libraries and baths, in Rome and enriching the churches with ornaments and sacred vessels. He built a monastery at St Lawrence's, where he was to be buried, beside the tomb of his predecessor, St Sixtus.

St SIMPLICIUS
(Elected 3 March 468; died 10 March 483)

Simplicius was born at Tivoli, not far from Rome. As Pope he witnessed what modern historians often regard as the fall of the Roman Empire in the West with the deposition of last Western Emperor Romulus Augustulus by the Goth Odoacer in 476, and also the collapse of imperial support for the Christological settlement of Chalcedon: neither of these events, however, was thought worth recording in his biography in the *Book of the Pontiffs*. Simplicius was nevertheless actively involved in support of Chalcedon, initially in support of Acacius, Patriarch of Constantinople, who opposed the occupation of the Sees of Antioch and Alexandria by opponents of Chalcedon, Peter the Fuller and Timothy the Weasel, in the 470s. After the death of the Emperor Leo I, imperial policy began to change, and under the Emperor Zeno, a Christological statement, devized by Acacius and Peter the Hoarse, called the Henoticon, was promoted in 482. On the basis of this Acacius received Peter the Hoarse, now Patriarch of Alexandria, into communion. Simplicius, alerted to this by the appeal of John Talaia, displaced at Alexandria by Peter's accession, protested to Acacius, but it does not seem that he ever knew much about the Henoticon. In Rome itself Simplicius was active in building, and in the pastoral organization of the Roman clergy.

St FELIX II (III)
(Elected 13 March 483; died 1 March 492)

On his deathbed, Simplicius had required that no election of a successor was to be made without consulting Basilius, a leader of the Roman aristocracy and chief minister to Odoacer. It seems likely that this was to ensure a smooth transition in the changed political circumstances in Italy. The man elected as his successor, Felix, is the first known aristocrat to have occupied the See of St Peter: he was a deacon, the son of a priest, and himself a widower, with at least two children, and an ancestor of St Gregory the Great. Felix inherited from Simplicius the Christological disarray following the issuing of the Henoticon. On his election, he sent an embassy to Constantinople, to announce his election to the Emperor Zeno (whom he addressed in warm terms) and both to encourage Acacius in the Chalcedonian Faith and also to summon him to Rome to answer in synod the charges of John Talaia. The envoys, Bishop Vitalis of Truentum and Bishop Misenus of Cumae, were arrested and coerced—and bribed—into entering into communion with Acacius and the legates of Peter the Hoarse, thereby frustrating the papal initiative. Their behaviour was reported back to Rome by the strictly Orthodox monks of the

Above: St Simplicius. *His pontificate saw the collapse of imperial support for the settlement of Chalcedon-and, at last, the end of Roman imperial power.*

Left: Flavius Anastasius, *Roman Consul, is portrayed in a sixth-century carving. Roman aristocrats filled positions of power under "barbarian" rule.*

monastery of the Akoimetoi (the 'sleepless monks'), and the envoys returned to face trial before a synod at which they were excommunicated and deposed. The synod also excommunicated Acacius: the sentence of excommunication was taken to Constantinople by Titus, who was also bribed at the capital, but not before the sentence had been delivered to the Akoimetoi, who pinned the decree of excommunication on Acacius' back while he was celebrating in Hagia Sophia. Acacius responded by excommunicating the Pope. On Acacius' death in 489, Felix communicated cordially with his successor, Fravitas, and offered to heal the schism on condition that Fravitas accepted the condemnation of the memory of Acacius, a condition acceptable neither to the Patriarch nor to the Emperor. Despite a renewed attempt at reconciliation after the accession of the new Emperor, Anastasius, in 491, the schism—it was called the "Acacian" schism and was to divide Christendom for thirty-four years—outlasted the Pope.

St GELASIUS I
(Elected 1 March 492; died 21 November 496)

Born in Rome of African descent, Gelasius had already played a major role in papal affairs before his election as Pope, for as Archdeacon and "Secretary of State" his was the mind behind the letters in his predecessor's name that spelt out Rome's position as defender of orthodoxy. He maintained this position during his own pontificate, appearing even more unbending and scornful of the wiles of the "Greeks". Within months of his accession, the Gothic "king" Odoacer was overthrown by the Ostrogoth Theoderic, who invaded Italy with the support of the Emperor Zeno. The Pope, along with the bulk of the Roman aristocracy, accepted the change of regime. Theoderic's embassy to the Emperor to secure the title "king"—on that occasion unsuccessful—also acted on Gelasius' behalf in the matter of the Acacian schism, but Anastasius' proffered compromise was rejected in a letter that has become famous for its distinction between priestly and secular power—sacerdotium and imperium—a distinction already traditional but destined to be an important influence on the medieval assertion of papal power. Others in Rome perhaps manifest a gentler attitude: at a synod held in Rome in 495, the surviving envoy, excommunicated for his frailty in 484, Bishop Misenus of Cumae, was absolved and restored to office. In Rome itself, Gelasius was active against heresies, especially Manichaeism, and also against the continued observance of pagan practices by the now Christian populace: he made determined attempts to outlaw the celebration of the Lupercalia (this may

have taken place under his predecessor, but the letter that survives condemning the practice is most likely from the pen of Gelasius). Like many popes, he was active in building. He is said to have built, among others, the Churchof St Euphemia at Tivoli: the dedication may be significant, as it was in a church dedicated to that Eastern saint that the Council of Chalcedon had been held. Gelasius' harsh, unbending stance may seem unattractive, but he was revered by those who knew him for his holiness and personal austerity, his charity to the poor and the pastoral support of his clergy. He was no mean theologian: several treatises against heresies are rightly attributed to him. Although neither the Gelasian decree nor the Gelasian sacramentaries are his, the reputation as a liturgist that led to these traditional ascriptions is not unfounded: several of the "Leonine" masses are probably the work of Gelasius.

ANASTASIUS II
(Elected 24 November 496; died 19 November 498)

With Gelasius' successor, there was a brief attempt to resolve the Acacian schism. Anastasius II, a Roman by birth, who had been one of the deacons behind the synod that restored Misenus, began his pontificate with a letter to the Emperor, in which he humbly announced his desire for reconciliation, the only condition being the condemnation of the memory of Acacius, though even over this he appeared open to negotiation. This was followed by an embassy to Constantinople, again an embassy jointly with Theoderic, who renewed his attempt to secure the title "king". In Constantinople, the envoy, Festus, persuaded the Churchof Constantinople to celebrate the feast of the Apostles Peter and Paul, and negotiated a deal whereby Theoderic was recognized as king in return for the Pope's acceptance of the Henoticon. This was almost certainly rejected by the bishops who accompanied Festus, but he promised to persuade the Pope to accept the compromise. This turn of events impressed the Bishop of Thessalonica—a see which at this stage was still under the jurisdiction of the Pope as belonging to one of the Western prefectures, and which had been denounced by Gelasius for entering into communion with Acacius—who sent his deacon Photinus to renew communion with the Roman See. He was admitted to communion by Anastasius, an act regarded as the last straw by those in Rome faithful

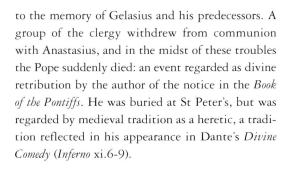

Left: The Apostles Peter and Paul. *Festus, Pope Anastasius II's envoy to Constantinople, was able to persuade the Church there to celebrate the feast of the two apostles, and also negotiated the recognition of Theoderic, Ostrogothic ruler of Rome, as king. However, the concessions made by Anastasius in pursuit of these ends caused him to be branded heretical.*

to the memory of Gelasius and his predecessors. A group of the clergy withdrew from communion with Anastasius, and in the midst of these troubles the Pope suddenly died: an event regarded as divine retribution by the author of the notice in the *Book of the Pontiffs*. He was buried at St Peter's, but was regarded by medieval tradition as a heretic, a tradition reflected in his appearance in Dante's *Divine Comedy* (*Inferno* xi.6-9).

St SYMMACHUS
(Elected 22 November 498; died 19 July 514)

With the death of Pope Anastasius, Rome faced an internal schism. On the same day, two men were declared Pope: at the Lateran basilica the deacon Symmachus, a Sardinian and a convert from paganism, was chosen, and at the basilica of S. Maria Maggiore the priest Laurentius. Both found support among the clergy and the senate. They appealed to Theoderic, the Ostrogothic king, himself an Arian, who laid down two criteria for his decision: priority of consecration and majority support. Symmachus fulfilled both criteria and was declared Pope; the Laurentians attributed his success to bribery. Symmachus thereupon called a synod in St Peter's to endorse this decision, and among the signatories was the archpriest Laurentius himself, who was given the See of Nuceria (Nocera) in Campania. The following year Theoderic made an official visit to Rome, where he was welcomed by the Pope and the Senate and entire people of Rome. A year later, however, a group of clergy and senators, led by Festus, the envoy who had compromised Anastasius and had led the Laurentian party after his death, made charges to Theoderic against Symmachus, the

Right: Theoderic the Great *(455-526), King of the Ostrogoths, an Arian, endorsed the pontificates of Symmachus, whom he supported against the self-proclaimed Pope Laurentius, and Hormisdas.*

first of which was that he had celebrated Easter according to the old Roman Easter-cycle, and not according to the Alexandrian one, as required by the Council of Nicaea. The king called Symmachus to answer these charges at a synod in Rimini. On his arrival, Symmachus discovered that there were other charges—unchastity and misappropriation of church property—and fled, taking refuge in St Peter's. At this point Laurentius was probably recalled to Rome by his supporters, and many of the clergy withdrew from communion with Symmachus and supported Laurentius. Again Theoderic was called on to intervene and appointed Peter, an Istrian bishop, to preside over a synod at which the charges against Symmachus could be heard. Although Symmachus appeared before the synod, he refused to acknowledge the authority of the synod to sit in judgment on him. There was deadlock. All this took place in the context of increasing violence. When the Pope set out to appear before the synod on 1 September 502, his party was set upon by a mob of Laurentian supporters; many were injured and two of Symmachus' priests killed. A further meeting of the synod simply dropped the charges against Symmachus. Symmachus then called a synod in St Peter's in November 502, which rejected the arguments of the Laurentians and further declared against all lay involvement in Church matters, the immediate object being the decree against the alienation of Church property promul-

gated by Basilius in 483. But all this resolved nothing: Laurentius returned to Rome, and with the support of Festus and others held the Roman Churches and ruled as Pope. The period from 502 to 506 was one of civil violence verging on civil war. A resolution was finally achieved by two deacons from outside Rome: Ennodius of Milan, who drew on the wealth of Milan, as well as his skill as an advocate, to persuade the court at Ravenna; and Dioscorus, an exile from Alexandria, who led the final embassy in 506. As a result of Theoderic's intervention, Festus handed over the Roman churches and Laurentius withdrew, and soon after died—of excessive fasting, it was said. Once victorious, Symmachus made sure that his party was firmly established. He ordained an exceptional number of clergy: 92 priests and 16 deacons, some of whom presumably replaced those expelled for their support of Laurentius. His building work was concentrated on the Vatican Hill, which he held throughout the troubles: indeed, he seems to have been the first Pope to make the Vatican his home.

St HORMISDAS
(Elected 20 July 514; died 6 August 523)

Hormisdas, a native of Campania, was a deacon at the time of his election, one of Symmachus' earliest diaconal appointments. After his election, he was approached by the Emperor Anastasius who was anxious for reconciliation between Rome and the East, not least because his continued support for the Henoticon had provided a pretext for rebellion against his rule. Hormisdas responded with two embassies in 515 and 517, both led by the Milanese deacon, Ennodius, who had been instrumental in gaining Symmachus' recognition, and who was now Bishop of Ticinum (Pavia): neither was successful, as the Emperor was not prepared to condemn the deceased Acacius. In 518, however, Anastasius died, to be succeeded by Justin, the son of a peasant from Dardania (in the Balkans), who had risen through the ranks to become commander of the imperial bodyguard. His nephew was Justinian, who is generally reckoned to have been the power behind the throne until he succeeded his uncle in 527. Immediately there was a change in imperial religious policy: the Henoticon was abandoned, and Chalcedon unequivocally supported. This was communicated to Hormisdas by the Emperor, who responded with an embassy, this time led (unoffi-

only were Acacius and his successors condemned, but the emperors Zeno and Anastasius as well. But this reunion did nothing to solve the problem the Emperor still faced of reluctance in the East to accept Chalcedon, and when a refinement of Chalcedonian orthodoxy emerged, Hormisdas was unable to respond positively. This refinement is usually called "theopaschism" (misleadingly, for it did not entail the passibility of the divine nature), and is associated at this stage with a group of Scythian monks (i.e., monks from modern Dobruja, the coastal region of Romania), led by John Maxentius. At the heart of Eastern reluctance to endorse Chalcedon was the fear that it compromised Cyril's stress on the unity of the Incarnate Christ. This fear the Scythian monks sought to meet by proposing the formula that "one of the Trinity suffered in the flesh" as a gloss on the Chalcedonian definition: this formula made clear that the person of Christ was the divine person who became incarnate, and not a product of the Incarnation. Justinian was convinced, and the monks made their way to Rome, where they received no joy from the Pope, although others endorsed their formula, including Dionysius Exiguus and Boethius. Papal opposition to the theopaschite formula was stiffened by Dioscorus (for whom Hormisdas had failed to secure the patriarchate of Alexandria) who regarded theopaschism as contrary to Chalcedon, and a vitriolic response by John Maxentius to a leaked letter from the Pope on the subject led to Hormisdas' formally communicating to the Emperor his rejection of theopaschism, but this had no effect on Justinian. Throughout Hormisdas maintained good relations with Theoderic. The *Book of the Pontiffs* records gifts to the Apostolic See during Hormisdas' pontificate from the Emperor Justin, Clovis the Frankish king, and Theoderic.

St JOHN I
(Elected 13 August 523; died 18 May 526)

Hormisdas' successor was John, a senior deacon, by now old and infirm, who almost certainly supported Laurentius until he was reconciled with Symmachus in 506. He was a native of Tuscany, and a friend of Boethius who dedicated three of his theological tractates to him, calling him his "saintly master and venerable father". On the advice of Dionysius Exiguus (a Scythian monk, now long resident in Rome, and a translator who made much Greek the-

Above: St John I, *aged and infirm, headed an embassy to Constantinople sent by Theoderic to seek better treatment for Arians. Although partly successful, he failed to satisfy Theoderic, and died in disgrace while under house arrest.*

Left: Clovis I *(465-511), King of the Franks, converted to Christianity by his wife, St Clotilda of Burgundy, championed orthodoxy against the Arian Theoderic the Great, by whom he was defeated at Arles.*

cially at least) by Dioscorus, the exiled Alexandrian deacon (now adopted by the Apostolic See), who had also been instrumental in securing Theoderic's support for Symmachus. The embassy was warmly welcomed in Constantinople, and the Pope's terms for reunion accepted, and even exceeded, for not

Right: Emperor Justinian I
(c.482-565) is shown with a model of Hagia Sophia (the Church of the Holy Wisdom), the great basilica (now a museum) built at his order in Constantinople in 532-537.

ology available in Latin), he introduced the Alexandrian computation of Easter, which had been the ostensible cause of the renewal of the Laurentian schism. The now elderly Theoderic had been unsettled by the change of religious policy in Constantinople, combined with the collapse of his alliances, through marriages, with the barbarian kingdoms of the West. Part of his response was to send a distinguished embassy to Constantinople, led by Pope John himself, to seek not only an end to Justin's policy of persecution of Arians and confiscation of Arian churches, but also the reconversion to Arianism of those Arians who had been forced to become Catholic. John's embassy was warmly received, and remarkably successful, but could not secure the Emperor's agreement to the reconversion of the forcibly-converted Arians. On their return to Italy, John and the rest of the embassy, in disgrace, were put under house arrest by Theoderic in Ravenna, where John soon died. At about the same time (probably later, though our sources are in conflict), Theoderic's unease about links between the Italian aristocracy and the Eastern capital, no longer divided by religious differences, led to the deaths of Boethius and his father-in-law, Symmachus, both executed for treason. All three—John, Boethius and Symmachus—were regarded as martyrs for Catholic orthodoxy, and there rapidly developed a cult of the martyred Pope. Shortly afterwards, on 30 August 526, Theoderic himself died, somewhat unfairly execrated as an Arian persecutor.

St FELIX III(IV)
(Elected 12 July 526; died 22 September 530)

The seven-week gap between death of John I and the election of Felix makes it clear that the election did not run smoothly. One of the versions of the *Book of the Pontiffs* says that he was consecrated at the order of king Theoderic, which suggests that, as in 498, there had been a contested election, and appeal had been made to Theoderic. It would seem that he chose the candidate popular with the people rather than the senate, and also someone favorable to the Gothic cause. Felix (like Symmachus) was liberal with his gifts to the poor, and is also said to have enriched the papacy, although no gifts are recorded from the Eastern court, as with his two predecessors: the most obvious source of this wealth would seem to be the Gothic court. Shortly after his election Theoderic died, and was succeeded by his young grandson, Athalaric, whose mother, Amalasuntha, initially acted as regent. One of Athalaric's edicts confirmed the right of the papacy to judge cases concerning the clergy: a sign of royal favor towards Felix. At his election, Felix, a Samnite by birth, was a deacon, one of those appointed by Symmachus, and probably the same as the Felix who accompanied the embassy to the East in 519. Like Symmachus, he conducted a large number of ordinations—four deacons and fifty-five priests (John had ordained no-one, and Hormisdas only priests)—which suggests a purge of the clerical ranks, as under Symmachus. His concern to secure the continuance of the pro-Gothic faction led to his nominating Boniface as his successor on his sickbed: an action that provoked outrage from the senate.

BONIFACE II
(Elected 22 September 530; died 17 October 532)

Despite Felix III's precautions, his death was followed by a contested election. The two candidates were the Archdeacon Boniface, Felix's nominee, a Roman by birth, but whose father bore a Germanic name, Sigibuld, and the deacon Dioscorus, the exiled Alexandrian, supporter of Symmachus, Hormisdas' unsuccessful candidate for the throne of Alexandria. The election took place in the Lateran basilica and Dioscorus secured a large majority; the pro-Gothic minority withdrew to the basilica of

Left: Justinian I, *like his predecessor and uncle, Emperor Justin I, was of Latin stock and thus deeply concerned with events in the West.*

Julius (S. Maria in Trastevere) where they elected Boniface. Dioscorus' accession to the papacy was ratified by the Emperor, but on 14 October he died. Boniface's triumph was eventually secured, and on 27 December the sixty priests who had supported Dioscorus condemned the memory of Dioscorus and declared their support for Boniface. Boniface seems to have devoted his pontificate to supporting the clergy (presumably to secure their support). Mindful of the fact that it was as a supporter of the Goths that he had become Pope, Boniface tried, like his predecessor, to designate a suitable successor, in

this case the deacon Vigilius. But the outcry was so great that he formally revoked his choice, and Vigilius was despatched to Constantinople as papal apocrisiarius (permanent representative at the imperial court).

JOHN II
(Elected 2 January 533; died 8 May 535)

The two-month gap between the death of Boniface and the election of John II suggests that the election was far from smooth. A letter from King

53

Right: Belisarius, *the general on whom Justinian chiefly relied to fulfill his dream of re-uniting the Eastern and Western empires, is shown with the Emperor and others in a sixth-century mosaic.*

Athalaric to the new Pope reveals that the election campaign had been a scandalous affair with widespread corruption: bribing of the factions in Rome, and of the royal officials involved in political confirmation of the election, as well as mass suborning of the Roman mob. The king announced that he was confirming a decree passed in 530 by the senate to prevent any future irregularities. The man eventually elected was not a Roman deacon (as with every other sixth-century Pope where we can be sure), but the parish priest of St Clement's on the Caelian Hill, Roman by birth, bearing the pagan name of Mercurius, which he changed to John lest it bring shame to the See of St Peter. On election he received from the Emperor Justinian a confession of faith and precious sacred vessels, an attention denied to either of his predecessors. In return the Pope accepted the theopaschite formula, and even excommunicated the Akoimetoi, for years the Pope's staunchest allies in Constantinople, for their refusal to accept it. Nonetheless his relations with the Gothic court seem to have been cordial.

St AGAPITUS I
(Elected 13 May 535; died 22 April 536)

On John's death, Agapitus, a Roman by birth, the son of a priest and relative, maybe nephew, of Pope Felix II, was quickly elected to the papal throne. He was an elderly man, a last survivor of the Symmachan old guard, who had been ordained deacon as long ago as 502 and only recently attained the rank of archdeacon. He began his pontificate in conciliatory fashion by publicly burning the public confession Boniface had extracted from the supporters of Dioscorus after Dioscorus' death. In the same year Anthimos, an opponent of Chalcedon, was appointed Patriarch of Constantinople, but Agapitus' election, which had already taken place, can hardly be seen as a reaction to that further challenge to Chalcedon in the East. Agapitus, however, was soon to meet Anthimos, though that was not the purpose of his visit to the imperial capital. The Emperor Justinian had grand ideas about the restoration of the Roman Empire. He had already restored to imperial rule North Africa, for long under the rule of the Vandals, and the murder of Amalasuntha on the order of her cousin Theodahad in 534 gave Justinian the pretext he needed for the invasion of Italy. Belisarius, the victor of North Africa, invaded Sicily in 535. It was as the envoy of

MAXIMIANVS

the panic-stricken Theodahad that Agapitus set out for Constantinople. Once there, in the spring of 536, Agapitus tackled the religious question. Justinian tried to coerce Agapitus into recognizing Anthimos as patriarch, but Agapitus insisted on a disputation between himself and Anthimos, in which he demonstrated the heretical views of Anthimus to Justinian's satisfaction. Anthimos was deposed and exiled, and Agapitus consecrated Menas to the patriarchal throne. A month later Agapitus died, but a synod held after his death, attended by his fellow envoys, confirmed the deposition of Anthimos and the election of Menas. Agapitus' body was taken back to Rome, and buried in St Peter's on 20 September 536.

St SILVERIUS

(Elected 8 June 536; deposed 11 March 537; abdicated 11 November 537; died 2 December 537)

Even before Agapitus' body had reached Rome, Silverius had been appointed his successor. His entry in the *Book of the Pontiffs* makes it clear that he was imposed by the Gothic King Theodahad, and not formally elected at all. Theodahad may have been bribed by Silverius, but the main reason for his appointment was his support for the Goths. Meanwhile Belisarius had invaded the Italian mainland; he advanced through Campania, and after taking Naples, made for Rome. Silverius, the pro-Gothic Pope, soon found himself at the mercy of the forces of the Empire. The accounts about what happened next are conflicting, but the following outline is probably right in essential details. Vigilius, the former papal apocrisiarius, now Archdeacon, whom Boniface had intended as his (pro-Gothic) successor, had arrived from Constantinople with the intention of replacing the pro-Gothic Silverius—as a pro-Eastern Pope acceptable to the Empire. Silverius' loyalty was clearly in doubt, and Rome itself was threatened by the Gothic army under the newly-elected King Witigis, so Belisarius had Silverius deposed on 11 March 537 and exiled to Patara in Lycia (in the southwestern corner of Asia Minor). The Bishop of Patara, however, appealed to Justinian over the uncanonical deposition of Silverius, and Silverius was ordered back to Rome to face trial. Back in Italy, neither Vigilius nor Belisarius cared to be bothered further with the issue of Silverius. He was exiled again, this time to

Above: St Silverius, *the favored candidate of the Gothic ruler Theodahad, may have owed his pontificate to bribery. He was deposed and exiled by Belisarius, and was at last forced to abdicate.*

Left: Totila, King of the Ostrogoths, *seen here kneeling before St Benedict, led the last surge of Gothic resistance to the Byzantine reconquest. He was defeated and killed in 552.*

the island of Palmaria in the gulf of Gaeta, where he was forced to abdicate the papal throne on 11 November, and a few weeks later died.

VIGILIUS
(Elected 29 March 537; died 7 June 555)

Vigilius, a Roman aristocrat, appointed papal apocrisiarius in Constantinople in 532 after having been unsuccessfully nominated by Pope Boniface as his successor, finally achieved the papal throne as the imperial nominee. His pontificate ushered in a new era for the papacy, for the defeat of the Goths, which was secured during his reign, brought Italy and Rome once more under the power of the Roman (or Byzantine) Emperor in Constantinople. The conquest of the Goths was not, however, achieved easily: after an initial success under Belisarius in 540, the Goths rallied under a new king, Totila, and were only finally vanquished under Narses in the early 550s. Nearly twenty years of constant warfare had devastated Italy, which was further ravaged by plague which was to remain endemic for the next two centuries. Vigilius' reign began with his sending letters affirming his orthodoxy to the Emperor and the Patriarch Menas, and beginning to repair the destruction caused by the siege of Rome, in the course of which he had been elected. This early stage reached its high-point in 544 when, at a great assembly of the Roman clergy and people, Vigilius received the dedication of a metrical version of the Acts of the Apostles, composed by the subdeacon Arator, who gave a series of public readings of this much-admired, though to our taste rather tedious, work. But Vigilius was quickly to learn what was entailed in being an imperial nominee. For Justinian's plans for the Empire included not only territorial expansion, which made Italy once again part of the Empire, but also a religious settlement that would heal the wounds left by the Council of Chalcedon in 451. One element of this was the theopaschite formula, which Rome had already accepted (see Hormisdas and John II); further elements were the condemnation of theologians of the so-called Antiochene school, whom the Monophysites abhorred, and condemnation of the great Alexandrian theologian, Origen, and his followers (this latter was, however, purely of concern to the East: our Western sources know nothing of it). The condemnation of the Antiochenes is known as the condemnation of the

"Three Chapters", since it involved the condemnation of the writings and the person of Theodore, early fourth-century Bishop of Mopsuestia, thought to be the teacher of Nestorius, whose condemnation Cyril of Alexandria had secured at the Council of Ephesus of 431, and certain writings (against Cyril) by Theodoret, Bishop of Cyrrhus, and Ibas, Bishop of Edessa. Theodoret and Ibas had, however, been among the fathers of the Council of Chalcedon: condemnation of their views looked to some like a roundabout way of calling in question the Council itself. In 544 Vigilius was reminded that his loyalty to the Emperor would involve condemnation of the Three Chapters. Vigilius refused: he was arrested and taken to Catania in Sicily to await further developments. While there he sounded out Western theological opinion, which was strongly against condemnation of the Three Chapters. After a year he was summoned to Constantinople. There his opposition to the condemnation of the Three Chapters wavered, once he realized how deeply committed to it the Emperor was. The story of the next few years is very tangled, with Vigilius and members of his entourage wavering in their attitude to the Three Chapters, and the imperial court doing everything it could to encourage, or coerce, support, especially among bishops in the newly-conquered Western provinces. In April 548 Vigilius issued a formal judgment (the Judicatum), in which he accepted the condemnation of the Three Chapters. The Western reaction to this was such that, in August 550, Vigilius withdrew it, while at the same time promising secretly to help the Emperor secure condemnation of the Three Chapters at a forthcoming council. A formally constituted Ecumenical Council was called: in June 552 the Pope and Emperor were reconciled; in May 553 the Council itself was opened. Vigilius sought a compromise, embodied in his Constitutum, which condemned Theodore of Mopsuestia, but not Theodoret or Ibas. This was refused by the council, which accepted instead the secret document containing the Pope's promise to condemn the Three Chapters. Having secured the condemnation of the Three Chapters at his council, Justinian set about suppressing all opposition: several prominent Western opponents were arrested and exiled, and Vigilius himself placed in solitary confinement on bread and water. By the end of the year Vigilius had weakened, and in February 554 he issued a second Constitutum which accepted the decisions of the

Above: Vigilius. *Having earlier failed to gain election as the nominated successor of Pope Boniface II, Virgilius finally achieved office as the favored candidate of the Roman (or Byzantine) Emperor in Constantinople.*

Fifth Ecumenical Council. Vigilius was released from his incarceration, but while on his way back to Rome, he died in Syracuse.

PELAGIUS I
(Elected September 555; consecrated 16 April 556; died 3 March 561)

Pelagius, a learned and noble Roman, had had an active career as a deacon before he ascended the papal throne: he had accompanied Agapitus to Constantinople, and remained there after his death; in 537 he had succeeded Vigilius as apocrisiarius, a position he held until 544. When Justinian issued his edict condemning the Three Chapters in 544, he had been in Rome and sought the support of Ferrandus of Carthage against it. He did not accompany Vigilius to Constantinople, but remained in Rome and played a major role in defense of the city against the Goths, and in negotiating with Totila to prevent a massacre. In 547 he went to Constantinople as Totila's envoy to negotiate peace, without success. In the affair of the Three Chapters, he remained opposed to their condemnation, sharing Vigilius' sufferings, and denouncing his final capitulation, until, in turn, he yielded to the imperial will which made his acceptance of the condemnation of the Three Chapters a condition for imperial support to his accession to the papal throne. He therefore arrived back in Rome a tainted candidate. The candidate with popular support was the priest Mareas, who had looked after Rome for much of Vigilius' long absence, but he died in August 555, leaving Pelagius unopposed. Such was his unpopularity, however, that it was more than six months before Pelagius could find even two (instead of the canonical three) bishops to consecrate him. Once established as Pope, he faced further opposition: a group of clergy in Rome itself withdrew from communion with him over his support for the condemnation of the Three Chapters, and outside Rome many bishops refused communion with him. He found it necessary to send an official declaration of his orthodoxy to the Frankish King Childebert in February 557 to secure his support. Pelagius also set about restoring the devastation wrought in Rome and Suburbicarian Italy by the Gothic wars, redeeming captives, rebuilding churches, restoring estates, appointing clergy. With the help of a lay banker, Anastasius, he reorganized the papal finances. His genuine success in relieving poverty

Above: Pelagius I, *a scholar and aristocrat, had written a brilliant* Defence of the Three Chapters, *but accepted their condemnation as the price of imperial support. He did not fully recover from the unpopularity this caused.*

Left: King Childebert I *of the Franks. Pelagius I was able to convince the Frankish ruler of his orthodoxy, but was never reconciled to the northern Italian bishops, who long remained in schism.*

Above: John III. *His reign saw the death of Emperor Justinian I in 565–and with it the end of the grand conception of a restored Roman Empire–and the invasion of Italy by the Lombards in 568.*

Left: The Abbey of St Germain-des-Prés *(originally the Monastery of St Vincent), Paris, is endowed by the Frankish ruler Childebert I, who brought back the revered tunic of St Vincent as a trophy from a campaign in Spain.*

and restoring normality must have contributed to winning over those who at first opposed him in Rome and Suburbicarian Italy, but the bishops of Istria (not just the modern Istrian peninsula, but Northern Italy round to Venice), under the leadership of the Archbishop of Aquileia, were to remain in schism from Rome for 150 years. As a deacon he had used his scholarly gifts make known in the West something of the wealth of Greek piety and theology by embarking on a translation of the Greek *Sayings of the Desert Fathers*; his theological acumen is manifest in his *Defence of the Three Chapters*, a work the brilliant argumentation of which must have been an embarrassment to him when, as Pope, he was forced to reverse his position in order to gain imperial approval.

JOHN III
(Consecrated 17 July 561; died 13 July 574)

John was a Roman aristocrat like his two predecessors; he may have changed his name to John, like John II, and, as in his case, such reverence for the memory of the martyred John I may indicate pro-Eastern leanings. It is likely that he is the same as John the subdeacon, who completed Pelagius' translations of the *Sayings of the Desert Fathers*. John's reign was notable for two events: the death of the Emperor Justinian, and the invasion of Italy by the Lombards. Justinian's death meant also the demize of his grand conception of a restored Roman Empire; his successors were more concerned with the threats of the Persians in the East and the encroachment of the Slavs on the Danubian frontier, than with Italy and the papacy. The invasion by the Lombards coincided with (and may have been occasioned by) the dismissal of Narses, the provincial governor who had finally defeated the Goths. The restoration of Roman rule in 554 meant the renewed burden of imperial taxes, and the oppressed Italians, angry at the wealth of the successful Narses, in 567 complained about him to the Emperor, who replaced him with Longinus. Narses retired to Naples. In 568 the Lombards invaded and established themselves in duchies throughout Italy, threatening both Rome, and the imperial provincial government centred on Ravenna. Eventually Roman (or Byzantine) rule was established through a military exarchate with its headquarters in Ravenna, which was defended by what Byzantine troops there were, leaving Rome cruelly exposed.

BENEDICT I
(consecrated 2 June 575; died 30 July 579)

Benedict was a Roman. The long gap between his predecessor's death and his election does not, as it would under the Goths, suggest trouble, for now papal elections had to be confirmed by the Emperor in Constantinople (and the date of "election" is, in fact, the date of consecration). Very little is known about Benedict's reign. Lombard raids and a siege of Rome caused a severe famine, which was relieved by supplies sent by the Emperor Justin II from Egypt. But Benedict made significant appointments: the future Gregory the Great was called from his monastery into the papal service and ordained deacon by Benedict, and he made sure of Rome"s ascendancy over Ravenna by securing the appointment of a Roman called John as Archbishop in the Western imperial capital.

PELAGIUS II
(Elected 26 November 579; died 7 February 590)

Benedict died during a Lombard siege, so Pelagius was consecrated before the imperial mandate had arrived (the official date of election is the date of the receipt of the mandate). He was a Roman, whose father, Unigild, bore a Gothic name. He immediately sent his apocrisiarius, Gregory, to Constantinople to seek support against the Lombards, and, when that was unavailing, wrote to Aunarius, Bishop of Auxerre, to seek Frankish sup-

port against the Lombards, with no greater success. In 585, however, the exarch in Ravenna negotiated an armistice with the Lombards which lasted for four years. He was actively engaged in building projects, probably moving the high altar in St Peter's to its position immediately above the relics of the apostle, and building the Church of S. Lorenzo fuori le Mure. He also turned his Roman family house into an almshouse. He made an unsuccessful attempt to repair the breach with the Istrian bishops over the Three Chapters controversy. It was also in his pontificate that the quarrel with John, Patriarch of Constantinople, broke out over his use of the title "œcumenical patriarch", a title the patriarchs of Constantinople had been using since the fifth century with the meaning "supreme within the patriarchate", but taken by the Pope to mean "universal patriarch" with pretensions to primacy.

St GREGORY I
(born c. 540; consecrated 3 September 590; died 12 March 604)

Gregory was a wealthy Roman aristocrat, belonging to a family that had already provided popes Felix II and Agapitus. Having received a good education, he entered the public administration and served as city prefect of Rome c. 572-4. On the death of his father, Gordian, he converted the family house on the Caelian Hill into the Monastery of St Andrew, which he joined as a monk. He also founded six other monasteries on family estates in Sicily. He was called from the severely ascetic life he was living as a monk (which ruined his health) and made deacon by Pope Benedict in 578; Pope

Above: Pelagius II *made a truce with the Lombard invaders but failed to heal the schism caused by the Three Chapters controversy. He also quarreled with the Patriarch of Constantinople.*

Left: Gregory I, *aided by followers of St Benedict, composes his* Dialogues. *This work, a valuable source for the understanding of medieval ideas of holiness, was especially popular in the East, where he was called "Dialogos."*

Above: King Reccared of Spain *(ruled 586-601), a Visigoth, is received into the Church. Pope Gregory I maintained a warm relationship with Reccared through Bishop Leander of Seville.*

Pelagius sent him to Constantinople as apocrisiarius the following year. In 585/6 he returned to Rome and his monastery, and seems to have acted as Secretary of State to Pope Pelagius. On Pelagius' death, he was elected unanimously to succeed him. Despite his reluctance, and indeed attempts to avoid the office, which included writing to the Emperor Maurice to persuade him to refuse his mandate, and maybe even flight, Gregory was consecrated to the Roman See. As Pope he continued to live a life of monastic simplicity, and expected the same of those who formed the papal household at the Lateran, replacing a papal court of powerful clerics and laymen with a community of monks. Faced with the collapse of public administration throughout Italy as a result of the Lombard presence, he was forced to fill the gap himself, negotiating peace treaties with the Lombards, paying the army, organizing the food supply, overseeing the

administration of the estates of the papal patrimonies, extending the patronage of the Roman See principally as a way of avoiding unregulated chaos. He established warm links with the newly-Catholic Visigothic King of Spain, Reccared, through his friend from Constantinopolitan days, Leander, Bishop of Seville, and also with Gaul, where he reestablished the papal vicariate of Arles. Gregory's attempts to bring the recalcitrant clergy of Istria to heel were thwarted by the Emperor Maurice. Relationships with the East proved more difficult, as he inherited, and continued to pursue, the quarrel over John of Constantinople's use of the title "oecumenical patriarch", which he persisted in regarding as an infringement of the privileges of the See of St Peter. Not entirely different was the quarrel with the Archbishop of Ravenna over his use of the pallium, which Gregory interpreted as a challenge to the Petrine claims of the Holy See. In 596

Right: Gregory I *calls for divine intercession to halt a plague that ravages Rome. His predecessor, Pelagius II, is said to have died from this plague, which Gregory's prayers at last averted.*

he sent a group of monks from his monastery of St Andrew, led by Augustine, to England to convert the Anglo-Saxons, and continued to guide that venture through his letters, through reinforcements in 601 when Mellitus was sent to became Bishop of London, and through granting Augustine the pallium as Archbishop of Canterbury. Alongside all this pastoral and administrative activity, he sought to give first place to a life of prayer and contemplation and wrote profoundly and simply on the Christian faith. His published homilies included series on the Gospels, on Job and on Ezekiel, but

his two most influential works were his *Pastoral Care* (*Regula Pastoralis*), a guide to the life and duties of a bishop, and his *Dialogues*, which provide a vivid account of the contours of medieval ideas of the holy. Translated into Greek by Gregory's successor, Zacharias, the *Dialogues* became very popular in the East, where Gregory, to whom the Liturgy of the Presanctified Gifts is ascribed, was given the epithet "Dialogos". In Rome itself, he certainly introduced certain changes into the liturgy, and may have established a school for the training of singers, but the so-called "Gregorian" sacramentary is mainly a later compilation. Book 2 of the *Dialogues* constitute a life of S. Benedict of Nursia, whose influence on Western monasticism was to be enormous, not least because of the reverence in which he was held by Pope Gregory. Gregory also promoted monasticism (it would be anachronistic to say "Benedictine" monasticism) by granting monasteries privileges and advancing monks to positions of ecclesiastical authority in Rome and beyond. Despite his worldwide fame, Gregory's memory was initially neglected in Rome itself, mainly, it is thought, because of the unpopularity of his "monasticization" of the papal court. Not until the late ninth century was anyone in Rome inspired to write his biography: his earliest biography was composed in the sixth century by an anonymous monk of Whitby in England, where his memory remained green. As he lay dying, Rome was facing a fresh siege and was already suffering from famine: the mob turned on the dying Pope

Left: St Augustine, *from Gregory I's monastery of St Andrew in Rome, was appointed by the Pope to lead a mission to convert England to Christianity. Here, he faces Anglo-Saxon nobles.*

Right: St Gregory I the Great. *He had been city prefect of Rome before entering a monastery, and strengthened the Church through his administrative skill as well as his holiness.*

· LES GRANDS PONTIFES ·

L'ÉCOLE DE CHANT GRÉGORIEN.

SAINT GRÉGOIRE 1ᵉʳ

Left: The School of the Gregorian Chant. *Although Gregory I may have founded a school for singers, the so-called "Gregorian" sacramentary is mainly a later compilation.*

Above: Sabinian, *undistinguished successor to Gregory the Great, was accused of profiteering at a time of food shortage. His funeral procession was threatened by an angry mob.*

and sought to destroy his writings, but were prevented by Gregory's disciple, the deacon Peter. On his epitaph he is described as the "consul of God".

SABINIAN
(Consecrated 13 September 604; died 22 February 606)

Gregory was succeeded by Sabinian, a deacon who had been born in Tuscany. His epitaph remarks that he achieved this position by working his way up the clerical ladder, which suggests that Sabinian was a representative of the career clergy opposed to Gregory's "monasticization" of the papal court. It is consonant with that that he is said to have "filled the church with clergy". He seems to have negotiated a truce with the Lombards, who were besieging the city when he was elected. But when war broke out again, he was accused by the mob of profiteering by selling grain from the papal granaries (instead of distributing it freely, as Gregory had done). He died suddenly, at the height of his unpopularity: it is traditionally related that his funeral procession had to make a detour in order to avoid disruption by an angry mob.

St BONIFACE III
(Consecrated 19 February 607; died 12 November 607)

The long vacancy of nearly a year before the consecration of Boniface may simply indicate an exceptional delay in securing imperial approval, but the fact that Boniface immediately held a synod which forbade simony in connexion with the papal election and any premature canvassing suggests that such behaviour had marked the election campaign. Boniface himself was a Roman who had been one of Gregory's deacons and had served as apocrisiarius, where he had secured from the usurper Phocas an affirmation of papal primacy in connexion with the controversy that had arisen over the title of "œcumenical patriarch".

St BONIFACE IV
(Consecrated 15 September 608; died 8 May 615)

Boniface IV was the son of a doctor from Valeria, who had been one of Gregory's deacons and dispensator (treasurer). He had worked closely with

Right: The Pantheon, *erected by Emperor Adrian in AD 118-128 to honor the old Roman gods, was converted into a Christian church (Santa Maria ad Martyres) by Pope Boniface IV.*

Above: St Deusdedit (Adeodatus I). *His reign was short and troubled: it saw a serious mutiny by Byzantine troops in Italy, an earthquake in Rome, and an epidemic in which the Pope himself died.*

Right: Emperor Heraclius battles with Chosroes II. *The Emperor's struggle with the Persian leader caused the imperial confirmation of Boniface V's election as Pope to be long delayed.*

Gregory, and his epitaph describes him as imitating the "merits and examples of his master Gregory". His pontificate was marked by serious famine, plagues and flooding. Nonetheless he found the time and energy to secure from the usurper Phocas the Pantheon which he turned into a Christian church dedicated to the ever-virgin St Mary and all the martyrs (the first such conversion of a pagan temple). He also ordained the remarkably large number of eight deacons, which suggests that the Gregorian diaconate was dying out, and Boniface stepped in to replenish it with more men after Gregory's heart. Boniface kept up Gregory's interest in the English Church and was also the recipient of a letter from the Irish monk Columbanus, then in Bobbio, who sought to persuade the Pope to repudiate his predecessors' condemnation of the Three Chapters.

St DEUSDEDIT (ADEODATUS I)
(Consecrated 19 October 615; died 8 November 618)

Deusdedit was a Roman, the son of a subdeacon, who had been a priest for forty years when he acceded to the papal throne. The *Book of the Pontiffs* speaks of his love of the clergy and his restoration of the clergy to their original places: which suggests that, like Sabinian before him, he reversed the monasticization of the papal court that had been effected by his predecessor. His pontificate saw a serious mutiny of the Byzantine troops in Italy (perhaps sparked off by news of the disastrous defeat of the Byzantine army in Palestine at the hands of the Persians), and an earthquake in Rome together with an outbreak of scab disease, during the course of which the Pope died. On his deathbed he made a bequest to the clergy of an *integra roga*, probably a full year's salary.

BONIFACE V
(Consecrated 23 December 619; died 25 October 625)

Boniface was a Neapolitan, but we know nothing else about him prior to his election as Pope. The long delay in the imperial confirmation of his election is doubtless due to the Emperor Heraclius' preoccupation with the Persians who were now occupying the Eastern provinces. Boniface evidently belonged to the pro-clerical party: like his predecessor he is recorded as bequeathing to his clergy a full year's salary. He also protected clerical rights: restricting the handling of relics to priests, and the assistants of deacons at baptisms to subdeacons, both roles on which the lower order of acolytes had encroached. He also protected the right of sanctuary. He kept up, too, his namesake's interest in the English Church. The *Book of the Pontiffs* speaks of him as being 'mild and compassionate': this is confirmed by his epitaph which tells of his distributing his personal fortune in charity.

HONORIUS I
(Consecrated 27 October 625; died 12 October 638)

Honorius' pre-papal career is unknown. His epitaph says that he followed in the footsteps of Gregory the Great. His building works included the conversion

Above: Severinus. *His very brief pontificate was marked by serious trouble between the imperial and papal powers, since Severinus refused to subscribe to the imperial religious policy defined in the Ecthesis–and further accused Pope Honorius of mis-appropriating papal funds. Severinus's chief opponent, Isaac, Exarch in Ravenna, came to Rome, banished the clergy, and plundered the treasury.*

of his family house near the Lateran into a monastery dedicated to the Apostles Andrew and Bartholomew, in evident imitation of Gregory. He also appointed an abbot, John Symponus, as his Secretary of State, and made the Monastery of Bobbio exempt from local episcopal jurisdiction by placing it directly under the Apostolic See: the first recorded example of this practice. All this suggests that he belonged to the Gregorian party, of which, however, he seems to have been the last representative. But his local importance is dwarfed by his unfortunate involvement in the continuing attempts by the Byzantine emperors to make Christological doctrine a political tool. The conquest of the Eastern provinces of the Byzantine Empire in the first part of the reign of the Emperor Heraclius (610-41) had exposed the weaknesses caused by the failure to heal the schism created by the Council of Chalcedon. To counteract Persian attempts to exploit this, a group of clergy led by Sergius, Patriarch of Constantinople, sought a compromise formula which is known as monenergism: the doctrine that, although in Christ there are two distinct human and divine natures, they are united in a single divine-human (or "theandric") activity (or energy: energeia). On Heraclius' reconquest of the Eastern provinces in the late 620s, this formula was used to incorporate the Churches of Armenia and Syria, where Chalcedon had never been popular. But the greatest success of monenergism was in Alexandria, where, in 633, the new Patriarch Cyrus presided over the reconciliation of those clergy, the majority, who had gone into schism over Chalcedon. Despite vehement protests from a monk Sophronius, soon to become Patriarch of Jerusalem, Sergius reported this great ecumenical advance to Honorius. Honorius had no opinion of theologians, whom he regarded as "croaking frogs", and in his reply remarked that in Christ we confess "one will". This became the basis of a refinement of monenergism called monothelitism, which received imperial endorsement in the Ecthesis of 638. Thus a Pope found himself an heresiarch.

SEVERINUS
(Consecrated 28 May 640; died 2 August 640)

The long delay, over a year and a half, between Honorius' death and Severinus' consecration as Pope was caused entirely by the new imperial religious policy, defined in the Ecthesis. The Exarch in Ravenna, Isaac, refused to confirm the election of Severinus, an elderly Roman, unless he subscribed to the Ecthesis. This he was unwilling to do, Rome having learnt more about the issues involved since the unfortunate letter of Honorius. Envoys were sent to Constantinople to negotiate and eventually secured the mandate for the consecration on condition that they would do their best to secure the Pope's signature to the edict. Meanwhile, Severinus faced attempts by the Exarch in Ravenna, Isaac, to harass him, and at the same time enrich himself from the papal treasury. His paymaster (chartularius), Maurice, alleged that Honorius had misappropriated funds intended to pay the troops, thus provoking an attack on the Lateran. Severinus and the clergy resisted, but eventually Isaac himself arrived, banished the clergy and plundered the treasury. With the return of the apocrisiarii, Severinus was consecrated, but in two months he was dead. It is not known what his final response was to the Ecthesis. The *Book of the Pontiffs* remarks on his gentleness and charity, and also his "love for the clergy", so it may be concluded that he belonged to the pro-clerical party.

JOHN IV
(Consecrated 24 December 640; died 12 October 642)

John, a native of Dalmatia and the son of a lawyer, who had risen to be Archdeacon of Rome, was soon elected to succeed Severinus. The attitude of Rome to the imperial Ecthesis was now clear, and John's first act was to hold a synod in Rome which condemned the Ecthesis and the doctrine of monothelitism. The new Patriarch of Constantinople, Pyrrhus, and the Emperor Heraclius were informed of the synod's decision. Heraclius wrote back, disowning the Ecthesis and blaming it on the former patriarch, Sergius. The Emperor was now a broken man, for the last decade of his life had seen a complete reversal of his fortunes, from his victory over the Persians and his triumphant restoration of the True Cross to Jerusalem, to the complete loss of the Eastern provinces to the newly insurgent Arabs, who within decades were to establish a new Islamic Empire, built on the ruins of the Eastern Byzantine provinces and the former Persian empire, with its capital in the former provincial capital of Damascus, that was to change forever the political geography

Above: Theodore I. *The Ecthesis controversy raged on throughout his reign. In 648, Constans II promulgated the Typos to replace it, but Theodore died before recording his response.*

Left: Damascus, *now capital of Syria, became during the reign of John IV the center of an Islamic empire embracing the Eastern Byzantine provinces and the former Persian empire.*

of the Mediterranean world. During his pontificate, John was noted for his efforts in redeeming captives from his native Dalmatia that had been overrun for some decades by Slavs and Avars, who had invaded from over the Danube.

THEODORE I
(Consecrated 24 November 642; died 14 May 649)

John's successor Theodore, whose election was speedily ratified, presumably by the Exarch in Ravenna, marks a new departure. He was a Greek, born in Jerusalem, whose father, also Theodore, had been a bishop. He was presumably one of the refugees from Palestine, which had fallen to the Arabs, and it is likely that it was from such exiles that Rome had become more deeply acquainted with the implications of the monenergist and monothelite controversy. The death of the Emperor Heraclius, together with the parlous state of the empire, had led to coup and counter-coup at the

imperial court, in which Pyrrhus lost his patriarchal throne and fled to North Africa. The political uncertainty provoked an attempt by Maurice to usurp the exarchate, that was foiled by the Exarch Isaac, who had Maurice beheaded, only himself to fall in battle to the Lombards after a distinguished eighteen-year exarchate. In North Africa, Pyrrhus encountered Maximus, a former Byzantine civil servant, who had now been a monk for thirty years, a great theologian to whom it now fell to lead the struggle against monothelitism. In a dispute, presided over by the Exarch of North Africa, Pyrrhus confessed himself persuaded of his error, and went to Rome, closely followed by Maximus himself, where he recanted and was received into communion by Pope Theodore. Maximus brought news of the condemnation of the Ecthesis by North African synods. Pyrrhus later made his way to Ravenna, where he embraced monothelitism once again, and was excommunicated by Pope Theodore, who signed the decree of excommunication with a pen dipped in the eucharistic chalice. Convinced

Above: St Martin I *called a synod that condemned the Ecthesis, Typos, and other imperial policies. Emperor Constans had him arrested, and sentenced him to die in exile.*

Above: St Vitalian *continued Eugene I's policy of conciliation with the imperial power. The highlight of his pontificate was the ten-day state visit to Rome of Emperor Constans in 664.*

that the Ecthesis had failed to bring about reconciliation, the Emperor Constans II promulgated in 648 a new edict, known as the Typos, which sought prevent any further discussion of wills or energies in Christ. Theodore died before formulating a response to this edict, which he would certainly have rejected.

St MARTIN I
(Elected 5 July 649; exiled 17 June 653; died 16 September 655)

Martin, an Umbrian from Todi, was elected to succeed Theodore. Earlier he had, as a deacon, served as Theodore's apocrisiarius in Constantinople, and so was well acquainted with the Patriarch Paul and the others involved in promoting monothelitism. Once elected, he proceeded to consecration without seeking imperial confirmation, a calculated rebuff to Constans II. He then called a synod which met in the Lateran basilica, attended by 105 bishops. Pope Martin himself, and senior Italian prelates, Archbishops Maximus of Grado and Deusdedit of Cagliari, played a major role, but it has recently been shown that the Latin version of the acts of the synod is a translation of the Greek version, and not vice versa, which suggests that the minds behind the synod were the Greek exiles, led by Maximus, who had recently arrived from North Africa where he had been in exile since 630.. The synod condemned monothelitism, the Ecthesis and the Typos, and the clerical architects of the policy: the patriarchs Sergius, Pyrrhus and Paul of Constantinople, and Cyrus of Alexandria. On hearing of this (to his mind) act of sedition, the Emperor Constans sent one of his chamberlains, Olympius, to Italy as exarch with instructions to arrest the Pope, and secure assent to the Typos from the bishops, laymen, and—significantly—from all foreign priests. However, on his arrival in Rome, Olympius discovered that support for the Pope was overwhelming. He tried to stir up schism, perhaps alleging an uncanonical election because of the Pope's failure to seek the imperial mandate, and failed to have him assassinated at mass at S. Maria ad Praesepe. Having achieved nothing, he made his peace with the Pope, and departed for Sicily to repel the Arabs. It was alleged at Pope Martin's trial, that there he declared himself Emperor, with the connivance of the Pope. However, he succumbed to an epidemic and died. The next Exarch, Theodore Calliopas, was more

successful, and in June 653 the Pope was arrested and taken to Constantinople. There he was charged with sedition, tried and sentenced to death. At the intercession of the Patriarch Paul, the sentence of death, that the sick Pope would have welcomed, was commuted to exile. In exile in the Crimea, Martin died on 16 September 655. More than the cold and hardship, and his own sickness, Martin suffered in exile from his abandonment by the Roman church, who proceeded to elect a successor on hearing of his condemnation. The intellectual leader of the opposition to monothelitism, Maximus, was doubtless arrested at the same time as the Pope, but he was not tried until 655, initially, like Martin, on grounds of sedition. After two periods of exile and attempts to break his resolve he was brought back to Constantinople and tried in 662, this time for heresy. Condemned, he had his right hand amputated and his tongue torn out, and was exiled to Lazica, in modern Georgia, near the Black Sea coast, where he died—Maximus the Confessor—on 13 August 662. Although their doctrine was vindicated at the Sixth Ecumenical Council of 680-1, no mention was made at that council of either of the men who had died confessors for that faith.

St EUGENE I
(Consecrated 10 August 654; died 2 June 657)

Eugene, a Roman by birth, was elected Pope while his predecessor was still alive, in exile in the Crimea. He was a mild and gentle man, and to begin with proved even more conciliatory than the imperial court could have hoped for. He sent envoys to Constantinople to negotiate, and in the summer of 655, they entered into communion with the new Patriarch, Peter, on the basis of a vague confession of faith in Christ. Peter responded by sending his customary synodical letter to Rome, announcing his election and including a confession of faith based on that agreed with the envoys. When this was read out during a service in S. Maria ad Praesepe, the clergy and the people rioted, and refused to allow the Pope to leave the church until he agreed to repudiate the letter. On hearing of this, the Emperor Constans threatened a repeat of his treatment of Martin, but he was prevented from carrying out such a threat – Eugene died and on the very day of his death ordered the customary distribution to be made to the poor, the clergy and the papal household.

St VITALIAN

(Consecrated 30 July 657; died 27 January 672)

Vitalian, a native of Campania, was as conciliatory towards the Emperor as his predecessor had tried to be. On his election Vitalian sent envoys to Constantinople with his synodical letter, and they returned with gifts of gospel books, bound in gold and decorated with pearls. Vitalian also wrote to Patriarch Peter of Constantinople urging his return to orthodoxy, but in such mild terms that Peter included his name in the diptychs, the first Pope to be honoured in this way since Honorius. The great event of Vitalian's pontificate was the state visit of the Emperor Constans, the first such visit since the deposition of the last Western Emperor. Unpopular at home, Constans sought to bolster his esteem further afield. He made his way through Greece, and sailed for Italy with an army of 20,000 in 664. There he attacked and sacked a number of Lombard cities, until Benevento stood firm. Making a treaty with the Lombards, he withdrew to Naples, whence he proceeded to Rome. There he was met by the Pope and his clergy at the sixth milestone, with the customary ceremonies. His visit of ten days went well, with no sign of any hostility towards the persecutor of Martin and Maximus. He left, having stripped the bronze tiles from the roofs of many buildings, including the Pantheon, and made his way to Sicily, where his presence was a burden to the people, until he was murdered there in July 669. Pope Vitalian continued to show the interest of his predecessors in the English Church, and in 668 sent Theodore, a Greek from Tarsus, who may have attended the Lateran synod of 649, to England as Archbishop of Canterbury

ADEODATUS II

(Consecrated 11 April 672; died 17 June 676)

Adeodatus was a native of Rome, and a monk, but the *Book of the Pontiffs* makes it clear that he made no attempt to monasticize the papal court. A sentimental interest in Rome in the fates of the confessors, Pope Martin and Maximus, who had suffered in the monothelite controversy, stimulated by the publication of the Greek monk Theodosius' *Hypomnesticon*, perhaps lies behind Adeodatus' refusal to accept the synodical letter of the new Patriarch of Constantinople, Constantine I.

Adeodatus engaged in building works, including the enlargement of the monastery to which he belonged, St Erasmus on the Caelian Hill.

DONUS

(Consecrated 2 November 676; died 11. April 678)

Little is known about the pontificate of Donus, a Roman by birth, already elderly when elected. He seems to have reached an agreement with Reparatus, Archbishop of Ravenna, as a result of which Ravenna's claim to ecclesiastical independence from Rome, granted by Constans II in 666, was abandoned. He is also recorded as having discovered a monastery of monks belonging to the Nestorian heresy (condemned at Ephesus in 431), whom he dispersed throughout other Roman monasteries in the hope that they would return to orthodoxy, replacing them with orthodox Roman monks. It was to Pope Donus that the Emperor Constantine IV addressed a letter proposing a General Council to resolve the Christological dispute, but Donus died before receiving it.

St AGATHO

(Consecrated 27 June 678; died 10 January 681)

Agatho was a monk, a native of Sicily, proficient in Greek as well as Latin. On receipt of the letter from the Emperor to his predecessor, proposing a General Council to resolve the Christological controversy, he

Above: St Agatho, *a scholarly monk from Sicily, devoted his reign to the resolution of the Christological controversy, along the lines proposed by Emperor Constantine IV to Pope Donus.*

Left: Jesus Christ *is portrayed between the Greek letters Alpha and Omega. These traditionally symbolize His nature: the first and the last; the beginning and the end.*

Above: The Council of Constantinople. *A fresco in the Vatican shows a scene at the great Ecumenical Council of 680-681, attended by Pope Agatho and Emperor Constantine IV.*

made preparations by having synods called in Milan, under the Archbishop Mansuetus, and at Hatfield (or Heathfield) in England, under the Archbishop Theodore, as well as a synod at Rome itself. At the Roman synod, the relinquishing by Ravenna of its ecclesiastical independence granted by the Emperor Constans II was also confirmed. Armed with these synodical decisions against monothelitism, a powerful delegation, including two future popes, and representatives of the Eastern refugees, set out for Constantinople. They were welcomed by the newly appointed orthodox Patriarch of Constantinople, George, and the sixth Ecumenical Council was held in the great domed chamber (the "Trullus") in the imperial palace. Despite the rearguard action mounted by Macarius, Patriarch of Antioch, monothelitism was condemned (though the martyrs to monothelitism, Pope Martin and Maximus the Confessor, were not honoured). Included among the heretics condemned

occupied the office of treasurer (arcarius) himself, until he became too ill. He also secured from the Emperor the abolition of the tax customarily paid to the exarch for confirming papal elections, but only on condition of returning to the older custom of confirmation by the Emperor himself. He continued the Roman interest in the English Church, and at a synod at Rome held in 679 upheld Wilfrid's appeal against deposition by the Archbishop of Canterbury, Theodore.

St LEO II
(Consecrated 11 August 682-3 July 683)

Leo was a Sicilian, described as being of great eloquence, learned in the Scriptures, and competent in both Latin and Greek. He was also a skilled chanter, who had been trained in the papal choir-school. The long delay in the confirmation of his election was due to the return to the practice of requiring confirmation from the Emperor, together with the lengthy negotiations needed to persuade the papal envoys to accept the condemnation of Pope Honorius by the the Sixth Ecumenical Council. In return the Emperor reduced the taxes on the papal patrimonies in Sicily and Calabria, and also the corn requisition from the patrimonies for the army. Leo received the acts of the council, and himself translated them into Latin. He also received confirmation from Constantinople of the abandonment of the ecclesiastical independence claimed by the Churchof Ravenna, which had already been negotiated by his predecessors.

St BENEDICT II
(Consecrated 26 June 684; died 8 May 685)

Benedict was a Roman, a priest who had been brought up in the papal choir-school. He is described as being a kind and gentle man, and a lover of the poor. During his pontificate, the Emperor Constantine IV revoked the newly-restored custom of requiring the Pope-elect to seek confirmation from the Emperor, and conceded that the newly-elected Pope should be consecrated without delay (that is, with exarchal confirmation). He secured the endorsement by the Spanish Church of the decrees of the Sixth Ecumenical Council, but only after lengthy scrutiny by the Spaniards. Benedict also restored and refurbished several of the Roman churches.

by the council was Pope Honorius, whose earlier foolish intervention had hitherto been given an innocuous interpretation (as affirming simply the undivided nature of Christ's human will) not only by the popes, but even by Maximus the Confessor. While the council was still in session, Pope Agatho died. He is recorded as having been of a cheerful disposition, and although he was a monk he promoted the Roman clergy. He seems also to have taken the finances of the Roman See in hand, and

Above: St Sergius I. *Although his election was accompanied by discreditable factional maneuvering, Sergius proved to be an able administrator and an enthusiastic builder.*

Above: John VI *was noted for learning and eloquence. His successful interventions in Italy's temporal affairs reflected the papacy.'s increasing political significance.*

Right: Emperor Justinian II *declared his support for the Ecumenical Council attended by his predecessor.*

Far Right: Christ depicted as a lamb *in the arms of St Agnes: such iconography was forbidden by the Eastern Church.*

JOHN V
(Elected 23 July 685; died 2 August 686)

John was a Syrian from Antioch, who had been one of the papal legates at the Sixth Ecumenical Council. He was Archdeacon, when elected by the full assembly of the Roman Churchin the Lateran Basilica. From there he went to the Lateran Palace to await confirmation by the Exarch. Already a sick man, he was unable to officiate at ordinations. He intervened in Sardinia, where the Archbishop of Cagliari, Citonatus, had consecrated a bishop for Turris (Porto Torres) without reference to the Holy See. During his pontificate the Emperor Constantine IV died, and was succeeded by his son Justinian II.

CONON
(Elected 21 October 686; died 21 September 687)

On the death of John V, there was a divided election: the clergy supporting Peter, the archpriest, and the army Theodore, the next most senior priest. To resolve the deadlock, they settled on a compromise candidate, the aged and saintly Conon, a priest, who had been born in Sicily. He was the son of a soldier of the Thrakesion theme (regiment) that was stationed there, which may have endeared him to the army. The new Emperor, Justinian II, announced to the new Pope his support for the

recent Ecumenical Council and reduced the tax paid on the papal patrimonies in Calabria and Lucania (modern Basilicata). Conon soon made the mistake of appointing a Sicilian deacon, Constantine, rector of the patrimony in Sicily (a post normally held by one of the Roman clergy), and allowing him the use of ceremonial saddlecloths (mappulae), a jealously guarded privilege of the Roman clergy: that, and the deacon's extortionate regime led to a revolt soon after the Pope's death, and Constantine's arrest and deportation to Constantinople. Old and sick during his pontificate, Conon, like his predecessor, was unable to officiate at ordinations, and died within a year of his election, leaving unrest among the papal tenants in Sicily and divisions still festering at Rome.

St SERGIUS I
(Elected 15 December 687; died 9 September 701)

As Pope Conon was dying, the Archdeacon, Paschal, wrote to the new exarch in Ravenna offering a bribe in return for his help in securing the election. However, at the election there was again division, this time between Paschal and Theodore, one of the unsuccessful candidates at the last election, now Archpriest. Both factions raced to secure the Lateran Palace, Theodore occupying the inner apartments, and Paschal's faction controlling the outer parts. Again there was a deadlock, and a compromise candidate was chosen, this time a young priest, Sergius, born in Sicily, the son of a Syrian from Antioch. Sergius' supporters stormed the Lateran Palace, and Theodore yielded to the new Pope. Paschal once again appealed to the exarch, offering him 100 pounds of gold. When the Exarch arrived, he discovered Sergius' overwhelming support, and so insisted on Sergius' paying him the 100 pounds in return for exarchal confirmation. Sergius proved an able man. He embarked on a programme of building, and also removed the relics of Pope Leo the Great to a more prominent position within St Peter's. As befitted one devoted to the memory of Leo, he stressed the privileges of the Holy See, consecrating the first Archbishop of Ravenna after the relinquishing of ecclesiastical independence, sending the pallium to Beortweald of Canterbury, and consecrating Willibrord, the missionary of the Frisians. He also received the submission of the Archbishop of Aquileia, thus bringing to an end the Istrian schism over the "Three Chapters". His pontificate also saw a crisis in relations with the Emperor. The new Emperor Justinian, like his namesake, wanted to assert his role as guardian of orthodoxy by holding a General Council. As there was no doctrinal issue to resolve, in 691 he convoked a council to complement the doctrinal decisions of the fifth and sixth councils with disciplinary decrees in the same domed chamber of the palace (the "Trullus") as the Council of 680-1 (a council therefore known as the "Trullan" or "Quinisext"—fifth-sixth—Council). The 102 canons of this council endorsed Church discipline as it was known in the Greek East (and is still the basis for the canon law of the Orthodox churches). This discipline was, by then, significantly different from the ideal (if not always the practice) in the West: in particular, in allowing the lower clergy (priests and deacons) to be married, and in forbidding the depiction of Christ as a lamb (since his true earthly form was that of a man), it departed from Western norms. Sergius refused to ratify these decrees as ecumenical, even though his envoys had given their consent. The Emperor's reaction (as on earlier occasions) was to dispatch an official, Zacharias, to secure the Pope's consent or to arrest him. But the army in Italy rose in support of the Pope, and the terrified Zacharias found sanctuary only under the Pope's bed. Zacharias' life was saved, but the army insisted on his expulsion from Italy. Despite his rejection of the Byzantinization of canon law, Sergius was enthusiastic about Byzantine and other Eastern liturgical ceremonies, enriching the four great feasts of the Mother of God (the Nativity, Presentation, Annunciation, and Dormition) with litanies and processions, and he may have introduced the feast of the Exaltation of the Cross (14 September) to Rome. He also introduced the singing of the anthem *Agnus Dei* ("Lamb of God") at mass: something that may have been intended as a rebuff to the canon of the Quinisext that forbade the imagery of Christ as a lamb.

JOHN VI
(Elected 30 October 701; died 11 January 705)

John, a native of Greece, is said to have been a man of great learning and eloquence. His pontificate is chiefly remarkable for the evidence it gives of the Pope's increasing political significance in Italy. On

one occasion, after the new Exarch at Ravenna had arrested certain prominent Roman citizens and confiscated their property, the troops planned to murder him as he was returning to Ravenna from Sicily via Rome, but were thwarted by the Pope's intervention. Similarly, when the Lombard Duke Gisulf invaded Campania and, after taking a number of cities, advanced on Rome, his advance was checked by priests, sent by the Pope, with ransom money to buy off his attack.

JOHN VII
(Elected 1 March 705; died 18 October 707)

John is the first example of the son of a Byzantine courtier to gain the papal throne: his father was Plato, a curator *sacri palatii* (governor of the imperial palaces on the Palatine), who had settled in Rome. In the same year that he was elected, Justinian II was restored to the imperial throne, and once more sought the papal confirmation of the decrees of the Quinisext Council. He sent copies of the decrees to Rome, requesting John to convene a synod and confirm those decrees that were acceptable, while rejecting those that were not. But John was so terrified of offending Justinian that he returned the decrees without making any amendments at all. He was a man of learning and culture, and a considerable patron of the arts. He restored and embellished several churches, and—particularly in S. Maria Antiqua—observed canon 92 of the Quinisext by avoiding the depiction of Christ as a

lamb, as well as imitating the image of Christ that Justinian used on his coinage. He often had himself depicted in such decoration, as the *Book of the Pontiffs* sardonically remarks. He began to build a new papal residence, near S. Maria Antiqua, at the foot of the Palatine, in what had become the Greek quarter of the city: it was there that he died. He maintained excellent relations with the Lombards, whose King Aribert restored to the Holy See the papal patrimony in the Cottian Alps.

SISINNIUS
(Elected 15 January 708; died 4 February 708)

Sisinnius was a Syrian by birth, and already a sick man when he was elected to the papal throne, so crippled with gout that he could not use his hands to feed himself. Consecrated after waiting three months for exarchal confirmation, he survived less than a month. He had the foresight, however, to have lime prepared for the rebuilding of the long-neglected walls of Rome.

CONSTANTINE
(Elected 25 March 708; 9 April 715)

Constantine was another Syrian. He began his pontificate, affirming the now-restored primacy over Ravenna by consecrating Felix Archbishop. Ravenna seems again to have sought independence, though the details are unclear. Shortly after his election, Constantine was formally invited to Constantinople by the Emperor Justinian. On his way, he met the new Exarch of Ravenna at Naples, who, on his way through Rome with the Pope on his way to Constantinople, seems to have plundered the papal treasury, murdering several officials, before dying of a horrible disease in Ravenna. On his arrival in Constantinople early in 711, the Pope was met with customary ceremony by the Emperor's young son and co-Emperor, Tiberius, the Patriarch Cyrus, and other notables. He met the Emperor at Nicomedia, where the Emperor kissed the Pope's feet and embraced him. The Pope celebrated mass the next Sunday in the Emperor's presence, and gave him communion. The official account is all sweetness and light, and draws a veil over the hard bargaining that went on behind the scenes, in which the deacon and future Pope Gregory II arrived at an acceptable version of the Quinisext decrees, which the

Above: Sisinnius, *already ailing and crippled by gout at the time of his election, died less than one month later. He did, however, take thought for the repair of the walls of Rome.*

Above: Constantine. *In 711 he traveled to Constantinople, where he achieved what appeared to be a successful reconciliation with Justinian II.*

Left: A golden cross *dating from the time of Justinian II. As Emperor, Justinian's conduct was often far from holy: he was noted for greed and for his cruelty towards all who opposed him.*

Above: The Baptism of Christ *is portrayed in a mosaic in Ravenna Cathedral. Ravenna was the seat of the Western Emperors in 402-751, and later became a papal possession.*

Pope ratified. Almost immediately afterwards, Justinian was murdered and the throne usurped by an Armenian, Philippicus, who sought to restore monothelitism. He convened a synod (which included distinguished churchmen, including the future Patriarch of Constantinople, Germanus, who resigned his throne over iconoclasm) which rejected the decisions of the Sixth Ecumenical Council. This policy was embodied in letters sent to the Pope now back in Rome, which provoked riots and the mob's rejection of Philippicus' image and his coinage; nor was the Emperor's name mentioned in the mass. The Exarch's attempt to enforce imperial policy in Rome resulted in violence and death on the streets of Rome, which was only quelled by the intervention of the Pope. Before long, however, news arrived of the overthrow of Philippicus and the accession of an orthodox Emperor, Anastasius II. Early on in Constantine's pontificate there was three years' famine. This time of want was, however, succeeded by a number of harvests of such abundance that the period of dearth was forgotten.

St GREGORY II

(born 669; elected 19 May 715; died 11 February 731)

Gregory was a Roman, the first after a series of popes of Eastern background. Brought up in the papal household, he was made subdeacon and sacristan (sacellarius) by Pope Sergius and placed in charge of the library; as deacon he accompanied Pope Constantine to Constantinople and negotiated the qualified acceptance by the papacy of the canons of the Quinisext Council. As Pope, he continued the rebuilding and adornment of Rome, restoring the city walls and reroofing the basilicas of St Paul's and St Lawrence Outside-the-Walls, as well as repairing many other churches. In 719 Wynfrith, a native of Crediton in Devon, who had been preaching the gospel in Frisia, visited Rome and was blessed by the Pope who gave him the name of Boniface. In 722 on another visit he was consecrated missionary bishop for the Germans by Gregory, who continued to keep in touch with him. In this Gregory was the beneficiary of the devotion to the papacy among the

Below: St John the Baptist baptizes Christ: *a mosaic on the dome of the Baptistery of Ravenna Cathedral. In the East, from 726, the imperially-approved policy of iconoclasm condemned such religious images as idolatrous.*

Anglo-Saxons that had been inspired by his namesake's mission of 596, and the subsequent papal concern for the English church. Gregory's pontificate saw a number of disagreements with the Emperor Leo III, who acceded to the throne in 717. Leo took over a much weakened empire and, early on in his reign, doubled the taxes, an act which threatened to bankrupt the Roman Church. Gregory led the Italian resistance to this increase in

taxes and provoked the opposition of the Exarch, which included attempts on his life, that were however quite without success, owing to the support the Pope commanded among the people as well as the army. Relations with the Emperor worsened over the imperial policy of iconoclasm, which began in 726. This policy, which, with a gap at the turn of the century, was to hold sway in the Byzantine Empire for nearly a century and a half, was an attempt to ban religious art as idolatrous (to begin with: later the grounds for iconoclasm became more sophisticated). Gregory refused to comply, despite the blandishments of the Emperor, and again commanded the support of the Italians. Despite the strained relationships between Emperor and Pope, Gregory remained loyal to the empire, defending imperial territory against Lombard incursions, and even supporting one of the Exarchs, Eutychius, with troops against a revolt in the Roman army, immediately after Eutychius' attempt, in league with the Lombard King Liutprand, to depose him—an attempt that was thwarted by Gregory's direct appeal to the Lombard King on grounds of their common faith.

St GREGORY III
(Elected 18 March 731; died 28 November 741)

Gregory, of Syrian origin, a learned and eloquent Roman priest, equally at home in Greek and Latin, was elected by acclaim during his predecessor's funeral, and consecrated five weeks later, after waiting for exarchal confirmation of his election (the last Pope to do so). He immediately wrote to the Emperor, denouncing iconoclasm, though the letter never got any further than Sicily, where the bearer of the letter was arrested and exiled. The following year Gregory called a synod, attended by 95 bishops, including the archbishops of Grado and Ravenna, to condemn iconoclasm, and excommunicate the iconoclasts. In retaliation the Emperor sent a fleet to Italy, but it foundered in the Adriatic and the expedition had to be abandoned. It was presumably also in retaliation, though it is difficult to establish any clear dates, that the Emperor Leo confiscated the papal patrimonies of Calabria and Sicily, thus depriving the papacy of one of its richest sources of income, and transferred the ecclesiastical provinces of Sicily and Illyricum from the jurisdiction of the papacy to that of the patriarchate of

Constantinople (this transfer of jurisdiction may belong to the reign of Leo's son, Constantine V). The Pope's repudiation of iconoclasm can probably also be seen in his programme of enriching and embellishing the Roman churches, as the *Book of the Pontiffs* details the erection of several splendid icons. Splendid twisted onyx columns, a gift from the Exarch, perhaps to indicate that iconoclasm did not entail any lack of rich ornamentation, were erected and promptly adorned with icons! Despite the antagonism beween Emperor and Pope, Gregory remained loyal to the Empire, ransoming the fortress of Gallese from the Lombard Duke Transamund and restoring it to the empire, as well as reinforcing the fortifications of Civitavecchia and the walls of Rome at his own expense. In 737, when Ravenna was actually taken by the Lombards, Gregory was instrumental in arousing support to regain it for the empire and restore it to the Exarch. However, Byzantine weakness in Italy led Gregory to involve himself directly in Lombard politics, seeking an alliance with the duchies of Spoleto and Benevento that posed the greatest threat to Rome. This brought upon him the wrath of the Lombard King, Liutprand, and in the ensuing conflict Rome was the loser. In 739, and again in 740—perhaps at the suggestion of Boniface who had visited Rome in 737—Gregory appealed for help to Charles Martel, mayor of the palace and thus effective ruler of the Franks, but to no avail.

St ZACHARIAS
(Elected 3 December 741; died 15 March 752)

Zacharias was the last of the "Greek" popes, a learned man who translated into Greek the *Dialogues* of Gregory the Great. He was consecrated eight days after the death of his predecessor, without waiting for either exarchal or imperial confirmation. Despite this he sent envoys with his synodical letter to Constantinople. There they found in possession of Constantinople not Constantine V, Leo's son and successor, but Constantine's brother-in-law, Artavasdus, who had usurped the throne and may have declared himself against iconoclasm. The Pope dealt with this state of affairs, as with the change of regime when Constantine deposed Artasvasdus in 743, with caution. However, Constantine V seems to have established friendly relationships with the Pope, giving him the impe-

rial estates of Norma and Ninfa, situated north of Rome, thus making some recompense for the loss of the papal patrimonies. The complete lack of mention of the iconoclast controversy in the life of Zacharias in the *Book of the Pontiffs* may mean that some kind of *modus vivendi* was reached between Emperor and Pope. But in Italy, Zacharias wsa confronted with the situation brought about by his predecessor's involvement in Lombard affairs. Faced with the advance of King Liutprand, the Spoletans and Romans made common cause and inflicted a defeat. From this position of strength, Zacharias arranged a meeting with Liutprand, abandoned his predecessor's policy of alliance with the duchies against the king, and offered to support the king in return for the cession of the cities he had taken. Liutprand, having defeated the duke of Spoleto with Roman support, reneged on his promise, so in 742 Zacharias set out to Terni to meet once again with the king. There a twenty-year peace treaty between Pope and King was agreed, and the Roman cities restored. Liutprand now turned his attention to the Ravenna Exarchate and took the city of Cesena. The Ravennans appealed to the Pope, who sent an embassy to Liutprand, without success. Again the Pope decided on a personal meeting, this time at the Lombard palace in Pavia. Again the Pope worked his magic on the king. But in 744 Liutprand died. Ratchis confirmed the peace treaty, but in 749, probably under pressure from his nobles, seized Perugia. Once again Zacharias inter-

Above: St Gregory III *denounced iconoclasm, excommunicated those who practised it, and embelished Roman churches with splendid icons.*

Above Left: Ratchis, King of the Lombards, *confirmed, but then broke, the peace treaty made between his predecessor, Liutprand, and Pope Zacharias.*

Above: St Zacharias. *The fall of Ravenna in 751, at the end of his reign, left the papacy at the mercy of the Lombards.*

Above: Stephen II (III) *was elected to succeed another Stephen, who had died before being consecrated. His anti-Lombard policies saw the establishment of the Frankish Carolingian dynasty.*

Below: Rome viewed from the Palatine Hill. *The Lateran Palace, restored and reestablished as the Popes' dwelling place by Zacharias, is seen to the left of this picture.*

vened and Ratchis withdrew. But his successor Aistulf conquered Ravenna itself in 751, and thenceforth Byzantine influence in Italy was confined to the south and Sicily, still Greek in language and culture. This left the papacy at the mercy of the Lombards, a race it had never trusted, even after their conversion to Catholicism. Soon the papacy was to turn to the Franks. In 752 Pepin, the Frankish mayor of the palace, sought the Pope's view on whether one should rule and another be king. The Pope thought not, and thus sanctioned the transfer of power from the Merovingian kings to the new Carolingian dynasty. It is not clear what pact there was, if any, between Pepin and the Pope: but it was the first step in an alliance that was to shape the future of European history. Under Zacharias, we see the beginnings of papal estates called domuscultae, lands, acquired (by gift or purchase) by the papacy, legally inalienable, and cultivated for the benefit of the papacy. In Rome itself, Zacharias engaged in much restoration, especially of the Lateran Palace which once again became the Pope's dwelling place.

STEPHEN II (III)
(Elected 26 March 752; died 26 April 757)

On Zacharias' death, one of the Roman priests called Stephen was elected to succeed him, but he died two days later. Not having been consecrated, he was not regarded as Pope either by the *Book of the Pontiffs* or any other medieval source: only in the sixteenth century did he come to be included in papal lists. After his death, another Stephen, an orphan who had been brought up in the Lateran,

and had risen to the rank of deacon, was elected Pope in the basilica of S. Maria ad praesepe. His immediate problem was the threat posed by the Lombards. Aistulf, having taken Ravenna, had attacked Istria and reached an agreement with Venice, and was now threatening Rome. Stephen sent an embassy, which included his brother Paul, who later succeeded him, to Aistulf, and a peace-treaty was drawn up in June 752. In his isolation, the Pope appealed to the Byzantine Emperor for help. Perhaps because of that, by October Aistulf once again attacked the Roman duchy; embassies from the Pope proved fruitless. It was now that the Pope seems to have turned to the Franks, sending a message secretly to Pepin through a pilgrim. Much is unclear about the nature of these negotiations, but in autumn 753, Stephen set out from Rome, initially to Pavia, to negotiate directly with Aistulf, and then, when that proved unsuccessful, with Aistulf's agreement he travelled beyond the Alps to the court of the Carolingians. Pepin and the Pope met at Ponthion on 6 January 754. Again much is unclear, but the upshot of their negotiations was that Pepin agreed to come to the aid of the Pope and the Roman people. The Pope went to St. Denis to rest and await the arrival of spring. At Easter Pepin's promise to help the Pope, now confirmed by the Frankish nobility, was ratified at a meeting held in Quierzy. In July, at St. Denis, the Pope crowned and anointed Pepin King of the Franks, and gave him the title "Patrician of the Romans" (Patricius Romanorum). The significance of these events is probably to be found in the Pope's injunction forbidding the Franks to seek a king from any other family. which thus established the Carolingian dynasty. The rest of 754 was spent trying to secure Aistulf's restoration to the papacy of the cities of the Roman duchy he had taken, together with Ravenna and the Pentapolis. In Spring 755, Pepin and the Frankish army crossed the Alps and defeated the Lombards. At the peace treaty, Aistulf agreed to Pepin's demands. The Pope returned to Rome, and Pepin to France. This first Peace of Pavia was soon abandoned by Aistulf, and on New Year's Day 756 Aistulf and his army were at the gates of Rome. Again Pepin crossed the Alps. On the way, in the Alpine passes, he was met by Byzantine emvoys who asked him to use his force to restore Ravenna to the Byzantine empire; Pepin replied that he was fighting for the love of St Peter, and the forgiveness of his sins. He sought to make

Above: St Paul I, *the brother of Stephen II (III), continued his predecessor's policy of seeking Frankish support. His administrative measures, though harsh, significantly strengthened the papacy.*

Right: A Carolingian monarch, *possibly Pepin "the Short" (c.715-768), disposes of one of his rivals. The Carolingian dynasty established by Pepin replaced the Merovingians as Frankish rulers.*

a second Peace of Pavia secure by the taking of hostages. On Aistulf's death, the Pope secured the kingship for Desiderius, in return for promises of the restoration of cities: promises that were not honoured. In the East, developments in the iconoclast controversy further alienated the papacy. In 754, the Emperor Constantine V called a large council in the imperial palace at Hieria. It claimed to be "ecumenical", and defined iconoclasm as Christian doctrine, defending it with sophisticated theological arguments. The Patriarch of Constantinople, Anastasius, died before it met, and so, with no papal legates, there were no representatives from any of the patriarchal sees. All these events of significance during Stephen's reign are, however, simply ignored by the *Book of the Pontiffs*.

St PAUL I
(Elected 29 May 757; died 28 June 767)

When Stephen died, he was succeeded by his brother, Paul, who had tended him in his last hours. Like him, he was an orphan from an aristocratic Roman family, brought up in the papal palace and ordained deacon by Zacharias. The election was divided, with a faction supporting the Archdeacon Theophylact; but the majority supporting Paul were able to impose their will. Paul complained to Pepin about the Lombard King Desiderius' refusal to honour the promises he had made to his brother, and was also anxious about attempts by the Byzantine Emperor Constantine V to seek an alliance with the Franks and the Lombards. Eventually Pepin secured a compromise, in which Pepin and Desiderius

Above: Constantine *is blinded. A layman, and in any case irregularly elected, Constantine was deposed with Lombard help. He and his followers were punished by blinding or execution.*

Right: St Peter *is shown with the heavenly keys. Among the bodies removed to Roman churches from the catacombs by Paul I was that of Petronilla, supposedly Peter's daughter.*

promised not to enter into an treaty with the Byzantines against the Pope, although Desiderius was allowed to keep the cities that had been promised to the papacy. Paul protested directly to the Emperor about the heretical council of 754, gave refuge to Eastern monks fleeing iconoclast persecution and supported the Eastern patriarchs against Constantinople. When Constantine V attempted to gain Frankish support for iconoclasm, Pepin called a synod at Gentilly, attended by Franks and Greeks, at which the Roman rejection of iconoclasm was upheld. Paul also allowed the Archbishop of Ravenna, Sergius, whom his brother had retained at Rome, to return to Ravenna, confident that Sergius had no interest in the restoration of the Exarchate. His pontificate was also important for the history of the catacombs, for he transferred many bodies from them to the churches of Rome, notably that of Petronilla, revered by the Frankish royal house as the daughter of the Apostle Peter. The entry in the *Book of the Pontiffs* for Paul is brief, and though eloquent about his care for the poor, and his building achievements—including the monastery of S. Stephen and S. Silvester, founded in his family home, which was given over to the use of refugee Greek monks—it is slighting about his achievements, perhaps because of his failure to secure the cities promised by Desiderius, and maybe also because of his harsh administrative regime. His achievements in consolidating papal power in changed political circumstances were real, and his conception of the papal office as "mediator between God and men, the searcher of souls" correspondingly exalted.

STEPHEN III (IV)
(Elected 7 August 768; died 24 January 772)

On Paul's death, Constantine, brother of Toto duke of Nepi, a layman, was elected: this was probably a reaction on the part of the lay aristocracy against Paul's harsh clerical administration. The election itself—not to mention the election of a layman—was irregular. Constantine found it difficult to gain recognition: his synodical letter to Pepin was unanswered. Two leaders of the clerical party—Christopher, the Secretary of State (*primicerius*), and his deputy Sergius—sought the support of the Lombard King Desiderius. With his army, they stormed Rome, Toto was killed and Constantine deposed: soon the ringleaders had either been mur-

dered or blinded. Once in command, the Lombards tried to elect their own candidate, Philip, but this was thwarted by Christopher, who realized that a Pope so dependent on the Lombards would be unacceptable to the Romans, and Stephen was elected. Stephen was a native of Sicily, who came to Rome as a boy and entered the new monastery of St Chrysogonus. He soon entered the service of the Pope in the Lateran, and was ordained priest of St Cecilia's, while still remaining on the staff of the Lateran. He was caring for Pope Paul when he died. Once elected, Stephen sent letters to Pepin, announcing his election, and requesting that he send bishops to a council to be held in Rome to ratify his election and the deposition of Constantine. In all this there was an element of dissembling, as Stephen had been one of the clerics who ratified the election of Constantine. The council duly met in

Rome in April 769, attended by twelve Frankish bishops and forty Italian bishops, or their representatives. This council ratified the election of Stephen and the deposition of the now-blinded Constantine, who piteously sought pardon, only to be worse treated when he pleaded precedents for his election as a layman. Constantine's ordinations were declared null and void. The council also passed a decree limiting future electors to the Roman clergy (the nobility and the people's role being limited to acclamation) and the candidates to those already cardinal priest or cardinal deacon (an early example of the use of the term "cardinal"). The question of religious images was discussed and the iconoclast Council of Hieria (754) was condemned. In 768 Charlemagne succeeded his father Pepin and, to begin with, sought an alliance with the Lombards. Alarmed, Stephen sought an alliance with the Lombard King Desiderius, at the cost of the lives of Christopher and Sergius, to whom he owed the papal throne. By the time of Stephen's death, the Franks were once again enemies of the Lombards, and the folly of Stephen's actions exposed.

HADRIAN I
(Elected 1 February 772; died 25 December 795)

Hadrian was an orphan of the Roman aristocracy, who had made his way through the Lateran administration and was deacon when elected Pope. His was an exceptionally long (nearly 24 years) and distinguished pontificate. Its early years saw the collapse of Lombard power in Italy. Under pressure from the Lombard King to make kings of the sons of Carloman, Charlemagne's brother, who had become a monk, Hadrian appealed to Charlemagne, who invaded Italy and deposed the Lombard king. On his visit to Rome in 774, while Pavia, the Lombard capital, was still under siege, Charlemagne promised three quarters of Italy to the Pope. After his victory, despite frequent letters from Hadrian, Charlemagne never fulfilled these promises, though several territories were conceded to Rome. The reason for this apparent bad faith is probably to be sought in the fact that Charlemagne did not so much destroy the Lombard kingdom, as add that kingdom to his own domains—and thus become protector of the papacy. Nevertheless this is the culmination of the period, beginning with the collapse of the Byzantine Exarchate of Ravenna, in which the papacy began to take on a political identity (whether called the Republic of St Peter, or anachronistically the Papal State): this is evident in Hadrian's dating his letters by his own regnal years, rather than by those of the Byzantine Emperor, and by his issuing his own coinage. Rome's position between two worlds—the Byzantine empire to the East and the emerging Frankish Empire to the West—is revealed in the (temporary) ending of iconoclasm and the calling of the Seventh Ecumenical Council at Nicaea in 787. A projected alliance between Charlemagne and the Byzantines had broken down, so the papal legates at the Ecumenical Council had to tread a fine line between orthodoxy and support for the Byzantine Empire. Rome achieved this by welcoming the condemnation of iconoclasm, but raising at the council the issue of the restoration of papal jurisdiction in Sicily and Illyricum (as well as the return of the papal patrimonies, though this was not an ecclesiastical matter), that had been transferred to Constantinople by Leo III. The decrees of the council were translated into Latin on Hadrian's initiative (a point emphasized by the *Book of the Pontiffs*), and dispatched to Charlemagne, whose theologians, on the basis of this text, attacked the decrees on the veneration of icons as tantamount to idolatry in a report known as the "Caroline Books" (*Libri carolini*). This judgment was, however, based on a mistranslation which erased the distinction made by the Greek theologians between worship (*latreia*) which is due only to God and veneration (*proskynesis*) which can be offered to creatures. At a synod held in Frankfurt in 794, attended by many bishops from the Frankish empire and beyond, as well as by papal legates, the decrees of Nicaea II were endorsed in terms drawn from Hadrian's letters, save for one clause that condemned the worship of icons, only to discover that this was in accord with the Greek of Nicaea. Thus Hadrian "expertly" (*solertissme*) defended orthodoxy, as the *Book of the Pontiffs* put it. Hadrian also engaged in a massive programme of rebuilding and adorning churches, and aiding the poor.

LEO III
(Elected 26 December 797; died 12 June 816)

Leo, an administrator and priest of S. Susanna, quickly elected to succeed Hadrian, was of obscure background: he was not a Roman, as the *Book of the Pontiffs* asserts, but perhaps a southern Italian. He did more than announce his election to Charlemagne: he sent him the keys of the confessio of S. Peter and the banners of Rome, thereby acknowledging his suzerainty. Although elected unanimously, there was opposition to him from the Roman nobility, and in April 799, while he was conducting one of the Rogation processions, he was attacked and left half-dead. Supporters spirited him out of Rome, and he made his way to Paderborn where he presented his case before Charlemagne. Charges had also been laid against him, of unchastity and perjury, which the king decided to investigate. Leo returned to Rome and in late 800 Charlemagne arrived on a state visit to give judgment. He was greeted at Rome with the ancient imperial ceremonies. Declaring it beyond his competence to judge the Apostolic See, he dismissed the charges against Leo. On Christmas Day, before mass, Charlemagne was, to his surprise, crowned Emperor of the Romans in front of the confessio of St Peter; the people knelt in obeisance, led by the Pope (for the first and only time in history). Imperial imagery applied to Charlemagne was not novel, and the fact that Irene, having blinded and deposed her son Constantine VI, was ruling in her own right (as a woman!) as Emperor at Constantinople made plausible the idea that the imperial throne was vacant; but there is no evidence that the Carolingian court welcomed the Pope's action. Indeed, for the most part, even in ecclesiastical matters, the Emperor seemed to take the initiative. It is the more surprising, then, that Leo resisted Carolingian pressure to introduce the *filioque* (the clause affirming the double procession of the Spirit from the Father and the Son, that was already a point at issue between Eastern and Western theologians) into the Nicene creed: a practice already well-established among the Franks, but rejected in Rome

Right: Leo III crowns Charlemagne *as Emperor of the Romans. In fact, at this ceremony, on Christmas Day in 800, it was the Pope who, for the only time in history, knelt before the Emperor.*

Above: Stephen IV (V) *sought to heal the divisions that had troubled the pontificate of Leo III, and recalled those opponents of Leo who had been banished by Charlemagne.*

Above: St Paschal I *was a determined opponent of iconoclasm- an attitude reflected in his rebuilding and magnificent embellishment of San Prassede and other Roman churches.*

as an innovation that would alienate the Greeks. Leo was immensely active in building work, and in the apse of the triclinium (the banqueting chamber) at the Lateran expressed his idea of imperial rule in two mosaics: one of Pope Sylvester and the Emperor Constantine before Christ balanced by one of himself and Charlemagne before St Peter. After Charlemagne's death there was another revolt against him, which Leo dealt with sharply, having the culprits executed on his own authority, thus taking a step further the papacy's claim to temporal sovereignty within its domains.

STEPHEN IV (V)
(Elected 22 June 816; died 24 January 817)

Stephen, born into the Roman nobility, had entered the service of the Lateran under Hadrian, and been made Archdeacon by Leo. Concerned to heal the divisions that had troubled his predecessor's pontificate, he recalled the opponents of Leo who had been exiled by Charlemagne in 800. Despite his brief pontificate, he made a visit to Charlemagne's successor, Louis the Pious, whom he met at Reims in October 816. There he crowned and anointed him Emperor, and concluded an agreement, the *Pactum Ludovicianum*, whereby all the territories that Rome had acquired under Hadrian were formally recognized as land under papal rule by the Emperor, who also agreed not to interfere in lands ruled by the papacy, except to help the oppressed, nor to intervene in papal elections. It also restored to the laity their active involvement in papal elections. The *Book of the Pontiffs* records the rich ornaments Stephen gave to several Roman churches.

St PASCHAL I
(Elected 24 January 817; died 11 February 824)

Paschal was a Roman, brought up in the Lateran, who at the time of his election was a priest. He announced his election to the Frankish Emperor Louis the Pious, and also confirmed the agreement that had been made between his predecessor and the Emperor, the so-called *Pactum Ludovicianum*. On the surface, it appears that relationships between Pope and Emperor during Paschal's pontificate were harmonious, the Emperor recognizing the Pope's rights within his territories, and the Pope supporting the Emperor in ecclesiastical matters. When Louis

divided his empire in 817, he had the Pope confirm it; and Ebbo, appointed by Louis to convert the Danes, visited Rome in 822, and received a papal blessing and appointment as papal legate in the North. Further, Paschal invited Lothar, Louis' son, then in Italy, to Rome and on Easter Day, 5 April 823, crowned him Emperor and Augustus, thereby strengthening the idea that emperors needed papal coronation. But it appears that Lothar's visit to Italy may have been in part to investigate complaints from those suffering from Paschal's rule, and Lothar's granting the abbot of Farfa exemption from papal taxes a sign that the Emperor was ready to intervene. A few months later a number of papal officials were murdered, and complaints were made against Paschal to the Emperor. Although Paschal was allowed to purge himself on oath before imperial envoys (as Leo had done before Charlemagne himself), it looks as if the Emperor's acceptance of papal temporal sovereignty was qualified. It was Paschal who received the formal envoy from the new Patriarch of Constantinople, who had been appointed in 815 to inaugurate a new phase of iconoclasm. He reacted by reiterating Rome's condemnation of iconoclasm: an action which gave great encouragement to the opponents of iconoclasm in Constantinople, led by Theodore, the Abbot of the Stoudios Monastery that had been closed for its opposition to the Emperor. Paschal also welcomed to Rome Greek monks fleeing persecution in Constantinople. His opposition to iconoclasm is also manifest in his rebuilding and decorating of churches in Rome, especially S. Prassede, among the magnificent mosaics of which Pope Paschal himself can still be seen depicted.

EUGENE II
(Elected 21 February 824; died August 827)

Eugene was elected as the candidate of the nobility to resolve what seems to have been a contested election. He was himself a Roman, drawn from the nobility, and Archpriest of S. Sabina, when elected. He communicated his election to Louis the Pious in Compiègne. Louis sent his son Lothar to Rome to deal with the disturbances from the time of the two previous popes. In Rome, Lothar published the *Constitutio Romana* which replaced the agreement between Pope and Emperor established by Stephen IV, the *Pactum Ludovicianum*. Scholars are divided on the significance of the *Constitutio*, but it is increas-

ingly regarded as a much more conservative agreement than it was formerly taken to be. It certainly established a degree of control over Rome by the Emperor with the appointment of two resident envoys, one by the Emperor, the other by the Pope, who were to report annually to the Emperor on affairs in Rome, and with the requirement that an oath of allegiance to the Frankish Emperor be made, in the presence of an imperial legate, before a Pope-elect could be consecrated. Otherwise it recognized the Pope's sovereignty within his realms, under the suzerainty of the Emperor. Eugene maintained Paschal's concern for the evangelization of northern Europe, and extended papal commendation to Anskar, the "Apostle of the North", and his companions. The Pope was also involved, although indirectly, in the attempt by Louis and the Byzantine Emperor Michael the Stammerer to establish a pact on the basis of a moderate iconoclasm, whereby images were allowed but not venerated. Louis

Left: Emperor Louis I "the Pious", *son and successor of Charlemagne, looks on as Pope Stephen IV (V) honors the Emperor's son, Lothar, during Louis' coronation at Reims in 816.*

sought papal agreement, but this was not forthcoming. Eugene also held a synod in Rome in 826, which passed a number of reforming measures, intended for the Frankish realms as well as Rome, covering clerical discipline, Sunday observance and marriage discipline, as well as seeking to promote education throughout Christendom.

VALENTINE
(Elected August 827; died September 827)

We know scarcely anything about Valentine, save for his entry in the *Book of the Pontiffs*, an encomiastic piece, mostly written while Valentine was still alive. Born into the Roman nobility, he served in the Lateran administration and was Archdeacon at the time of his election. His pontificate lasted for only forty days.

GREGORY IV
(Elected late 827; died early 844)

Gregory was of aristocratic Roman birth, and at the time of his election was the priest of S. Marco. Before being consecrated, he had to take the oath of allegiance before an imperial legate, as prescribed by the *Constitutio Romana*. The bond between Pope and Emperor meant that the Pope became caught

up in the tangled succession of the Carolingians. In 833 Louis the Pious' sons rebelled, and Gregory was certainly seen as lending support to Lothar, the eldest of the three brothers, though he maintained his concern was for peace and the unity of the empire. He travelled to France with Lothar, and before the two sides engaged battle in Alsace, Gregory left Lothar's camp to negotiate with Louis. His meeting with Louis was constructive but was rendered nugatory, because Lothar had persuaded many of his father's supporters to desert and Louis was deposed. Again, after Louis' death in 840, Gregory was involved in trying to keep harmony among the brothers, sending George, Archbishop of Ravenna, as his envoy. But matters were settled by battle, Lothar being defeated at Fontenoy in 841 by Charles and Louis the German. In 831/2 Gregory received in Rome Anskar, the "Apostle of the North", who had been evangelizing Denmark since 826, and gave him the pallium as Archbishop of the Nordic people and the office of papal legate. Gregory built a fortress, called Gregoriopolis, at Ostia, now threatened by the Arabs, who, having taken Sicily, were now a constant threat to the southern coastal area of Italy. He also, like most popes, engaged in extensive rebuilding and decoration of the Roman churches, including his own former *titulus* where in the apse his own portrait in

Above: Valentine, *of whom little is known other than that he was a member of a noble Roman family and a Lateran administrator, died when his pontificate had endured for only forty days.*

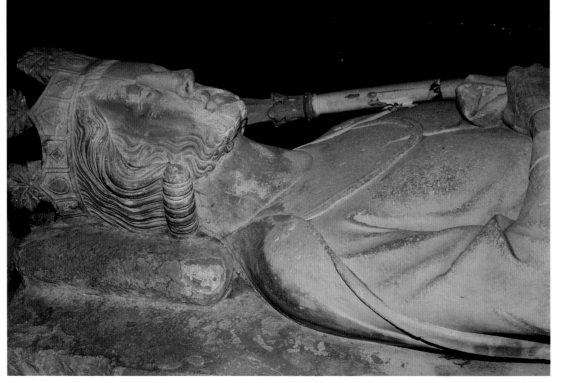

Left: The tomb of Emperor Louis I "the Pious". *The* Pactum Ludovicianum *he made with Stephen IV (V) confirmed the papal title to extensive territories acquired during the reign of Adrian I.*

Above: Sergius II's *election incurred the wrath of Emperor Lothar, who sent his son Louis to invade Italy. Much of the ailing Sergius' power was wielded by his unscrupulous brother Benedict.*

mosaic survives. Gregory also encouraged the adoption of Roman liturgical uses throughout the Carolingian Empire, in 832 receiving Amalar of Metz, and in 835 seeing the observance of the feast of All Saints (fixed by Gregory III on November 1) extended throughout the Frankish realms.

SERGIUS II
(Elected January 844; died 27 January 847)

Sergius was from the Roman nobility, a close relation of Stephen IV, who after the death of his widowed mother had been brought up in the choir school, and had advanced rapidly through the ranks of the Roman Church to become Archpriest (now a specific office, not simply the senior priest). At the time of his election he was elderly and gout-ridden, the candidate of the nobility in a divided election in which a deacon John, otherwise unknown, had been the popular candidate. He was consecrated without waiting to take the oath required by the *Constitutio*, doubtless to secure his position in the face of popular unrest. The Emperor Lothar was displeased at the flouting of the *Constitutio*, and sent his son Louis, then King of Italy, to punish the Roman nobles for their action. On their way to Rome, they pillaged papal territory, and Sergius forestalled an attack on Rome itself by meeting Louis with all the ancient honours due to a visiting Emperor. At a synod held in Rome, Sergius was upheld as Pope, but required to take the oath of allegiance to the Emperor, though an attempt to make him swear allegiance directly to Louis was rebuffed. Louis was crowned King of the Lombards, anointed and girded with the sword by Sergius. Sergius' ill-health meant that papal affairs were effectively conducted by his unscrupulous brother Benedict, a source of much resentment. The sacking of Ostia by the Arabs in 846 and the consequent plundering of St Peter's and St Paul's, both outside the Roman walls, was regarded by the *Book of the Pontiffs* as divine vengeance for actions of Sergius and his brother.

St LEO IV
(Elected 10 April 847; died 17 July 855)

Leo was a Roman by birth, educated in the monastery of St Martin close to St Peter's, who had risen through the Lateran administration to become priest of SS. Quattro Coronati at the time of his election. Arab fleets were still harassing the coast when Leo was elected, and for this reason he was consecrated without waiting to take the oath of allegiance to the Emperor. Much of Leo's pontificate was devoted to church building, not least to restoring St Peter's that had been plundered by the Arabs. In S. Clemente he had frescos painted where his portrait still survives. But he also sought to secure Roman territory against future Arab attack, rebuilding the walls of Rome, constructing the Leonine city to protect St Peter's (at the command of, and helped with cash from, the Emperor Lothar), as well as organizing the fleets, garrisoning the ports, and rebuilding Civitavecchia at Leopolis. Leo's relations with the Frankish Emperor are not entirely clear. There was no reaction to his consecration without taking the oath; in 850 Louis II was anointed in Rome as Emperor. The affair of Anastasius, the scholarly priest ordained by Leo, who seems to have pursued an independent career despite papal fulmination and excommunication, seems bound up with papal-imperial relations, as Anastasius was intruded as imperial candidate for the papacy on Leo's death. In France itself, Leo's struggle with Hincmar of Reims over the nature of papal authority in France proved to be but the beginning of a long wrangle, Hincmar claiming as Archbishop of Reims an authority more extensive than Leo would allow, and not that of a virtual papal suffragan. Leo's pontificate saw also the beginnings of a long struggle with the patriarchate of Constantinople. Ignatius, appointed Patriarch in 847, held a synod at which Gregory Asbestas, Bishop of Syracuse, who had fled to Constantinople following the Arab invasion, was deposed (possibly a piece of unfinished business from the iconoclast controversy that had ended in 843). Leo, who refused to accept the alienation of Sicily from papal jurisdiction by the Emperor Leo III, regarded this action as an infringement of his own authority, and refused to confirm it.

BENEDICT III
(Elected 29 September 855; died 17 April 858)

Benedict was a Roman, educated at home, who entered the Lateran administration and by the time of his election was priest of S. Callistus. He was elected unanimously in Rome, and envoys were sent from Rome to the Emperor Louis II to secure his

Above: St Nicholas I *owed his election largely to the support of the Emperor, but nevertheless insisted that the imperial function was to protect the Pope—but not to interfere in papal affairs. As a result, his relations with the imperial family were stormy, involving a further punitive expedition to Rome by Louis*

Right: King Æthelwulf of the West Saxons *kneels before Benedict III. On pilgrimage from England, the Anglo-Saxon monarch stayed for one year in Rome. With him was his youngest son, Alfred (849-899)—who perhaps acquired in Rome some of the wisdom that was to dignify his rule as King Alfred the Great.*

confirmation and the two imperial envoys before whom Benedict would swear the oath of allegiance before his consecration. On their way to the Emperor, they were persuaded to change their allegiance to the candidate favored by the Emperor, Anastasius, the cardinal priest excommunicated by Leo. When they returned with the imperial envoys, they made their way to Anastasius at Orte, and then conducted him to Rome. They entered first the Leonine City, where they destroyed the sentences of excommunication that Leo had set up before St Peter's and the adjacent sacred images, and then proceeded to the Lateran for Anastasius' consecration. Amidst the rioting of the people, no bishops could be found to consecrate Anastasius, and eventually the envoys accepted Benedict, received his oath, and he was consecrated. Anastasius seems to have lived in obscurity during Benedict's pontificate, but became Pope Nicholas' secretary, and papal librarian under Hadrian II. Like his predecessor, Benedict devoted himself to building and restoration, and repaired S. Paolo fuori le mura, devastated by the Arabs in 846, which had been neglected by Leo. Probably on the very day of Benedict's consecration, Lothar the Emperor died, and the final agreement whereby the three sons of Lothar—Charles, Lothar II and Louis II—shared out Provence and Italy was claimed by Benedict to be the result of his intervention. The troubles concerning Hincmar of Reims and Ignatius of Constantinople continued through Benedict's pontificate, which also saw the year-long stay of Æthelwulf, King of the West Saxons, and his son Alfred, in Rome on pilgrimage.

St NICHOLAS I
(Elected 24 April 858; died 13 November 867)

Nicholas was a native of Rome, and brought up by his father who saw that he received a good education. He served in the Lateran administration, and was made deacon by Benedict, to whom he was very close. Louis II, having just left Rome when he heard of Benedict's death, returned and made sure that Nicholas was elected Pope. After election at the Lateran, he was immediately taken to St Peter's, where in the presence of the Emperor he was consecrated. With Nicholas Pope, Anastasius returned to favor and became his secretary. Despite being the imperial candidate, Nicholas had an exalted view of

the papal office: the Pope was St Peter's representative, archbishops and synods were to execute his decisions; the Emperor was to protect him, and not to interfere in papal affairs. The consequences of this understanding of his office can be seen in his relationships with the imperial family, with senior prelates in France and Italy, and with Emperor and Patriarch in Constantinople. In 860 Lothar II divorced his wife; two years later a synod held at Aachen authorized his remarriage, and a further synod held in Metz in 863, attended by papal legates, confirmed it. When the archbishops of Trier and Cologne brought the decision of the synod to Rome, Nicholas held a synod that quashed the synod of Metz and deposed the two archbishops. Lothar ordered his brother Louis II to undertake a punitive expedition against Rome, in which blood was shed within the city of Rome itself. The two archbishops were released, but Nicholas conceded nothing. The years following saw repeated attempts to coerce the Pope, but Nicholas refused to accept Lothar's divorce, or the reinstatement of the deposed archbishops. With Hincmar of Reims and with several bishops in Italy, Nicholas stood by his rights, as he saw them, to receive appeals from those disciplined by bishops and archbishops, to make his own decision and have it enforced. With Byzantium the issue was partly the Pope's right to hear appeals from Constantinople, especially over the deposition of Patriarch Ignatius and his replacement by the learned scholar Photius, and partly—ostensibly—the disputed jurisdiction over "Illyricum", i.e. the Balkan peninsula south of the Danube, though here a much greater issue was at stake: the future allegiance of the Slav peoples, now beginning to turn to Christianity. These issues were entangled. In 865 Khan Boris of Bulgaria converted to Christianity, in its Byzantine form. To preserve his independence from Byzantium, he wanted his new Bulgarian church to have a patriarch. This Constantinople could not grant, and Boris turned to the Pope. He received letters from both Nicholas and Photius, and by the time of Nicholas' death was still undecided. This was, however, conceived of as a matter of jurisdiction, not faith: the two halves of Christendom were not yet alienated. Evidence of this is found in Nicholas' friendly relations with Cyril and Methodius, Byzantine missionaries in Moravia, who as Nicholas was dying were travelling to Rome at Nicholas' invitation for the ordination of several of their company.

ADRIAN II
(Elected 14 December 867; died c. 24 November 872)

Adrian, an aged priest of S. Marco, belonging to the nobility and related to two earlier popes, Stephen IV and Sergius II, was the compromise candidate in a divided election. He had twice before refused the office of Pope. As the imperial envoys were already in Rome, he was consecrated the following Sunday in St Peter's. Hadrian inherited a good deal of unfinished business from Nicholas. Over Lothar's divorce, he relented and agreed that the question could be reopened at a synod to be held in France; but Lothar died on his way back from Rome before it could convene. He also admitted the deposed archbishops of Trier and Cologne to communion. On Lothar's death, Hadrian involved himself unsuccessfully in settling the succession, which went to Charles the Bald, rather than Louis II, whom he favored. In the year of Hadrian's election, Basil the Macedonian usurped the Byzantine throne and, anxious for the support of Rome, reinstated Ignatius as patriarch. Hadrian welcomed Basil's decision and also his intention to hold a council in Constantinople to settle the whole matter. This council, held 869-70, and reckoned the Eighth Ecumenical Council in the West, accepted Nicholas and Hadrian's decisions in favor of Ignatius, and also once again condemned iconoclasm. It also saw a resolution of the issue of the religious allegiance of Bulgaria. Khan Boris had sent an embassy to the council, which arrived in time for the last session. They asked the council to decide between Byzantium and Rome. Given the overwhelming Greek presence at this council, it decided, hardly surprisingly, in favor of Byzantium. Ignatius later consecrated an archbishop for the new Bulgarian church, who had exceptional rank in the Byzantine hierarchy, which went some way towards meeting Boris' demand for a patriarch. Hadrian also welcomed the brothers, Constantine and Methodius, and their disciples, whom Nicholas had invited to Rome. They arrived bearing the relics of Pope Clement I which they had discovered in the Crimea. They stayed in Rome for some time, Constantine becoming a monk with the name Cyril and Methodius, already a monk, being ordained priest by the Pope. They persuaded the Pope of the value of Slavonic as a liturgical language, and celebrated in Slavonic in Rome. After Cyril's death in 869, Methodius, now consecrated by the Pope Archbishop of Sirmium (Sremska Mitrovica) with responsibility for the former provinces of Pannonia I and II as well as Moravia, returned to Moravia together with his disciples with the intention of extending his work to the region around Lake Balaton. But Methodius faced opposition from the East Frankish missionaries, was imprisoned, and finally saw his mission in Moravia fail.

JOHN VIII
(Elected 14 December 872; died 16 December 882)

John, a native of Rome, had been for twenty years Archdeacon on his election as Pope. An immediate problem was the continuing threat from the Arab fleets in the Mediterranean. He extended the fortifications to embrace S. Paolo fuori le mura and established a small, defensive papal fleet. On the death of Louis II, he encouraged the Romans to acclaim his uncle, Charles the Bald, preferring him to his half-brother Lothar the German. He crowned him in Rome at Christmas 875. In return Charles recognized an extension of the papal territories, and forewent the right to keep resident envoys in Rome. Soon after John faced opposition in Rome itself, and protected himself by excommunicating the leaders in their absence. They included Formosus, Bishop of Porto, who had been Nicholas' envoy to Bulgaria and was later to become Pope himself: in 878 John had him degraded and exiled. Lothar's son, Carloman, invaded Italy to assert his right to the imperial throne; Charles, retreating across the Alps, died. John temporized, and Carloman's supporters took Rome and imprisoned the Pope. He refused to accept Carloman, and eventually escaped to Provence. His attempts to find an alternative to a German Frank failed: Louis the Stammerer, crowned in September 878, died a few months later, and Boso, whom he crowned in 880, was soon defeated. In the end, he had to settle for Louis the German's son, Charles the Fat, whom he crowned Emperor in February 881. But though thwarted as to his choice of Emperor, his actions went a good way towards establishing the Pope as effective arbiter of the imperial office. The Arab threat forced John to seek a rapprochement with Byzantium. But in 878 the Emperor Basil had restored Photius to the patriarchal throne, and wanted Rome to recognize him. John agreed, and sent legates to a council that met in the Great Church of Hagia Sophia, presided over by Photius. Photius refused to apologize, as the

Pope had required, and the Council ratified the Seventh Ecumenical Council, annulled the synods that had condemned Photius, and endorsed the original form of the Niceno-Constantinopolitan creed (without the *filioque*), which caused Rome no problem as the *filioque* had not yet been added to the creed used in the papal court. John accepted all this, and agreed to a compromise over the Bulgarian question, as a result of which Bulgaria was technically subject to Rome, while the Greek missionaries were not to be disturbed. But he secured the military aid he needed from the Byzantine Empire, the power of which was once again in the ascendant. The conflict with Hincmar continued, but John did not have the resolve of Nicholas, and backed down like Hadrian. He defended Methodius, the apostle of Moravia, in his clash with the German clergy and obtained his release from prison; in 880 he sanctioned Methodius' continued use of the Slavonic liturgy. John has the distinction of being the first Pope to be assassinated.

MARINUS I
(Elected 16 December 882; died 15 May 884)

Marinus was from Tuscany, the son of a priest, who entered the Lateran administration and was made deacon by Nicholas I. He was one of three legates who represented Hadrian II at the Council of Constantinople in 869-70, which condemned the deposed Patriarch of Constantinople, Photius. He also displeased the Emperor Basil by adhering strictly to his instructions as legate. Later he became Archdeacon and treasurer (*arcarius*), and also Bishop of Caere (Cerveteri) in Etruria. John VIII used him as an envoy in his negotiations with Charles the Fat. When he succeeded John as Pope, he was the first Pope to have been transferred from another episcopal see, in violation of the ancient canons. Marinus was consecrated without reference to the Emperor Charles the Fat, but when he visited Italy in 883, Marinus met him and secured his recognition. He also pardoned those bishops who had been exiled by John VIII for plotting against him. It was once maintained that Marinus had refused to send the customary synodical letter to Photius, once again Patriarch of Constantinople, and that the so-called "Photian schism" was renewed; but it is now clear that this is false. Both men were indeed keen on reconciliation. Very little is known of his pontificate (he has no entry in the *Book of the Pontiffs*, nor do his predecessor or successor), but he intervened in a dispute between the Archbishops of Reims and Sens over a recently founded monastery, and maintained good relations with the English King, Alfred the Great, granting a tax exemption to the English quarter in Rome.

St ADRIAN III
(Elected 17 May 884; died mid-September 885)

Adrian was a native of Rome. We know little that is clear about his succession to Marinus, and indeed very little at all about his pontificate (again he has no entry in the *Book of the Pontiffs*). He seems to have supported the policies of John VIII, and is recorded as having had blinded one of those exiled under John, whom Marinus had allowed to return. Like John and Marinus, he maintained peaceful relations with Byzantium, sending the Patriarch Photius the customary synodical letter. In 885 he was summoned by Charles the Fat to attend an imperial diet at Worms to settle the succession on his illegitimate son Bernard. Adrian set out, leaving Rome to the protection of the imperial envoy John, Bishop of Pavia. He died on the way near Modena, and may, like his predecessor John VIII, have been murdered. Perhaps significantly, his body was not brought back to Rome, but buried in the Abbey of Nonantula.

ALFRED

Above: St Adrian III, *another Pope of whom little is known, was a native of Rome. It seems probable that his rule was harsh, and possible that his death, while on the way to attend an imperial diet at Worms, was met at the hands of an assassin.*

Above left: King Alfred the Great of Wessex. *The learned English monarch maintained a warm relationship with Pope Marinus I, and himself undertook the translation of works by Pope Gregory I the Great and other leading theologians from Latin into Anglo-Saxon.*

Below: Stephen V *was elected by popular acclamation to succeed Adrian III, and is said to have used his own great wealth to make up the considerable losses incurred when the Lateran was pillaged following the death of his unpopular predecessor.*

STEPHEN V
(Elected September 885; died 14 September 891)

Stephen, a member of the Roman aristocracy,
entered the Lateran under Adrian II and was
Cardinal Priest of SS. Quattro Coronati when he was
elected by acclamation to succeed Adrian III. His
entry in the *Book of the Pontiffs* (the last such, and
only in some manuscripts) reports that he found the
Lateran pillaged, by this time apparently a regular
custom on the death of a Pope, and goes on to
record the vast expenditure of his own personal
wealth to make good the losses, as well as his pastoral devotion and concern for the liturgy (including an increase in the use of incense at matins in St
Peter's). His election was opposed by Charles the
Fat who sent an envoy to depose him. Once convinced of Stephen's support he left well alone.
Stephen needed military support against the continuing Arab raids, and appealed for help to the
Emperor, who had not the resources. On the death
of Charles the Fat (deposed in 887 because of a
shameful agreement he made with a Viking army
besieging Paris) the empire of Charlemagne disin-
tegrated. Stephen initially sought the support of
Arnulf, Charles' nephew, King of the East Franks,
but he was occupied elsewhere. He found support
in Guido III, Duke of Spoleto, who had usurped the
Italian throne in 889, and whom, under coercion,
he crowned as Emperor in 891. He also maintained
close links with Byzantium, and sought military aid
from the Emperor. When the Emperor Basil died
and his successor Leo the Wise deposed Photius,
Stephen accepted the new patriarch, Leo's brother
Stephen, without demur. In the year of his election,
Methodius, the "Apostle of Moravia", died and designated his disciple Gorazd (who had been ordained
in Rome) as his successor, but under the influence
of the German clergy the Pope summoned Gorazd
to Rome, forbade the Slavonic liturgy, and
appointed Methodius' suffragan, Bishop Wiching of
Nitra, administrator of the metropolitan See. The
band of Methodius' disciples made their way East,
where they settled in Bulgaria and were instrumental in the introduction there of a fully Slavonic
form of Christianity, with Slavonic scriptures and a
Slavonic liturgy following the Byzantine rite, with
the result that Slav Christianity, which in the next
century was to spread to Russia, was to be loyal to
Byzantine Orthodoxy and thus increasingly
estranged from Rome.

· LES GRANDS PONTIFES ·

NICOLAS LE GRAND EXCOMMUNIE PHOTIUS.

Édition de la CHOCOLATERIE d'AIGUEBELLE (DRÔME)

SAINT-NICOLAS LE GRAND.

Above: Nicholas I *excommunicates Patriarch Photius of Constantinople, who had become irritated by the success of the future Pope, Formosus, in converting the Bulgarians to Latin-rite Christianity. Photius believed the region was under his jurisdiction. This led to schism between the Churches of east and west.*

Below: Formosus *presided over the Church at a time of many battles for control of the papacy. As a man, Formosus was an ascetic and a zealous missionary. After his death, his successor Stephen subjected his corpse to great indignities in an attempt to discredit his papacy.*

FORMOSVS·I·PAPA

FORMOSUS
(Born c.815, elected October 6, 891; died April 4, 896)

It is possible, even probable, that Formosus was Roman born. He was a man of talent, created Bishop of Porto by Nicholas I c.864 and sent by him as a missionary to the Bulgarians. His missionary activity was an enormous success, converting the region not just to Christianity but to Latin-rite Christianity, much to the irritation of Patriarch Photius of Constantinople who believed the territory fell under his jurisdiction. The King of the Bulgarians wanted Formosus to remain as an archbishop, but this Nicholas refused and recalled him to Rome. He cannot have been in disgrace – he continued to play a prominent role in the life of the Roman Church and successive Popes used him on important diplomatic missions – but he had powerful opponents who accused him on several charges, chief among them being the desire to change Sees, a thing still theoretically disapproved of, and of being ambitious for the papacy.

In 876 he had to flee Rome with a group of supporters, and remained in exile until recalled in 883 by Pope Marinus – who had himself changed his See to accept the Bishopric of Rome. During his time in exile Formosus had gathered allies among those who were sympathetic to German interests, including Guy III, Duke of Spoleto. Unfortunately for Formosus, however, his chief rival for the papacy in October 891 was Sergius, a deacon of noble Roman birth, who was one of the leaders of the Spoletan faction in the city: Sergius' opposition was effectively neutralized, at least for the remainder of Formosus's pontificate, by his being promoted to

the see of Caere. The new Pope's loyalties were therefore divided, if not actively inclined against the Spoletan domination of Rome. Duke Guy had, however, already defeated his only serious contender for power over Rome, Berengar, Marquis of Friuli, and had been crowned Emperor. Formosus had little choice but to recognize the fact, which he did in 892 by recrowning Guy at Ravenna and creating Guy's son Lambert co-Emperor. Berengar had taken refuge with Arnulf, the King of the East Franks in the region which became Germany, and Formosus now turned to Arnulf for support. There was a modest invasion led by Arnulf's son which proved unsuccessful. Arnulf looked for another opportunity, which came when Guy died in 894. Arnulf invaded, but had not calculated on resistance being shown by Guy's widow Agiltrude, and by his son Lambert. As Arnulf advanced, Agiltrude retreated to Rome, threw Formosus in prison, and appointed Boniface Pope in his place, a man who had been twice reduced in the ranks, first as a subdeacon and then as a priest, because of his immorality. Arnulf arrived outside the city in October 895 and laid siege until the following February. Members of the Spoletan faction, including Agiltrude and Lambert, escaped Rome relatively unscathed and lived to fight another day; on February 22, 896 Arnulf was crowned Emperor by a grateful, and reinstated, Pope Formosus on the steps of St Peter's. Agiltrude and Lambert withdrew to their fortress at Spoleto. Arnulf planned to attack them there, but the campaign came to nothing after he suffered a stroke, and returned to Germany. Formosus himself died shortly afterward, on Easter Day.

Though Formosus' pontificate was dominated by battles over control of the papacy, in his personal life he was something of an ascetic, even a holy man and, in his early career, a zealous missionary. He had done nothing to merit the indignities which his successor Pope Stephen was to visit on his corpse. The fact that he had changed Sees, from Porto to Rome, gave his enemies a chance to claim that the ordinations he had carried out while Pope were invalid, a problem which survived into the next century.

BONIFACE VI
(Consecrated April 11?,896; died April 26?, 896)

It seems likely that Boniface, who had been promoted as an antipope under Formosus, was elected by a Roman mob simply out of hostility to the Formosan faction, and out of enmity toward the German Emperor Arnulf. His rule was, however, very short. He lived just a fortnight as Pope, dying of gout and being buried at the entrance to St Peter's.

STEPHEN VI (VII)
(Consecrated May 896; died August 897)

Stephen had been Bishop of Anagni, promoted to that office by Formosus. He too, therefore, was technically guilty of the same offence as Formosus, mov-

ing from one See to another. This problem he attempted to resolve through one of the most macabre acts in the history of the papacy: he put on trial the corpse of Formosus, which was dug up, sat upon a chair and dressed in papal vestments before being condemned – a deacon was deputed to speak for the late Pope, but simply admitted his errors. Three fingers of his right hand – those he had used in blessing – were cut off, his vestments stripped off, and his mutilated body thrown into the Tiber, from which a hermit rescued it, and gave it burial. He was condemned as a usurper, and all his acts were annulled – including that of elevating Stephen to the See of Anagni. This meant that Stephen was no longer "bigamous," because his first consecration had been invalid. All these events took place in the presence of Agiltrude and Lambert who had returned to Rome when it became clear that Arnulf's health was going to prevent him returning to Italy. Even his representative and the small garrison under his charge quit the city. Spoletan power was therefore re-established, and Rome freed from foreign influence. This state of affairs did not last long. The "synod of the corpse," as Formosus' posthumous trial came to be called, occurred in February or March. Six months or so later Stephen was himself deposed. The condemnation of Formosus and the nullifying of all his acts as Pope was a serious threat to the stability of the Roman Church, and especially to all those clerics who had received office under him. There was a revolt against his authority. He was seized, stripped of his papal vestments and thrown into prison where he was shortly afterward put to death by strangulation.

ROMANUS
(Consecrated August 897; deposed November 897)

Romanus was a priest of one of the Roman Churches when he was elected to replace Stephen, possibly even before Stephen's death – the dates are not known exactly. He was, presumably, elevated through the machinations of the Formosan faction in Rome, and his coins are inscribed with the name of the Emperor Lambert. A few of his acts as Pope are recorded, though they are not of great significance in the history of the Church, and a contemporary chronicler has a few lines about him which suggest he was a virtuous man. Perhaps too virtuous, and not sufficiently active against the

Above: Theodore II *was instrumental in reversing the decision of the "synod of the corpse" held under Stephen VI (VII). Theodore declared Formosus's election to the papacy valid and all his acts valid. Theodore then had the body of Formosus re-interred with honor in its tomb in St Peter's.*

Below: John IX *did much to restore both the Roman Church and the city of Rome itself to its former power and majesty. One of his finest acts was to restore friendly relations with the Patriarchate of Constantinople.*

Spoletans. After a very few months in office he was, one account records, confined to a monastery.

THEODORE II
(Consecrated and died November 897)

The Formosan faction may have been unhappy with Romanus because of his relative inactivity. After Romanus was deposed a Roman was elected about whose previous career almost nothing is known. Theodore took swift action. He summoned a synod whose purpose was to reverse the "synod of the corpse." Not only was the body of the deceased Pope returned in honor to its tomb in St Peter's, Formosus's election to the papacy was declared valid, and all his acts therefore approved, restoring thereby the status of those clerics whose authority had been undermined during the pontificate of Stephen. Unfortunately for the Formosans, Theodore died after less than three weeks in office.

JOHN IX
(Consecrated January 898; died January 900)

The election of John was a turbulent one. Sergius, who had renounced the see of Caere to which Formosus had promoted him, to get him out of the way, was elected by followers of Stephen. John, a monk of Lombard ancestry who had been ordained by Formosus, had the support of the Formosan party, and particularly of the Emperor Lambert. His predecessor had attempted reconciliation, and John continued the same strategy. At a gathering in St Peter's attended by bishops from northern Italy the "synod of the corpse" was once again condemned though those who had taken part were pardoned – except, that is, for Sergius and some close followers of his. Three bishops had by now been elected to the papacy: it was somewhat anachronistic that John should once again attempt to ban the practice, but the synod also attempted to bring some order into papal elections by requiring the attendance of an imperial representative and insisting that the election was the responsibility of the clergy and bishops. Another synod in Ravenna, attended by 120 bishops, endorsed the decisions taken in Rome. The Emperor Lambert was in attendance. He was recognized as overlord, and every Roman citizen was allowed the right of appeal to him.

John set about restoring Rome, especially the

Lateran which had been damaged by fire. But, he complained, it was difficult to transport to the city the materials needed, so unsafe was the countryside. It was at least in part to achieve security that John came so much to rely on the young Emperor. When Sergius allied himself with the Marquis of Tuscany and challenged Lambert's rule over Italy, Lambert defeated him in battle. But hopes for a more stable Italy were dashed when in October 898, Lambert was killed in a hunting accident. There could be no hope of support for the Pope from the dying Emperor Arnulf. Berengar of Friuli revived the hopes he had seen dashed during the pontificate of Formosus. He was supported by Lambert's mother Agiltrude and other Italian nobles, but in September 899 his army was overwhelmed by an invasion of Magyars into Italy. Among other acts of his impressive pontificate, Pope John attempted, with some considerable diplomatic acumen, to restore friendly relations with the Patriarchate of Constantinople.

BENEDICT IV
(Consecrated May/June 900; died August 903)

Little is known of Benedict – even the date of his election is uncertain – except that he was of distinguished Roman ancestry, and had been ordained by Formosus. At the end of August 900 he held a synod in the Lateran which confirmed certain acts of Formosus and of the late Pope. The death of Lambert during John's reign left a political vacuum in Italy. Benedict turned to Louis, the King of Burgundy and Provence, who in October 900 had proclaimed himself King of Italy, a title which Berengar of Friuli also claimed. In February 901 Benedict crowned Louis as Emperor, but eighteen months later Louis's army was defeated by that of Berengar and the Emperor was forced to swear never to return to Italy, as he was driven back into France. There was speculation that Berengar had Benedict assassinated, but there is no evidence of this.

LEO V
(Consecrated August 903; deposed September 903; died early 904)

Leo was a priest in a town some distance south of Rome, which makes it difficult to understand how he came to be elected, except possibly as a compromise candidate. If that is so, it seems that there may have been a split in the Formosan faction to which Leo undoubtedly belonged, because he was thrown into prison by Christopher, a priest of S. Damaso, one of the traditional parish churches of the city, after only a month in office. He was then assassinated in prison along with Christopher during the pontificate of Pope Sergius.

SERGIUS III
(Consecrated January 29, 904; died April 14, 911)

Something of Sergius' earlier career has already been told above (*cf* Formosus *and* John IX). After the "synod of the corpse", which he attended, he claimed to have been reduced back to the rank of deacon, and was ordained priest by Stephen VI. He always regarded his election to the papacy after the death of Theodore as valid: January 29, 904 is the date of his consecration after he had marched on Rome with the support of Duke Alberic of Spoleto (a Frank who had murdered the late Emperor Lambert's son and seized the duchy for himself), and thrown Christopher into prison – having him shortly afterward strangled, along with Pope Leo. There were therefore no rival claimants to the papal throne. It was an extremely difficult time for Rome. Saracen attacks in southern Italy had robbed the monasteries of their income, and religious life had gone into decline. Instead, the papacy came increasingly to rely upon lay people in the administration of the city and the papacy. Prominent among them was the house of Theophylact. Theophylact was both treasurer of the papal revenues and commander of the papal armies. He and his wife Theodora were regarded at the time as relatively pious: most contemporary criticism was reserved for their children, particularly for Marozia, their fifteen-year-old daughter who, it was said, was Pope Sergius' mistress, and by whom he had a son who was later to become Pope John XI. The story, told by a hostile chronicler, seems unlikely – Sergius was well into his fifties by the time he became Pope. His was, it seems, an active pontificate, though few details remain. He wanted to offer the imperial crown to his old ally Berengar of Friuli but was prevented from doing so by an alliance of Theophylact, Alberic of Spoleto, Adalbert of Tuscany, and Archbishop John of Ravenna, all of whom, it seems, wanted Rome to have no imperial ambitions but to

play a role in Italy similar to the other duchies. Sergius endowed churches within the city, and a convent or two, and attempted to restore those religious institutions outside Rome which had been damaged in the raids of the Saracens. He also restored the Lateran, largely destroyed in the reign of Stephen VI, and dedicated it to St John. It was to become the usual burial place of Popes. His support was solicited by the Eastern Emperor Leo VI who, in search of an heir, married a fourth time and was condemned by the Patriarch Nicholas I. Sergius decided in favor of the Emperor, and the Patriarch was deposed, a course of events which was to cause problems for Sergius' successors.

ANASTASIUS III
(Consecrated c.June 911; died c.August 913)

It is recorded that Anastasius was Roman by birth, the son of Lucian, but little else is known about him. It is always presumed that this shadowy figure owed his promotion to Theophylact. In his pontificate the Patriarch Nicholas was restored, who promptly complained about Sergius's decision against him: the Pope's name was removed from the Patriarchal diptychs, and Constantinople and Rome drifted further apart. Berengar of Friuli, whom Pope Sergius had hoped to create Emperor, was mollified when certain bishops in his territory were granted privileges by Anastasius.

LANDO
(Consecrated c.August 913; died c.March 914)

Again, little is known of Lando except that his father was a wealthy Lombard landowner from an area just northeast of Rome. As with Anastasius, it is presumed that the Theophylact family was behind his election and short pontificate.

JOHN X
(Consecrated March/April 914; deposed May 928; died 929)

The choice of John as Bishop of Rome was remarkable. While it was no longer unusual for someone already a bishop to be transferred to the See of Rome, John had ruled the important Archdiocese of Ravenna for nine years before he came to Rome. Before Ravenna he had been offered the diocese of

Above: **Sergius III** *was rumored to have taken a fifteen-year-old mistress although this seems to have little basis in fact. During his papacy, Sergius restored the Lateran which was to become the usual burial place of Popes.*

Below: **Lando** *was a somewhat obscure figure and little is recorded about his short term of office, which lasted for less than a year.*

Bologna but had refused it, possibly on the advice of Theodora, the wife of the papal treasurer Theophylact. There has been a suggestion that Theodora and John were lovers, but there is no evidence for this. The fact that John was close to King Berengar of Italy must have been an argument in his favor. It is not surprising that the Roman noble families wanted a tried and tested bishop after two rather inconsequential pontificates, and especially now that the Saracens were in danger of overrunning the city.

Shortly after John's election a band of Saracens was defeated in a skirmish to the north of Rome. Pope John with Alberic of Spoleto united to pursue the Saracens into their camp at the mouth of the River Garigliano. Other Italian armies joined them as they marched south. Of particular significance was the support of leaders of the states of Southern Italy which owed allegiance to the Byzantine Emperor, and the presence of the Byzantine navy, which prevented the Saracens either leaving by, or being reinforced from, the sea. They were decisively defeated in a battle in which Pope John himself took part, and John and Alberic returned as heroes to Rome, where Alberic married Theophylact's eldest daughter Marozia, thus strengthening the bonds between Spoleto and the Roman nobility. But this alliance threatened the independence of the Pope, and he tried to counterbalance the power of the nobles by, in 915, giving the imperial title to his old friend Berengar who took the traditional oath to defend the privileges of the Church. This policy backfired on Pope John, however, when in 924 Tuscany and Lombardy rebelled against Berengar and invited Rudolf of Burgundy to become King of Italy. Berengar brought in Hungarian mercenaries to defend his authority, and they promptly overran much of Italy. Berengar was murdered that year, and more or less at the same time Theophylact died. Alberic, it seems, tried to use the Hungarians to bolster his own authority but was himself assassinated by the Romans. Pope John tried to re-establish his own power by appointing his brother Peter to the marquisate of Spoleto and to the offices held by Theophylact, and by collaborating with Hugh of Provence, who had become King of Italy. But Peter was unpopular with the Romans because of his association with the hated Hungarians, and Marozia reclaimed her family's former position in the city by marrying, in 927, Guy of Tuscany, one of the most powerful of Italian mag-

nates and the half-brother of Hugh of Provence. At the end of the year she had Peter murdered in the Lateran before his brother the Pope's eyes, and, the following year, had Pope John himself flung into prison where, in June 928, he was suffocated. To concentrate only on the political events of John's pontificate, important though they be, is to do him an injustice. Although in one instance he approved, for political reasons, of the appointment of a five-year-old to the archbishopric of Rheims, his concern for the re-establishment of the authority of bishops in France and Germany was real enough, and he also, in 923, mended relations with the Byzantine Patriarch, Nicholas the Mystic, broken at the time of Pope Sergius. He struggled, but failed, to bring back Croatia and Dalmatia under the authority of Rome with a Latin, rather than a Slav, liturgy, and was remembered at Rome for completing the restoration, and decoration, of the Lateran.

LEO VI
(Consecrated May 928; died December 928)

Undoubtedly elevated to the papacy by Marozia, Leo was of the Roman nobility, son of a major figure, Christopher, in the papal administration, and by the time of his "election" Cardinal Priest of Sta Susanna. He was by then already an old man and he died even before his imprisoned predecessor had been murdered.

STEPHEN VII (VIII)
(Consecrated December 928; died February 931)

Like his predecessor, Stephen, a priest of the Church of Sta Anastasia, Stephen owed his promotion to the papacy even before the death of his predecessor-but-one to Marozia, daughter of Theophylact. Like his immediate predecessor he was a stop-gap until Marozia's own son was old enough to succeed to the Bishopric of Rome. Although he reigned for over two years, remarkably little is known about him.

JOHN XI
(Born c.905; consecrated March 931; died December 935)

John XI was the eldest son of Marozia by, it has been alleged, Pope Sergius III. This was the opportunity for which Marozia had been waiting: a con-

Above: **John X** *His papacy was characterized by much political activity but his achievements included re-establishing good relations with the Byzantine Patriarch, Nicholas the Mystic, and the completion of restoration of the Lateran.*

Above: **John XI** *was alleged to be the son of Sergius III and Marozia, and was said to have been made Pope at her instigation, and the real power was generally felt to lie in her hands.*

temporary observer remarked that John's role as Bishop of Rome was purely ceremonial. The real power lay in the hands of his mother, who had taken over the titles, and the authority, of her father Theophylact. He did, however, confirm the protection of the Holy See over the abbey of Cluny on the petition of its abbot Odo, and guaranteed the freedom of the Cluniac monasteries to elect their own abbots. The Cluniacs were later to play an important role in the reform of religious life in Rome. Quite probably on the instigation of Marozia, John also gave his approval to the consecration, at the age of only sixteen, of the son of the Byzantine Emperor as Patriarch of Constantinople, and sent bishops over to take part in the ceremony. Although it was Marozia who exercized power, she needed the support of a husband. After the death of Alberic of Spoleto she had married, in 928, Guy of Tuscany, but in 931, he too, died. Marozia next married – contrary to the law of the Church because he was Guy's half-brother – Hugh of Provence, King of Italy, who turned up to the ceremony with his army. The marriage festivities were to take place in Castel Sant'Angelo, the mausoleum of Adrian on the north bank of the Tiber near the Vatican. Alberic, Marozia's son by her first marriage, quarrelled with his new stepfather and called upon the Roman militia. They surrounded Castel Sant'Angelo and drove Hugh and his troops from the city. Marozia was imprisoned by her son, quite possibly as a nun in the convent of Sant Maria in Campo Martis, endowed by Alberic for that purpose. Her marriage to Hugh was apparently annulled. Pope John was also imprisoned, probably a form of "house arrest" in the Lateran where he was permitted to carry out liturgical functions. His brother – or half-brother, if John was indeed an illegitimate child – took over total control of the city.

LEO VII
(Elected January 3, 936; died July 13, 939)

After the imprisonment of Marozia by Alberic during the pontificate of her son John XI, Alberic took charge of the papacy. Evidence suggests that he was personally devout, and interested in the monastic reform of which Cluny was the outstanding example. Leo was a Roman by birth, Cardinal Priest of S. Sisto, and may possibly have himself been a monk. Certainly he favored monasticism and continued the papacy's support for Odo and promptly

invited him to Rome to foster monastic reform in the city and its immediate environs. This Odo did with, on occasion, the support of Alberic's troops to enforce change on recalcitrant monks. He was also used to negotiate peace between Alberic and Hugh of Provence, sealed by the marriage of Alberic to Hugh's daughter Alda. The reform movement spread beyond Italy. Leo appointed the Archbishop of Mainz legate to all Germany with a brief to restore the observance of Church law among the clergy, as well as banning superstitious practices. He also ordered that all Jews in Germany who refused to be baptized should be expelled. Leo died with a reputation for sanctity.

STEPHEN VIII (IX)
(Consecrated July 14, 939; died October 942)

The choice, inevitably, of Alberic who was the effective ruler of Rome, Stephen came from a Roman family and was Cardinal Priest of SS. Silvestro and Martino. He continued support for monastic reform, which Alberic favored, not least because it restored agriculture in the region around the city. One major political act was his backing for Louis IV, crowned King of France in 936, against a well-supported rebellion. He sent Bishop Damasus as his representative to persuade the people of France to recognize Louis on pain of excommunication. He also restored to his See, and granted the pallium to, Archbishop Hugh of Rheims, a gesture which also helped to defuse the opposition to Louis. At the end of Stephen's pontificate there was a conspiracy against Alberic by two cardinal bishops who wished to restore the power of the clergy over Rome. It was hatched with the connivance of Hugh of Provence who had vainly attempted in the summer of 941 to take the city by force. The Pope's involvement in this plot is unclear, though there is some suggestion that he ended his days in prison.

MARINUS II
(Consecrated October 30, 942; died May 946)

Marinus was a Roman, and Cardinal Priest of S. Ciriaco, but beyond that little or nothing is known of him before his elevation to the papacy under the patronage of Alberic, the ruler of Rome after his coup against his mother Marozia and Hugh of Provence in the pontificate of John XI. A contemporary chronicler recorded that he did not do any-

Above: **Leo VII** *was a Roman by birth and may possibly have been a monk himself. His interest lay in monastic reform; he made efforts to rid the Church of superstitious practices.*

Above: **Stephen VIII (IX)** *continued support for monastic reform and backed King Louis IV of France against a rebellion by threatening the rebels with excommunication.*

thing without Alberic's permission, and what little can be discovered about his pontificate bears this out; even his coins bore Alberic's name on the reverse. He continued the support for monasteries, and especially for monastic reform, which had become a hallmark of Alberic's policy.

AGAPITUS II
(Consecrated May 10, 946; died December 955)

Even less is known of the early career of Agapitus than of his predecessor. He was a Roman by birth, and undoubtedly owed his appointment to Alberic. He did, however, make an effort to loosen Alberic's control over the city and did not limit himself to purely ecclesiastical affairs. These nonetheless loomed large. He continued papal support for the monastic reforms associated with the French abbey of Cluny, but chose monks from the German abbey of Gorze to reform the monastery attached to the Roman basilica of St Paul's-Outside-the-Walls. He showed a particular interest in Germany and was an admirer of its king, Otto I of Saxony. Early in 948 he sent Bishop Marinus to the court of Otto, and Marinus presided, alongside Otto and the French King Louis IV, over a synod at Ingelheim in the June of that same year which excommunicated or threatened to excommunicate those rebelling against the rule of the French king, decisions which were later endorsed by Agapitus himself. Earlier, Agapitus had extended the jurisdiction of the Arch-Bishop of Hamburg over Denmark and other northern lands which were only now being converted to Christianity. In 951 Otto was invited to Italy with Alberic's approval – his activities in northern Italy weakened the power of Alberic's old rival Berengar who claimed the title of King of Italy. Berengar submitted to the German king, acknowledging himself as his vassal, and Otto came south in 952, as if on pilgrimage to the city but in reality seeking the imperial crown. He sent ambassadors to Agapitus not, significantly, to Alberic, but Alberic's authority over the Pope prevailed and the imperial title was refused because it would have undermined the power of Alberic over Rome and the Church of Rome. Otto retired back to Germany to bide his time, but conscious that the power of his family was now threatened, Alberic attempted to secure the succession of his sixteen-year-old son Octavian, not only as secular ruler of Rome but as spiritual ruler

as well. In 954, when he fell mortally ill after twenty-two years as Prince, he summoned the leaders of Rome and made them swear to elect Octavian as Pope after the death of Agapitus, thus combining in the one person both spiritual and civil authority in the city. Agapitus himself survived Alberic by some two years and was able to strengthen his pro-German policy, conferring the pallium on Otto's brother Bruno, the Archbishop of Cologne in 954 and, the following year, creating the archbishopric of Magdeburg – originally founded by Otto in 937 as a monastery – with oversight of the mission to the Slavs including authority to define ecclesiastical boundaries in those territories. The prestige of the Bishopric of Rome was much heightened during Agapitus's term of office, and pilgrimages to the city, frowned upon by Alberic, began once more.

JOHN XII
(Born c.937; consecrated December 16, 955; died May 14, 964)

The name John was taken by Octavian when he succeeded to the papacy on the death of Agapitus. Octavian was the illegitimate son, and political heir, of Alberic who had ruled Rome from 932 to his death in 954. On his deathbed he had obliged the Roman nobility not only to accept Octavian as the Roman "Prince and Senator," Alberic's titles, but also as Pope in contravention of the 450-year old canon which forbade one Pope to be elected while his predecessor was still alive. Octavian was sixteen when his father died, eighteen when he became Pope. His manner of life undoubtedly gave rise to scandal; his death was attributed – admittedly by a hostile witness – to a fit of apoplexy brought on during an act of adultery, but he was probably no worse than many bishops of the day. Perhaps more significantly he was remembered as choosing his friends from among grooms of the Lateran stables rather than from among the Roman aristocracy. In his public life, however, he continued his father's policy of supporting monasticism, he upheld the privileges of the Church, threatening excommunication against anyone trying to seize ecclesiastical property, and had contact with ecclesiastics particularly in Germany but even in far-flung places such as Britain and Spain. He also attempted, though in vain, to regain control over lands well outside Rome, some territories, indeed, he was losing to power of the German king, intrigued against him, seeking an accommodation with Berengar through the mediation of his son Adalbert. Otto returned to Rome, Adalbert and John fled, and the German ruler placed Leo, an official in the Lateran and still at the time a layman, on the papal throne. This he achieved through a synod convoked for November 6 which accused John of gravely immoral conduct and declared him deposed on December 4. Otto then withdrew from Rome and the following February John returned to rule until his death three months later. Leo was put to flight, and all his acts as Pope were declared void.

LEO VIII
(Consecrated December 6, 963; died March 1, 965)

Leo was a lay man and protoscrinarius, or chief notary, in the Lateran when, on December 4, 963, he was elected by a Roman synod to replace John XII. The charges against John were of immorality, but the real reason for his deposition was his rebellion against the German King Otto I whom he had, less than two years before, created Holy Roman Emperor. Leo was therefore seen as subservient to Otto, something to which the Roman populace took exception. His elevation to the episcopacy from the lay state took place in a period of two days. At his consecration he swore fidelity to the Emperor, and it seems likely that the "Ottonian privilege," that no Pope should be consecrated without the agreement of the Emperor or his representatives, came into being at that time. As a Pope, Leo was insignificant. When Otto withdrew from Rome he was chased from the papal throne by his deposed predecessor, and John, in a synod held in St Peter's on February 26, declared all Leo's acts invalid. John died on May 14 and Otto attempted to reinstall Leo. Before he could do so, however, the people of the city elected and installed the Cardinal Deacon Benedict. Otto was furious, and laid siege to Rome, reducing the population to starvation. When he entered Rome Leo once again became Pope and, at a synod on June 23, 963, Benedict was reduced to the rank of deacon and sent off into the custody of the Archbishop of Hamburg. Though he reigned for another eight months or so, Leo's pontificate has left little record, though a number of documents promoting the idea of imperial authority over the Pope were later written to read as if

Above: John XII *was the subject of much scandal during his papacy including a rumor that he had incestuous relations with his mother. He was also very fond of horses, hunting and gambling. His lifestyle did much to bring the papacy into disrepute.*

Berengar, King of Italy, who was plundering areas to the north of the city. John needed support and he turned, as his predecessor Agapitus would have liked to have done, to the German King Otto I. In August 961 Otto entered Italy; by the end of January 962 he was outside the walls of Rome. In February he was crowned Emperor in St Peter's, and struck a bargain with the Pope which secured imperial protection for the papacy and its territories – now extended to cover large areas of Italy – though imperial officials were to be associated with papal ones in the administration of the Church's estates. The Pope was to swear an oath of fidelity to the Emperor before he was consecrated. These matters settled, Otto turned his attentions against Berengar. Pope John, however, threatened by the

OTTO DER GROSSE

Above: Otto the Great was crowned Emperor in St Peter's in February 962 by John XII and agreed a pact with the Pope which ensured imperial protection for the papacy and its territories which were spread over large areas of Italy. A supporter of Leo VIII, Otto later laid siege to Rome and deposed Benedict V in order to have Leo reinstalled as Pope.

they came from this period. Leo is traditionally considered a legitimate, rather than an antipope, but as he was elected during the lifetime of his predecessor it is difficult to find justification for this.

BENEDICT V
(Consecrated May 22, 964; deposed June 23, 964; died July 4, 966)

A Roman by birth, a man of virtue and of learning, Benedict was a cardinal deacon when the people of Rome chose him as Pope on the death of John XII instead of reinstalling Leo VIII as the German Emperor Otto I had wanted. Otto laid siege to the city and reduced its population to starvation before entering it and putting Leo back on the papal throne. Benedict was formally deposed at a synod

on June 23, 964, and was sent off into the custody of the Archbishop of Hamburg. If Leo was a legitimate Pope, it is difficult to see why Benedict was not an antipope, but he has traditionally been included in the list of Roman Pontiffs.

JOHN XIII
(Consecrated October 1, 965; died September 6, 972)

On the death of Leo the Romans wanted the restoration of Benedict V, but this the Emperor Otto I denied them. After a five-month delay John, a member of the Roman nobility, formerly papal librarian and now Bishop of Narnia was appointed under the patronage of Otto. John began his pontificate in a high-handed manner, and in December the Romans revolted. They imprisoned the Pope in the Castel Sant'Angelo, then exiled him to the Campagna. He, however, managed to escape and made his way to Otto's camp. The following November, with the support of the army of Count Pandolph of Capua, John returned to Rome. He was well received by the populace who by their actions had reason to fear the anger of the Emperor. Otto arrived in the city a month or so later and wreaked vengeance on its citizens. Some leaders of the people were put to death, others exiled; the bodies of two nobles who had died before his arrival were taken from their tombs and thrown out on to the street. A year later a grateful Pope crowned Otto's twelve-year-old son, Otto II, as co-Emperor. In the meantime John and the Emperor had spent Easter together in Ravenna where, on March 31, a synod was held at which Otto guaranteed that the exarchate of Ravenna would be restored to the papacy. The synod also insisted on clerical celibacy, gave support to the monastery of Cluny, confirmed Magdeburg as an archbishopric with oversight of the ministry to the Slavs, and gave the archbishop responsibility for the establishment of diocesan boundaries in the territories newly converted to Christianity. Otto had territorial ambitions in Italy itself, in the south which was traditionally under the protection of the Byzantine Emperor. A marriage was arranged, and performed on April 14, 972 by Pope John, between the son of the Emperor Otto I and the Princess Theophano, niece of the Byzantine Emperor John I, who was crowned as Otto II's Empress. Despite the tensions between the Emperor of the East and the Emperor of the West

Above: John XIII *enjoyed the support of Emperor Otto I and it was due to this that John was reinstated as Pope after he had been imprisoned and exiled. John later crowned Otto's son as co-Emperor.*

Above: Benedict VII *excommunicated Boniface VII who staged a coup in Rome in the summer of 980. Benedict was able to regain the city the following year with the help of Emperor Otto II.*

over their respective territorial ambitions in southern Italy, John had the most peaceful – and longest – pontificate in the second half of the tenth century.

BENEDICT VI
(Consecrated January 19, 973; died July 974)

It seems likely that Benedict was elected Pope not long after the death of his predecessor: the delay between election and consecration accounted for by the need to receive confirmation of the election from the Emperor Otto I, who was at the time in Germany. Benedict was a Roman, son of a man who had become a monk. When he was elected he was Cardinal Priest of S. Teodoro. His election was opposed by the Crescentii family who backed a candidate of their own, the Cardinal Deacon Franco. Their leader, Crescentius I, was the son of Theodora the Younger, and therefore the great grandson of Theophylact whose family had dominated the papacy in the first half of the tenth century. At first, the Crescentii had to bow before the imperial will, but the death in May 973 of the Emperor Otto I seriously weakened Pope Benedict's authority. The Crescentii, quite probably with the support of the Byzantine Emperor, rose against Benedict and imprisoned him in Castel Sant'Angelo, despite the protests of the imperial representative who attempted to have Benedict released. Franco was elected and consecrated Pope in his place, taking the name Boniface VII: to secure his authority he had Benedict strangled by a priest called Stephen. Little of ecclesiastical significance is known of Benedict's eighteen-month pontificate, though he continued the Ottonian policy of supporting monastic reform, and the reform of the clergy at large, as well as strengthening the Church in Germany.

BENEDICT VII
(Consecrated October 974; died July 10, 983)

After the strangulation in prison of Benedict VI, the imperial representative at Rome refused to recognize the intruder into the papacy, the Cardinal Deacon Franco, who had taken the name of Boniface VII. Boniface fled the city, and Benedict was elected with imperial approval. As one of Rome's nobility and connected to, if not actually a member of, the Crescentii family he was widely accepted. Before his election he had been Bishop of Sutri. Immediately after becoming Pope Benedict held a synod which

excommunicated Boniface. Boniface had, however, fled south, to Byzantine-held territory, and managed to stage a coup in Rome in the Summer of 980, though, with the help of the Emperor Otto II, Benedict regained the city the following March. Shortly afterward he held in St Peter's basilica, with the Emperor in attendance, a synod which roundly condemned simony. This was perhaps not remarkable in itself, but Benedict was sufficiently sure of himself to send to the bishops of the Christian world a letter (an "encyclical") announcing the fact.

He was, indeed, a reforming Pope. Like many of his predecessors he supported the monastic reforms inspired by the Abbey of Cluny, the general tendency of which in France was to support their independence of monarchs and local bishops and nobility. In Germany, however, though he equally supported monastic reform, he put this in the hands of the king and bishops. He gave special authority to the Archbishops of Trier and of Mainz, including the privilege for the latter of crowning German kings. He also gave to one German prelate a Church (or "title") in Rome, the first time a foreign bishop had been granted such a concession. During his pontificate the Patriarch Sergius of Damascus fled to Rome after his city had been seized by Islamic forces. Benedict refounded the monastery of SS Boniface and Alexis on the Aventine for the Patriarch, and this became a center for relations with the Eastern, and especially the Slav, Churches. It was a sign of Benedict's high standing that Sergius had come to Rome. The Bishop-elect of Carthage did likewise, seeking consecration at the Pope's hands. Benedict's relations with the Byzantines, however, were more difficult. He was closely associated with the anti-Byzantine policy of Otto, and he set up a Latin-rite archbishopric in Byzantine territory in southern Italy. He was buried in the basilica of Sta Croce in Gerusalemme.

JOHN XIV
(Consecrated December 983; died August 20, 984)

The Pope consecrated to succeed Benedict VII was Peter Canepanova, Bishop of Pavia (where he had been born) and a close ally of the Emperor Otto II. Soon after John's consecration Otto returned to Rome from southern Italy, dying of malaria – he died in the Pope's arms, after receiving absolution. John had no power-base among the Roman nobility,

Above: John XV *began the practice of canonization by Popes when he declared Bishop Ulrich of Augsburg to be a saint. Before this point such canonizations had been the prerogative of local bishops.*

and no defense when Boniface VII, an antipope since the pontificate of Benedict VI, returned from Constantinople and, in April 984, succeeded in overthrowing Pope John. John was imprisoned in Castel Sant'Angelo where he died, some reports say of starvation, others that he had been poisoned.

JOHN XV
(Consecrated August 985; died March 996)

The antipope Boniface VII, who had seized power in Rome from John XIV in April 984, managed to hold on to the pontificate until his death in July 985. Otto III was still in Germany being cared for by his mother, the Byzantine Princess Theophano, and was in any case too young personally to play any part in the politics of the papacy. Instead, the Crescentii family, in the person of John Crescentius, came to the fore. Their candidate was a Roman, Cardinal Priest of San Vitale, a learned man and the son of a priest named Leo. Though popular, at least at first, with the Roman nobility and senior priests, John did not have the support of the lower clergy because of his avarice and the way he promoted his family. The support of the Crescentii also disappeared when John Crescentius died in 988 to be succeeded as head of the family by his brother Crescentius II who took over all temporal authority in the papal estates. For a time Pope John had the distant support of Theophano in Germany. She came to Rome in the winter of 989/990 to assert her son Otto III's imperial claims. Her presence for

a time strengthened the Pope, but Theophano died in June 991 and his position deteriorated. In March 995 he fled the city, taking refuge in Sutri, when he sent an appeal for support to the fifteen-year old Otto III in Germany. Otto moved south, but the mere threat of his presence was enough to make the Romans invite Pope John back to the Lateran. Otto kept up his advance, arriving in Pavia to celebrate Easter, but by that time the Pope was dead of a fever.

Though dominated by politics, John's decade-long pontificate was an important one for other reasons. The stature of the papacy had risen under his recent predecessors: one of his more remarkable achievements was to mediate, and achieve peace, in 991 between Richard Duke of Normandy and King Aethelred II of England. He attempted, through his legate, to summon the French bishops to Rome when, in 991, they deposed Arnoul, Archbishop of Rheims, replacing him with Gerbert of Aurillac, who was later to become Pope Sylvester II. The French protested at this papal intervention in what they regarded as their affair, and declared that John had overstepped his authority, making him no better than a heretic. In fact, four years later, John managed to have Gerbert removed from office. Gerbert left Rheims and made his way to the German court. John continued his predecessors' support for the ecclesiastical policy of the German court and, in an act which has become one of the best-known offices of the papacy, declared Bishop Ulrich of Augsburg to be a saint worthy of honor by the whole Church: hitherto such "canonizations" had been the responsibility of local bishops.

GREGORY V
(Born 972; consecrated May 3, 996; died February 18, 999)

At the death of Pope John XV a group of Roman nobles travelled to Ravenna, where the German King Otto III had arrived, to inform him of the Pope's death and formally ask his advice on the choice of a successor. To their astonishment Otto insisted on the election not of a Roman, or even of an Italian, but of his relative Bruno who was accompanying him as one of his chaplains. This was the first time a German, a "foreigner" to the city of Rome, was to be elected its bishop. Bruno, who was the son of Otto's cousin the Duke of Carinthia, was only twenty-three years old. He was, however, well-educated and generally talented, and when he

Right: Aethelred II of England. *Pope John XV was the mediator between Aethelred and Richard, Duke of Normandy in 991 which brought peace. This act of mediation marked a significant rise in the status and influence of the papacy at this time.*

arrived in Rome in the company of Otto's chancellor and archchancellor, there was no hesitation in his elevation to the papacy. Otto himself was not far behind, and on the feast of the Ascension, May 21 that year, Otto was crowned as Emperor. One of his first acts was to banish Crescentius II for his illtreatment of Pope John XV but, eager to win favor with the Roman nobility, Gregory asked that the sentence be remitted. His generosity proved an expensive mistake. Gregory also attempted to demonstrate a degree of independence of the Emperor by asking for the restoration to the papal estates of the Pentapolis, five towns (Rimini, Pesaro, Fano, Senigallia and Ancona) with their associated territories which, in the pontificate of Stephen II (III), Pepin had handed over to the Roman See. Otto III would not grant this, and likewise refused to renew the pact by which his grandfather, in the pontificate of John XIII, had undertaken to defend the estates, and the privileges, of the bishopric of Rome. Indeed, soon after his crowning, the new Emperor withdrew from Rome, leaving Gregory feeling vulnerable: he asked his protector to return, but Otto refused to do so, instead recommending the Pope to the protection of two Italian nobles, the Dukes of Tuscany and Spoleto.

In the autumn Gregory was forced out of Rome, and had to flee to the safety of Spoleto. In his absence John Philagathus, a Greek from Calabria and by this time the Bishop of Piacenza, was elected an antipope with the backing of Crescentius. Bishop John had served in various offices under Otto I, and then as tutor to the young Otto II. He had been sent to Constantinople to negotiate a marriage for Otto III to a Byzantine princess, and had returned with a Byzantine emissary, Leo, just at the time of Gregory's expulsion from Rome. John Philagathus took the title of Pope John XVI. At about the same time as this election of an antipope, Gregory in Pavia was holding a synod in which the ban on selling ecclesiastical offices for money (the crime of "simony") was renewed, as was the ban on arranging the succession to the papacy during a Pope's lifetime. He also renewed the suspension from office, first issued by his predecessor, of those French bishops who had connived at the appointment of Gerbert of Aurillac, Gregory's successor in the papacy, to the Archbishopric of Rheims. Although he made a couple of attempts to take Rome by force, and although the antipope was not recognized by the bishops of the West, Gregory had to remain

outside the city until Otto returned to Italy. Once back in Rome, Otto had the antipope mutilated and imprisoned, Crescentius was beheaded and a dozen of his closest collaborators hanged. Gregory and Otto from then on worked for the most part together, the Pope agreeing to confer the pallium on Gerbert, who was a friend of Otto's, when the Emperor made him Archbishop of Ravenna.

SYLVESTER II
(Born c.945; consecrated April 2, 999; died May 12, 1003)

With the choice of Sylvester as Pope, the bishopric of Rome had its first Frenchman as its head. Gerbert had been born in the Auvergne and educated first in the monastery of Aurillac, then at Vichy, and finally at Rheims, where he went on to teach in the cathedral school. He was possibly the greatest scholar of his day, skilled particularly in astronomy, mathematics and music. Impressed by his learning, the Emperor, in 980, made him Abbot of the monastery of Bobbio. At this task he was not a success and went back to Rheims, where he was partly instrumental in making Hugh Capet the King of France. He might have expected a reward for this

Above: Gregory V *renewed several important tenets of the Church during his term of office, notably the ban on selling ecclesiastical offices for money, and the ban on arranging the papal succession during the lifetime of the incumbent.*

Left: Sylvester II *was restricted to ecclesiastical affairs after the death of Otto III. Sylvester did, however, make attempts to enforce celibacy on the clergy, as a way of preventing lands being diverted away from the ownership of the Church.*

service, and was disappointed when Arnoul, who was son of the Carolingian King Lothair, was appointed to the archbishopric of Rheims. Arnoul, however, was not loyal to Hugh Capet, and the king deposed him, putting Gerbert in his place. Gerbert and his supporters tried to argue that this was a French matter, and that the Pope had no standing in the dispute over Rheims, but many, Pope John XV included, thought otherwise and Gerbert was removed from office. He went off to the court of Otto III, who, in the pontificate of Gregory V, had him made Archbishop of Ravenna in 998.

The choice of the name Sylvester reflected the Pope's sympathy for ambitions of Emperor Otto who made Rome rather than Germany his permanent home, for Sylvester I had been, according to legend, close to Emperor Constantine. The imperial ambitions were Otto's, but they had an important ecclesiastical dimension. In the winter of 999/1000 Otto went on pilgrimage to visit the tomb of Adalbert who had been martyred near Danzig in 997 after evangelizing parts of Prussia, Hungary, and Russia, in what is now Poland. He was buried at Gniezo in Poland, and Otto took with him a papal privilege making Gniezo the metropolitan See of the, as yet non-existent, Polish Church. This brought Poland under the aegis of Rome; it also extended Otto's imperial claims. A similar policy was pursued in Hungary, where Sylvester made Esztergom the metropolitan See and declared Stephen to be a king by sending him a crown. Otto made overtures – unsuccessful as it turned out – to the Venetians, and it is also likely that he sent envoys to Kiev: Bruno of Querfurt was consecrated Archbishop in Rome in 1002 to have charge of missions to the East. But by that time Otto was dead. He died in January 1002 when still only twenty-two. He died, moreover, outside Rome: the Romans had risen in revolt against the domination of their city by foreigners, Pope and Emperor, and had driven them both out of the city. John II Crescentius was now in command of Rome and although he allowed Sylvester to return after Otto's death, the Pope was restricted to ecclesiastical affairs. He showed himself in general a reforming Pope, denouncing simony and tried to enforce celibacy on the clergy: clerical marriage, after all, diverted lands which were donated away from the Church. One particular success for Sylvester compared to his predecessor Gregory, the Pentapolis, which Gregory had sought and had been refused by

Otto, was now made over to the bishopric of Rome, though the Emperor insisted that he was doing so of his own free will and not because of any claims arising from the alleged "donation" of Constantine.

JOHN XVII
(Consecrated May 16, 1003; died November 6, 1003)

John II Crescentius was in effective control of the city of Rome at the death of Pope Sylvester II. The Roman-born John Sicco, in all probability a relative of the Crescentii family, was his appointee, but beyond that scarcely anything is recorded of him, so short was his pontificate. The manner of his death is not known, though there is nothing to suggest it was anything but natural.

JOHN XVIII
(Consecrated 25 December 25, 1003; died June/July 1009)

Another John, John Fusanus, was appointed by John II Crescentius, the virtual ruler of Rome, to

Above: **John XVIII** *continued the practice of his namesake John XV by declaring five Polish martyrs to be saints. His pontificate also saw an improvement in relations with Constantinople.*

Left: **King Henry II of Germany.** *In May 1004, he traveled to Pavia to be crowned King of Italy during the papacy of John XVIII. Later, good relations were established between Henry and Pope Sergius IV.*

be Pope after the short pontificate of John XVII. More is known about Fusanus than about his predecessor: at his election he was Cardinal Priest of St Peter's, the son of Ursus and Stephania, and possibly a relative, like John XVII, of the Crescentius family. In May 1004 the German King Henry II traveled to Pavia to be crowned King of Italy. One chronicler reports that the Pope was eager that Henry should come as far as Rome, but that proposal was vetoed by Crescentius whose power in the city would have been undermined by Henry's presence, and especially by the grant to him of imperial authority. Henry stayed away, but Pope John busied himself with the affairs of the German Church, creating in 1007 a new bishopric at Bamberg, as Henry wanted, to be a base for missionary work among the Slavs: he put it under the protection of the Bishopric of Rome. He took firm action in France when two bishops refused to acknowledge the papal privileges accorded to the Abbey of Fleury-sur-Loire; he summoned them to Rome on pain of excommunication, and threatened the King of France, Robert the Pious, with an interdict if he did not make them go to Rome. Continuing the precedent set by John XV, John XVIII declared five Polish martyrs to be saints venerated right across the Church. In his pontificate there seems to have been an improvement in relations with Constantinople, possibly a consequence of the authority over the Pope of the pro-Byzantine John II Crescentius. There is no suggestion that John XVIII was for any reason imprisoned, but shortly before his death he appears to have withdrawn to a monastery, that of St Pauls-Outside-the-Walls, where shortly afterward he died. It is possible that he abdicated his office as Pope when he became a monk.

SERGIUS IV
(Consecrated July 31, 1009; died May 12, 1012)

At his consecration as Bishop of Rome, Peter, Bishop of Albano for five years, changed his name to Sergius out of respect for the Prince of the Apostles (there has still not been a Pope called Peter). The nickname by which he had been known was unfortunate: he was called "Peter Pig's Snout." He came from Rome itself, the son of a shoemaker also called Peter, married to Stephania. His appointment he owed to John II Crescentius, who had

dominated Roman politics since shortly before the death of Pope Sylvester II. One, perhaps the only, way at the time for a pontiff to break the Crescentian hold was an alliance with the German King Henry II, but this, John II Crescentius managed to prevent. Sergius did, however, have good relations with Henry, and sent representatives to the consecration of the cathedral at Bamberg: his predecessor had approved the establishment of the diocese. News that on October 18, 1009 Islamic forces had occupied Jerusalem and seized the Holy Places, arrived in Rome during the pontificate of John XVIII, but the Pope's chief political preoccupation, so far as one is recorded, was to attempt to persuade the Italian dukedoms to form an alliance to drive the Arabs out of southern Italy. In this he was not successful. Less than a week after Sergius' death John II Crescentius also died. The coincidence of their deaths has led some to speculate that they were murdered, but of this there is no evidence.

BENEDICT VIII
(Born c.980; consecrated May 17, 1012; died April 9, 1024)

The death of John II Crescentius shortly after that of Pope Sergius left a political vacuum in the city, into which stepped the family of the Counts of Tusculum, wresting power from the Crescentians. This did not happen without a struggle. The Crescentians promoted one Gregory, about whose antecedents nothing is known and who disappears from history after he tried, and failed, to win over to his side the German King Henry II; the Tusculum arranged for the election of Theophylact, one of the three sons of Gregory of Tusculum, and a direct descendant of the papal treasurer Theophylact (see under Sergius III) through his daughter Marozia. On his election he changed his name to Benedict VIII. Little is known about this latest Theophylact except that, on his election, he was still a layman. He was, however, an astute politician. His brother took over the civil government of Rome while the Pope won over the Roman nobility and organized the forcible suppression of the Crescentians. When Henry II refused to support Benedict's rival it was probably because Benedict himself had fairly successfully made Rome his own, and was already engaged in managing the Church. One of his earliest acts was to confirm the privileges of Henry's much-favored bishopric of Bamberg,

Above: **Sergius IV.** *At his consecration as Pope, Peter, Bishop of Albano, changed his name to Sergius IV. During the whole history of the papacy there has never been a Pope who took Peter as his name, out of respect for the Prince of the Apostles.*

Above: Benedict VIII *was a man of action rather than a spiritual figure. One story has it that, during battle, he personally slew the wife of the Moslem leader (depicted). He was one of few Popes who took part in campaigns against enemies of the papacy.*

minimum ages for ordination. Thus Benedict began as a reforming Pope, and he was, like several of his predecessors, an admirer of the monastic life as propagated by the Abbey of Cluny, but his chief concerns were political.

In Rome there was the constant threat of the Crescentii. These he actively suppressed. Then there were the Arabs. These he managed to defeat on land and at sea, taking part in the campaigns himself. That was in north Italy. In the south the Byzantines were once again strong. Benedict encouraged Norman mercenaries to unite with those uneasy with Byzantine rule, but the allies were defeated. Feeling under threat, Benedict now made his way to the Emperor in Bamberg – his arrival there creating something of a sensation. In 1019 he held a synod at Goslar where, inspired by the Emperor, Benedict issued decrees against marriage, or the concubinage, of clerics of whatever rank. Henry accepted the Pope's request that he march south to defend the papacy, renewing formally the Ottonian privilege (*see under* Leo VIII). In fact the campaign of 1022, though initially a success, resulted in no long-term gains of territory. At Pavia in a synod held on May 1, 1022 the decrees of Goslar were repeated, but more of the Pope's thinking was revealed. The children of clerical marriages were to be reduced to the status of serfs for, as he disarmingly pointed out in a sermon at Pavia, clerical children could readily lead to the alienation from the Church of ecclesiastical property. Benedict was a man of action rather than a spiritual figure, while the Emperor, who had at one time wanted to become a monk and who died soon after the death of the Pope, was in 1146 declared a saint. His wife Cunegundis entered a convent a year to the day after Henry's death, and was canonized in 1200.

JOHN XIX
(Consecrated April 19, 1024; died October 20, 1032)

When Benedict died he was immediately (the Tusculani ensured that he was) succeeded by his brother Romanus. Romanus at the time was still a layman, and he had to be rushed through ordination in a single day, taking the name of John. His election was assisted by the liberal distribution of money, making nonsense of his brother's decrees against simony, but he managed to win over the nobility of Rome to his side, even including the

something which could not fail to commend him to the German king. A further attraction for Henry was the invitation to visit Rome and to be installed as Emperor. He and his wife came, and they were duly crowned on February 14, 1014. On the way down to Rome, Henry's half-brother Arnold had been, with the approval of the Pope, appointed as Archbishop of Ravenna; he was consecrated in the course of a synod held in Rome immediately after the imperial coronation. One other concession of some consequence was made by Benedict. It was the practice in Germany to recite the creed at mass. Benedict agreed that in this Rome would follow the German custom, but that meant including in the liturgy the much disputed (with the Greeks) term "filioque". From Rome, Pope and Emperor moved to Ravenna where another synod was held, reforming abuses in the lives of clerics and laying down

Above: John XIX *was the brother of Benedict VIII, his immediate predecessor. He was successfully elected due, in part at least, to the liberal distribution of bribes.*

arch enemies of the Tusculani, the Crescentii. There is a story that the Byzantine Emperor, Basil, and the Patriarch of Constantinople, Eustathius, sent representatives to Rome asking the Pope to agree to Eustathius and his successors calling themselves the "ecumenical" patriarch (*see under* Pelagius II). John was willing to accept, given the lavish gifts they had brought (that much, in the Pope's case, rings true), but that John was prevented from agreeing by an outcry, especially from monasteries.

BENEDICT IX
(Born c.1005; consecrated October 21, 1032; deposed September 1044; reigned 10 March 10 to May 1, 1045, November 8, 1047 to July 16, 1048; died 1055/56)

Two of his uncles had been Popes, and Theophylact was put on the papal throne by the simple expedient of distributing largesse to the clergy and people of Rome. This was done by his father, Alberic III, Count of Tusculum, who also ensured that another of his sons took over the civil government of the city. The new Pope chose the name of Benedict. At his election he was still a layman and, according to some sources, only twelve years of age, though that is not now generally believed by historians of the period. Whatever his personal life – and it was reputed to have been scandalous, at least for a Pope – he carried out the public duties of his office well, holding synods, consecrating bishops, supporting the reform of communal life. Politically he got on well with the Emperor Conrad II and, initially, with Conrad's successor in 1039, Henry III. There had, however, been some small signs even in the time of Conrad, that Benedict wanted to loosen German influence on the papal court. Then, at a synod held in Rome in April 1044 he restored to the Archbishop of Grado the status of Patriarch, and simultaneously withdrew it from Grado's arch-rival Aquileia, in a direct reversal of a decision made by his predecessor. This was not a purely ecclesiastic matter: the Archbishop of Aquileia was Eberhard, formerly the chancellor of Henry III. The German king was not pleased. He gave support to Benedict's enemies in Rome, and it was from this time in particular that stories of Benedict's dissolute life began to spread. At the beginning of September there was an uprising against Benedict and he had to flee from the city. On 24 January the following year the Crescentii, believing themselves once more in the

ascendant, had Bishop John of Sabina installed in the Lateran as Pope. He took the name Sylvester III. By March 10 Benedict was back in power, but even he seems to have felt that his grasp of it was weak. He may also have been alarmed at the thought that Henry III would shortly make his way to Rome. Benedict's solution was, apparently, to abdicate his office. He did so in favor of the devout John Gratian, his godfather, who had charge of a community of canons at the Church of St John at the Latin Gate, and in favor of a very large sum of money to serve as his pension. The new Pope (*see below*) took the name of Gregory VI. There were now three men with a claim to the papacy: Sylvester III who had no real ambition for the post and whom one might have thought was an antipope though he is not treated as such; Gregory VI whose title to the office was dubious and possibly simoniacal; and Benedict, who claimed to have abdicated. When Henry III arrived in Italy he called synod at Sutri on December 20, 1046, summoning all three contenders to the pontificate to appear before him. Benedict did not appear but the other two did, and Henry deposed them. Then, four days later, he held a further synod at Rome where Benedict was deposed. This left, in Henry's view, the bishopric of Rome conveniently vacant and Suidger, Bishop of Bamberg and a member of Henry's entourage, was made Pope on December 24, taking the name of Clement II. There were, therefore, no longer three, but four men with a claim. Clement died in October 1047 and Benedict, seizing the opportunity when Henry was back in Germany, made another return to Rome on November 8 with the support of Boniface of Tuscany and Guaimar V of Salerno. Some eight months later, under pressure from Henry III, Boniface turned against Benedict and put Poppo, Bishop of Brixen, on the papal throne. Poppo took the name Damasus II. This time Benedict withdrew for good, but unlike the one-time Sylvester III, he never gave up the title of Pope. He survived five more Popes before his death, probably at the end of 1055.

SYLVESTER III
(Consecrated January 20, 1045; deposed March 10, 1045; died 1063)

It is difficult to know why Bishop John of Sabina should not be regarded as an antipope, but as Sylvester III he is included in the official lists. He

Above: **Gregory VI**. *Although some confusion surrounds the legitimacy of Gregory VI's papacy, he was widely regarded as the true Pope. He was, however, deposed by King Henry III and died in exile.*

Above: **Clement II** *was something of a reformer during his time of office, condemning simony and imposing a penance on clergy who let themselves be ordained by known simonists. Unusally, on his death his body was interred in the cathedral at Bamberg rather than in Rome.*

was the candidate of the Crescentii when they saw their opportunity to overthrow the Tusculani, who had controlled the papacy since the time of Benedict VIII. He was excommunicated by the exiled Benedict IX and when Benedict returned, Pope Sylvester simply went back to his original See. The German King Henry III formally deposed him at the synod of Sutri on 20 December 1046, and he was sentenced to be imprisoned in a monastery for usurping the papal throne. What seems most likely, however, is that once again he returned to his See, and apparently carried on as before. He died in the office of bishop.

GREGORY VI
(Consecrated May 1 1045; deposed December 20, 1046; died late 1047)

Unlike Sylvester, it is possible to argue that Gregory was a legitimate Pope. If Benedict IX had indeed abdicated then Gregory's election was valid – except for the facts that he been nominated by his predecessor, Benedict, and that, it was alleged, his election had been accomplished by bribery. But John Gratian, Archpriest of the Church of St John at the Latin Gate and in charge of a community of canons there, was a devout man, highly respected in the circles of those who were working for reform in the Church. He was a close friend of Hildebrand, a cleric on the staff of the Lateran, who was later to become Gregory VII, one of the greatest of reforming Popes. He was widely regarded as the legitimate Pope, even in Germany, but when the German King Henry III entered Italy in 1046, though he first met Gregory courteously at Piacenza, on December 20 he deposed him, along with Sylvester II, at the synod of Sutri. Gregory was exiled to Cologne, and Hildebrand went with him. Gregory outlived the Pope whom Henry created, Clement II, but only just. He died toward the end of the year, still in exile.

CLEMENT II
(Elected December 24, 1046; died October 9, 1047)

The choice of name by Suidger, Bishop of Bamberg, on his appointment to the See of Rome by King Henry III after the king had deposed all other contenders at the synod of Sutri in 1046, was significant. Clement was the name of a very early pontiff: Suidger's adoption of it indicated a desire for the supposed purity of the early Church. Clearly, but paradoxically, this could only be done were the pontiff to be freed from domination either by the Roman nobility or by the German king. A tract "On the making of Popes" *(De ordinando pontifice)* written soon after the synod of Sutri claimed that no lay person could appoint bishops or have control over Church property. On the contrary, it was argued, the king was subject to bishops. Suidger, even though he took this early Christian title, had been far too close to Henry throughout both their careers to adopt so radical a stance. On Christmas Day he was enthroned, and then crowned Henry and his Queen Agnes as Emperor and Empress. On 5 January Clement and Henry held a synod which embarked on a reforming program, condemning simony and imposing a penance on clergy who let themselves be ordained by known simonists. The penalty for the latter crime, however, was slight: just forty days penance. But whatever plans Clement may have had came to nothing. He went off with Henry into southern Italy on what could be seen as a reforming tour. He returned to Rome and spent the summer months there, which was probably bad for his health. He left again the early fall, but died in the Monastery of St Thomas at Pesaro. His body was interred in the cathedral at Bamberg: despite being Pope, he had never ceased to be that city's bishop as well.

DAMASUS II
(Consecrated July 17, 1048; died August 9, 1048)

When Clement II died, Benedict IX was still alive and with a claim to the papal throne, and so was Gregory VI, in exile in Cologne. The Bishop of Liège even recommended to Emperor Henry III that Gregory be reappointed which, since he was to die shortly afterward, would have been unfortunate. As it was, Henry chose another prelate who had been part of his entourage when he came to Italy in 1046: Poppo, Bishop of Brixen in the Tyrol. Poppo does not seem to have been particularly eager to be Pope, and retained the bishopric of Brixen until his death. His hesitations may have arisen from a fear that, as an imperial nominee, he would be popular neither with those in Rome who were backing reform, nor the Roman nobility who had lost control of the papacy to the Emperor. Meanwhile

Benedict IX re-emerged and, with the support of Boniface of Tuscany, once more took over the papal throne. Poppo seems not to have been too distressed by this event, and went back to Henry to tell him what had happened. Boniface asked Henry that Benedict be recognized. Henry was having none of this challenge to his authority. He told Boniface that if Poppo was not made Pope he would come back to Italy to ensure it happened. Boniface promptly had Benedict expelled once again from Rome, and Poppo consecrated. As a sign of his commitment to the supposed purity of the early Church, he took the name Damasus. Whether he would indeed have carried out a reforming program no one will know, because within a month of his consecration he died at Palestrina, where he had gone to escape the heat of the Roman summer. He was buried in Rome, in the Church of St Laurence-Outside-the-Walls.

St LEO IX
(Born June 21, 1002; consecrated February 12, 1049; died April 19, 1054)

The appointment of Bruno of Toul to be the successor of Damasus II was a major step in the reform of the papacy. He was born in Alsace, of the family of the Counts of Egisheim. He was educated at Toul in Lorraine, and became bishop of the city in 1026, and remained so until appointed Pope – in fact he retained his See until 1051. As Bishop of Toul he was very involved in the reform of monasteries in his diocese. He was also associated with those who believed in the non-interference of the monarchy in ecclesiastical affairs. It was, therefore, something of a paradox that, in December 1048, he should be named as Pope by his cousin the Emperor Henry III. It seems that he was hesitant to accept, and agreed to do so if he were to be elected by the people of Rome. He went to Rome barefoot, dressed as a pilgrim, and was elected by acclamation, thus satisfying one detail at least of his reforming program. This program he put into operation almost immediately. He held a synod in the Lateran in April at which clerical marriage or concubinage was condemned and all bishops who could not demonstrate they were innocent of simony were deposed from office. There was also an attempt to declare that all ordinations by simoniacal bishops were invalid. Such a decision would have been contrary to what had been taught by St Augustine of Hippo in

the fifth century and would have caused immense confusion, as well as depriving the laity of the services of very many of the clergy. In the end Leo had to be content with issuing the same penalty, of forty days penance, that had been imposed by Clement II.

In all his years as Pope, Leo stayed in Rome perhaps for only some six months. Soon after the synod he was on the road – to Pavia, and onward into Germany then on to France, holding synods as he went, to impose upon the Church as best he could his vision of reform. That at Rheims in 1049 has been hailed as the beginning of the Gregorian reform which reached its peak under his friend Hildebrand when he became Gregory VII. It asserted a Pope's rights over the universal Church, and the right of the clergy and people to elect their prelates. It was particularly important to assert this in France where the king was much less sympathetic to the reforms than was the Emperor oper-

Below: St Leo IX *brought major changes to the Church, including the assertion of a Pope's rights over the universal Church. His papacy also saw the beginnings of what came to be known as the College of cardinals. On his death he was proclaimed to have been a saint.*

ating in Germany and in Italy. In all this Leo was not operating alone. There was a movement for reform of the clergy within the Church at large, and some of its most powerful protagonists had entered Rome with the new Pope, among them two of his successors, Frederick of Liège (Stephen IX) and Hildebrand (Gregory VII). This group of men became an unofficial advisory body to Pope Leo and formed the nucleus of what came to be the College of Cardinals. One of them, Humbert of Silva Candida, he made Archbishop of Sicily, then in the hands of the Saracens.

Leo was eager to establish in southern Italy a league which would restrain the Normans who had settled there. In 1052 the Pope visited the Emperor in Germany to win his support. This was granted, up to a point, but Henry was dissuaded by his chancellor, Gebehard of Eichstätt, from sending military assistance to Leo. Instead the Pope recruited his own troops, and set off at their head, trusting in the support of the Byzantine representative in Italy to raise an alliance with Byzantine forces. On June 16, 1053 the papal army was overwhelmed by the Normans and the Pope taken captive. He was held prisoner at Benevento, which, just before the disastrous expedition, Henry had ceded to him. In an effort to regroup the alliance, Archbishop Humbert went to Constantinople to see the Emperor. Unfortunately for Leo's delegation, the Patriarch, Michael Caerularius, was anything but sympathetic, especially to a man who claimed to be Archbishop of Sicily, a territory traditionally within the Byzantine sphere of influence. The situation deteriorated to the point of Humbert, in the Church of Hagia Sophia, excommunicating the Patriarch. It was July 16, 1054: later the same month Michael Caerularius excommunicated the Latins who had, by that time, left for Italy. It was the formal break between Rome and Constantinople. By that time Leo had been released by the Normans. He was however, a broken man and died little over a month later. Almost immediately after his death he was acknowledged to have been a saint.

VICTOR II
(Born c.1018; consecrated April 13, 1055; died July 28, 1057)

The man chosen to succeed Pope Leo IX was the man who had, indirectly caused his death. As chancellor to Henry III, Gebehard, Bishop of Eichstätt,

ΒΕСΤΆΤΗ ΆΥΓΌΥСΤΑ

X̃C

Left: Emperor Constantine I,
*depicted with the enthroned Christ, was
the first Roman ruler to embrace
Christianity. The break between Rome
and the Church in his city of
Constantinople came at the end of the
reign of Leo IX.*

Above: The Church of Hagia Sophia *in Constantinople which saw Archbishop Humbert of Sicily excommunicate the Patriarch, Michael Caerularius. This led, in turn, to the Patriarch excommunicating the delegation headed by Humbert which had been sent by Pope Leo IX. These events marked the formal break between Rome and Constantinople.*

had dissuaded the Emperor from sending troops to support Leo in the battle, which he lost and after which he was imprisoned, against the Normans in southern Italy. Gebehard came from a noble Swabian family, had been made Bishop of Eichstätt in 1042, an office which he retained throughout his papacy, and a counsellor to the Emperor less than a decade later.

His appointment came after prolonged negotiations with a delegation from Rome headed by Hildebrand, the future Gregory VII. The lengthy delay – it was almost a year between Leo's death and

Gebehard's acceptance of the office at Regensburg in March 1055 – possibly arose from the Roman desire to have one of their own group of reformers as Pope. The Emperor, however, was facing a major political crisis in Italy. Boniface of Tuscany, the one-time patron of Benedict IX, had died and his widow had married Godfrey of Lotharingia. Duke Godfrey, Henry's over-powerful vassal, was threatening imperial control of central Italy: Henry, who could not have been happy with the appointment of Godfrey's brother Frederick, who was one of Leo's closest supporters, as chancellor of the Roman

Church, needed a strong ally in Rome such as he knew Gebehard to be.

Gebehard, as had become the custom, adopted the name of one of the early Popes to signify his reforming intentions. The reform did indeed continue, with a synod at Florence, attended by both Pope and Emperor, which deposed unworthy bishops, attacked those of the clergy who failed to observe celibacy or were simoniacal, and fulminated against the alienation of Church property. That was on June 4, 1055. The following year there were synods at Toulouse and – presided over by Hildebrand – probably at Chalon-sur-Soâne. Despite these synods, the dominating factors of Victor's pontificate were political. The Emperor had strengthened the Pope by giving into his charge the Duchy of Spoleto and the Marquisate of Fermo. He also marched south into Italy in such force that Godfrey fled, his wife and step-daughter (the future Countess Matilda) were taken hostage, and Frederick, Godfrey's brother, took refuge in the abbey of Monte Cassino. The Emperor then retired back to Germany. Pope Victor, however, conscious of the growth of Norman power in the south, went off to visit the Emperor to persuade him to send reinforcements into Italy. It never happened. The Emperor died, entrusting the care of his son Henry IV to his trusted one-time chancellor. With the Empire potentially weak, Victor had to win over the late Emperor's enemies, especially Godfrey of Lotheringia. This he did by restoring Tuscany to him, and by making his brother Frederick both a cardinal and Abbot of Monte Cassino: Godfrey became a considerable ally of the Roman Church. Shortly afterward Victor died at Arezzo, and was buried at Ravenna.

STEPHEN IX (X)
(Elected August 2, 1057; consecrated August 3, 1057; died March 29, 1058)

The death of Victor II was unexpected. It occurred when the Empire was at its weakest, and those in Rome felt they could proceed to an election of a successor to Victor without consulting the German court. The reform group in Rome, those who had come to the city in the entourage of Leo IX, turned eventually to Frederick of Lotharingia, Cardinal Priest of S. Crisogono and Abbot of Monte Cassino. Frederick was the son of a Duke of Lotharingia, and had been a canon and archdeacon at Liège before joining Leo's party and coming to Rome. He was the brother of Godfrey of Lotharingia, now also Duke of Tuscany, and it is likely that, given the minority of King Henry IV of Germany, those in Rome considered Godfrey something of a surety against the menace of the Normans in the south of Italy. Stephen did not, however, wish to alienate the German royal family: he sent Hildebrand to them to seek their retrospective approval. Stephen died before Hildebrand could return: recognizing that he might die, he had instructed that no successor be elected before Hildebrand got back. His reign was too short to give much indication of what Stephen's reform program might have been, though at a synod in Rome issued strict decrees against the marriage of clerics. He also, and despite his protests, made Peter Damiani a Cardinal: Peter was perhaps the most important theoretician of the reform movement. He was, however, preoccupied with the situation in the south. He organized an embassy to the Emperor in Constantinople to seek his help – though it never went – and in March 1058 he traveled to Florence to consult his brother, Duke Godfrey: he may even have considered giving Godfrey the imperial crown. He died in Florence, and was buried there.

NICHOLAS II
(Born c.1010; elected December 6, 1058; installed January 24, 1059; died July 20, 1061)

Stephen IX had insisted that the electors of his successor should wait upon the return from Germany of Hildebrand. This delay allowed a group of disaffected Roman nobles to elect John, Cardinal Bishop of Velletri, as Pope. He took the name Benedict X. It was a clever choice: John was himself a reformer, a member of the Tusculani family, and had already been mentioned as a possible Pope when Stephen was chosen. But Peter Damiani, the Cardinal Bishop of Ostia to whom it fell to enthrone him, would not do so. The reformers refused to recognize Benedict and fled the city. Instead they chose, in an election held in Siena, Gerard, Bishop of Florence, who had originally come from Lotharingia. The electors acted under the influence of Hildebrand, and they had the backing of Godfrey of Lotharingia, the Duke of Tuscany. Godfrey accompanied the new Pope, who chose the name Nicholas II after one of the most vigorous defenders of the rights of the See

Above: Victor II *reformed a number of aspects of Church practice at the synod of Florence in 1055 which deposed unworthy bishops, attacked non-celibacy among the clergy and condemned simony.*

Below: Nicholas II. *During his relatively short period of office, Nicholas made peace with the Normans, which strengthened the military power of the papacy in southern Italy.*

of Rome. Godfrey conducted Nicholas to Rome, accompanied by Guibert, the chancellor of the German court whose presence gave implicit imperial approval, though this approval had not actively been sought.

In April, at a synod held in Rome, there was promulgated a decree legislating for future papal elections. The cardinal bishops were to gather, then to include other cardinals before making known their choice. Their decision had to be assented to by the other Roman clerics, and by the people of the city. Nicholas recognized, however, that the election might have to be held, as his own had been, outside Rome. It was decreed that the election might be held elsewhere if need be, but that the person then chosen had all rights over the See of Rome. The rights of the imperial family were referred to only in passing, and they could be forfeited if misused. Although the Emperors might still have a role to play, that role was subject to ecclesiastical authority, and was not above it. Nicholas had acted firmly in the matter of papal power, but he was still weak militarily, and was threatened by the presence near Rome of the anti-Pope Benedict. The solution proposed by

Hildebrand and Desiderius, Abbot of Monte Cassino, was to make peace with the Normans in the south of Italy. This was done, and on August 23 two Norman princes, Robert Guiscard and Richard of Aversa, swore fealty to Nicholas at the synod of Melfi, thereby making the papacy the feudal lord of much of southern Italy. Richard promptly stormed the fortress in which the antipope Benedict was taking refuge, and delivered him to Nicholas. He was formally deposed and imprisoned, probably at a synod held in April 1060.

Nicholas was now in complete control. He issued a series of reforming decrees. Already in 1059 the laity had been forbidden to attend mass celebrated by priests living in concubinage, and such clergy were banned from holding Church property. Lay people who had gained control of tithes were ordered to return them to the bishop, and no priest was to accept a church from a lay person. A later decree, probably issued at the instigation of Hildebrand, insisted that clergy serving a church should live a common life. Simony was, naturally, once again prohibited and punished, but in this regard Nicholas was careful to distinguish degrees of guilt. Shortly before Nicholas's death

Below: The Battle of Hastings.
Pope Alexander II backed William of Normandy, sending him a banner of St Peter, under which William fought and defeated Harold of England at Hastings in 1066. Alexander felt that William was more committed to ecclesiastical reform than Harold, reform which the Pope was keen to see implemented across Europe.

there was a breakdown in relations with the German court. Why this should have happened is unclear. However there is no doubt that the dispute was bitter. Nicholas's decrees were condemned, and the court refused to receive the Pope's emissary. This dispute was to have an influence on the election of Nicholas's successor.

ALEXANDER II

(Elected September 30, 1061; died April 21, 1073)

The man chosen to succeed Nicholas II, Anselm, Bishop of Lucca, came from a noble family living near Milan. He had been a pupil of Lanfranc of Bec and had been invested with the bishopric of Lucca by Emperor Henry III in 1056. Ever since that time he had been used by successive Popes as an ambassador to the German court. It was in all probability that familiarity with the imperial family which recommended Anselm, who was a known reformer, to the reformers in Rome anxious to build bridges after the dispute at the end of Nicholas's pontificate. But he was also known to Godfrey of Lotharingia in whose sphere of influence lay the city of Lucca. That, too, was a recommendation. The niceties of Pope Nicholas's 1059 election decree may have been observed, but the Roman nobility and some disaffected Lombard bishops turned to the young King Henry IV to ask for the appointment of an anti-reform prelate, Peter Cadalus, Bishop of Parma. At his election by an assembly in Basle, he took the title Honorius II. By dint of superior military power Honorius seized Rome, and Alexander took refuge in Lucca – he remained its bishop until his death. Godfrey of Lotharingia had to come to Rome in support of Alexander, and drive out the antipope, who retired to Parma. It fell to the German court, in particular to Archbishop Anno of Cologne, to decide between the rival candidates: Anno, a reformer himself, opted for Alexander. The Pope's troubles were not yet over. Honorius again invaded Rome in May 1063, and both contenders for the title were summoned to a synod at Mantua, convened by Anno on the advice of Cardinal Peter Damiani, to determine the rightful claimant. Honorius refused to go, but Alexander went, presided, and was acclaimed – though he first had to swear he had not been simoniacally elected. Honorius remained in his diocese, claiming the title of Pope until the end of his days. Alexander could

now get on with his policy of reform. In England it had dramatic effect because William of Normandy solicited the Pope's support against Harold of England, accusing Harold of perjury. Alexander backed William, sending him a banner of St Peter under which he fought the Battle of Hastings.

The Pope's favor was bestowed on William not because of the perjury but because he was, of the two men, the more committed to ecclesiastical reform. There was backing for the reform movement in Spain, where the Pope encouraged the efforts of the Christian kings to win the peninsula back from Islam: the King of Aragon placed his country under the feudal protection of the papacy and brought in the Roman liturgy. In southern Italy the Byzantines were driven from their last foothold by the Norman knights, now vassals of the papacy. They also moved to occupy Sicily, so that new territories fell under papal control. Alexander sent special blessings to the knights who undertook these crusades in Italy and in France. In Germany, however, the situation was very different. There, during the minority of Henry IV – he was declared of age in 1065 – the bishops took the opportunity to enrich themselves and their relations at the expense of the bishoprics and monasteries. The loss of independence by the monasteries was very much resented, because some of them had been in the vanguard of reform. Matters came to a head, however, over the See of Milan.

There was at Milan a radical reform movement called the Pataria, whose fanatical zeal verged on the revolutionary. Successive reforming Popes had attempted to restrain its members without curbing its zeal, and in Pope Nicholas's time a delegation from Rome had persuaded Archbishop Guido to adopt a reforming stance. From this, Guido soon fell away, reviving the energies of the Pataria, the movement now spreading beyond the confines of Milan. Archbishop Guido decided to resign his office, and Henry appointed a priest called Godfrey in contravention of the rights of the people of Milan. They in turn elected – on the death of Guido – a priest, Atto, who was recognized by Pope Alexander as the rightful Archbishop of Milan. Henry refused to abandon Godfrey and not he, but five of his councillors, were excommunicated at the Rome synod in 1073. There was inevitably to be a clash between the Pope and King Henry. This occurred dramatically in the pontificate of Alexander's successor.

Above: **Alexander II.** *His chief desire was for reforms in ecclesiastical affairs. In Spain he encouraged efforts to win back the peninsula from Islam; he sent blessings to the Normans in southern Italy who drove out the Byzantines; and he hoped that his support for William the Conqueror would see changes in England.*

Above: **King Harold of England** *who was defeated and killed at the Battle of Hastings by William of Normandy, who enjoyed the backing of Pope Alexander II.*

Above: St Gregory VII *had a vision of a Crusade against the Turks which would recapture the Holy Sepulchre for Christendom. The First Crusade was eventually launched by his successor, Urban II.*

St GREGORY VII
(Born c.1020; elected April 22, 1073; consecrated June 30, 1073; died May 25, 1085)

Gregory VII was one of the most significant architects of change in the history of the papacy. He was born Hildebrand, of a modest Tuscan family. He was educated in Rome, in Sta Maria all'Aventino and the Lateran. He became chaplain to Gregory VI and went into exile with him to Cologne in 1046. In 1047, when Gregory died, he seems to have entered the Monastery of Cluny. Leo IX called him back to Rome and made him treasurer of the Roman Church and prior of the Monastery of St Paul. Under successive Popes it became customary to send Hildebrand on missions. He went to France in 1054 and again in 1056 and to Germany in 1057. His advice was taken on matters of papal policy. He was the natural choice to succeed Pope Alexander II.

He took the name of Gregory out of respect for Gregory the Great. He set out to be a reformer. The *Dictatus Papae*, a curious little document in its format – possibly surviving from notes – is nevertheless a bold statement of papal claims to plenitude of power in the Church and supremacy over the secular authorities. He took a high line on the effect of the succession from Peter in conferring personal holiness on a Pope. He claimed the right to depose all princes, whether temporal or spiritual, and to have all Christians as his subjects. He also claimed supreme legislative and judicial power. The drive to stop the widespread practice of simoniacal ordination and to enforce clerical celibacy had begun under his predecessors. He continued the policy vigorously, re-enacting decrees on these subjects at the Lenten synods of 1074 and 1075 and pursuing matters in a practical way when there was attempted resistance on the ground in France and Germany. The most far-reaching of his moves was the prohibition of lay investiture. He was anxious to clarify in favor of the Church a good deal of the confusion which was arising about the exact boundaries of the roles of Church and State in the making of a bishop. There were three stages: the choice or election of the individual to fill the vacant bishopric, the consecration, and the handing over of control of the "temporalities" or lands and possessions of the See.

The consecration was clearly a sacramental act, which only the Church could perform, and the temporalities appeared to be in the gift of the secular authorities. But the election could be interfered with by either Church or State, and the actual ceremony of consecration was being muddled by the handing over of ring and staff, symbols of pastoral office, by the king or Emperor rather than by the Church authorities. Gregory wanted to see not only a proper separation of roles, but also a great diminution of what had become in practice the secular control of the process. Emperor Henry IV slowly awoke to the implications of Gregory's policy, and from 1075 he asserted himself by making his own nominations to the See of Milan and to Sees in Germany, and also to Ferme and Spoleto. Gregory reproved him. The Emperor called a synod of German bishops at Worms in 1076 at which the bishops deposed the Pope, and Henry called upon him to abdicate. The bishops of Lombardy allied themselves with the bishops of Germany. Gregory responded by excommunicating Henry which meant that Henry's subjects were no longer under a duty to obey him. The Emperor partly capitulated, and in the winter of 1077 came to the castle of the Countess Matilda of Tuscany at Canossa, where the Pope was staying, in humiliating circumstances in order to receive absolution. There followed three years of maneuvering, while Henry and his rival, and elected anti-king, Rudolf of Swabia struggled for supremacy, with Gregory partly holding the balance of power. In 1080 Gregory again excommunicated Henry and recognized Rudolf as King.

Henry convoked another council of imperial bishops in June 1080 at Brixen, to depose Gregory and then elect Guibert of Ravenna as (antipope) Clement III. He was willing to bargain, because he wanted to be crowned as Emperor. But Gregory responded firmly to the threat, though losing the support of some of the cardinals in the process. Henry captured Rome in March of 1084, evoking the indignation of the Roman people against Gregory. Gregory himself was rescued by the Norman Robert Guiscard, but he had to go into exile in south Italy and Sicily, where he died.

Gregory had more success in his relations with the King of England, William I, and Philip I of France, whom he pressed less hard. He persuaded Alfonso VI of Castile to accept the liturgy of Rome. He had a vision of the Crusade, which Urban II would eventually launch, to recapture the Holy Sepulchre for Christendom and rescue the Eastern Empire itself from the Turks, thus restoring the two Churches, in schism since 1054, to union. To this end he kept on good terms with the Eastern Emperor, Michael VII Dukas.

It was Gregory VII, too, who brought the controversy over what was later to be known as transubstantiation to a temporary settlement, by gaining an acceptance from Berengar of Tours, who had hitherto argued that there was no "substantial" change in the bread and wine at the Eucharist, that such a change did indeed occur.

Bl VICTOR III

(Born c.1027; elected May 24, 1086; consecrated May 9, 1087; died September 16, 1087)

Victor III was born as Daufer or Dauferi into the family of the Lombard Dukes of Benevento. He became a monk at Benevento, under the name

Desiderius, then spent a period in the service of Leo IX. In 1055 he became a monk at Monte Cassino, and in 1058 he was made abbot. As such he was very successful. Under his rule the abbey was rebuilt and acquired new property; he expanded the library; he fostered learning among his monks. He was a writer himself, the author of a book on the miracles of St. Benedict.

Nicholas II made him Cardinal Priest and Papal Vicar of the southern Italian monasteries in 1059. He was successful in establishing friendly relations with the Normans and in 1080 was able to achieve a reconciliation between Gregory VII and Robert Guiscard, the Norman Duke of Apulia. His relations with Gregory VII were upset two years later by an unsuccessful attempt at mediation between the Pope and Henry IV, as the tensions of the Investiture Contest over the balance of power of Church and State began to build up. Gregory took refuge with Desiderius, however, when he had to flee from Rome in 1084.

Desiderius was elected as Gregory's successor a year after Gregory's death at Salerno in 1085. He was not consecrated at once: there was rioting in Rome because he was not the preferred choice of the Gregorian faction. He turned his back on the disturbances and returned to Monte Cassino. Norman

Above: **Bl Victor III** *instigated the Council of Benevento in 1087 which reiterated a number of important principles of Church law. Victor's papacy was brief – he was taken ill during the Council and died at Monte Cassino.*

Left: **William I of England,** *who had been favored by Alexander II. William's successor, William II was one of the sovereigns of Europe who recognized the claims of Urban II over those of "antipope" Clement III, in return for certain concessions.*

Above: Philip I of France, *who was excommunicated by Urban II at the Synod of Clermont in 1095. It was at that same synod that Urban called for the First Crusade to recover the Holy Places for Christendom.*

Below: Bl Urban II at Cluny. *Prior to becoming Pope in 1088, Urban II had joined the Clunaic Order and later became prior at Cluny.*

troops accompanied him on his return to Rome the following spring, and he was consecrated on May 9 when the city had been temporarily captured from the supporters of the antipope Clement.

But Rome still would not have him, although he had the support of Jordan of Capua and Countess Matilda of Tuscany, and he had to go back to Monte Cassino, leaving Clement's supporters still in control of Rome. He was back in the city in July and despite failing health managed to hold a Council at Benevento in August. This was a Council of some importance because it seems to have reiterated a number of the main principles of the Gregorian pontificate – the prohibition of lay investiture, the declaration that simoniacal ordinations were invalid. He was ill during the Council, and retreated to die at Monte Cassino.

Bl URBAN II
(Born c.1035; elected March 12, 1088; died July 29, 1099)

Odo of Lagery was born of a noble family at Châtillon-sur-Marne. He was a student at Rheims, and a pupil of Bruno of Rheims, the founder of the Carthusian Order. Odo became a canon at Rheims and then archdeacon. About 1068 he joined the Cluniac Order and later became Prior of Cluny. He

moved on to the papal household under Gregory VII. About 1080 he was appointed Cardinal Bishop of Ostia and was papal legate in Germany from 1084-85. During the period of the Investiture Contest he proved to be extremely useful to Gregory VII, presiding at a synod at Quedlinburg in Saxony in 1085 which laid an anathema on the antipope Clement III.

After the death of Victor III, Odo's election as his successor was delayed by the fact that Clement III's party had control of Rome. Odo took the name Urban II, and set about establishing the legitimacy of his position as the true Pope. That was a very urgent necessity, since he had to face both the hostility of the antipope's party and also that of the Emperor.

At Melfi in 1089 he reaffirmed Gregory VII's rulings against clerical marriage and simony and also against lay investiture. In practice he was pragmatic in dealing with the cases where the Gregorian rules had been breached, instructing his legate in Germany to take a moderate line. He was willing to accept as bishop someone who had been elected in a canonically acceptable way, but who had been invested by a lay sovereign. Though to some degree such moderation calmed the tensions within the Church it did not improve relations with the Emperor. Henry IV invaded Italy in 1090–92 and Urban was forced to give up Rome to Clement III and retreat to Norman territory in south Italy. He won his way back by typically pragmatic means, through bribery and diplomacy, obtaining control of Rome in 1093, the Lateran in 1094 and Castel Sant'Angelo not until 1098.

He had to cement his position not only in relation to the Emperor but also with other sovereigns. William II of England (1087–1100) required concessions before he would recognize him, and Urban had to allow him the right to give his permission before papal legates could enter England.

He did not press things too hard in France, where Philip I (1060–80) had contracted an adulterous marriage, and won a degree of French support in that way. His relations with the Normans of southern Italy and Sicily were uniformly positive and on more than one occasion they gave him support and shelter.

After 1095 Urban was safe enough to hold a series of successful synods. In March 1095, at Piacenza, he made declarations condemning Berengar of Tours' teaching against the developing doctrine of transubstantiation and he sought to have the ordinations of the antipope Clement III and his successors declared void. It was at this synod that he first made a call to the Christians of the West to help the Eastern Emperor Alexius I Comnenus (1081–1118) who had sent an appeal for defenders of the faith to come to his aid against Muslim incursions. Urban already had an established track-record in Spain, where he had been supporting efforts to reconquer the Christian lands held by the Moors. The Holy See now had jurisdiction over Aragon and Catalonia. In 1088 Urban had been in a position to restore the archbishopric of Toledo, and when the new archbishop was consecrated, Urban made him primate of all Spain.

But the call to engage in holy war against Islam in the Middle East was of another order. At a further synod held at Clermont in November 1095 he launched the First Crusade. He did so with a promise of a "plenary indulgence" (which meant complete forgiveness of all punishment due to sin) to all who took the Cross and either died on the crusade or won their way to Jerusalem. This was an unprecedented enlargement of papal claims to the power to grant indulgences and set a further precedent in the sense that it appears to have been the first time a complete "indulgence" was offered.

Anselm of Canterbury turned to Urban for protection in his long dispute with William II of England, finally running to him in exile. In 1098, during the period Anselm remained in the Pope's entourage, Urban held a council at Bari. One of Urban's purposes was to try to mend the schism of 1054. He found Anselm useful as a theologian apologist who could address the theological issues which now separated the Eastern and Western Church, notably the dispute over the procession of the Holy Spirit, the "filioque".

Urban's pontificate saw substantial moves forward in the evolution of the papal curia, and its diplomatic and epistolary functions; it also began increasingly to resemble a royal or imperial court. Pope Urban was declared "blessed" in 1881.

PASCHAL II
(Elected August 13, 1099; died January 21, 1118)

Paschal was born Rainerius in an obscure family and entered the religious life as a boy. He was made Abbot of S. Lorenzo fuori le Mura by Gregory VII,

and Cardinal Priest of S. Clemente about 1078, so he had clearly caught the eye of those in high places. He was still being noticed in the time of Urban II, who sent him on a mission to Spain. He became Paschal II within two weeks of the death of his predecessor, Pope Urban II.

It was not an easy moment to ascend the papal throne. The Investiture Contest was at its height; there was an antipope (Clement III) and the Emperor (Henry IV) was hostile. Paschal appears to have combined a timidity and compliance which had got him on in earlier life with a lack of strategic skill born of an inability to move with events. However, the problem of the antipope and his successors was successfully dealt with by removing, with Norman help, Clement III from Rome by brute force. There were to be three more during the pontificate: Theodoric, Cardinal Bishop of Albano; Albert, Cardinal Bishop of Silva Candida; and Maginulf – who styled himself Sylvester IV – Archpriest of S. Angelo.

The Emperor's mind was now concentrated not on supporting more antipopes but on getting his way in the matter of lay investiture of bishops and abbots with ring and pastoral staff. Much turned on

Above: Urban II at the Synod of Clermont. *Urban instigated the First Crusade with a powerful and impassioned pleae to rescue Byzantium and free the Holy Places from Islamic control.*

Below: Paschal II. *It was during Paschal's reign that the First Crusade, proposed by Urban II at Clermont, had its initial success, when Jerusalem was captured in 1099.*

Right: Peter the Hermit *led the First Crusade to the Holy Land. Peter was an untidy and fiery character from Picardy who was a spell-binding orator. His eloquence persuaded many thousands of ordinary people to join in the long and arduous journey to take on the Turks. The first expedition ended in disaster.*

Below: The First Crusade. *In this illuminated manuscript, the Christian Crusaders are depicted bombarding the walls of Nicaea with the severed heads of the enemy. Nicaea eventually surrendered and the Crusaders went on to take Jerusalem.*

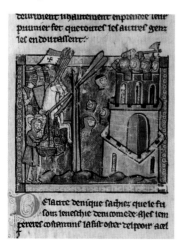

that for the maintenance of a balance of power between Church and State, one that was favorable to the secular side. Paschal opposed him by prohibiting lay investiture in the same terms as Urban had done, and by keeping in being the ban on Henry IV which Gregory VII had imposed.

He supported the revolt of Henry IV's son, which overthrew the Emperor in 1105–06. But Henry V as new Emperor (1106–25) proved no more willing than his father to relinquish lay investiture.

Paschal now employed the method of condemnation by Council, to that end holding synods at Guastalla (1106), Troyes (1107), Benevento (1108) and the Lateran (1110).

The new Emperor needed his crown and he came to Rome for his coronation in a mood for settlement. Paschal's proposal was for a mutually beneficial "trade". There should be free elections of bishops and abbots and no more lay investiture; in return the Church would hand back the property (*regalia*) which came from the secular authorities and keep only ecclesiastical revenues. But when this Concordat (Sutri, 1111) was announced there was public outcry and the coronation was halted.

Henry arrested Paschal and held him in prison for two months until he conceded the right of lay investiture before the consecration of a bishop, releasing him only on condition the coronation was completed and Henry V was not to be excommunicated. This agreement was known as the Privilege of Ponte Mamolo 1111.

Paschal annulled the privilegium of 1111 at the Lateran Synod of 1112, and withdrew it in 1116, because it was politically and ecclesiologically essential for him to go back to prohibiting investiture. Meanwhile solutions were being arrived at on the home territory of the kings of France and England and the principle beginning to emerge on which a long-term resolution would stand. Ivo of Chartres, a canon lawyer of sophistication, suggested that the "temporalities" and the "spiritualities" should simply be separated in the process of making a bishop, and that each party should keep to its own natural area of jurisdiction.

It was during Paschal's reign that the First Crusade had its success: Jerusalem was captured in 1099. Paschal made the mistake of supporting the further incursions of the Norman Bohemond into the lands of the Eastern Emperor. This was especially ill-timed, since the Emperor, Alexius I, was anxious to mend the schism which had divided the Eastern and the Western Church since 1054.

The years 1116–18 were a period of unrest in the city of Rome, during which Paschal was forced to leave the city. He did, however, manage to return there just before his death, which occurred in Castel Sant'Angelo.

GELASIUS II
(Elected January 24, 1118; died January 29, 1119)

Gelasius was born John of Gaeta, and spent his boyhood as a monk at Monte Cassino. There he was a pupil of Alberic, who was an important influence on the developing contemporary art of letter-writing (*ars dictaminis*). Gelasius became an author himself: three *Lives* of saints survive. He was made cardinal deacon in 1088 and chancellor in 1089, by Pope Urban II. That placed him in the papal chancery, where letter-writing was a necessary applied art, and for thirty years he appears to have been influential in improving the style and form of papal communications and the secretarial standards of the papal civil service. He was a loyal servant to Paschal II, going into imprisonment with him in 1111 and defending his position at the Lateran Synod of 1116.

His own papal reign was dramatic and disturbed. No sooner was he elected than he was attacked and imprisoned by Cencius Frangipani and his family, who had long been hostile to Paschal II and therefore disliked those who had been faithful to him. Although Roman pressure freed him, he had to leave Rome in a hurry to escape the invasion of the Emperor Henry V. The warfare in the midst of which he was becoming a pawn continued, and he set sail for France on 23 October 1118. His chief acts while he was in France were to give his sanction to the founder of the Premonstratensian canons, Norbert, to preach freely anywhere, and to hold a synod at Vienne. He died at the Abbey of Cluny, with the Investiture Contest still unresolved.

CALLISTUS II
(Born c.1050; elected February 2, 1119; died December 14, 1124)

Callistus II was born Guido, the son of William, Count of Burgundy, and was made Archbishop of Vienne in 1088. He was a strong reforming leader, who actively disapproved of the concession Paschal II had made on investiture to Henry V. That won him a following, who ensured that on the death of Gelasius II at Cluny, Guido was elected by a small group of cardinals who had been with the late Pope in France. His coronation as Callistus II at Vienne took place rapidly, on February 9.

As Pope, Callistus proved a fair strategist. The time was ripe for a settlement of the Investiture Dispute. The first attempt failed, because the terms were not crisp enough. Callistus breathed fire again and reimposed the anathema on Henry V (at Rheims in October 1119) . The Pope then made his way to Rome, where he overcame the resistance of the supporters of the antipope Gregory VIII and incarcerated him.

At Würzburg towards the end of 1121 there was an agreement with the German princes that Callistus would be recognized as Pope in Germany. Callistus welcomed ambassadors from them in the early weeks of 1122 and in return sent his own plenipotentiaries to Germany to negotiate.

The result was the Concordat of Worms of September 1122. Its thrust was a separation of the temporalities from the spiritualities. Its effect was to save the face, and the honor, of both sides. The German Emperor gave up the right to invest with ring and staff, since these were conceded to be symbols of the bishop's spiritual authority, of his marriage to his Church and of his pastoral office. The Emperor was to allow canonical election and freedom of consecration. In return, Callistus would permit the Emperor to be present when elections to bishoprics and abbeys in Germany took place. The Emperor was to be allowed to invest the elected bishop or abbot with the temporalities, symbolized by the sceptre, which was clearly his to give. If there was a dispute over an election the Emperor was to decide it.

If the election took place outside Germany the Emperor did not need to be present and investment with the temporalities could be deferred for up to six months. Callistus felt a justified sense of satisfaction with this pragmatic and ecclesiologically satisfactory solution, and frescoes to celebrate it were placed on the Lateran walls.

His final significant act was to hold the First Lateran Council in 1123, which produced a number of re-enactments of earlier disciplinary canons and renewed the plenary indulgence Urban II had offered to crusaders who persevered and who sought to provide protection for pilgrims.

HONORIUS II
(Elected December 21, 1124; died February 13, 1130)

Lamberto Scannabecchi was of modest birth, from near Bologna. He had some reputation for learning. In 1117 he was chosen by Paschal II to be cardinal

Above: Gelasius II, *whose papacy lasted little over a year. Toward the end of his reign he was exiled in France, where he died at the Abbey of Cluny.*

Above: Callistus II *was responsible for the First Lateran Council in 1123 which reiterated a number of disciplinary canons and restated the plenary indulgence of Urban II which had been offered to the Crusaders.*

Bishop of Ostia. He had remained in the papal entourage, going with Gelasius II to France and continuing as a respected adviser to Callistus II. He had been important as a negotiator in arriving at the Concordat of Worms of 1122.

Honorius II emerged as Pope from a chaotic scramble for control of the papacy after the death of Callistus, between the Frangipani family and the Pierleoni family and their candidates, with the installation of the would-be Celestine II, the candidate of the Pierleoni, being interrupted by armed supporters of the Frangipani. Both families had to be squared before Honorius could be elected and enthroned.

It was clear to all parties that there was now a new phase of development. With the Investiture Contest to all intents and purposes settled and the relationship of Church and State in a new, if uneasy balance, the papacy needed to establish its position in relation to the Church itself. Honorius began by supporting Lothar III, Count of Supplinburg, as candidate for the German crown after the death of the Emperor Henry V, and anathematizing his rival, Conrad, and Conrad's supporter, Anselm, the Archbishop of Milan, who had already crowned Conrad King of the Lombards. In France he played a waiting game and that encouraged King Louis VI to resolve his conflicts with the ecclesiastical hierarchy. England was coaxed into allowing in papal legates after 1125. The Normans in southern Italy were more resistant to his diplomatic devices, but he was able to obtain an oath of fealty from Roger II of Sicily in return for papal recognition in 1128.

Honorius' chancellor was Aimeric, and it was he who had been largely instrumental in ensuring Honorius' election, and who was clever enough to ensure the relatively smooth election of Innocent II when Honorius died.

The two worked systematically for reform in the Church. They supported and sanctioned the newly active orders of canons, especially the Premonstratensians; Honorius approved the Knights Templar as an order, under their new distinctive rule.

INNOCENT II
(Elected February 14, 1130; consecrated February 23, 1130; died September 24, 1143)

Innocent II was born Gregorio Papareschi, into a Roman family of some standing. In 1116 he was appointed Cardinal Deacon of Sant' Angelo in Pescheria by Paschal II. After undertaking several diplomatic missions, he was appointed one of the negotiators who won the Concordat of Worms in 1122, and in the following year he was sent as legate to France.

His election and enthronement were carried out in great haste on the very night Honorius II died by a minority of the cardinals led by Aimeric the chancellor. The majority of the cardinals objected when they learned what had happened, and chose

Below: St Bernard of Clairvaux *was an important supporter of Innocent II and an outspoken critic of heresy. He was vocal in his suport for the Second Crusade, and when it failed blamed the lack of purity of the soldiers.*

Above: Innocent II. *His papacy was marred by schism when Anacletus II was consecrated as the rival "antipope." The support of Bernard of Clairvaux was vital in his attempts to be recognized as the legitimate incumbent.*

Above: Celestine II *was the unanimous choice of the cardinals to become Pope following the death of Innocent II. His papacy lasted less than six months.*

Pietro Pierleoni, who had been with Innocent as legate in France, as Anacletus II.

On February 23, both Pope and antipope were consecrated. Eight years of schism followed. Anacletus could call on an alliance with Roger II of Sicily, whom he bribed with the crown of Sicily, with Apulia and Calabria. He was also in control of Rome. Innocent fled to France in exile, but it was his claim which was most widely recognized throughout Europe – partly because the canons regular were able to influence opinion in many countries. Norbert, the founder of the Premonstratensians, was now Archbishop of Magdeburg, and in that capacity he won over the German bishops and King Lothar III. He also had powerful support in Bernard of Clairvaux, who persuaded the English and French kings to give their voices to Innocent.

Lothar's support became crucial when, in the spring of 1131, Innocent met him and offered him the promise of the Empire in return for military support to enable him to win control of Rome. Lothar wanted more, in the shape of a return of the rights surrendered by the secular power at the Concordat of Worms, but he did not get his way.

Innocent held a synod at Rheims to anathematize Anacletus and in the spring of 1133 Lothar marched on the city of Rome as he had promised. He was not able to evict the Anacletan party from St Peter's, and therefore the coronation Innocent had promised him had to be conducted in the Lateran. Lothar was still pressing for concessions about investiture, and Innocent gave him the right to the homage of bishops and abbots before they took possession of the temporalities at the hands of the Emperor.

Rome proved too hard to hold on to, and after Lothar's return to Germany, Innocent was forced to move to Pisa, but there he held a synod at which he excommunicated Anacletus, together with Roger II of Sicily. Bernard of Clairvaux again proved helpful, winning Milan for Innocent in 1136. Lothar returned to Italy in the same year but the expedition was largely abortive, and Lothar died on his way back to Germany in 1137.

Meanwhile Innocent and those supporting him were trying to persuade Roger of Sicily to change allegiance. In 1138, on January 25, Anacletus died, and although his supporters immediately elected a successor in Victor IV, he did not last long, resigning on May 29. The Pierleoni capitulated and made

their submission to Innocent, and he was at last able to begin on the real work of his papacy. In 1139 he held a Second Lateran Council. Its main task was to tidy up the confusion of decisions and actions which had arisen during the schism, by annulling everything Anacletus had done and all his ordinations. More positively, it consolidated recent reform legislation by republishing it. In 1140 the Council of Sens made a second formal condemnation of Peter Abelard as a heretic and Innocent II confirmed what it had done.

The remaining years of his pontificate saw more conflict. In July 1139 Roger II defeated the Pope in battle, took Innocent prisoner, and forced him to acknowledge Roger as King of Sicily. In addition there was a serious rift with the French King in 1141 over an episcopal appointment, and then in 1143 there was rioting in the city of Rome where the populace set up a commune.

CELESTINE II
(Elected September 26, 1143; died March 8, 1144)

Guido of Città Di Castellor in Umbria was a former pupil of Peter Abelard and perhaps one of the first academic importations into the papal service: such importations were to become the regular thing by the time of Innocent III. Callistus II adopted him in that way, and in 1127 he was appointed to the position of Cardinal Deacon of Sta Maria in Via Lata by Honorius II.

In 1131–32 he was a papal legate in Cologne and legate in France (1139–40). He was an active supporter of Innocent II's claims. Only in the matter of Peter Abelard did he seriously disagree with Innocent's policy, a stance which earned him a reproving letter from Bernard of Clairvaux. His election followed hard on the death of Innocent II; he was the cardinals' unanimous choice from the five candidates Innocent had named as possibilities he would favor to succeed him.

During his short pontificate, Celestine lifted the interdict on Louis VII of France which Innocent had imposed in 1141. In addition, he did not ratify the treaty made at Migniano in July 1139, in which Innocent had, under duress, recognized the sovereignty of Roger II in Sicily and southern Italy but before his death – he was already an old man when he was elected – Celestine had to reopen negotiations with Roger.

Above: Lucius II. *His pontificate lasted for less than one year. Having failed to gain the support of Emperor Conrad III, he was killed while leading his forces against Roman insurgents who sought a government of their own for the city.*

LUCIUS II
(Elected March 12, 1144; died 15 February 1145)

Gherardo Caccianemici was born at Bologna and joined the canons regular, entering the congregation of S. Frediano at Lucca. He became a member of the curia and Callistus II made him Cardinal Priest of Sta Croce, to which he brought a community of regular canons. He was friendly with Bernard of Clairvaux and Peter the Venerable of Cluny. He served Honorius II as legate in Germany and was instrumental in the 1125 election of Lothar III as king. It was he who ensured that Norbert, the Premonstratensians' founder, should become Archbishop of Magdeberg. In 1130 he worked with Aimeric, the papal chancellor, to support Innocent II against Lothar when they were in dispute over Monte Cassino. Innocent II made Gherardo chancellor when Aimeric died in 1141.

His own accession to the papacy was relatively uncontroversial, at least by the standards of elections in the immediate past, although he faced controversy in Rome. His reign was short. He was able to achieve some consolidation in the Iberian peninsula, particularly in establishing more firmly the primacy of Toledo and receiving Portugal as a fief of the Holy See. Like other Popes before him, he found that he needed to improve relations with Roger of Sicily, whose family went on making attacks on the Papal States. He asked for help from the new German Emperor, Conrad III, against the Roman people who were seeking a government of their own for the city, but Conrad had troubles of his own at home and would not come. Lucius decided to take the initiative himself, but was killed in an attack he was leading against the insurgents.

Bl EUGENIUS III
(Elected February 15, 1145; died July 8, 1153)

No time was lost in electing Eugenius III after the sudden death from stoning of Lucius II. Eugenius, born Bernardo Pignatelli, had been prior of St Zeno in Pisa. Meeting St Bernard he was overwhelmed and became a Cistercian monk. He was Abbot of SS Vicenzo and Anastasio, a Cistercian monastery outside Rome, at the time of election.

Bernard regarded his election with alarm, because he did not consider Eugenius to possess the acumen and forcefulness to carry his responsibilities

Right: St Bernard of Clairvaux *preaches the Second Crusade, proclaimed by Pope Eugenius III in 1145. St Bernard's sermon at Vézelay in 1146, in the presence of King Louis VII of France, shown here in an illustration dating from around 1490, won the French monarch to the cause.*

well. He wrote him an open letter, which became the first book of the *De Consideratione*, to warn him not to spend all his time hearing legal cases. It was, he told him, important for a Pope to keep a balance between his practical duties and his spiritual life. The *De Consideratione* gradually lengthened to five books, becoming one of the most important statements of the day on the powers and duties of the papacy. Bernard took a strong line on papal plenitude of power, and he created an ecclesiology of the papacy which incorporated much of the development adumbrated in the Gregorian reforms. He also included reflection on the "two swords" analogy of the relationship between Church and State, first used by Pope Gelasius I. Luke's Gospel describes the incident where two swords were produced at Jesus' arrest, and Jesus said: "*satis est*" ("It is enough."). This text was taken as justification for the theory that it is the divine intention there should be two kinds of power in the world, the spiritual and the secular. The debate then turned on their ownership, whether God entrusts both to the papacy, the Pope giving one to the Emperor at his coronation, or whether God gives each his own sword directly.

Because Rome was held by the people's commune, Eugenius had to begin his pontificate outside the city, being consecrated some twenty-five miles away at Farfa. He took up residence in Viterbo and though, by the Christmas of 1145 he was briefly in Rome, early 1146 saw him in retreat again in Viterbo. Eugenius was also faced with trouble in the crusading kingdoms. The Turks captured Edessa from its Christian masters in 1145, and a group of Armenian bishops came to Eugenius to ask for help against the Eastern Emperor. He proclaimed a Second Crusade in 1145, by sending a bull to Louis VII of France. The bull was renewed on March 4, 1146, with a commission to Bernard of Clairvaux to preach the crusade. Eugenius himself traveled to France to make the call in person. He had not intended the German Emperor to become involved because he was in need of his assistance with the now familiar papal problems of the insurgency of Rome and relations with Roger of Sicily, but Bernard won him for the Crusade.

The Second Crusade failed, with two results which created difficulties for Eugenius. The first was the loss of face. The second book of Bernard's *De Consideratione* was directed at the implications. Bernard had rather the same problem as had faced

que la terre sainte z le pup
ple vpistiens y demourans
feussent secourus et gardés
contre ses impetueuly assaulx
de leurs trsfautaires et aues
emeins. et ouuant se trefor
de leglise donna plain pardon
et remission de pune z de
coulpe de tous pehes atous
et a bung chasaun de ceulp q

en faueur et pour audier la ter
re sainte prendroient lenseigne
de la sainte Croy z yroient
en cestu uoyaige. Et combien
que yeust lors et diuerses
partes de vpistiente plusieur
seigneurs ducreurs z prelats
Toutefois lesaulsit uoir
estan temps vertuely comme
lespesaic journal au point du

Above: King Louis VII *and Emperor Conrad III enter Byzantium (Constantinople) during the Second Crusade. The failure of this Crusade (1145-48) added to the domestic and foreign problems of Pope Eugenius III.*

Augustine in *The City of God*, when he had to explain how God could allow a Christian Roman Empire to fall to barbarian invaders. The only answer was to see a lesson in it, and Bernard argued that God had meant to teach Christian Western Europe that it was not yet spiritually worthy to succeed in a holy war.

The second result was to compound the problem about Byzantium. Roger of Sicily and Louis VII of France pressed for a crusade against Byzantium itself, and Bernard supported them, but Eugenius was well aware that this was hardly the best way to mend the schism of 1054 and did not commit himself to the project.

Eugenius' interests in rapprochement with the Eastern Church led him to urge Burgundio of Pisa

to produce Latin translations of some of John Chrysostom's homilies and of John of Damascus's *De Fide Orthodoxa*. These were significant additions to the tiny store of Greek patristic material then available in the West.

Eugenius' period in office coincided with significant developments in the struggle of the mid-twelfth-century Church to deal with heresy, particularly academic heresy. This was something new, in that there were now schools of a new sort, proto-universities, in which issues of academic freedom of speech were beginning to arise. Among the free-speakers was Gilbert of Poitiers, who was tried at Rheims in 1148 for his teachings on the Trinity, with Bernard of Clairvaux acting as prosecutor for the Church. Hildegard of Bingen, the abbess who had been publishing her visions, was also scrutinized at this synod. The Synod of Rheims was called with an invitation in which Eugenius explored Bernard's encouragement to take a strong line on the "two swords". Eugenius claimed for the papacy a supreme authority in things temporal as well as things spiritual. Rheims was not Eugenius' only reforming synod. He held others at Paris (April– June 1147) and at Trier (1147–8). In Ireland Eugenius set up four metropolitan Sees and in English affairs he was an interventionist Pope. He was supportive of Archbishop Theobald of Canterbury in his disputes with the king and he deposed William Fitzherbert from the See of York.

In June 1148 Eugenius condemned the dissident Arnold of Brescia to excommunication. Here the thrust of his displeasure was practical as well as to do with the need to discourage the anti-establishment opinions Arnold was spreading. Arnold had been pardoned in 1146, but had formed an alliance with the Roman commune and was speaking of the Pope as "the man of blood". The Roman commune was making overtures to Conrad III, and he was to come to Rome for his coronation in 1152. He died

before he could arrive, however, and Eugenius entered negotiations with his successor, Frederick I Barbarossa. Frederick sent him notice of his election and promised the Pope his protection. He did not ask for Eugenius' approval of his election, but Eugenius prudently gave it.

It was agreed at the Diet of Würzburg, in October 1152, that Frederick should make an expedition to Italy. This proved useful to the Pope, because Rome's commune was persuaded by Frederick to allow Eugenius to install himself in the city. In March 1153 he made the Treaty of Constance with Frederick. This was in part a mature version of the Concordat of Worms agreed under Callistus II. Each sovereign power undertook to protect the other's sovereignty or "honor". The Pope promised to crown the Emperor and in return Frederick promised not to make peace with the Roman commune or the Normans without agreement with the Pope. The two stood solidly together in the subject of not making concessions of territory to the Eastern Empire. Eugenius died (at Tivoli) before Frederick was able to come to Rome for his coronation. Eugenius was declared blessed in 1872.

Above: **Anastasius IV** *improved papal relations with the Roman commune and settled disputes that had arisen between the papacy and Frederick I Barbarossa and with the Church in England.*

Below: **Frederick I Barbarossa** *receives Venetian ambassadors.*

Above: Adrian IV *is notable for being the only Englishman ever to become Pope. He traveled to France and became prior at Avignon where he was noticed by Rome. His was a difficult papacy and it is said that just before his death he expressed regrets over ever leaving England.*

ANASTASIUS IV
(Elected July 8, 1153; died December 3, 1154)

Anastasius IV was a Roman by birth, with the family name of Corrado. He rose from apparent obscurity to become Cardinal Priest of Sta Pudeziana sometime between the years 1111 and 1114. In 1125 he was acting on Honorius II's behalf in a controversy involving the Abbey of Farfa, and again in 1127, in a similar controversy involving Monte Cassino. Toward the end of 1126 he was made Cardinal Bishop of Sta Sabina. During the period when the antipope Anacletus II was in control of Rome he was a supporter of Innocent II, lingering in the city during the periods of Innocent's absence in exile. In 1147–9 and again from 1150–2 he acted as Eugenius' vicar. His election as Pope took place on the day Eugenius died, and he was enthroned in the Lateran on July 12. The Roman commune allowed him to stay, which bespeaks the good relationship he had established over the years with the people of the city. He proved himself a peacemaker in other ways, too, mending relations with Frederick Barbarossa over the appointment to the See of Magdeburg and repairing the damage done by the extended dispute over the election to the See of York. He sent Nicholas Breakspear, who was to be the next Pope, as legate to Scandinavia with the result that Peter's Pence began to be paid by Norway and Sweden. He was buried in the Lateran basilica.

ADRIAN IV
(Born c.1100; elected December 4, 1154; died September 1, 1159)

Adrian IV is notable for being the only Englishman to become Pope. He was born Nicholas Breakspear, near St Albans and became a monk at St Albans abbey. He then traveled to France as a student, where he settled among the canons regular of St Rufus, Avignon, eventually becoming prior there. He came to papal notice because his community complained to Rome that he was too strict. Eugenius perceived Nicholas as an able man who might be useful to him, and made him cardinal bishop of Albano. He showed his talents to good effect as papal legate in Scandinavia in 1150–3. He reformed and reorganized the Church there and established a metropolitan See at Trondheim. When Eugenius died he was unanimously elected Pope.

His first act as Pope was to renew the Treaty of Constance with Frederick I Barbarossa. That he saw to be important not only because he needed Frederick's help with the Roman commune but also because the Treaty constituted a stance on the monarchical claims of the papacy, which he believed important to maintain. He placed Rome under an interdict until it expelled Arnold of Brescia who had been excommunicated by Eugenius. In 1155, with Frederick's help, he had Arnold executed.

Frederick was as ambitious a monarchist as Nicholas, but for the supremacy of the Empire over the papacy. He had a vision of a restored Carolingian Empire, of a return to an era before the Gregorian reforms had altered the balance between Church and State. Accordingly, when he and Adrian first met at Sutri in 1155, he was reluctant to show the Pope the deference etiquette demanded. When he crowned Frederick, Adrian changed the wording of the service so as to make plain the Emperor's subordination to the Pope.

In this uncomfortable situation, Adrian shifted his alliances. In 1156 he concluded the Treaty of Benevento with William I of Sicily, recognizing William's authority as King over southern Italy. In return for this William acknowledged Adrian as his feudal suzerain and undertook an annual tribute payment.

Frederick responded to this new alliance by considering himself now free to disregard the Treaty of Constance. At the Diet at Besançon in 1157 there was a noisy dispute over whether the Pope had intended to treat Frederick as his vassal. The following year at the Diet of Roncaglia, Frederick asserted imperial rights over north Italy in a manner which trod on the toes of the papal prerogatives Adrian was claiming. Adrian threatened to excommunicate Frederick unless he rescinded the decrees of Roncaglia. It was at this difficult juncture that Adrian died.

It is said that at the time of his death he confided in his. countryman, John of Salisbury that he wished he had never left England. It seems clear that his difficult tenure on the papal throne had taken its toll. Adrian IV was perhaps unfortunate in that he was the first Pope to encounter the strength of personality of Fredrick Barbarossa at the beginning of a struggle which was to last for more that twenty years. Adrian's friend and supporter, Cardinal Roland, was to become his successor, Alexander III.

Left: The Peace of Venice. *In 1177, Alexander III and Frederick I Barbarossa at last became reconciled. Frederick, who had formerly supported the antipopes Victor IV and Paschal III, now recognized Alexander as rightful Pope.*

Below: Frederick I Barbarossa is *hailed by his subjects at Aachen. This city was the center of the realm which Frederick renamed the Holy Empire (later called the Holy Roman Empire).*

ALEXANDER III
(Born c.1105; elected September 7, 1159; died August 30, 1181)

He was born in Siena and, according to later tradition, of the Bandinelli family, and was named Rolandus. He taught theology at Bologna around 1140, and a theological treatise, the *Sententie Magistri Rolandi*, has been attributed to him. For a long time he was identified with the Master Rolandus of Bologna who wrote a treatise, or *Summa*, on the famous compilation of Church law, Gratian's *Decretum*, but this is no longer agreed by historians. Eugenius III made him a cardinal in 1150, when he was a canon of Pisa Cathedral, and in 1153 put him in charge of the Chancery, the office which drew up all official papal documents. He was sent on papal diplomatic missions, negotiating with the German Emperor in 1153, and was a close advizer of the English Pope, Adrian IV. After Adrian was driven out of Rome by rebels in 1154, Cardinal Rolandus was a leading figure in the faction of cardinals who favored a political alliance with the King of Sicily as a means to reinstate him. He helped make an accord with Sicily at Benevento in 1156, and in 1157 was one of two papal envoys sent to berate the Emperor at Besançon for his failure to support the Pope. They carried a letter from Adrian which reminded the Emperor that the Pope had crowned him and would offer him other *beneficia*. The imperial chancellor, Rainald of Dassel, interpreted this to mean that the Emperor received his power from the Pope. When the Emperor and his circle expressed outrage, Cardinal Rolandus supposedly retorted: "From whom does [the Emperor] hold his empire if not from the lord Pope?" But it is not certain that he said these words and they do not accord with the more moderate view of the relationship between papacy and empire which he later expressed as Pope.

Rolandus was elected Pope by a majority vote, but a pro-imperial minority of cardinals supported another candidate, Octavian. An imperial envoy, Otto of Wittelsbach, orchestrated support for Octavian in Rome, where he was declared Pope Victor IV while Alexander had to flee the city. Alexander now began an eighteen-year campaign for recognition as the one true Pope. In 1160, the Emperor, Frederick I Barbarossa, called a council of bishops at Pavia, supposedly to decide who was rightful Pope, but in effect to secure obedience to Victor IV. Alexander III did not even attend, claim-

ing that the Pope could be judged by nobody. The council's decision was not accepted by the kings of France and England, and Alexander won wide support outside the German empire. He declared that Frederick and his antipope were excommunicate and the Emperor's subjects were released from obedience to him. Frederick reacted by invading Italy in 1162, attacking Milan and other Lombard cities which supported Alexander. He also sent envoys to persuade the kings of France and England to abandon Alexander but failed in this aim. Alexander might have claimed that the Pope had given power to the Emperor and he could also take it away. In 1084, Pope Gregory VII had deposed the Emperor on these grounds. But Alexander did not depose Frederick nor did he use as Pope the language of papal supremacy attributed to him at Besançon. Instead, he criticized Frederick for dividing the Church and oppressing the papacy which it was the duty of Emperors to protect. Even when imperial propaganda declared that Frederick had received his power from God by the election of princes, Alexander continued to show incredible restraint and even sought reconciliation with Frederick.

Meanwhile, resistance to the imperial antipope was growing and even some German bishops were going over to Alexander's cause. Alexander felt sufficiently confident to return to Rome in 1165 from exile in France where the papal court had been based at Sens for three years. To maintain control of the situation, Frederick called an assembly at Würzburg where he required the German princes and bishops to swear obedience to a new antipope, Paschal III, Victor IV having died in 1164. The bishops who refused were driven from office. Frederick then launched a new military campaign in Italy which was so successful that he had taken Rome and expelled Alexander from the city by 1167. On July 22 of that year Frederick and his wife were crowned in Rome by Paschal III. Alexander then received an offer of aid from the Byzantine Emperor, Manuel I Comnenus, who proposed the union of the Western Catholic and Eastern Orthodox Churches under papal control if the Pope would allow him to remove Frederick and declare him joint ruler of the Western German and Eastern Byzantine empires. The Pope would not accept such terms, still hoping for reconciliation with Frederick. His moderation was rewarded by a sudden turn of events. Malaria ravaged the imperial army, even killing off important figures like

Above: Frederick I Barbarossa. *Excommunicated by Alexander, he reacted by invading Italy in 1162, attacking Milan and other Lombard cities which supported the Pope. Alexander eventually sought reconciliation with Frederick.*

Left: Alexander III *receiving and blessing the Doge of Venice after the legendary victory over Frederick I Barbarossa who had reacted badly to the Pope's declaration of excommunication. Frederick invaded much of Italy before he was eventually defeated.*

Rainald of Dassel, and the Emperor was forced to retreat to Germany. This reversal encouraged the league of north Italian cities which had been forming in reaction to imperial attacks. Alexander, who had fled to Benevento in Sicilian territory, had cultivated anti-imperial sympathies among these cities since he was Cardinal Rolandus and now secured their firm support. The Milanese even named a new city Alessandria in his honor in 1168.

Frederick tried to divide the Pope from his allies by seeking separate peace talks with him but Alexander insisted on a settlement which included the Lombard cities. Papal envoys worked to maintain the alliance and Alexander III threatened spiritual sanctions against any cities of the league which attempted to break away or form new alliances. His efforts bore fruit for, in 1176, the Emperor, who had undertaken a third invasion of Italy, was roundly defeated by the Lombard league at the battle of Legnano and agreed to seek peace with the Pope and his allies. In the Peace of Venice (1177), Frederick recognized Alexander as the rightful Pope and made truces with the Lombard cities and Sicily. He was absolved from excommunication and performed the ritual of leading the Pope's horse by its bridle in recognition of his title. This did not signify the utter defeat of the Emperor, however, for Frederick withdrew at Venice the promise made in preliminary negotiations at Anagni to allow the Pope to recover the lands in Tuscany which the Empress Matilda had bequeathed to the Roman Church, a source of grievance between papacy and empire since the early twelfth century. He also obtained immunity for the German Church from recriminations against clergy who had opposed Alexander. The Pope was no doubt so weary of conflict and desperate for peace that he was prepared to accept such terms. In his final years, he even allowed Frederick to exercize unhampered control over the German Church. Church unity was more important to Alexander though it had been won at the expense of compromises which would create problems for his successors.

In the very period when Alexander had been most vulnerable in his conflict with the Emperor, in 1164–70, there had arisen the Becket crisis. In 1164, Henry II had stated in the Constitutions of Clarendon certain customary royal rights which Thomas Becket, Archbishop of Canterbury, perceived as contrary to the freedoms of the English Church. The king's most controversial claim was

that clerks who committed crimes should be tried in the royal courts; Becket held that they should be judged only by the Church courts. The Pope condemned the Constitutions and supported Becket, whom he welcomed as a fellow exile in France. His support of Becket, nonetheless, threatened to drive Henry over to the Emperor's side, and Frederick tried to exploit the situation, sending envoys to

Above: *The assassination of Thomas Becket, Archbishop of Canterbury, in 1170. This act caused Henry II to surrender his claims over the English Church in 1172 at the peace of Avranches.*

negotiate a marriage alliance with Henry's family in 1165. The Pope not only valued Henry for political support but also financial. When the papal court in exile could no longer draw revenues from papal territories in Italy, which had fallen into the hands of imperial supporters, one of the few regular sources of income was the payment of Peter's Pence from England. Hence, the Pope sought reconciliation between Henry II and Becket in order to keep the king on his side. Becket was a thorn in the Pope's side and it has often been said that he was more useful to Alexander dead than live since his assassination in 1170 brought the king to surrender his claims over the English Church in 1172 at the peace of Avranches and created a valuable symbol of the Church's struggle for liberty from secular control.

Alexander has been criticized for being cautious and conciliatory in his dealings with the secular powers, but given the circumstances in which he found himself his approach was perhaps more prudent than the reckless one adopted by Becket. He conceived Church and State as distinct but interdependent powers in the world, and sought their cooperation. His moderate attitude was informed by and in turn influenced contemporary legal thought in the Church. He was an effective administrator and reformer of the Church. He made statements of Church law in hundreds of letters and issued legislation at the Councils of Tours (1163) and Lateran III (1179), much of which formed a substantial part of the law of the Catholic Church until early in the twentieth century. The Third Lateran Council, in particular, decreed that a candidate who obtained at least two-thirds of the votes in the College of Cardinals was to be recognized as the duly-elected Pope, a ruling intended to consolidate the victory which Alexander had won in 1177. The Council, which brought together clergy from all over Christendom, marked the restoration of Church unity and was the crowning achievement of his pontificate, which came to an end with his death.

LUCIUS III
(Born 1097; elected September 1, 1181; died 25 November 1185)

Born at Lucca, Ubaldus Allucingolus is thought to have been a Cistercian monk before being made Cardinal by Innocent II in 1141. He certainly endowed the Cistercians with privileges and valued

their support as Pope. He was a member of the faction of cardinals who favored a political alliance with Sicily after 1153 and helped make the papal accord with the King of Sicily in 1156. He was a loyal agent of Alexander III and his chief representative in peace negotiations with the Emperor in 1177. He was elected Lucius III the day after Alexander's death, and as Pope pursued the same conciliatory policy toward the empire as his predecessor. He lost many of the political advantages which the papacy had won in 1177. He failed to prevent the collapse of the papal alliance with the Lombard cities which became pro-imperial in 1183; symbolically the city named Alessandria after Alexander III was renamed Caesarea. He also raised no objection to the marriage in 1184 of the German Emperor's son, Henry, to the heiress of Sicily, Constance, which later gave rise to the union of the empire and Sicilian kingdom, representing a threat to papal territorial interests in Italy for much of the following century.

In 1184, Lucius attempted to negotiate with the Emperor at Verona on issues left unresolved by the Peace of 1177. Emperor Frederick I offered the papal court a share of his Italian revenues in return for the dropping of papal claims to the lands in Tuscany which the Empress Matilda had bequeathed to the Roman Church. Lucius declined, but they agreed on a new crusade to the Holy Land and on measures against heresy, issuing together the decree *Ad abolendam*, which defined heresies and recognized the cooperation of Church and State as the means to fight them. It marked a watershed in papal legislation against heresy. Nonetheless, the peace which the council at Verona was meant to secure was ebbing as Lucius rejected Frederick's request to crown his son as co-Emperor and decided to judge the disputed election of the Archbishopric of Trier rather than back the imperial candidate. A new conflict between empire and papacy was brewing at Lucius' death.

URBAN III
(Elected November 25, 1185; died October 19, 1187)

Urban III was born Ubertus Crivelli of a noble Milanese family. He was made a cardinal in 1182 and was Archbishop of Milan when he was elected Pope almost unanimously on the day of Lucius's death. Such haste is explained by the contemporary tension between papacy and empire, and Ubertus was chosen since he was the staunchest foe of the

Above: **Lucius III** *joined with Emperor Frederick I in proclaiming a new crusade and in creating new legislation to combat heresy. However, toward the end of Lucius' life, tensions between papacy and empire had begun to surface.*

Above: **Urban III** *was elected Pope on the day of his predecessor's death due to his opposition to the Emperor. Relations between the two deteriorated throughout Urban's reign.*

Emperor in the papal court. His attitude was probably influenced by the imperial destruction of his native Milan in 1162 and his association with the martyred champion of ecclesiastical liberty, Thomas Becket, during the latter's exile in France. As Pope, he fulfilled his predecessor's deathbed wishes and refused to crown the Emperor Frederick I's son as co-Emperor. The Emperor provocatively responded by arranging the wedding and coronation of his son in Milan where Urban still held the archbishopric. Relations deteriorated further as Urban decided against the imperial claimant to the archbishopric of Trier and consecrated his rival in spite of a promise to Frederick. Imperial troops then laid siege to the papal court in Verona and occupied papal lands in central Italy. The Pope had allies among the German bishops, but, leaving nothing to chance, Frederick summoned them to an assembly which denounced the papal disturbance of the rights of the empire and German Church and sent envoys to the Pope. Urban tried to declare Frederick excommunicate but was frustrated by the Veronese, and so decided to issue the sentence in Venice, but he died *en route* there on the night of 19 October.

GREGORY VIII

(Born c.1110; elected October 21, 1187; died December 17, 1187)

Albertus Morra was born at Benevento, becoming a regular canon and a trained church, or canon, lawyer. He was made a cardinal in 1155 by Adrian IV and was sent on many missions by the Pope, negotiating Henry II's reconciliation after Becket's murder. He was appointed head of the papal secretariat, the Chancery, in 1177 by Alexander III, and still held this post when he was unanimously elected Pope. He seems to have been chosen to appease Frederick I whom the previous Pope had done so much to confront: the view was attributed to him that the Emperor did not hold his power from the Pope. He re-established peaceful relations with the Emperor who lifted the siege on the papal court at Verona. One of his first acts was to launch the Third Crusade to recover the Holy Land, Jerusalem having fallen to Saladin three weeks before his election. He called upon the Emperor and other princes to lead the expedition, and was still making energetic preparations for it and was busily reforming papal government when he died having been Pope for only fifty-seven days.

CLEMENT III

(Elected December 19, 1187; died April 10, 1191)

The Roman-born Paolo Scolari had been a candidate in the papal election of October 1187, but was disqualified on health grounds. Even when he was successfully elected, the cardinals feared for his imminent death especially after the short-lived Gregory VIII. His Roman connections no doubt influenced his election, for he could use them to negotiate the return of the papal court to Rome. Indeed, he made a treaty with the Roman senate to this effect in 1188. Clement kept favor with the Roman nobility by promoting many of its members to the cardinalate, and sought to recover papal lands in central Italy. He also set about promoting the crusade called by Gregory VIII and sought to establish the peace in Christendom necessary for its launch. Clement won Emperor Frederick I over to the crusade but at the cost of agreeing to crown his son as co-Emperor, which Clement's predecessors had refused, and overruling Urban III's choice of candidate in the Trier archbishopric, appointing the imperial chancellor instead. The papal legate, Henry of Albano, secured peace between Richard I of England and Philip II of France and their participation in the crusade. Frederick I died in 1190 *en route* to the Holy Land and his son, Henry VI, claimed the succession. But the King of Sicily had died childless the year before and Henry VI was married to his aunt, the nearest claimant to the title. This raised the specter of the encirclement of the papacy by a union of the kingdom and empire. Determined to avoid this, Clement recognized Tancred as King of Sicily. Henry invaded Italy and Clement promised to crown him, but the Pope had already died before Henry reached Rome.

CELESTINE III

(Born c.1105; elected April 10, 1191; died January 8, 1198)

Born of a noble Roman family, Hyacinth Bobo studied theology under the controversial Paris master, Peter Abelard, and had served the papal court for sixty-five years prior to becoming Pope. He was sent on papal missions to Spain (1154–6 and 1172–4) and to the German Emperor (1158). In the 1160s when Alexander III was campaigning for recognition as Pope and Louis VII of France was his firmest supporter, Bobo was a valuable intermedi-

Above: **Clement III** *was committed to the crusade which had been called by Gregory VIII and worked to secure peace between Richard I of England and Philip II of France and their participation in the campaign.*

Above: **Celestine III** *was aged eighty-five years old when he was elected to the papacy. He was seen as a compromise candidate as the cardinals were divided regarding the Emperor.*

ary between the papacy and France. He was aged eighty-five and had been a cardinal for forty-seven years when he was elected as Pope on April 10, 1191, the day of his predecessor's death. His hasty election was determined by the arrival of Henry VI in Rome who sought coronation as the German Emperor by the Pope. Henry was also claiming the kingdom of Sicily through his wife.

The cardinals were bitterly divided between those who wished to appease the Emperor and those who wished to prevent his intended union of empire and kingdom, which would surround papal territory. Bobo was chosen as a compromise candidate and as a Roman favored by the Roman majority in the college of cardinals. He crowned the Emperor, but the divisions in the college and his own moderation made agreement on a policy toward the empire difficult and Celestine could only take decisive action when one faction or another dominated. For example, in 1192 he recognized Tancred as the King of Sicily when many of the cardinals who would have preferred Henry VI were absent. But, in 1193, when all were present, he failed to act against Henry for holding Richard I of England prisoner. Richard was a crusader and as such came under papal protection, but most of the cardinals feared that support for Richard would strengthen ties between the Emperor and Richard's greatest enemy, the King of France. Even when Henry VI invaded Sicily on the death of Tancred and his heir in 1194 and had himself crowned king, the Pope remained cautious, merely breaking off diplomatic relations with the imperial court.

Negotiations, however, were soon resumed. Celestine was eager for peace with Henry but at the same time refused to recognize Henry as King of Sicily or his new-born son's hereditary succession to the elected office of Emperor, refusal which threatened the chances of peace. In 1196, Henry even offered to join a new crusade and raise a crusader army at his own expense if the Pope would crown his son. Celestine ignored this request and complained of Henry's violation of papal rights in the Sicilian Church but he agreed to send envoys to promote a crusade in the empire. In 1197, events turned in the papacy's favor, for Henry had to overcome a rebellion of his Sicilian subjects, which may or may not have enjoyed papal approval, and shortly afterward died. Fearing for his son's inheritance threatened by the revolt and lack of support among German princes for his succession, Henry left a will

which required papal recognition of his son as the new Emperor in return for restoration of papal lands in central Italy, including those bequeathed to the Roman Church by the Empress Matilda and long withheld by the Emperors. It also commanded respect for papal rights in Sicily, binding his successor to swear obedience to the Pope as the overlord of Sicily, a papal claim which he had never acknowledged in his lifetime. If the will was authentic, and it has been doubted, then it offered generous concessions long desired by the papacy, and the imperial vacancy represented an ideal opportunity for the Pope to make them a reality.

The anti-imperial faction now had the upper hand in the papal court and negotiated an alliance with the north Italian cities, but Celestine was too

Above: King Richard I of England *was taken prisoner by Henry VI. As a Crusader, Richard was entitled to papal protection, but for political reasons Pope Celestine III failed to act decisively.*

139

ill to take advantage of the situation. The English chronicler, Roger of Howden, claimed that the dying Celestine had made a novel proposal to the cardinals that he would resign if they would elect his own choice of successor, Cardinal John of St Prisca, but they refused. It would have been an unprecedented move and Howden's story is dubious; there are no other accounts of it. In fact, the cardinals chose a thirty-seven year old to succeed Celestine, who at his death was aged ninety-two.

INNOCENT III
(Born c.1160/61; elected January 8, 1198; died July 16, 1216)

Born Lothar Conti dei Segni into an aspiring Roman family, Innocent III was one of the most significant Popes of the Middle Ages. As a young man, he studied theology at Paris under Masters Peter of Corebeil and Peter the Chanter. Their emphasis on pastoral care has been seen as a formative influence on the future Pope. He also spent some time at Bologna, famous for the study of Roman and canon law, but it is uncertain that he acquired much legal training there, even though as Pope he was to make an important contribution to the law and legal thinking of the Church. He was made a cardinal in 1189 by his relative, Clement III, and his early career is mainly noted for his writing of theological tracts and sermons. He was elected Pope by a majority vote; aged 37 years, he was one of the youngest Popes ever.

He was perhaps chosen to be a dynamic successor to the weak, aged Celestine III, and certainly soon put forward his own distinctive program. He had a high conception of the papal office. In a sermon, he described himself as higher than man but lower than the angels, occupying an intermediary position between heaven and earth. He was the first Pope to use the title, Vicar of Christ, signifying that he was Christ's representative on earth and not merely St Peter's successor. He claimed the right to intervene in both spiritual and temporal affairs, modeling himself on the biblical Melchizedek who was both king and priest. He thus created an elaborate rhetoric of papal power, and historians have long disagreed over its interpretation. An older school of thought represented by the Germans, Hauck and Haller, viewed him as a political Pope bent on world domination, his interventions in secular affairs intended purely to translate his ideology

of papal hegemony into reality. More recent historians, notably Tillmann and Maccherone, have drawn more attention to his zeal for Church reform and argued that his political interventions were guided by spiritual motives. Certainly, he denied any intention of usurping the power of secular princes, accepting that they had a divinely appointed role in the right ordering of Christian society. Nonetheless, Innocent did consider their power subordinate to his own, and that on those occasions when they neglected justice or when a matter was disputed among them and no other superior could be referred to, the Pope could intervene. Whatever his motives, and they were probably sincere, his idea of papal power and his practical application of it was to inspire his successors and shape their policy for the rest of the century.

At his accession, Innocent was handed the political advantage of an imperial vacancy. In 1197 the German Emperor Henry VI had died, leaving, in papal guardianship, his tiny son Frederick as heir to the Sicilian kingdom. The boy's mother had immediately recognized papal overlordship in Sicily. Innocent extended papal claims to lands in central Italy, which had long been disputed between empire and papacy, and so laid the foundations of the Papal State. This provided the territorial base and financial security which the Popes had long craved. It was crucial to Innocent that Henry's successor in the empire respect papal claims both in Italy and Sicily, and since two rival claimants to the imperial crown had divided support among the German princes, Innocent saw the chance to influence events to his advantage. Philip of Swabia, the candidate who enjoyed the widest support, had allowed himself to be nominated instead of Frederick, his nephew, because the princes had considered the boy too young, and he was determined to protect his family's interests. Philip conceded papal claims in central Italy but disputed papal overlordship and guardianship of Sicily. Henry VI had planned the union of the empire and kingdom as Frederick's inheritance, which the papacy perceived as a threat, and Philip's attitude revived this fear. As his attempts to sway Philip failed, Innocent came to back the rival claimant, Otto. He asserted the right to examine the suitability of each candidate for imperial office on the grounds that it was the Pope who crowned the choice of the German princes. In effect, Innocent was extending to the empire the rules for election of bishops, according

Above: Innocent III, *first Pope to use the title Vicar of Christ, described himself as higher than man but lower than the angels. Young and dynamic, he claimed both spiritual and temporal authority.*

‡ INNOCENTIVS EPS SERVVS SERVORV DI. OILECTIS FIL... PRIORI ET FRIB IVXTA
SPECV BEATI BENEDICTI REGLARE VITA SERVANTIBVS IN P·P·IN. INTER HOLOCAVSTA
VIRTVTV NVLLV MAGIS EST MEDVLLATV QVA QD OFFERTVR ALTISSIMO DE PINGVEDINE
CARITATIS. HOC IGIT ATTENDENTES. CV OLI CAVSA DEVOTIONIS ACCESSISSEM AD LOCV SOLI... I

to which an ecclesiastical superior could reject those nominees whom he judged unfit for office. Philip was unfit, Innocent maintained, because of his past persecution of the Church and his excommunication by Celestine III. In his responses to the events that followed, Innocent's skills as a diplomatist can be seen. He secured the support of King John of England for Otto, but at the same time was careful not to antagonize Philip and the German princes by declaring spiritual sanctions against them, for

Otto's success was far from certain. When papal forces withstood an invasion of central Italy led by Philip, Innocent still sought peace with him and secured favorable terms: renunciation of imperial claims over Sicily and confirmation of papal rights there and in Italy. The peace was jeopardized, however, by Philip's sudden murder in 1208 and the prospect of a claim from young Frederick who had just come of age. Innocent, who had been ready to drop Otto, now put his hopes in him but they were

Right: St Dominic *debates with Cathar heretics, while condemned books fuel a fire like those soon to be associated with the Inquisition (established not long after the saint's death in 1221). Innocent III, who defined heresy as treason against God, proclaimed a campaign against the Cathars in 1208. This Albigensian crusade, so called from the Cathar stronghold of Albi, southern France, was savagely prosecuted by papal forces led by Count Simon IV of Montfort. Cathar communities were massacred and many condemned heretics were burned alive.*

misplaced. No sooner had Otto been crowned by the Pope in 1209 than he turned against his ally, invading Sicily and papal lands in central Italy. Innocent excommunicated him and reluctantly accepted Frederick as a rightful claimant to the empire in order to secure French support against Otto. Frederick was elected in Germany and issued the Golden Bull of Eger in 1213, promising to safeguard the rights of the papacy and the Church. The defeat of Otto by the French at Bouvines in 1214 removed one threat to papal security, but the question of the union of empire and kingdom in Frederick remained unresolved at Innocent's death and was to provide the basis of future conflict between papacy and empire.

Innocent's diplomatic concerns were not, however, confined to the empire, but extended to every kingdom. He made a new king in Bulgaria and was recognized as overlord in the kingdoms of Aragon and Portugal. He intervened in the marriage cases of Spanish kings and, most notably, that of Philip II of France, to whom Innocent denied a divorce for fifteen years before the king agreed to cohabit with his legal wife. In England Innocent intervened in the disputed 1205 election of the Archbishop of Canterbury and imposed his own candidate, Stephen Langton. King John, however, would not accept Langton, and Innocent finally placed England under interdict, a sentence suspending Church services and designed to turn the king's subjects against him, and excommunicated John. In 1213, when John faced the threat of invasion from France and a baronial revolt at home, he submitted to Innocent, offering the Pope overlordship of his domains in exchange for political support. In 1215, Innocent annulled Magna Carta on the grounds that the barons extracted it from John in prejudice of his rights. Clearly, where kings respected their obedience to the Pope and ecclesiastical liberties, Innocent was a staunch defender of their authority. His intervention in England cannot be separated from his spiritual concerns, for he acted against John in defense of ecclesiastical liberty, specifically freedom of episcopal elections from lay control, and even his interest in Sicily was motivated by a desire to liberate the local Church from royal influence.

Though Innocent's political thought and activity continue to interest historians, more attention is now rightly given to his pastoral achievements. The high point of his reign was the Fourth Lateran Council in 1215, which assembled over 1200 churchmen from all over Christendom "to form the largest council yet held in the history of the church." Among its many reforms, it required all the faithful to attend confession and receive the Eucharist at least once a year at Easter; formulated a new creed, stating that salvation could be gained only inside the Catholic Church; and approved transubstantiation, the doctrine that the bread and wine of the mass once consecrated by a priest became the body and blood of Christ. This statement of orthodox belief reflected the teachings of Innocent's Paris masters and his concern with the growth of religious dissent, or heresy. Early in his reign he had defined heresy as treason against God and extended to its adherents and their supporters penalties provided in Roman law against political traitors: loss of public office and confiscation of property.

The Fourth Lateran Council introduced further anti-heresy measures, for example granting those who fought heretics the same spiritual rewards accorded to crusaders. Indeed, the military campaign against the Cathar heretics of southern France called by Innocent in 1208 is often known as the Albigensian crusade (Albi was the main center of

Below: St Francis of Assisi *kneels before Innocent III, who recognized the Franciscan Rule in 1210. With the saint are his first followers, the twelve disciples known as the First Order. Francis, a former soldier, was called by God to a life of poverty and self-sacrifice in 1208. He was canonized in 1228, two years after his death, by Gregory IX.*

Above: St Francis, *whose order of Franciscan monks was unofficially recognized by Pope Innocent III in 1210. Joy of poverty and an emphasis on humility and simplicity were their main principles of belief. Francis traveled widely extoling the virtues of this way of life, even preaching to the Sultan of Egypt in 1223 which resulted in improved conditions for Christian prisoners in his dungeons.*

Right: The Fall of Constantinople *in 1204 was a major feature of the Fourth Crusade instigated by Innocent III. The city was sacked and the booty shipped back to Europe. Count Baldwin of Flanders was proclaimed Patriarch and there was a superficial unification of Greek and Roman Churches. However, the crusade ended in failure and it was not until 1212 that another (The Children's Crusade) was eventually launched.*

Catharism in the Midi). It was fought with great brutality, involving indiscriminate massacres at Carcassone and Bèziers, and allegedly drew the participation of northern French barons more with the lure of land-grabbing than of spiritual rewards. Innocent disapproved of its methods but welcomed its effect: Cathars and their patrons were crushed in southern France. Though he intensified the Church's persecution of heresy in collaboration with the secular power, Innocent also accommodated new religious movements inside the Church. He approved the Humiliati, formerly classed as heretics, and recognized the eccentric St Francis and his followers, giving them freedom to preach. Innocent saw the energy which such groups could release within the Church, and perhaps felt that they could draw back into the Church those attracted to heretical groups similarly devoted to poverty and preaching. He certainly encouraged the Cistercian missionaries in the Midi and St Dominic and his companions to imitate the poverty of the Cathars and engage in debate with them, while preaching the orthodox faith.

Innocent is recognized as one of the great lawyer Popes of the Middle Ages. Although he probably had little formal legal education, he quickly mastered the administration of judicial business on becoming Pope. He sat three times a week hearing cases, and contemporary lawyers praised his skills in summing up and noted his judgements. His vast output of letters included many legal decisions, which were collected by lawyers. In 1210 Innocent approved the first official compilation of Church law, assembling rulings from the first twelve years of his reign, and sent it to the University of Bologna for use in law schools and courts. This, together with his Fourth Lateran decrees ("his" since the Council largely approved without debate the legislative program that he set before it) was to form a substantial part of the law of the Catholic Church until early in the twentieth century. Contemporaries saw him as a compassionate judge, sympathetic to the poor, widows, and orphans. He tried to curb bribe-taking at the papal court, sacking corrupt officials, and to reduce the costs of litigants by delegating cases to local judges and opposing frivolous appeals designed to protract cases. He centralized power in the Church, intervening in the jurisdiction of bishops, reserving many classes of cases to the Pope, and appointing papal plenipotentiaries abroad, limiting the powers of local bishops.

Above: Count Baldwin of Flanders *established himself as Latin Emperor of Byzantium in 1204. In 1205 he was defeated by a Bulgarian-aided Greek uprising and died in captivity.*

Right: Honorius III *hears a sermon from St Francis. The Franciscan Order grew rapidly after its recognition by Innocent III, and in 1219 its first General Chapter was attended by some 5,000 friars. Faced with demands to moderate his original Rule, Francis resigned leadership of the Order to work on a more complex but less demanding Rule, approved by Honorius III in 1223.*

Innocent's concerns with the wider world included Christian missions to the Baltic, support for the *Reconquista* – the recovery of Spain from Islam – and the launching of a crusade to recapture Jerusalem from Muslim rule. As soon as he was elected Pope, he imposed a special tax on the clergy to aid a new expedition to the Holy Land. His plans were, however, to be thwarted by the guile of the Venetians contracted to ship the crusaders to the East. The Venetians diverted the Fourth Crusade to the Dalmatian coast, requiring the crusaders to earn their passage by conquering lucrative ports for them. Innocent tolerated this in the hope that the army would continue to Jerusalem, but instead it went to Constantinople to support a pretender to the Greek throne. In 1204, there the crusade became bogged down and its military leaders fell out. The result was that the city was sacked, the booty shipped back to Venice, and Count Baldwin of Flanders established himself as Latin Emperor of Byzantium. This was hardly the outcome Innocent intended, though he did accept the superficial union of the Greek and Latin Churches under papal primacy which it brought. In fact, Greek clergy continued their customs in spite of the Latin take-over. The political question of the empire and other issues then distracted Innocent from launching a new crusade. In 1212, there was the ill-fated "Children's Crusade", and in 1215 the Pope proclaimed a new expedition to Jerusalem to depart in 1217. The crusaders had lost freedom of decision in the Fourth Crusade because inadequate fund-raising made them too dependent on the Venetians. Innocent was determined to make better provision this time. He was preaching the crusade in northern Italy when he died at Perugia.

Innocent III's reign is often seen as the apogee of the medieval papacy and the closest the vision of papal monarchy came to realization. In fact, Innocent was more often responding to events than controlling them, such that he rarely succeeded in making his bold claims for papal power into a reality. His defense of papal rights in Italy was spirited, but left a difficult inheritance for his successors. His most positive legacy was the Fourth Lateran reforms, though these had barely begun to be implemented at his death. It is best, perhaps, not to see him as either political or pastoral, but to view both as conflicting aspects of his personality which contributed to the underlying tension between the temporal and spiritual characteristic of his reign.

HONORIUS III
(Elected July 18, 1216; died March 18, 1227)

Like his predecessor, Cencio Savelli also came from an upwardly-mobile Roman noble family, entering the service of the papal household under the patronage of Cardinal Hyacinth Bobo. The latter's election as Pope in 1191 brought Cencio rapid promotion. He was not only made a cardinal but combined two of the most powerful offices in the papal administration, chancellor and chamberlain, which gave him charge of official correspondence and finances. In 1192, as chamberlain, he was responsible for compilation of the *Liber Censuum*, an *ad hoc* survey of the rents and payments due to the Roman Church. It was more of a symbolic than working document, asserting papal fiscal rights in central Italy threatened by the territorial claims of the German Emperors and in the face of large-scale evasion of dues eased by inefficient collection. It was a bold attempt to rectify the parlous state of papal finances in the late twelfth century, not helped by Celestine's creation of many new cardinals all requiring incomes.

The other testimony to Cencio's activity as chamberlain are the bronze doors, now in the cloister of S. Giovanni in Laterano at Rome, which he commissioned for the papal palace, as the inscription on them records. He was passed over in the papal election of 1198, despite his proven administrative record, and accepted election only reluctantly on July 18, 1216, three days after his predecessor's death.

The new Pope was described as of "mature age", though his date of birth is unknown: the apse mosaic of S. Paolo fuori le Mura at Rome, which he commissioned, shows him as a white-haired figure. Honorius was left a difficult legacy by Innocent III. He had to continue many projects which his predecessor had initiated before his untimely death. The far-reaching legislation of the Fourth Lateran Council (1215) still had to be implemented, and many churchmen little understood and neglected its reforms. The mendicant groups of St Dominic and St Francis recognized by Innocent were left to be approved as religious orders by Honorius in 1217 and 1223 respectively. Innocent had accepted King John's offer of papal overlordship in England which bound the Pope to defend the king's rights against his rebellious subjects. John died in 1216, leaving his infant son under papal guardianship, and

Honorius dutifully sent legates to help sustain the boy's claims against the rebels and successfully persuaded Philip II of France not to invade and install his own son on the throne of England.

Honorius also had to promote the Fifth Crusade, called by Innocent in 1215 for 1217, the fate of which was largely bound up with the big political question left unresolved on Innocent's death, the union of the German empire and Sicilian kingdom in the person of Frederick II. Popes since the late twelfth century had perceived this union as a threat to their territorial claims in Italy, and Honorius was no exception. Frederick had promised Innocent to designate his son as king of Sicily and to fight on crusade, which indicated a willingness to co-operate with the papacy. But, by 1220, Frederick still had not joined the Fifth Crusade, by then seriously bogged down in Egypt, and had his son crowned as king in Germany without papal approval while still maintaining his personal rule in Germany and Sicily. Honorius negotiated with Frederick, who in return conceded temporary possession of the lands in Tuscany long withheld by the Emperors from the Roman Church. He promised to join the crusade in 1221, and insisted that he would administer the empire and kingdom as separate political entities. To his credit, Frederick did indeed send a large fleet to relieve the crusaders but it arrived too late to save the enterprize, the failure of which was blamed on Frederick's nonfulfillment of his crusading vow and Honorius' inability to hold him to it.

In 1223, Honorius agreed to Frederick's proposal of a new crusade for 1225. Honorius sent preachers to promote it across Europe and Frederick prepared a fleet to carry the crusader army. The Pope even approved Frederick's marriage to the daughter of the exiled Latin King of Jerusalem, though he required that Frederick name his son, rather than himself, as heir to Jerusalem. Various delays put the launch of the crusade back to 1227, and Honorius threatened excommunication if Frederick did not fulfill his vow this time. Relations between Pope and Emperor remained cordial nevertheless, and both worked to establish peace in unruly Lombardy so as to speed the departure of the Sixth Crusade. It still had to be realized when Honorius died. He has been criticized as weak and conciliatory in his dealings with Frederick, but he could be firm on the principal issues and his avoidance of the confrontational approach favored by his successors did maintain peace, the prerequisite of a successful crusade.

Left: St Dominic *is shown with three of his emblems – book, lily and rosary. It is a tradition that he introduced the rosary after receiving the first from the Virgin.*

Below: St Francis, *surrounded by episodes from his life, displays the stigmata which appeared on his body while he prayed in 1224.*

Above: Emperor Frederick II, *seen here on one of his coins, gained possession of Jerusalem for the Christian crusaders in 1228, but incurred papal wrath because he accomplished this through political negotiation rather than by battle.*

Right: Gregory IX *was, from the moment of his election, at verbal or actual war with Emperor Frederick II, whom he first excommunicated in 1228, over the respective papal and imperial rights. In 1239, a fragile alliance between Pope and Emperor collapsed: Gregory again excommunicated Frederick, calling him the Antichrist, and proclaimed a Holy War against him. Its lack of success contributed to Gregory's death.*

He was foremost an able ecclesiastical administrator, demonstrated as Pope by his promulgation on 2 May 1226 of an official collection of Church law, the *Compilatio Quinta*, which among other things outlawed trial by ordeal.

GREGORY IX
(Born c. 1170; elected March 19, 1227; died August 22, 1241)

Hugolino was born at Anagni and was trained in theology at Paris and in canon law, probably at Bologna. Descended from the family of the Conti dei Segni, he was a close relative and trusted adviser of Innocent III, who made him a cardinal in 1198. A deeply spiritual man, he was an early patron of the Franciscans, being instrumental in securing their papal approval, and even considered becoming a friar himself until St Francis dissuaded him. He was a leading figure in the administration of Innocent III and of his successor, Honorius III, and deeply distrusted the German Emperor, Frederick II, whom Honorius had tried to appease. Once Hugolino was elected Pope, the day after Honorius' death, he adopted an approach to Frederick strikingly different from that of his predecessor.

Hugolino took the name of Gregory, recalling an earlier Pope who had defied and even deposed an Emperor, Gregory VII. Gregory IX immediately reminded Frederick of his promise to go on crusade in 1227 on pain of excommunication. By the summer, Frederick had a fleet ready to transport the crusader army which had been gathering in southern Italy, but then disaster struck. A plague spread through the army, and even Frederick himself was affected. He set sail but soon returned, claiming continued ill health, and directed the fleet to go on without him. He sent envoys to explain to Gregory that he would rejoin the crusade in early 1228, but Gregory would hear no excuses and declared him excommunicate. The conciliatory approach of Honorius was over. Gregory issued letters to Frederick and other princes, denouncing his repeatedly broken crusading promises, his oppression of the Sicilian Church, his continued personal union of the German empire and Sicilian kingdom which the papacy had long tried to separate, and his ingratitude to the Roman Church which had been his guardian as a child. Gregory even implied that disease among the crusaders was Frederick's fault because he kept them waiting too long to embark

in the pestiferous summer heat! Despite his excommunicate status, Frederick rejoined the crusade in 1228 and negotiated a truce with the Muslims, granting the Christians possession of Jerusalem. Reasonable as this may sound to modern ears, his peace with the infidel was condemned in the West as a betrayal of the crusading spirit.

Meanwhile Gregory had launched an invasion of Sicily, closely modeled on the crusade. In 1229 Frederick hurried back to restore control over his kingdom. The Pope had released his subjects from obedience, and in Sicily Frederick was even rumored to be dead. Frederick soon put down rebellion in Sicily and even conquered Italian territory disputed between the empire and papacy. After protracted negotiations, Gregory agreed to peace in 1230. For the next six years, the Pope and Emperor tried to co-operate, and Gregory even supported Frederick against a revolt in Lombardy led by his own son in 1234. Their fragile alliance crumbled over the issue of Lombardy. Both claimed rights there and favored differing strategies in dealing with the unruly Lombards. Gregory urged Frederick to seek peace by negotiation, but Frederick preferred to subjugate Lombardy by force and mistrusted papal ambitions in the area. Gregory reminded him that he was subject to papal authority and that the Emperor received his power from the Pope. Frederick continued his campaign in Lombardy, and invaded Sardinia, subject to the Roman Church. The provocation was too much. In March 1239, Gregory again excommunicated Frederick in spite of discouragement from certain cardinals. The sentence oddly made no mention of Lombardy, but of Frederick's continued abuse of the rights of the Sicilian Church. A war had been declared and at first it took the form of words, both sides trading insults and appealing for the support of European princes. The Pope condemned Frederick as an atheist and the Antichrist. Imperial propaganda declared the Pope a false prophet and "a Pharisee seated on a chair of pestilence, anointed with the oil of wickedness." Frederick then began a war of arms, invading papal lands in central Italy and marching on Rome. In early 1240 Gregory staged a procession through the city, displayed its holy relics, and passionately called upon the Romans, who were far from loyal to his cause, to defend their Church. He called this a Holy War, a crusade, and it was the first which a Pope had proclaimed against a political foe inside Christendom.

Frederick did not besiege Rome, however. Despite the calls of some cardinals for peace talks, Gregory summoned a general council of the Church to meet at Rome in summer 1241, the object of which was to condemn Frederick before the world. In April 1241, Frederick's fleet intercepted a convoy of ships carrying delegates to the council and probably money raised for Gregory's cause. The council was never to meet, and Gregory, trapped in the summer heat of Rome by Frederick's armies, died a broken man. His provocative approach brought war between empire and papacy on two occasions in his reign and no practical advantage to him, but he had a canon lawyer's keen sense of the rights of the papacy and the Church and was determined to assert them.

His other achievements deserve attention. He commissioned his chaplain, Raymond de Peñafort, to produce a single compendium of Church law from the existing collections of papal legislation, adding to it nearly 200 decrees of his own. Promulgated in September 1234, the *Decretales Gregorii IX* carried legal force among Catholics until 1918. Gregory's own laws included numerous provisions against heresy, and he laid the foundations of the papal inquisition. The war in southern France on the Cathar heretics and their patrons, sanctioned by Innocent III, had been concluded with the peace of Paris in 1229, but pockets of heresy still held out in the Midi. Though it was the duty of local bishops to inquire into heresy, pressure of other business meant that they could not devote sufficient energy to this task. Therefore, Gregory appointed inquisitors to enforce anti-heresy laws in the Midi in 1233. The "inquisition" did not yet mean an institution but a legal procedure which did not demand the usual strict standards of proof otherwise required in Church law. No accuser need be presented whose word could be contested in open court. In fact, suspected heretics had little right of defense, and could be convicted by hearsay evidence alone. Many inquisitors were not even lawyers but friars who had long preached against heresy, and their inquisitorial activity was often resented by local civic authorities and layfolk, so much so that Gregory had to suspend it more than once. Nevertheless, his pursuit against heresy found willing collaborators among secular princes. Even Frederick II had passed laws in Sicily in 1231, stating that those convicted of heresy by the Church should be handed over to the secular power for punishment – including death. In 1235, when the Pope was his ally, he offered to persecute the Cathars who had fled into northern Italy from the Midi. The subsequent conflict between Frederick and the Pope was exploited by the Cathars, who associated themselves with imperial allies to secure protection from the inquisition which in 1234 Gregory had established in northern Italy. Cathars also fled from France into Spain where the King of Aragon organized his own inquisition with Gregory's approval, entrusting local bishops with its prosecution. Gregory was more tolerant of the Jews, but nonetheless ordered examination of their law books and the burning of any found to contain error. He also sponsored Christian missions to the Baltic, many of which involved forced conversion as well as peaceful preaching. Thus, under Gregory, intolerance and persecution of non-Christians came to typify ever more strongly medieval Christian society.

Below: The Decretales Gregorii IX. *Gregory IX approves the compendium of Church law, supplemented by many of his own decrees, promulgated in 1234. The Decretales were in force until 1918.*

Above: King James I of Aragon, *here seen entering Valencia in 1238, established an inquisition in his realm with the approval of Pope Gregory IX.*

Below: Celestine IV *died only seventeen days after the suffering imposed during his election.*

CAELESTINVS IV. Gaufridus Casti lioneus Mediolan. creat. die 22. Sep: tem. an. i241. Sed: dies 17. Obijt 8. Oc: tob 1241. Vac. Sed. an. i. men. 8. d. 15.

CELESTINE IV
(Elected October 25, 1241; died November 10, 1241)

Goffredus Castiglioni was born at Milan, and was a Cistercian monk for forty years before he entered the College of Cardinals in 1227. On the death of Gregory IX in August 1241 the College numbered only nine and was divided between those wishing to continue Gregory's policy against Emperor Frederick II, whose army surrounded Rome, and those preferring to negotiate with Frederick. The Emperor tried to influence the election of Gregory's successor in his favor, but Matthew Orsini, senator of Rome, was equally determined to speed up the election in his disfavor, and so confined the cardinals in a tumbledown Roman palace called the Septizonium, promising to release them only when they had reached a decision. They prevaricated for weeks despite the appalling conditions of their confinement, in which one of them died. They resisted all outside pressure before finally siding with the moderate Goffredus in the first conclave, or enclosed

election, in papal history. Celestine IV was elected on October 25, 1241 and died seventeen days later on November 10, his demise probably brought on by the suffering of the conclave.

INNOCENT IV
(Elected June 25, 1243; died December 7, 1254).

Sinibaldo Fieschi was born in the late twelfth century, the youngest son of a Genoese noble family. He received his early education in Parma before going on to excel in Roman and canon law studies at Bologna, where he subsequently taught law. His Bolognese teachers contributed significantly to doctrine on papal power, and their ideas would influence his thinking and policy as Pope. His legal talent secured him the office of "auditor" in 1226, hearing disputes referred to papal justice. He assisted Cardinal Hugolino as an adviser, and when the latter became Pope in 1227 he promoted Sinibaldo to the cardinalate and vice-chancellorship of the Roman

Above: The Council of Lyons.

Fearing that Frederick II intended to renege on their fragile agreement, and might seek to take him prisoner, Innocent IV excommunicated the Emperor in 1245.

Church, further rewarding him in 1235 with the rectorship of the Marches, the office of governing papal lands in eastern Italy.

In 1240, Sinibaldo was recalled to Rome to support Gregory's conflict with the German Emperor. The conflict was left unresolved on Gregory's death in 1241, and the Emperor tried to influence the papal succession in his own favor. An election in 1241 made a Pope who lasted barely three weeks, and an eighteen-month vacancy followed before the cardinals elected Sinibaldo at Anagni near Rome on 25 June 1243. Both the cardinals and the Emperor, Frederick II, expected the new Pope to negotiate peace, and Innocent duly proposed terms which Frederick accepted, tough though they were. Frederick was to restore lands conquered from the papacy, recognize the spiritual leadership of the Pope, and provide support for a crusade and the campaign against Mongol invasions in eastern Europe. A meeting was arranged between Emperor and Pope for mid–1244, but Innocent never kept the appointment, fleeing instead to Genoa and then to Lyons, accompanied by the cardinals.

Lyons was to remain the seat of papal government until 1251. Innocent fled perhaps because he feared that Frederick in a personal meeting would force

him to accept less generous terms, even hold him captive. Innocent was not one for compromize, and it is possible that he already planned to revive Gregory's idea of a council at which Frederick could be condemned. Frederick had thwarted Gregory's council in Rome by seizing its delegates, and Lyons perhaps appeared a safer venue.

In December 1244 Innocent summoned a general Council of the Church to meet at Lyons on June 28, 1245. It was to deal with pressing issues facing the Church, which, apart from the matter of Frederick, included the unrecovered Holy Land, the Mongol attacks, religious dissent or heresy, and the union of the Greek and Latin Churches. Before the small gathering of delegates who assembled, the charges against Frederick were read out: suspected heresy; sacrilege in seizing the delegates of Gregory's Council; perjury; violation of the peace. Frederick was represented at the Council by an envoy who defended him and insisted on his desire for conciliation. Frederick was making for Lyons but on July 17, before he could answer in person to the Council, Innocent declared him excommunicate and stripped of all his titles, releasing his subjects from obedience to him. Innocent was perhaps encouraged by the presence of German bishops who were ready to elect a new Emperor who would be prepared to submit to the Pope. And in 1246 they chose Henry Raspe as the papal anti-Emperor.

Meanwhile, Innocent was preaching a crusade against Frederick, another unfulfilled project of Gregory IX's which he revived. King Louis IX of France, Innocent's nominal protector in Lyons, preferred that the Pope launch a crusade to recover Jerusalem and negotiate with Frederick. He tried to act as a mediator between Pope and Emperor in 1245 and 1247, but failed to dissuade the Pope from his war upon Frederick. Most German princes still favored Frederick, and in early 1247 the anti-Emperor died. Frederick's cause was still strong, and he aimed to unite his allies to defeat the papal armies active in Sicily and Lombardy. He intended to advance on Lyons and force peace talks with the Pope, but in 1248 he was caught off guard by a rebellion of his subjects in Parma. A siege failed to break the city, and the citizens laid waste to the imperial encampment, optimistically named Vittoria. Encouraged by Frederick's setback, the rebel electors chose Count William of Holland to succeed Henry Raspe.

In 1249 Louis IX left on crusade, depriving Frederick of a mediator with the Pope. Frederick managed to restore order in Sicily but before he could seize victory in the conflict, he fell ill and died on December 13, 1250, naming his son, Conrad, as his heir and appointing his illegitimate son, Manfred, as regent of Sicily. Innocent sought to take advantage of the new situation, supporting William of Holland against Conrad. He launched an invasion of Sicily but was opposed by Manfred. The Pope sought a champion who would conquer and hold Sicily as a papal fief, and made unsuccessful overtures to Richard of Cornwall, brother of King Henry III of England, and Charles of Anjou, brother of Louis IX. Conrad died in 1254 leaving an infant son, Conradin, and offering submission to the Pope in order to guarantee Conradin's inheritance. Innocent was overseeing a new offensive against Manfred when he died suddenly at Naples, like Frederick too soon to clinch victory.

Because of Innocent's prolonged struggle against Frederick, his political ideas have long interested historians, and he has been seen as the most extreme exponent of papal supremacy in temporal affairs. The anti-imperial pamphlet *Eger cui lenia* (1245) asserted that the Pope received from God dominion over both temporal and spiritual affairs, including rule over the empire, and that since Frederick as an excommunicate stood outside the Church where no power was sanctioned by God, the Pope was justified in withdrawing the imperial power which he had bestowed on him. It is uncertain that Innocent composed this text though it emanated from his circle. His ideology is better sought in the canon law commentary which he amazingly found time to write during 1245–51. It has been argued that Innocent's commentary simply built upon traditional papal claims, in particular expanding on ideas of Innocent III, and that it expressed a conventional view of power as divided between temporal and spiritual rulers, respecting the kingly office.

Innocent also developed an interpretation of world history, however, in which God had bestowed government of human society to a succession of representatives, the prophets and kings of the Old Testament, Christ and finally St Peter and his suc-

Below: **King Louis IX of France** *attempted to mediate between Frederick II and Innocent IV, but withdrew from the dispute in 1249, when he set out on a crusade to recover Jerusalem.*

Above: King Henry III of England *shared Louis IX's disquiet over Innocent IV's obsessive dispute with Frederick II. Innocent vainly offered the rule of Sicily to Henry's brother, Richard of Cornwall.*

the empire if its leadership fell vacant. Other contemporary events also shaped the concerns of his commentary. Contacts with the Mongols moved him to an enlightened essay on the property rights of non-Christians, which was consulted when churchmen in the sixteenth century debated the rights of indigenous peoples in the New World. His commentary was unusual in that it also treated his own laws besides those of his predecessors, offering a unique insight into a Pope's legislative motives, and included discussion of his ban on the excommunication of organized communities. The nineteenth-century historian Gierke traced back to this source the origins of the legal idea of the fictitious person, such that a community could act and be prosecuted as if an individual in law. Historians have since argued that although Innocent did conceive of organized society in abstract terms, he nowhere spoke of it as a fictitious person.

Besides his significant contribution to legal thought, Innocent also issued three collections of legal rulings, which reveal an increasingly conscious and autocratic sense of papal law-making. These were incorporated into Boniface VIII's law book, the *Liber Sextus* (1296), and remained in force among Catholics until 1918.

Also noteworthy are Innocent's attitudes toward the Jews and heretics. For much of his reign his stance was comparatively liberal, curbing the activity of the inquisition and lifting the ban on the Jewish law code, the Talmud, many copies of which had been burned in 1242 at Paris on the orders of Gregory IX. Innocent even ordered protection for Jews of Lyons, accused in 1247 of ritually murdering a Christian child. A year later, however, he renewed the condemnation of the Talmud, and in 1254 laid down tough new anti-heresy provisions in Lombardy, the first to allow inquisitors to use torture. This change was perhaps encouraged by the wane of Frederick II, who had hitherto obsessed Innocent as the anti-Christian enemy, but also by the influence of the friars, many of whom were inquisitors and converters of Jews. Innocent favored them with many privileges and sent them on Christian missions as far as Africa and the Mongol court in the East. Because they were dependent on papal support, they espoused papal primacy in the Church, to the distaste of bishops and parish clergy who resented growing papal centralization as the diminution of their local jurisdiction. Bishop Grosseteste of Lincoln, for example, decried

cessors, the Popes. He conceived society as an organic body under the direction of one person. This was a hierarchical society in which princes occupied a necessary but subordinate position to the Pope, who could intervene to correct them where their actions were endangering the divine ordering of society and the attainment of its ultimate goal, salvation. These views were doubtless encouraged by the war of propaganda and arms with Frederick, and Innocent's commentary claimed the papal power to examine the suitability of the Emperor and to hold

Innocent's use of "provisions", the reserving of Church offices to papal nominees, arguing that many of those thereby appointed were unworthy of the priesthood and negligent of their flocks. Frederick II, outraged by his deposition, even accused the Church under Innocent of abandoning its founding principles in pursuit of worldly ambition and greed. Even pious princes like Henry III and Louis IX worried about Innocent's sense of priority. Indeed, it is debatable whether his uncompromising obsession with Frederick set the papacy on the right path in these years, for it was to involve him and his successors more deeply in political concerns and less in religious reforms. Innocent IV was a determined, energetic and intelligent Pope, but perhaps a misguided one.

ALEXANDER IV
(Elected December 12, 1254; died May 25, 1261)

Born toward the end of the eleventh century, Rainaldus Conti dei Segni came from a Roman noble clan which had produced two earlier Popes, Innocent III and Gregory IX. Gregory, his uncle, made him a cardinal in 1227. Rainaldus was Cardinal Bishop of Ostia on his election as Pope. Though one chronicler described him as "scholarly and pacific", Alexander was led by his cardinals to continue Innocent IV's war against the Staufen, the descendants of the German Emperor Frederick II who had died in 1250. In Germany he supported Count William of Holland, whom Innocent IV had backed as an alternative Emperor to Frederick. On the count's death in 1256, Alexander favored King Alfonso X of Castile to succeed him. The German princes at first elected Alfonso but later transferred their support to Richard, Earl of Cornwall, brother of King Henry III of England, who consolidated his position by having himself crowned King of the Romans, or Emperor-designate, and winning over the Pope in 1257.

In Sicily, Frederick's illegitimate son, Manfred, had assumed control ostensibly on behalf of Frederick's rightful heir to the kingdom, his grandson Conradin. However, his coronation as King of Sicily in 1258 gave the lie to his true ambitions, and German supporters of Conradin saw him as a usurper. Innocent IV had distrusted Manfred and was launching a war to establish papal rule in Sicily when he died in 1254. Alexander tried to resume this campaign but its failure in 1255 only encouraged Manfred. The Pope needed a champion who would conquer Sicily and hold it from the Pope as his overlord. Innocent's favor had fallen on Edmund, the younger son of Henry III, and Alexander confirmed this choice. He required Henry to send troops to Italy and a vast sum of money to the papal trea-

Above: **Alexander IV**, *nephew of Pope Gregory IX, was described as a peaceful scholar. Nevertheless, he vigorously pursued the papal campaign against the descendants of Emperor Frederick II.*

Left: **King Alfonso X of Castile** *became Alexander's chosen candidate for the imperial throne, but was abandoned by the German princes in favor of Richard, Earl of Cornwall.*

Above: Urban IV *proclaimed a crusade against Manfred, illegitimate son of Frederick II, but died while fleeing from the advance of Manfred's Ghibelline (antipapal) forces into Italy.*

Below: The Mass at Bolsena. *A miraculous occurrence at Bolsena in 1263 inspired Urban IV to institute the feast of "Corpus Christi".*

sury by late 1256. The plan was impracticable, for the sum demanded was more than Henry could afford and his son, a nine-year old boy, was hardly an ideal candidate. However, the Pope was too stubborn and the king too blindly optimistic to abandon the project immediately, and it was instead twice postponed to allow the king more time to raise money from taxes. The "Sicilian business" was to provoke discontent among Henry's barons into rebellion, and by December 1258 the Pope decided to drop Edmund. Manfred, in the meantime, had exploited the situation, seizing control of most of Italy, including papal lands. Because of this, and because of political instability in Rome, Alexander spent little time in the city. He found himself politically isolated in the peninsula and had still not decided on a new champion by his death. He was a gentle but weak figure, and his hostility to Manfred ineffectual. He failed to support the last Latin Emperor of Byzantium who was overthrown by a Greek claimant, perhaps since the Latin Emperor saw Manfred as an ally and his Greek foe had tempted the Pope with the promised reunion of the Greek and Roman Churches.

URBAN IV
(Born c.1200; elected August 29, 1261; died October 2, 1264)

Jacques Pantaléon was the son of a humble shoemaker of Troyes and was educated at his local cathedral school and then at the University of Paris. He

was appointed a canon of Lyons where in 1247 he came to the attention of Innocent IV, whereafter his rise was rapid. Innocent sent him to Germany on diplomatic business and to the Baltic on Christian missionary work. In 1253, he became Bishop of Verdun and, in 1255, Patriarch of Jerusalem. His intervention among the squabbling groups in the crusader kingdom was decisive, and he came to Rome in 1261 to secure papal support for his efforts, only to become the choice of the cardinals to succeed Alexander IV, being elected three months after the latter's death. Alexander had been indecisive, and Urban's energy, his long experience in ecclesiastical administration and his wide knowledge of political affairs strongly recommended him to the cardinals as one to tackle the challenges facing the papacy. He added fourteen new cardinals to the College, including several Frenchmen, to ensure its continued support. He also set about recovering papal control over central Italy and influence in Tuscany and Lombardy, which had all fallen under the sway of Manfred, self-styled king of Sicily. Disorder in Rome obliged him to reside in Viterbo and Orvieto, and without a papal champion to overthrow Manfred the Papal State remained insecure. In 1262 King Louis IX of France was approached. He refused to conquer Sicily for himself or his son, but did not object to his brother, Charles of Anjou, being asked. Negotiations were delayed, however, by the arrival in the West of the exiled Latin Emperor of Byzantium who sought the recovery of his throne with Manfred's support. A reconciliation

between Urban and Manfred was attempted but failed, and overtures to Charles were renewed. Terms were agreed and Charles was accepted as the papal champion in June 1263. Meanwhile, Manfred and his Ghibelline (antipapal) allies had overrun papal lands in the Marche and were closing on Rome. Urban gave Charles all the concessions he wanted on the original terms in order to secure his immediate intervention. Urban proclaimed a crusade against Manfred but, before Charles could arrive to lead it, the Pope had already died fleeing from Manfred's armies. In his final year, he instituted the feast of "Corpus Christi" (Body of Christ') in response to the miracle of Bolsena. In 1263, when a priest who doubted the Church's teaching that the bread and wine of the mass were the body and blood of Christ, had celebrated mass at Bolsena, the communion bread had bled onto the altarcloth. The cloth was immediately brought to Urban at nearby Orvieto, who declared the event a miracle.

CLEMENT IV
(Born c.1200; elected February 5, 1265; died November 29, 1268)

Guy Fulquois was the son of a lawyer of Saint-Gilles in the Rhone valley, and himself became a lawyer, entering the service of the Counts of Toulouse. He advised Count Alfonso and his brother, king Louis IX of France. After the death of his wife in 1247 he took holy orders and was appointed archdeacon of Le Puy. He rose rapidly in the Church, becoming Bishop of Le Puy in 1257, and two years later Archbishop of Narbonne. In 1261 he was promoted Cardinal-Bishop of Sabina, and in 1262 was sent on papal business to England. He arrived back at the papal court in Perugia on February 15, 1265 to learn that he had been elected Pope ten days earlier. Following the death of the previous Pope, the cardinals, split into French and Italian factions, had deliberated for four months until one of them proposed that two commissioners decide, one from each faction, and their choice of Guy was accepted by the others. Guy's close contacts with the French court clearly suggested that he was the ideal candidate to continue the papal alliance with Charles of Anjou, brother of Louis IX. The previous Pope had solicited his intervention against the upstart king of Sicily, Manfred, whose armies had occupied the Papal States and, by the spring of 1265, were besieging Rome. Charles relieved the city, and in June 1265

the Pope sent a delegation of cardinals to invest him with the kingdom of Sicily. But first he had to conquer it. The Pope set about raising funds for him, even pawning treasure and Church property to secure loans. By the end of the year there was enough money to finance a campaign, and Charles' main army was already marching down through northern Italy from France. Charles was crowned King of Sicily at St. Peter's in January 1266 by cardinals acting for Clement. Soon after, Charles led his army against Manfred, who was slain on 26 February 1266 at the battle of Benevento. Charles extended a general amnesty to Manfred's supporters, and resistance soon crumbled. Charles took no reprisals, but his new subjects complained to the Pope of his cold, efficient rule. Clement admonished him, especially about the heavy taxes which he was imposing to pay off his campaign debts.

The Pope had hoped for a subservient client king in Sicily, but Charles was very ambitious. He turned his attention to northern Italy, and most of Tuscany was his by mid-1267. Though Clement may have feared the encirclement of the papacy by an Italy uniting under Charles instead of Manfred, he was still dependent on Charles, and a very real danger was emerging from Germany. Conradin, grandson of the German Emperor Frederick II (d. 1250), asserted his hereditary claims to the empire and Sicily. In April 1267 Clement sent letters to the German bishops, excommunicating all who dared support Conradin's election as Emperor. By the late summer of 1267 Conradin's supporters had stirred up rebellion in Sicily, and Clement urged Charles to return there from Tuscany. In October, Conradin crossed the Alps and won allies in Tuscany.

Above: King Louis IX of France (St Louis) *sets sail on his last crusade, during which he died, in 1270. A monarch of legendary piety, he was canonized by Boniface VIII in 1297.*

Below: Clement IV. *His papacy saw the end of the Staufen imperial dynasty. Conradin, grandson of Frederick II, was defeated and captured in 1268, and Clement approved his execution.*

Below: Bl Gregory X *was crusading in the Holy Land when told of his election in 1271. He showed himself to be less preoccupied with territorial politics in Italy than his predecessors in office, and devoted much energy to seeking reunion between the Roman and Greek Churches and to urging a new crusade.*

Conradin's progress south was slow, giving Charles time to crush revolt in Sicily and return to defeat Conradin on August 29, 1268 in the Battle of Tagliacozzo. Within two months Conradin had been captured, tried, and beheaded. Clement approved the execution for it marked the end of the Staufen imperial dynasty which, for over a century, the papacy had perceived as a threat to its own territorial claims in Italy. A month later Clement himself died. His concerns outside Italy had included continued dialogue with the Greeks over the union of their Church with Rome and support for the holy wars in the Baltic and in Spain.

Bl GREGORY X

(Born 1210; elected September 1, 1271; died January 10, 1276)

Tedaldo Visconti came from Piacenza and entered the service of Cardinal Pecorara of Palestrina in the late 1230s, accompanying him on papal missions to France. On the Cardinal's death in 1245, Tedaldo was already Archdeacon of Liège and may have participated in the General Church Council of Lyons I. From 1248 to 1252 he pursued theological studies in Paris before returning to Liège. In 1259 he joined the household of another cardinal, Ottobuono

Fieschi, serving on his mission to England from 1264 to 1268. From England he went to the Holy Land in the entourage of Prince Edward, the future Edward I of England, and it was there at Acre in 1271 that the news of his election as Pope reached him. The previous Pope, Clement IV, had died three years earlier, and a long vacancy had followed, in which rival factions of French and Italian cardinals failed to agree on a successor. French royal pressure had finally persuaded them to seek a compromise candidate, and on the advice of the Franciscan leader, St Bonaventure, they were confined to the papal palace of Viterbo on bread and water until they reached a decision. They appointed a committee of six who chose Tedaldo. His election came as a surprise to him, and he was reluctant to abandon the crusade, preaching the recovery of Jerusalem before his departure. He arrived in Viterbo on February 10, 1272 and was consecrated as Pope on March 27 at Rome. His first act was to summon a General Church Council to meet on May 1, 1274 to discuss reform, the Union of the Eastern and Western Churches, and a new crusade. The agenda clearly set him apart from his predecessors, who had been more concerned with territorial politics in Italy than a wider vision of Christendom, promoting papal supremacy in temporal affairs rather than pastoral

It was in Edward's (then Prince Edward) entourage that Tedaldo Visconti was crusading when he learned of his election as Pope Gregory X. One of Edward's chief advisors, Thomas of Hereford, was canonized in 1320 – despite having been excommunicated by the Archbishop of Canterbury in 1282.

Above: Bl Innocent V, *a scholarly Dominican and a leading figure in the Council of Lyons called by Gregory X, was the first of his Order to achieve the papacy. He was beatified in 1898.*

reforms. That is not to say Gregory did not intervene in politics, for he urged the German princes to fill the long-vacant imperial throne and in 1273 approved their choice of Rudolph of Habsburg. Meanwhile he paved the way for the reunion of the Churches at the Council by negotiating with the Greek Emperor, Michael VIII, who promised the submission of the Greek Church to the Pope. At Gregory's invitation Michael sent envoys to the Council, which Gregory had decided to hold at Lyons. They swore obedience to the Pope, though the union was not supported by most of Michael's subjects, lay or clerical. The Council also drew up fund-raising measures for a crusade. Its most significant decree laid down rules for papal elections which still apply today. Doubtless occasioned by the circumstances of Gregory's own election, it required the cardinals to wait for absent colleagues no more than ten days after a Pope's death before proceeding to an election in "conclave", meaning they were confined until a new Pope was chosen. Gregory was busy making peace among princes to prepare for a crusade when he died.

Bl INNOCENT V
(Born c.1215; elected January 21, 1276; died June 22, 1276)

Peter of Tarentaise in Savoy entered the Dominican order c.1236 and studied theology at Paris from 1248 to 1254, becoming a master there in 1259. He alternated spells of teaching at Paris (1259–64, 1267–9) with leadership of the Dominicans in France (1264–7, 1269–71). A theological commentary and other writings are attributed to him. He was nominated Archbishop of Lyons by Gregory X in 1272 and played an important part in the Council which that Pope held there, preaching reunion with Rome to the Greeks. He was Cardinal-Bishop of Ostia when he was elected Pope according to the new rules laid down at Lyons (1274). He favored Charles of Anjou, King of Sicily, and his ambitions in Tuscany and Greece, though this threatened papal relations with the Greek Emperor and the German Emperor-elect, who had interests in Tuscany. Innocent V successfully arranged peace between the Genoese and Charles just four days before his death. In 1898 he was beatified by Leo XIII.

ADRIAN V
(Elected July 11, 1276; died August 18, 1276)

Born Ottobuono Fieschi at Genoa, he was made a cardinal in 1251 by his uncle, Innocent IV. He was sent on papal missions to England in 1254 and again from 1264 to 1268, when he negotiated peace between King Henry III and his barons. His family connections suited him to the task of promoting the 1271 papal-Angevin alliance in Italy. He was elected Pope after Charles of Anjou, King of Sicily, had confined the cardinals in a conclave, pressuring them into choosing one friendly to his cause, Ottobuono being an old ally. He died before he could be consecrated as Pope.

JOHN XXI
(Born c. 1205; elected September 13, 1276; died May 20, 1277)

Peter Juliani Rebolo was born at Lisbon, the son of a doctor. He studied at Paris c.1228-35, and later taught medicine at Siena. He was renowned for his philosophical, theological and medical writings. His most influential work was the *Tractatus*, or *Summulae Logicales*, disseminated in hundreds of manuscripts and editions down to the 1600s. It formulated theories of language important to the development of logic and adopted by such later thinkers as Thomas Aquinas and William of

Above: **Nicholas III** *owed his election partly to a riotous mob that demanded an Italian Pope. He incurred criticism for his excessive nepotism (the promotion of relatives to Church offices).*

Ockham. The *Thesaurus pauperum*, a popular medical manual, is also attributed to him though not securely. His fame as an intellectual is greater than that as Pope. He held appointments in the Portuguese Church before he was made a cardinal in 1273 and three years later elected Pope. Charles of Anjou, King of Sicily, had influenced the election of his predecessor, Adrian V, by confining the cardinals in a conclave. He did not succeed on this occasion for the proceedings were dominated by a cardinal opposed to Charles. However, this cardinal persuaded his colleagues, who divided into pro-Charles Frenchmen and anti-Charles Italians, to choose a neutral figure from Portugal. John XXI was not unfriendly toward Charles, approving his scheme to establish himself as King of Jerusalem and supporting his interests in northern Italy. John also sought to maintain the union of the Greek Church with Rome. In January 1277 he ordered an investigation into errors taught at the University of Paris, which resulted in his condemnation of 219 false doctrines. John revoked the decree on the conclave, perhaps because Charles had abused it, but his successors revived it. He died after the ceiling of his bedchamber in the papal palace of Viterbo collapsed on him.

NICHOLAS III
(Born c.1215; elected November 25, 1277; died August 22, 1280)

John Gaetano Orsini was a scion of the powerful Roman noble family. He was made a cardinal by Innocent IV in 1244 and on his election as Pope Nicholas III was the most senior figure in the college. He had played a decisive role in the election of his predecessor, John XXI. A six-month vacancy had followed the latter's death, during which the conclave had been evenly split between the French and Italian cardinals. Orsini was leader of the Italian faction, and his election in Viterbo was hastened by the rioting of the townsfolk who demanded an Italian Pope. He used his family connections to establish more direct control over Rome and papal lands in central Italy. His initial concern was to persuade Charles of Anjou to resign as senator of Rome after his ten-year term in office expired in 1278. Charles agreed, and on June 18, 1278 Nicholas issued the *Constitutio super electione senatoris urbis*, which forbade the election of any foreign potentate as senator of Rome in future and

limited tenure of office to one year. Nicholas installed his brother as senator, Charles having resigned on August 30, and also replaced Charles' men with his own relatives in other administrative posts of the Papal State. His family policy even extended to the college of cardinals where his new appointments included a nephew and another brother. He was thereby assured loyal agents, though it set a much-criticized pattern of nepotism at the papal court. Much of his reign was taken up with diplomatic schemes to reconcile Charles of Anjou, King of Sicily, and Rudolph of Habsburg, German Emperor-elect, concluding in a peace signed in May 1280 which appeared to satisfy the competing interests in Italy of both rulers and the Pope. Nicholas was also concerned that the Union of the Greek Church with Rome declared at the Second Council of Lyons (1274) was not being realized in practice. The Greek Emperor faced opposition from both his lay and clerical subjects on the issue, and was using severe measures to enforce obedience to the Union. Nicholas found his reassurances unconvincing and sent two envoys to demand strict observance of ten new conditions of the Union. The Emperor persuaded the Greek bishops to sign a declaration of obedience to Rome, but Nicholas realized from his envoys' report that the Union lacked genuine popular support. Nicholas also attempted to resolve another inherited problem, the controversy within the Franciscan movement over poverty. Some of the order lived in property-owning convents which the others considered a betrayal of their founder's ideals. Nicholas attempted to satisfy both sides by issuing the bull *Exiit qui seminat* (1279) which declared that the Pope was sole owner of all possessions of the friars and defended their pursuit of poverty as following the example of Christ. Nicholas moved the papal residence to the Vatican, adding to its palace and to St Peter's.

MARTIN IV
(Born c.1215; elected February 22, 1281; died March 28, 1285)

Born Simon of Brie, near Angers, he served as chancellor and adviser to King Louis IX of France before being appointed a cardinal in 1261. Successive Popes valued the confidence in which he was held by the French court, using him on numerous diplomatic missions to France. Simon

Above: **Martin IV** *was elected with the militant support of the French faction. His French partisanship tarnished the image of the Pope as a universal arbiter.*

promoted the candidature of King Louis' brother, Charles of Anjou, for the Sicilian throne and successfully negotiated the alliance between Charles and the papacy in 1264. Following the death of Pope Nicholas III in 1280, the conclave was again split between French and Italian factions, but Charles intervened to secure his ally Simon's election, stirring up hostility to the Orsini, the previous Pope's relatives, thus dividing the Italian party, and surrounding the papal palace at Viterbo with his troops until the cardinals confined there reached a decision. Their choice of Simon, leader of the French faction, ended a six-month vacancy. The new Pope pursued an unashamedly nationalistic policy, immediately creating four French, but only two Italian cardinals, and restoring Charles to the senatorship of Rome which Nicholas III had made him resign. Martin never resided in Rome, leaving the running of the city to Charles, and lived instead at Orvieto and Perugia. At Martin's invitation Charles reinstated his own officials in the Papal State, ejecting the Orsini with whom Nicholas III had replaced them, and sent troops to help put down revolt in papal lands near Bologna. Rebel villages responded by burning effigies of the Pope.

In 1281 he abandoned at a stroke the failing Union of the Greek Church with Rome by declaring the Greek Emperor a heretic and backing Charles' enterprise to revive Latin rule over Byzantium. While Charles was preparing this campaign, the Sicilians rose in revolt against his rule in Easter 1282. They petitioned the Pope to take their towns under his protection as free communes, but he refused, as always identifying Charles' cause with his own. This drove the rebels to obtain the support of King Peter III of Aragon, who had long had designs on the island. Martin reacted by excommunicating Peter and the rebels, proclaiming a crusade against them and declaring Peter deposed as ruler in Aragon and Sicily. Charles had to redirect his forces away from the Byzantine expedition toward the reconquest of Sicily, and both he and Martin successfully persuaded King Philip III of France, Charles' nephew, to invade Aragon and install his third son, Charles of Valois, on its throne. However, before any of these plans could be realized, Charles died in January 1285, followed in the same year by the French king, by Peter of Aragon and by Martin himself. Martin's French partisanship only succeeded in tarnishing the image of the Pope as a universal arbiter set above national politics to keep peace among princes, and in alienating public feeling in Italy and Sicily. He also provoked opposition within the Church by championing the Franciscans. In 1281, his bull *Ad fructus uberes* granted them freedom to preach and hear confession without the consent of local clergy.

HONORIUS IV
(Born 1210; elected April 2, 1285; died April 3, 1287).

James Savelli sprang from a Roman family which had already produced Pope Honorius III, his granduncle, and in whose honor he took his name as Pope. He had been made a cardinal by Urban IV and had served as an instrument of papal policy toward Charles of Anjou, being one of the cardinals sent by Clement IV to invest him with the kingdom of Sicily in 1265. He was elected a month after Martin IV's death, and was probably intended by the cardinals as a contrast to his intransigently pro-French predecessor. He made peace with the central and northern Italians, whom Martin had antagonized, and reverted to Nicholas III's policy of appointing relatives, rather than Charles' men whom Martin had preferred, to official posts in the Papal State. Nonetheless, he continued Martin's policy of supporting the restoration of Angevin rule in Sicily, overthrown by local rebels with the support of the Aragonese. Unlike Martin, he sympathized with the grievances of the rebels and attempted to appease them by issuing two bulls in 1285, in which as overlord of Sicily he guaranteed them the freedoms they had enjoyed under William II of Sicily, in particular freedom from excessive taxation, a bugbear of the Angevin regime. The rebels, however, would not return even to reformed Angevin rule. James of Aragon promised them the same freedoms and had himself crowned their king in February 1286, sending envoys to the Pope offering allegiance and seeking recognition. Honorius responded by excom- municating him and his supporters and disciplining the bishops who crowned him. Meanwhile, Charles of Anjou's heir, Charles of Salerno, was held prisoner in Aragon and was negotiating the island of Sicily away to his captors in return for his freedom and retention of southern Italy. Honorius refused to approve Charles' treaty with the Aragonese, settled in February 1287, and the island's political future was still unresolved on his death.

Above: St Louis. *An episode in the life of Louis IX of France, the crusading monarch. He and his two brothers are seen as prisoners of the Saracens: captured after his defeat in battle at Mansura in 1250, he was released on payment of an enormous ransom.*

Above: Honorius IV, *great-nephew of Honorius III, succeeded the pro-French Martin IV. He was able to mollify the central and northern Italians whom Martin had antagonized, but failed to negotiate peace in Sicily.*

NICHOLAS IV
(Born September 30, 1227; elected February 22, 1288; died April 4, 1292)

Born Jerome Maschi of Ascoli, he was the first Franciscan Pope, having entered the order as a young man and become its leader in 1274. Nicholas III made him a cardinal in 1278 and Martin IV promoted him cardinal-bishop of Palestrina in 1281. An eleven-month vacancy followed the death of his predecessor, during which the anti-French cardinals opposed election of a Pope favorable to the Angevin cause in Sicily. They and the pro-French cardinals eventually agreed on Jerome as a compromise candidate. The new Pope proved no more flexible over the issue of Sicily than his predecessors, repudiating a treaty in which the Angevins signed the island over to its Aragonese occupiers. Nicholas urged Charles of Anjou to reconquer the island, crowning him King of Sicily in 1289. In fact the fate of Sicily was being decided by negotiations between France, Aragon, and Charles over which the Pope had little true control; the island was nonetheless left open to Angevin invasion on his death.

Nicholas had more success in developing a policy on governing the Papal State, and was the first Pope to give the matter proper thought. He was also the first Pope born in the new papal lands, and thus took a keen personal interest in their administration, accepting governorship of many papal towns including his native Ascoli, which he exercised through deputies. Unlike Honorius IV or Nicholas III, he appointed few of his relatives as placemen and instead sought an alliance with one of the most powerful landed families in the Papal State, the Colonna, promoting its members to many offices. His main concern was to counter the rise of the signori, warlords who were taking over local government in the Papal State from the communes and provoking opposition, anarchy and conflict. He sold communal rights to many of those towns in the Marche where the signori maintained their strongest forces.

His prime innovation, however, was the decree *Celestis atitudo potentie* (July 18, 1289) which assigned half the papal income to the cardinals, a move that reflected the rising importance of the cardinals in papal government and gave them a more direct concern in the welfare of the Papal State. He also had a personal interest in the Franciscans, approving the third order of the movement, the lay confraternities, and regulating their dress and conduct in 1289. In the same year he sent a Franciscan mission to China, headed by Giovanni di Monte Corvino (1247–1328), which was to result in a large convert community with its own bishops.

St CELESTINE V
(Born 1215; elected July 5, 1294; abdicated December 13, 1294; died May 19, 1296)

Born Peter of Isernia, he became a Benedictine monk at Faifoli, near Benevento, in *c*.1230, but soon abandoned his monastic community to live as a hermit on Mount Morrone, where his ascetic zeal attracted many followers. In 1259 he had a church built for them on the Mount, and in 1264 they were recognized by Urban IV as an offshoot of the Benedictine order. By the 1280s there were thirty-six convents of "Celestinians", as they would later be called, patronized by the local ruler, Charles of Anjou, and others.

The circumstances of this aged hermit's election as Pope were unusual. After the death of Nicholas IV in the spring of 1292, the Italian majority in the college was divided between rival Orsini and Colonna cardinals which prevented any immediate agreement on a successor. The vacancy lasted twenty-seven months before Peter of Morrone was suggested, probably under Charles' influence, and the cardinals elected him, moved as if "by divine inspiration." They soon realized their mistake, for Celestine was totally unsuited to the administrative demands of papal office and completely under Charles' control. He appointed twelve new cardinals, all nominated by Charles, and allowed Charles to use papal revenues to fund his planned campaign against Sicily. Most of the privileges and letters of appointment issued by Celestine had to be recalled and revoked by his successor, possibly at Celestine's own request.

Recognizing his own incompetence, he discussed the possibility of resignation with the cardinals, and on December 13 freely abdicated. It was an unprecedented act, and Paris theology masters defended its legitimacy. Two Colonna cardinals supported by radical Franciscans objected, but their views won little intellectual support. Celestine's successor, Boniface VIII, fearful that the hermit might become a focus for opposition, had him held in custody at Castello di Fulmone, where

Above: Nicholas IV, *the first Franciscan Pope, improved government of the Papal State by increasing the importance of the cardinals and checking the power of local signori (warlords).*

Above: St Celestine V. *Although a holy man who had lived for years as a hermit, Celestine was unsuited to papal office. He was unable to resist the demands of his patron, Charles of Anjou, to make use of papal resources for his political ends.*

Above: Boniface VIII. *His reign marked the end of the papal ambition, initiated by Innocent III, towards universal monarchy, for he was worsted in an ideological struggle with the King of France.*

he died. It seems that he had been well treated there, but rumors soon circulated, and the English poet John Gower later gossiped that Boniface had called outside Celestine's papal bedchamber at night for him to resign, speaking through a trumpet, pretending to be the voice of God. Celestine was canonized by Clement V on May 5, 1313.

BONIFACE VIII
(Born c.1235; elected December 24, 1294; died October 11, 1303)

Benedict Caetani came from a landed family at Anagni near Rome. His reign marked the last major crisis in relations between Church and State before the Reformation and ended the dream, pursued by his predecessors from Innocent III onward, of universal papal monarchy. His conflict with the King of France has been viewed as a clash of personalities, and though Boniface was an irascible character, prone to cutting remarks and outbursts of temper, it was in essence a clash of ideologies. Boniface defended a traditional papal view of world order, in which the Pope was universal judge able to intervene in the affairs of princes. This view was totally out of step with the contemporary reality of emerging national monarchies, where a king was increasingly perceived by political theorists as a supreme and independent authority within his own kingdom; and this was a view that was challenged by princes, supported by propagandists and machineries of government to rival those of the Church as never before.

Benedict Caetani entered the Church as a young man, becoming a canon in the cathedrals of his native Anagni and, in 1260, of Todi, where his uncle was bishop. He studied canon law at Bologna probably in the early 1260s, before serving on a papal mission to France under Cardinal Simon of Brie in 1264, and another to England under Cardinal Ottobuono Fieschi in 1265. In 1281 Simon became Martin IV and made him a cardinal. In 1290 he represented Nicholas IV at the Council of Paris, defending papal rights granted to the Franciscans against the criticisms of French bishops. His part in persuading Celestine V to resign in 1294 made him enemies among the radical Franciscans and their patron, James of Colonna, and would be cited against him by political opponents. He succeeded Celestine as Pope eleven days after the latter's abdication. In a letter announcing

his election, he emphasized the papacy's role in bringing unity to Christendom, and he was to intervene in many political disputes in the name of peace. He attempted to resolve the conflict of James of Aragon and Charles of Naples over Sicily, persuading James to relinquish the island in 1295, but James reneged on his promise, and when in 1302 Charles failed to reconquer Sicily Boniface had to ratify the peace, recognizing Aragonese rule there. In 1299 he tried without success to arbitrate between England and Scotland. When Albert of Habsburg sought papal recognition of his election as German Emperor, Boniface at first refused but yielded in 1303, restating the claim that the Emperor derived his power from the Pope.

The greatest political struggle of his reign was with France, and began in 1296. He had sought peace between France and England in 1295, when they were preparing a war against each other, and it concerned him that both were levying taxes on clergy in order to finance the conflict. In 1215 Innocent III had prohibited taxes on the clergy without papal consent, but in practice, kings raised money from ecclesiastical sources during the thirteenth century with little papal disapproval, especially when the money was to support a "just war": the kings of France and England each saw their war against the other as just. Boniface decided on a fight of principle and in 1296 issued the bull *Clericis laicos*, forbidding rulers on pain of excommunication to tax clergy without papal approval. The provision of a penalty to enforce the ban was novel. King Philip the Fair of France reacted by suspending the export of treasure and currency from his kingdom, effectively depriving Boniface of much-needed revenues from the French Church. Boniface protested but became increasingly conciliatory in his letters to Philip. By 1297 he was also facing opposition closer to home. The Colonna family were jealous of the favors and lands which Boniface was granting his relatives in the Papal State. The two Colonna cardinals were in contact with Boniface's foes in France and at the Aragonese court in Sicily. One of them, James, was patron of radical Franciscans who expressed doubts on the validity of Celestine V's resignation and hence of Boniface's succession. Matters came to a head when a Colonna attacked a papal baggage train carrying treasure. Boniface summoned the Colonna cardinals, who thereupon fled to their castle of Longhezza whence they issued manifestos proclaiming

Above: Albert (Albrecht) of Habsburg. *Boniface VIII at first refused to recognize Albert as German Emperor. He did so in 1303, but maintained that the Emperor derived his power from the Pope.*

Right: Boniface VIII and St Louis. *Boniface canonized Louis IX of France (called in Italian St Ludovico) in 1297. At that time he was making conciliatory overtures to King Philip the Fair of France, grandson of Louis IX.*

Below: Philip the Fair of France *receives notice of his excommunication by Boniface VIII. Boniface died before he was able to put the measure into effect.*

Celestine's abdication illegal, and calling for a general council to judge Boniface's legitimacy as Pope. They accused him of corrupt appointments and of not consulting the cardinals, of claiming mastery over kings, and of killing Celestine as well as usurping the papal office. Boniface announced sanctions and a crusade against the Colonna. Though the cardinals backed him, he was concerned that the Colonna could win French royal support for a council and therefore made a concession to Philip on the tax issue. In the bull *Etsi de statu* he allowed Philip to raise taxes from the clergy without papal consent when the king judged that a national emergency necessitated it. *Clericis laicos* was still to apply fully to other kingdoms and in 1298 was republished in the *Liber Sextus.*

The *Liber Sextus* was a law book, incorporating conciliar legislation and judicial decisions issued by the papacy since 1234, and compiled by three experts on Church law commissioned by Boniface in 1296. It differed from earlier compilations in that many of its rulings were written specifically for it by the current Pope in order to resolve disputed points of law, and it thus came close to a modern law code. Its publication marked a high point of Boniface's reign. Another such was his announcement of the first Jubilee, or "Holy Year" in 1300. It brought thousands of pilgrims to visit the shrine-churches of Rome, drawn by an indulgence promising three years off Purgatory.

Encouraged by this success, Boniface was ready for the fresh challenge Philip of France was presenting. In 1301 Philip tried and imprisoned Bishop Bernard of Pamiers on charges of treason. This violated Church law which reserved judgment

of bishops to the Pope, and Boniface wrote a reprimand to Philip which began "Listen son ..." and went on to remind him that he was subject to the Pope, accusing him of gross abuses of ecclesiastical liberties. Boniface may have only intended this "subjection" to apply to spiritual matters, but crude forgeries of his letter circulated in France attributing to him the claim that Philip was subject to him in temporal matters also. Boniface summoned French bishops to meet in Rome to discuss the state of their Church, but Philip forbade them to go and called a rival assembly of his lay and clerical subjects at Paris to win popular support. At the assembly Philip's chief minister accused the Pope of claiming that the king's power was derived from him, when in fact it came directly from God. The nobles sent a letter calling the cardinals to support France against Boniface, but the clergy merely wrote querying his claims over France. Barely half the French bishops dared to attend his council and it accomplished little.

In November 1302, Boniface issued the bull *Unam Sanctam*, a conservative statement of Church unity and papal supremacy, declaring that obedience to the Pope was essential to salvation. It was written in highly metaphorical language and made no reference to the current political conflict, though it did claim that temporal power was subject to the spiritual, suggesting that kings were subordinate to the Pope. There was no longer hope of compromise. Philip reacted by having copies of *Unam Sanctam* burned in France and sending his new minister, Nogaret, to arrest Boniface on charges of erroneous religious beliefs, sodomy, simony, murdering Celestine, and usurping his office, which accusations had been recited before a royal council at Paris. Boniface, meanwhile, retired from Rome to his native Anagni and prepared to excommunicate Philip. Before he could do so Nogaret arrived and stormed Anagni. Boniface was seized, but Nogaret was unsure what to do with him and had to restrain a Colonna from slaying him. The townsfolk rose and put Boniface's captors to flight. Boniface himself, however, never recovered and died a month later in Rome, by this time a broken man. In 1311, Philip secured from Clement V a vindication of his, and his agents', actions as being driven by just Catholic fervor. He was also granted a posthumous trial of Boniface, at which none of the charges against him were conclusively proven.

· LES GRANDS PONTIFES ·

EXCOMMUNICATION DE PHILIPPE LE BEL.

BONIFACE·VIII·

Edition de la CHOCOLATERIE d'AIGUEBELLE (DRÔME)

B1 BENEDICT XI

(Born 1240; elected 22 October 1303; died 7 July 1304)

Niccolò Boccasino was elected in the aftermath of the assault on his predecessor, Boniface VIII, at Agnani, led by Guillaume de Nogaret, minister of Philip IV, the Fair, of France, and Sciarra Colonna, head of the powerful Roman family and kinsman to two deposed cardinals. The attack was the dramatic climax of a quarrel between Pope and king. Originally about royal rights to tax and to judge the clergy, it had escalated into a dispute about the nature of papal sovereignty and whether it included temporal jurisdiction. What was needed was a neutral candidate, who had administrative and diplomatic experience. Niccolò had been loyal to Boniface, one of two who had not deserted him at Agnani, but was not related to any of the great Italian families and so was acceptable to France. His origins were humble: he was the son of a notary from Treviso. As a Dominican, he had been the provincial for Lombardy and became master general of the Order in 1296. Boniface had used him to negotiate peace between France and England in 1297, and his elevation to the Sacred College as Cardinal-Bishop of Ostia followed the next year. As Cardinal he was sent as legate to Hungary to support the claim of Carobert of Anjou to the throne. His credentials seemed perfect. Here was someone who might be able to resolve the quarrel with France without compromising papal sovereignty.

The French were demanding the posthumous trial of Boniface by a general council and his deposition for usurpation and heresy. The extreme Franciscans, known as the Spirituals, and their allies the Colonna cardinals rejected the legitimacy of the resignation of Celestine V, the Franciscan Pope, and thus of Boniface's election. In the hope of averting the threat of a general council, Benedict adopted a conciliatory approach. He modified the severity of *Clericis laicos* (1296), by which Boniface VIII had forbidden royal taxation of the clergy. He lifted the excommunication of the two rebellious Colonna cardinals, although without reinstating them to the Sacred College. He also absolved Philip and his family from all blame for the crimes perpetrated at Agnani, and revoked Boniface's measures against France, its king and its ministers - all, that is, except Nogaret and Sciarra Colonna. The Pope summoned Nogaret to appear before him on charges of sacrilege, backing his command with

threats of excommunication, but he died before the trial could take place.

There were other problems, especially in faction-ridden Italy. Benedict was able to restore peace neither to Florence and Tuscany, nor to Rome, which he was forced to abandon for the safety of Perugia.

As a Dominican, the Pope supported the right of the mendicant friars to preach and hear confession in the parishes. This had been curtailed by Boniface's bull *Super cathedram* (1300), which Benedict revoked in *Inter cunctos* (1304). He was opposed to the Spiritual Franciscans, and imprisoned the famous theologian-turned-preacher Arnold of Villanova.

Benedict was a scholar who had lectured in theology at Milan and Venice and had written several scriptural commentaries. He was a gentle, peace-loving man, but this did not mean that he was weak. He was loved by the people, and after his death miracles occurred at his tomb in San Domenico in Perugia. He was beatified by Clement XII in 1736.

CLEMENT V

(Born c.1260; elected 5 June 1305; died 20 April 1314)

On the death of Benedict XI the cardinals at Perugia were split between those for and against Boniface VIII. The election of Bertrand de Got, archbishop of Bordeaux, ended an eleven-month deadlock. He was not a cardinal, and the hope was that he would be impartial. The son of a Gascon noble, born at Villandraut (Gironde), he had stud-

Above: A Knight Templar. *Philip IV (the Fair) of France coveted the wealth of the Templars, a crusading order. Part of the price Pope Clement V paid for Philip's abandonment of serious charges against the late Boniface VIII was papal approval of the violent dissolution of the order.*

Below: Philip IV (the Fair) *receives advice from his counselors. Pope Benedict XI had gone some way to appease Philip: Clement went much further, displaying open French bias in the appointment of cardinals, and in 1309 moving the seat of the papacy "temporarily" to Avignon.*

Above: King Edward I of England. *French-born Bertrand de Got, the future Pope Clement V, served as a royal clerk at the court of Edward I, who was also Duke of Aquitaine, and during his reign was able to perform many useful services for the English monarchy.*

November 1305. In December he created ten new cardinals, nine of them Frenchmen, some related to him, and this bias was reinforced in 1310 and 1312. He intended to return to Rome, but French pressure, political circumstances, and poor health – he probably had cancer – prevented him, and in March 1309 he settled, "temporarily", at Avignon, where the papacy was to stay, with one brief interval, for nearly seventy years.

Philip IV had two related aims – to get the military order of Knights Templars dissolved, in order to acquire their wealth, and to see Boniface VIII posthumously condemned by a general council. Proceedings against Boniface were reopened in 1310, but due to papal prevarication and political circumstances, in 1311 the accusers withdrew, agreeing to leave the matter to Clement. Philip thereafter used the threat of resuming the trial as a weapon against Clement whenever it suited him. One condition for withdrawal was almost certainly the suppression of the Templars at the Council of Vienne (1311-12). In 1307 Philip had the Templars arrested, and their false confessions of blasphemy, idolatry and sodomy, extracted by torture, were placed before the Pope. He dissolved the order, though without condemning it, in 1312: its property went to the Hospitallers. Clement also had to annul all papal acts contrary to French interests and release Guillaume de Nogaret and Sciarra Colonna from their excommunications. He also agreed to canonize Celestine V, although he did so under his private name of Pietro da Marrone, so that the validity of Celestine V's resignation, and of Boniface's subsequent election, would not be impugned.

Clement defied Philip by approving the election of Henry of Luxemburg as King of the Romans in 1309 in opposition to Charles of Valois, Philip's brother. Henry VII undertook a disastrous Italian expedition prior to his imperial coronation. This reawakened violent hostilities between Guelfs and Ghibellines. In Rome, Henry was resisted by troops of the papal vassal Robert of Anjou, king of Naples. With difficulty – the Vatican was occupied by Robert's troops – reluctant legates crowned Henry in June 1312 at St John Lateran. On his way to attack Robert of Naples, in defiance of Clement's orders, the Emperor was struck down by fever and died. Clement restated the dependence of the empire on the papacy in a controversial bull, *Pastoralis cura.*

ied canon and civil law at Orléans and Bologna and had held several canonries before becoming vicar general to his brother, the Archbishop of Lyons. He was also a royal clerk in the service of Edward I of England, Duke of Aquitaine. In 1294, already a papal chaplain, he was sent on a mission to England to dissuade Edward from going to war with France. In 1295 he became Bishop of Commignes, and in 1299 Archbishop of Bordeaux, in Edward's duchy. As Pope he performed many useful services for the English monarchy, including the annulment of the baronial measure the Confirmation of the Charters (1297). But Bertrand had even closer links with the French court, soon translated into subservience. His coronation took place at Lyons, in the presence of Philip IV, in

Right: **Robert of Anjou**
("the Wise"), *King of Naples,*
a patron of the arts, led the
Guelf (pro-papal) forces.
Nevertheless, he opposed Clement
V's endorsement of Henry of
Luxembourg as king of the
Romans in 1312, sending
troops to occupy the Vatican.

Clement increased papal taxation and provisions (appointments to benefices), adding new categories of benefice reserved for papal appointment. This sparked English protests at the Parliament of Carlisle (1307). As a scholar he founded the Universities of Perugia and Orléans; as a legist he added a collection of decretals, the Clementines, to the corpus of canon law.

JOHN XXII
(Born c.1244; elected 7 August 1316; died 4 December 1334)

Jacques Duäsne, aged seventy-two, was elected as a stopgap after a stormy two-year conclave, but defied expectations by his authoritarianism, his energy and efficiency, and by living to about ninety. Born at Cahors, of a bourgeois family, he studied law at Montpellier and Paris. After holding various ecclesiastical offices he became Bishop of Fréjus (1300), Bishop of Avignon (1310), Cardinal-Priest of San Vitale (1312), and Cardinal-Bishop of Porto (1313). He was also chancellor to Charles II of Anjou (1308) and then to Robert of Naples,

John was soon drawn into the controversy about the absolute poverty of Christ and his followers, an idea followed by the extreme Franciscans, the Spirituals. During its course he issued a series of bulls, including *Cum inter nonnullos* (1328), which declared it heretical to say that Christ and his Apostles had owned nothing. This prompted many to accuse John himself of heresy, and drove some of the Spirituals into schism. The minister general, Michael of Cesena, with William of Ockham and others, fled from Avignon to the court of Louis of Bavaria, John's enemy. As head of a vast governmental organization, the Pope could hardly say that Christ, whose earthly vicar he was, had been propertyless. John canonized Thomas Aquinas in 1323 partly for his orthodox views on property.

John considered that during an imperial vacancy, administration of the empire reverted to the papacy, to be regranted when he formally approved the election of a King of the Romans. Election by the German princes conferred no such right. In 1314 there had been a disputed election between Louis of Bavaria and Frederick of Austria. Louis triumphed over his rival, but John did not approve his election. Nevertheless, Louis appointed an imperial vicar in Italy, for which John excommunicated him. Louis replied by rejecting John's claim to con-

firm imperial elections, and declared John a heretic for his views on apostolic poverty. Supported by the Spiritual Franciscans, he went to Rome, where, in 1328, he had himself crowned Emperor by city officials, who represented all Romani (Christians), "deposed" John XXII, and appointed an anti-Pope, Nicholas V, Peter of Corbara, OFM, before being forced to leave the city. John continued to press, unsuccessfully, for Louis's abdication after his return to Germany.

John was a lawyer, and officially published Clement V's collection of canon law, the Clementines. Later a collection of his own decrees, the *Extravagantes Johannis XXII*, became part of the corpus of ecclesiastical law. As an able administrator, few curial departments escaped his reorganization. He increased the use of provisions (papal appointments), but limited the number that

Below: St Thomas Aquinas (1225-74), the Dominican philosopher and theologian, defended the right of the Church to hold property. Partly because of this defense, he was canonized in 1323 by Pope John XXII, who was under attack by opponents of the doctrine.

171

Right: Petrarch *(Francesco Petrarca) (1304-74), the great poet, lived as a boy in Avignon, seat of Pope John XXII. In manhood, he returned to the city as one of the leading intellectuals brought there by papal patronage. But later he lamented corruption at the papal court.*

DOMINVS FRANCISCHVS PETRARCHA

could be held by one person. He imposed the payment of annates, the first year's revenue of a benefice where the holder had been provided, to all countries, and reorganized the taxation system. He died leaving the papal coffers full.

When the impossibility of a move to Rome became obvious, John started to build up Avignon as an intellectual and artistic center, founding the papal library and attracting people such as Marsilius of Padua and Petrarch to the city. He promoted his nephew, who was Bishop of Avignon, to the Sacred College, and himself moved into the episcopal palace. Like Clement V, he was a nepotist, especially when appointing cardinals

John was determined to extend papal authority through missionary activity, and he established bishoprics in India, Anatolia, and Armenia. He also set up an archbishopric with six dependent sees in Sultanieh (Iran).

Towards the end of his life he aroused theological controversy by his preaching on the Beatific Vision. He maintained that the souls of the blessed would not enjoy the vision of God after death, but must wait until the Day of Judgement and the reunion of body and soul. This led to further accusations of heresy, especially by William of Ockham. In his deathbed confession John retracted the view, claiming that he had advanced it in his private capacity as a man, rather than officially as Pope.

BENEDICT XII

(Born c.1280-5; elected 20 December 1334; died 25 April 1342)

Jacques Fournier, a Cistercian of humble background, from the Toulouse area, had been a Master of Theology at Paris before becoming Abbot of Frontfroide (1311), Bishop of Pamiers (1317) and then of Mirepoix (1326). At Pamiers he had been a rigorous inquisitor of Albigensian heretics, a role immortalized through the survival of his inquisitorial register dealing with the people of Montaillou (Comté de Foix). Perhaps as a reward he was elevated to the Sacred College in 1327 as Cardinal-Priest of Santa Prisca.

Benedict was a considerable reformer of the religious orders, especially the Cistercians, Benedictines and Franciscans, and tried to impose strict observance of their rules. Among other things, he introduced measures to control wandering monks, to ensure regular visitation of houses,

to improve the training of novices and to set up houses of study in every country. His bull regulating the Benedictines, *Summi magistri* (1336), remained in force until the Reformation. He also regulated the clergy: he sent away empty handed many who flocked to Avignon hoping to acquire benefices; he limited pluralism and non-residence; he forbade the holding of benefices *in commendam* (the temporary enjoyment of revenues of a vacant benefice), and he revoked all "expectative graces" (promises of provision before benefices became vacant). He undertook reforms within the curia and was parsimonious, inflexible, and untainted by nepotism: a Pope must be "like Melchizedek, who had neither father nor mother nor kindred".

Benedict assembled a crusading force, led by Philip VI of France, but was forced to cancel the expedition when he failed to prevent war between France and England. Ostensibly at least Benedict adopted a conciliatory attitude to the usurping Emperor Louis of Bavaria, who sent several embassies to the curia. Reconciliation, however, was no guarantee that Benedict would have confirmed his election as King of the Romans. In any event, the negotiations failed, initially due to the opposition of Philip VI and Robert of Naples, then due to the alliance Louis formed with Edward III of England against France, and, when this was replaced by a French alliance, due to Louis's usurpation of papal powers: he procured the marriage of his son to the heiress of the Tyrol, although she was already married. He not only annulled her first marriage, but also issued the necessary dispensation for the second marriage to take place, because the couple were too closely related according to canon law. Benedict's refusal to lift the interdict imposed on Germany and to reconcile Louis to the curia had prompted the celebrated Declaration of Rhense in July 1338, in which the imperial electors asserted that someone elected as king of the Romans did not need papal confirmation before administering the empire. Papal coronation and conferment of the imperial title did not add to his powers. Louis himself confirmed this the next month in *Licet iuris*.

When a combination of French pressure and political unrest in Italy made a return to Rome impracticable, Benedict gave the Popes a settled home by building the papal palace, which was also to house the many departments of the curia, and he had the papal archives brought from Assisi.

Above: **John XXII**. *Although seventy-two at the time of his election, he reigned for eighteen years. He opposed the election as king of the Romans of Louis of Bavaria, who responded by setting up an antiPope, Nicholas V, at Rome.*

Above: **King Edward III of England**. *His declaration of war on France in 1337 forced Pope Benedict XII to cancel plans for a crusade led by the French king Philip VI. Edward formed a brief alliance with the Roman Emperor Louis of Bavaria.*

Above: Benedict XII, *a sound theologian and skillful administrator, undertook necessary reforms among the religious orders, especially the Benedictines, Cistercians, and Franciscans, and forbade such priestly irregularities as pluralism.*

Below: Clement VI. *Although famous for the princely splendor of his court at Avignon (he purchased the city for the papacy and made it the artistic and intellectual center of the Christian world), Clement was also noted for his toleration, charity, and chastity.*

Before his election Benedict had been a leading theologian at the curia, involved in both the Apostolic Poverty and the Beatific Vision disputes. In 1336 he issued the constitution *Benedictus Deus,* stating that the souls of the blessed enjoy the vision of God immediately after death, thus correcting the unfortunate view of John XXII. Most of his theological tracts remain unpublished.

CLEMENT VI
(Born 1291; elected 7 May 1342; died 6 December 1352)

Pierre Roger, born at Maumont, in Corrèze, entered the Benedictine monastery of La Chaise Dieu aged ten. At fifteen he was sent to the University of Paris to study arts, philosophy, theology and law. Here he excelled as a preacher and theologian, advizing the Pope and participating in a series of spectacular disputations. Such was Pierre's brilliance that he was awarded the mastership in theology, a chair, and the licence to teach at only about thirty, below the customary age. He subsequently became Abbot of Fécamp (1326), Bishop of Arras (1328), Archbishop of Sens (1329), Archbishop of Rouen (1330) and Cardinal-Priest of St Nereus and Achilleus (1338). He was also president of the Chambre des Comptes and an indispensable councillor of Philip VI.

Clement's immediate problem was the Anglo-French war. The partiality of Pope and cardinals, and their monetary and diplomatic support for France, meant that papal efforts at peacemaking, especially those of 1344, were unsuccessful, and the imposition of truces, such as Malestroit (1343) and Calais (1347), aroused English resentment. Equally resented were papal provisions. Clement claimed authority to appoint to all ecclesiastical offices and benefices, and in the first half of his pontificate provided several foreigners to English benefices. Anti-papal parliamentary protests led to legislation – the Ordinance of Provisors (1343), and the First Statute of Provisors (1351).

Clement refused to recognize Louis of Bavaria as Emperor. He engineered the election of Charles of Moravia, later King Charles I of Bohemia, to whom he gave his approval as king of the Romans in a rousing sermon at Avignon in 1346. Despite his stringent oaths of obedience, Charles proved a disappointment.

In Italy, Clement was faced with rebellion by the Archbishop of Milan, Giovanni Visconti, who occupied papal Bologna. In Naples there was turmoil under his ward, the inexperienced Queen Joanna, especially after the nocturnal murder of her husband, Prince Andrew of Hungary. In Rome there was popular revolution, led by the demagogue Cola di Rienzo, the "tribune of the people" in 1347. Elsewhere there was conflict between Hungary and Poland, between Poland and Lithuania, and between Aragon and Venice, on the one hand, and Genoa, on the other.

In the Levant, the Turks, who held Egypt, Syria and Asia Minor (excluding Cilician Armenia), had reached the Bosporus, opposite Constantinople. They threatened both the remaining Latin strongholds and Cilician Armenia, only partly loyal to Rome and threatened also by the Mamelukes. In 1344 Clement initiated a naval league, the "Holy League", which captured Smyrna (Izmir) from the Turks. This was followed by an undistinguished crusade led by Humbert, Dauphin of Vienne, in 1345. The Turks threatened Constantinople also, and gave the Byzantine Emperor and the Pope common ground for negotiations about the healing of the Schism, though these ultimately came to nothing.

Despite pressure, Clement refused to go to Rome, even for the Jubilee of 1350. He highlighted Avignon as the artistic and intellectual capital of the Christian world. He bought the city from Queen Joanna of Naples, added a spectacular extension to the papal palace and patronized writers, artists and scholars. He preached powerful sermons in consistory, many on political themes. His bull authorizing the Roman Jubilee year laid the foundations for the doctrine of Indulgences.

Clement was generous to the poor, a friend to sufferers from the plague of 1348, especially the Avignonese, and a protector of the Jews. There is no evidence of his alleged sexual misconduct.

Although he lived in splendour like a Renaissance prince, had humanist interests, and was a nepotist, Clement was not a "renaissance Pope". His expressions of the theory of papal monarchy were traditional and extreme enough to lead to a palace revolution among the cardinals. They drew up an electoral pact, imposing conditions on whoever might be elected the next Pope, limiting his exercize of authority in their favor. If implemented it would have destroyed papal sovereignty and transformed the government of the Church into an oligarchy.

INNOCENT VI
(Born 1282; elected 18 December 1352; died 12 September 1362)

The Limousin Etienne Aubert, born near Pompadour, had been a professor of law at Toulouse and chief judge of the seneschal's court there for the French king. He became Bishop of Noyon (1338), then Clermont (1340), Cardinal-Priest of St John and St Paul (1342), cardinal-bishop of Ostia (1352), and finally Grand Penitentiary at the curia and Administrator of the See of Avignon.

If the electors had hoped for a pliable pontiff in this elderly man, they were disappointed. Innocent speedily annulled the electoral pact, drawn up by them and designed to limit the exercize of papal authority in their favor, although he had conditionally subscribed to it. In July 1353 he declared it to be a violation of canon law and in diminution of the papal plenitude of power. He then set about reforming abuses at the Curia, cutting down his household and curbing the excesses of the cardinals. This was necessary since Clement VI had left an empty treasury, and the papacy faced enormous expenditure in connection with its Italian wars. At one point Innocent was reduced to selling papal silver and art treasures according to weight rather than artistic value. Like Benedict XII he tried to limit pluralism and non-residence among the clergy. He also turned his reforming zeal towards the religious orders, especially the Spiritual Franciscans, some of whom were burned at the stake, the Dominicans and the Hospitallers. Despite reforming tendences, however, Innocent was a nepotist.

From the time of John XXII the Popes had realized the necessity of recovering the Papal States in Italy (the lands where the Pope exercized temporal sovereignty) from local tyrants and returning them to the control of the Holy See. In 1353 Innocent appointed the experienced Cardinal Gil Albornoz, ex-Archbishop of Toledo, as his legate in Italy and Vicar General of the Papal States and charged him with this task. Although he managed to recover most of the territories, starting with Rome and the Patrimony of St Peter and moving gradually north to the Romagna, the Church's hold on Bologna, dominated by Bernarbo Visconti, was not completely secured. Albornoz unified the customs and laws of the different territories, and in effect forged them into the Papal State, through his celebrated Aegidian Constitutions.

Unlike previous Emperors, Charles IV had little interest in establishing his authority in Italy. He was crowned Emperor by Innocent's legate in St Peter's, on Easter Sunday 1355, and left the City immediately, as promised to Clement VI in return for confirmation of his election. But this did not mean that he subscribed to papal theories of Emperorship. In his Golden Bull of 1356, which described the election procedure, there was no mention of papal confirmation.

Innocent was unable to prevent the renewal of hostilities between England and France, leading to the Battle of Poitiers (1356) at which John II was taken prisoner by the Black Prince. The Pope helped to negotiate the Treaty of Brétigny (1360), which caused a lull in hostilities for some years. After 1356, however, a horde of unpaid mercenaries was let loose on France, forming themselves into companies of violent freebooters. On two occasions Avignon itself came under attack. The second time Pont-Saint-Esprit was seized and communications with the city were cut. The Pope fortified it with walls and battlements.

Innocent failed to reconcile Aragon and Castile. The military turmoil throughout Europe prevented him from mounting a crusade, and his negotiations to heal the Byzantine schism were unsuccessful.

B1 URBAN V
(Born 1310; elected 28 September 1362; died 19 December 1370)

Partly due to the growth of a "Limousin" party (the Roger and Aubert families) within the Curia, and opposition to it, the cardinals had to look outside the College when their elected candidate, Hugues Roger, brother of Clement VI, refused office. Guillaume de Grimoard, born at the castle of Grizac (Lozäre) of noble parents, received the tonsure at the age of twelve and studied law at Montpellier and Toulouse. He joined the Benedictines, was professed at St Victor of Marseilles, and after further study and the award of a doctorate, lectured in canon law at Montpellier and Avignon. He later became Vicar General at Clermont and Uzäs, Abbot of St Germain of Auxerre (1352) and St Victor of Marseilles (1361). He was sent as papal legate to Italy on at least four occasions. Devout, austere, but politically naive, he continued his Benedictine way of life at Avignon. He was implusively generous, not only to scholars

Above: **Innocent VI** *curbed the power of the cardinals and made economies in the papal household necessitated by the extravagant expenditure of Clement VI. Although unsuccessful in peace-making abroad, he did much towards recovering the Papal States in Italy.*

Above: **Urban V** *fulfilled one of his primary ambitions when he made a triumphal entry into Rome in 1367. The papacy's return to Italy was short-lived: Roman opposition to French cardinals, and political intrigues, forced a return to Avignon in 1370.*

Above: The Battle of Poitiers, *19 September 1356. Unhorsed, King John II of France defies his English enemies. Taken prisoner, he was released in 1360, but, unable to raise the demanded ransom, honorably returned to captivity, dying in London in 1364.*

and artists – he is said to have maintained 14,000 students at his own expense – but in his rebuilding of churches and abbeys, and the founding of universities. His reforms, which continued those of Benedict XII and Innocent VI, penalized pluralists, insisted on the holding of provincial councils, halved the rate of tenths, and restricted both the greed of court officials and the excessive luxury of the papal court.

Urban's related aims were to mount a crusade against the Turks, both to recover the Holy Land and to assist the Byzantine Empire in the hope of a reunion of East and West, and to return the papacy to Rome. The crusade declared in 1363 had little support and limited success. Urban mistakenly imagined that the free companies of unemployed mercenaries who were terrorizing France and Italy might be directed against the Turks. Peter de Lusignan of Cyprus, flushed with triumphs in Cilicia, took Alexandria in 1365, but was unable to hold it.

A condition for return to Rome was peace in Italy. In Northern Italy Cardinal Gil Albornoz continued to campaign against Bernarbo Visconti of Milan. When success was near, the Pope, misjudging the situation, relieved Albornoz of his authority and made a shameful peace with Bernarbo (February 1364). He continued to thwart the cardinal, whose final act was the formation of a successful league against the free companies in the south, which brought the peace that enabled Urban to return to Rome.

Despite the opposition of the French King and cardinals, Urban left Provence and made a triumphal entry into Rome on 16 October 1367. There he received both Charles IV, whose queen he crowned empress, and the Byzantine Emperor John V Paleologus, who renounced the schism and submitted to papal authority in the hope of securing help against the Turks. Despite this, permanent reunion was not achieved. The Pope also undertook major restoration work in the dilapidated city and tried to reform abuses among both clergy and laity. But Roman goodwill evaporated when Urban created six French cardinals, one English and only one Roman in 1368. Hostility between French and Italians, threats of invasion of the Patrimony of St Peter by Bernarbo Visconti, the intrigues of the

Romans with Perugian rebels and the renewal of war between France and England in 1369 prompted Urban to return to Avignon. Ignoring the prophetic warnings of St Bridget of Sweden that his death would result, he arrived in late September 1370. Within three months he was dead. He was beatified in 1870.

GREGORY XI
(Born 1329; elected 30 December 1370; died 27 March 1378)

Pierre Roger de Beaufort, born at Maumont, in Corräze, was the nephew of Clement VI. As such, his ascent was rapid. At eleven he became a canon of Rodez and Paris, and at nineteen Cardinal-Deacon of Santa Maria Nuova (1348). He studied law at Perugia under the great jurist Baldus de Ubaldis. He was a scholar who, like his uncle, was interested in humanism and enriched the papal library with classical and religious works. He was also pious and, despite his frail health, strong-minded. He showed his concern for the religious orders by saving the Dominican missionaries in the East from extinction and introducing constitutional reforms into the order as a whole, and by restoring discipline to the Hospitallers. His concern for the purity of the faith was shown by his campaigns against heresy in France, helped by Charles V, and in Spain, Portugal, Germany, and Sicily. At Rome in 1377 he condemned nineteen propositions from the work of the English heretic John Wyclif.

Gregory knew that neither the pacification of Italy nor the healing of the Eastern Schism could be accomplished from Avignon. In May 1372 he announced to the cardinals his intention of returning shortly to Rome. But circumstances conspired against this. The papal coffers were empty: he could afford to finance neither the journey nor his wars in Italy. The Papal State was in turmoil. Perugia had been subdued in 1371, but from 1372 to 1375 the papacy was involved in trying to destroy the ambitions of Bernarbo Visconti of Milan in Piedmont and the Romagna. Meanwhile Florence felt threatened both by the Visconti and the prospect of a revitalized Papal State if the Pope were to return to Rome. The refusal of papal officials to export grain to Tuscany during the famine of 1375 provided a pretext for Florence to unite with the surrounding powers and to incite the towns of the Papal State to rebel. In May 1376

Gregory sent Cardinal Robert of Geneva (later anti-Pope Clement VII) at the head of a force of Breton mercenaries to reconquer the papal territories. Once achieved, it was imperative that Gregory should return to rule his lands personally and to settle the war – the War of the Eight Saints – with Florence. Peace negotiations eventually took place at Sarzano through the mediation of Bernarbo Visconti, but Gregory died before they were completed.

The critical situation in the Anglo-French conflict also detained the Pope in Provence. His nuncios managed to achieve a year's truce in the spring of 1375, and he wanted to negotiate a permanent settlement. However, he was never able to realize this laudable ambition.

Gregory's relationship with England was a difficult one. The issues at stake were papal provisions (appointments to benefices) and taxation (to finance the Italian wars), the exercize of papal jurisdiction, and a series of English anti-papal statutes. Discussions were taking place about these also from 1372 to 1376.

Gregory finally set sail for Rome in September 1376, and after a lengthy and dangerous journey arrived on 17 January 1377. The atmosphere soon became threatening, due to the atrocities of Robert of Geneva's mercenaries against the town of Cesena. The cardinals begged Gregory to return to Avignon. He weakened and agreed to do so by the autumn of 1378, but he died on 27 March 1378 – a sign, some said, that his intention had displeased the Almighty.

Left: John Wyclif *(c.1329-84), an English priest, attacked papal abuses in De Domino Divino (1376). He issued the first English translation of the Bible, and spread his teachings through "worker priests" called Lollards. In 1377, Gregory XI declared his writings heretical.*

Below: Gregory XI *shared his immediate predecessors' ambitions to restore the Papal State in Italy. He entered Rome in 1377, but opposition provoked by the excesses of his military leader, Robert of Geneva, made him decide on a return to Avignon.*

Above: The Palais de Papes, Avignon. *The papal seat from 1309 to 1376, the palace at Avignon became the center of European religious and cultural life.*

Below: Urban VI. *Gregory XI died before he could return to Avignon, and Urban's election in Rome saw mob violence that may have deranged him.*

URBAN VI
(Born c.1318; elected 8 April 1378; died 15 October 1389)

The conclave which elected Bartolomeo Prignano consisted of sixteen cardinals, eleven French, four Italians, and a Spaniard. Six had been left at Avignon. The first conclave at Rome since 1303, it was held amongst popular uproar, with armed bands invading the papal palace to demand a Roman, or at least an Italian, Pope and riots induced by the fear that the papacy might return to Avignon. Representatives of the city's regions called on the evening of 7 April 1378, and rioting broke out again in the morning.

At a hurried ballot all but one of the votes were cast for Prignano, Archbishop of Bari, regent of the chancery and an acceptable alternative to another Limousin Pope, since he came from Naples but had spent many years in Avignon. Before his consent could be secured on the afternoon of the 8 April, the crowd burst in, and were calmed only with the disinformation that the elderly Roman cardinal, Tebaldeschi, had been elected. Tebaldeschi was immediately enthroned, protesting, by the mob. Twelve cardinals returned next day and confirmed the election of Prignano who was enthroned on Easter Sunday, 18 April. Notification was sent to Avignon, to the Emperor, and to the Christian princes. There were no immediate complaints about

the validity of the election, although within days notes of caution were being sounded within Rome and in diplomatic communications within Christendom.

It became disputed, partly because Urban immediately manifested aggressive intransigence, truculently denouncing the style of living of the cardinals and upholding the church's independence of secular authority. Abusive tirades were delivered against important diplomatic representatives. Urban arrogantly threatened to create enough Italian cardinals to guarantee that any proposal to return the Curia to Avignon would be thrown out. His mind is thought likely to have become paranoiacally deranged by his election.

The French cardinals withdrew gradually to Anagni, where the Curia was transferred for the summer, and considered the position. The more moderate proposed imposing co-adjutors on Urban, while the more radical proposed seizing him. On 2 August, moved more by Urban's aggressive obstinacy than by defects in electoral procedure, they declared the April election invalid, made under duress by the threat of mob violence, and on 9 August they informed the Christian world that Urban, who refused conciliation, had been deposed.

Discussions at Fondi in the kingdom of Naples in mid-September 1378, held under the protection of Queen Joanna I, rejected the immediate convocation of a council in favor of a new election on 20 September, which resulted in the appointment of Cardinal Robert of Geneva, neither French nor Italian, as Clement VII, subsequently regarded as an "antipope", officially considered never legitimately to have been endowed with the primatial jurisdiction. His coronation on 31 October inaugurated the Western schism. A massive series of depositions and hearings, notably at Rome in March and November 1379, favoring the validity of Urban's election, and at Barcelona in that May and September, repudiating it, justified serious doubts about its validity. Further hearings were conducted. They culminated in a great judicial process at Medina del Campo, south of Vallodolid, from November 1380 to May 1381, which decided in favor of Clement.

Clement was backed by France, Burgundy, Savoy, Naples, and Scotland, and, after a delay of nearly ten years, also by Aragón and Castile. Urban was recognized by England, most of Italy, and, with exceptions, by German-speaking and central Europe.

Portugal switched four times between the two allegiances. Senior prelates changed sides. Junior prelates petitioned both sides for advancement. The rival claimants strove vigorously for recognition, excommunicated each other, and went to war in the Italian peninsula. Urban was victorious near Marino on 29 April 1379 and captured Castel Sant'Angelo, forcing Clement to retreat first to Naples, and then to Avignon in June 1379. Urban had already appointed a new Curia with twenty-nine cardinals on 17 September 1378.

Thereafter his principal preoccupation was to secure the sovereignty of Naples for a nephew. In 1380 he excommunicated and deposed Joanna of Naples, replacing her with his protector, her cousin Charles of Durazzo, whom he crowned in Rome before quarrelling with him over his nephew's claims. His incapacity was such that Charles, with the connivance of six cardinals, sought to place Urban under a council of regency. Urban found out, and had six cardinals imprisoned and tortured, before being besieged by Charles and forced, after imprisonment at Nocera, to flee to Genoa where five dissident cardinals were executed.

Charles died in February 1386, and Urban moved that December to Lucca and then, in the following October, to Pisa, from where he attempted to gather an army to win back Naples, now of Clementine obedience. Forced by lack of funds to abandon his ambition, Urban retired to Rome in October 1388, where he alienated the people. He died, perhaps poisoned, the following year.

Left: St Catherine of Siena
(Caterina Benincasa) (1347-80), a Dominican mystic, was foremost among those who persuaded Gregory XI to return to Rome in 1377. Her influence was great, for her holiness had been manifested by her reception of the stigmata in 1375.

Ecclesiastically, he had extended the feast of the Visitation to the universal Church and inaugurated a holy year at thirty-three year intervals, the duration of the life of Jesus.

CLEMENT VII
(Born 1342; elected 20 September 1378; died 16 September 1394)

Retrospectively regarded as invalidly appointed, the circumstances of his election are set out above. His mother was a cousin of the French king, and he had been a diocesan administrator, a canon of Paris, then Bishop of Thérouanne, then Cambrai, before being created cardinal in 1371. He had led Gregory XI's mercenary army against Florence, and had been responsible for atrocious massacres, notably at Cesena in February 1377.

Clement was elected on the first ballot, with the concurrence of the three Italian cardinal envoys of Urban VI, who did not vote. The Curia went over to his obedience and he was backed by Joanna of Naples. When, despite considerable military strength, he was defeated by Urban VI near Marino in April 1379 and his garrison in Castel Sant'Angelo was forced to surrender, he found himself too unpopular with the people of Naples to stay. On 22 May, he left for Avignon, where he kept an efficient administration and a court lavish in luxury.

He was an able diplomat who strove hard for universal recognition, but he did not hesitate to pursue his principal ambition, his re-establishment in Rome, at the cost of allowing the domination by France of the whole Italian peninsula. Even before leaving Naples, by bulls issued at Sperlonga, he invested Louis I of Anjou, son of the French king, with much of the northern part of the Papal State, proposing a kingdom of Adria, to induce him to provide military support for his ambitions. But the expedition to conquer Naples from Charles of Durazzo foundered after Louis's death in 1384. Charles was murdered in February 1386, and the struggle was resumed by Louis II of Anjou, acclaimed King of Naples in July 1386.

Charles V of France died in 1380. His son, Charles VI, a minor born in 1368 whose personal government dated from 1388, promised to conduct Clement to Rome, and the prospect of a French papal fiefdom of Adria was reborn. In 1389 Louis d'Orléans, brother of the French king, married a member of the Milanese Visconti family, due to inherit the state of Milan. Nonetheless, Clement's run of success was halted by the death of Urban VI, resentment of whom had been the force behind defections to Clement's allegiance. Nothing came of the projected thrust to Rome, although Orléans was promised extensive papal territory, the Marches of Ancona, Romagna, Ferrara, Ravenna, Bologna, Perugia, and Todi. Clement's ambitions received a further serious setback when, in 1400, Ladislas of Sicily, son of Charles of Durazzo, ousted Louis II of Anjou from Naples, and restored the kingdom to the Roman allegiance.

Clement's expenditure had been kept high by his princely style, his wars, his diplomatic missions, his patronage, and not least by the huge indemnities needed to buy off Raymond of Turenne, the nephew of Gregory XI, whose armed bands harried and seized from 1386 to 1392 persons and property near the papal territories in Provence. Opinion hardened that the schism could be ended only by the resignation of both claimants, but that solution was acceptable to neither. Clement believed himself to be the rightful Pope, prayed for the ending of the schism, and hoped in vain that the Roman conclave would determine it by electing him Pope on the death of Urban VI.

BONIFACE IX
(Born c.1350; elected 2 November 1389; died 1 October 1404)

Little is known of the early life of the Neapolitan aristocrat, the compromise candidate first created cardinal deacon and then cardinal priest by Urban VI. The Roman cardinals had not hesitated to proceed to a conclave, and the youthful Pietro Tomacelli was an acceptable compromise candidate between a Roman and a Florentine, neither of whom could command a two-thirds majority.

Boniface re-established the allegiance of the Papal State, excommunicated and was excommunicated by his Avignon rival, Clement VII, denounced as sinful the notion of calling a general council to resolve the schism, and welcomed back to his obedience several senior ecclesiastics who had been driven to support Clement by the outrageous behaviour of Urban VI. Boniface gave full support to Ladislas of Sicily in Naples, and had him crowned king at Gaeta on 29 May 1390, so turning against Louis II of Anjou and the French. Ladislas struggled for a decade before he could enter Naples in 1400 and restore the kingdom to the Roman obedience.

In 1392 Boniface was briefly forced to retire from Rome to Perugia and Assisi, although the Romans, fearful of a removal of the papacy from Rome, swiftly re-admitted him. A plot in 1398 allowed Boniface to abolish the republic at Rome, and to have the city administered by a senate appointed by himself. He did little to end the schism beyond promising in 1390 to accord to Clement VII and his cardinals favorable treatment, if Clement renounced his claim to the papacy. On Clement's

Below: Boniface IX. *The coronation of Boniface IX, elected in 1398 as Rome's answer to the discredited Clement VII, is shown in a near-contemporary manuscript painting. Boniface re-established the allegiance of the Papal State, but did little to heal the schism, other than promising Clement and his cardinals favorable treatment if Clement renounced his claim to the papacy.*

Above: A Gentleman Hawking;
*a wall-painting in the Palais de Papes
at Avignon, begun by John XXII in
1316 and completed in 1370. Benedict
XIII, the last Pope to occupy the Palais
de Papes, was driven out by rebellious
cardinals in 1403.*

death he rejected attempts by his successor, Benedict XIII, to negotiate. He lost the allegiances of Sicily and Genoa, and retained that of the German King Wenceslas only by authorizing him to raise tithes on ecclesiastical property, and by promising to crown him Emperor if he came to Rome. When in 1400 Wenceslas was deposed in favor of Rupert, the Elector Palatine, Boniface first delayed the requested approval and then falsely claimed that he had authorized the deposition.

The extent and manner of his taxation, and of his sale of benefices and of rights to reversions, and of his extension of jubilee indulgences, and of financial substitutions for the pilgrimages involved, were universally regarded as scandalous. His principal assistant in devising these exactions was the later John XXIII, who commanded more support than either of his rivals during the period when there were three claimants to the papal throne. Boniface did receive envoys from his rival, Benedict XIII, in 1404, although he had no intention of treating his rival as an equal. At the second of two meetings in September 1404, the exchanges became violent. The condition of Boniface, ill with the stone, swiftly deteriorated, and when he died Benedict's envoys were imprisoned and released only against huge ransoms.

BENEDICT XIII
(Born c.1328; elected 28 September 1394; deposed 26 July 1417; died 23 May 1423)

On the death of Clement VII, the Avignon cardinals met in conclave and, leaving unopened letters from Charles VI advocating a postponement, proceeded to an election. All twenty-one took an oath to work, if elected, for the end of the schism, and undertaking to abdicate whenever a majority should consider it appropriate. They unanimously elected the canon lawyer, Pedro de Luna, who had taken the oath only with reluctance.

De Luna had been made a cardinal by Gregory XI, and had become a resolute supporter of Clement VII only when he became convinced of the invalidity of the election of Urban VI. It was de Luna who, as legate to the Iberian peninsula for eleven years, won Aragón, Castile, Navarre and Portugal to the Avignon obedience. Irreproachable in character and behavior, he had reformed the University of Salamanca and presided over several reforming synods. When legate to France and other powers in

1393 he favored ending the schism by the abdication of both claimants to the papacy, a solution which commanded a handsome majority in both colleges of cardinals. De Luna declared that, if elected, he would follow that route.

Once elected, however, he came to hold obstinately to the legitimacy of his claim. He remained resolutely committed to a path of negotiation in spite of the powerful pressure on him to stand down, which started with a powerful deputation from Charles VI including the Dukes of Berry and Burgundy, the king's uncles, and his brother, and continued with an Anglo-French mission in June 1397, resulting from a rapprochement between England and France, and a German one in May 1398. He now declared the abdication of a legitimate Pope sinful. No progress was made through scheming and negotiation during most of 1396, but it was only in July 1398 that the exasperated French court withdrew its obedience, and in consequence the major source of Benedict's revenues. Eighteen of the Avignon cardinals also withdrew allegiance, as did Castile, politically close to France, and Navarre.

The cardinals, at Villeneuve-lès-Avignon, had the papal palace across the river bombarded, and Benedict was virtually imprisoned from 1399 until March 1403, when he escaped in disguise into Provence. Opinion in France now swung in favor of summoning of a council. Provence returned to Benedict's obedience, as did Castile, the cardinals and, finally, France. Benedict undertook to abdicate should the Roman claimant die, resign, or be deposed. Further negotiations with Boniface IX foundered, but on the accession at Rome of Gregory XII, the two claimants agreed on 21 April 1407 to meet at Savona before 1 November. It was Gregory's fault that the meeting never took place, but in May 1408, after the assassination of Clement's strongest French supporter, the Duke of Orléans, the French court again withdrew obedience, declared neutrality, and ordered Benedict's arrest.

He escaped from Portovenere, where he had sailed when Gregory called off the Savona meeting, to Perpignan, where he now set up court. At this point, his cardinals joined with those who had seceded from Gregory XII and jointly on 29 June 1408 summoned a general council to meet in March 1409 at Pisa. Both claimants refused invitations to attend, and Benedict called his own council at Perpignan. At Pisa, both claimants were condemned and deposed on 5 June 1409, and a third Pope,

Alexander V, was elected. Benedict, his obedience reduced to Scotland, Spain and Portugal, fought on, excommunicating his opponents and the new pope.

During the Council of Constance, held from 1414 to 1417, the German King and later Emperor Sigismund went in vain to Perpignan to obtain an abdication. Benedict retired to the impregnable fortress at Peñiscola on the Valencian coast, which he proclaimed to be the true church. The Council again deposed him on 26 July 1417, but he continued to have supporters, and in 1422 created four new cardinals. He died, a nonagenarian at Peñiscola, where his crozier and chalice are still displayed.

CLEMENT VIII
(Born c.1360; elected 10 June 1423; abdicated 26 July 1429; died 28 December 1446)

On the death of Benedict XIII, the Western schism had been over for six years, and the Avignon obedience had dwindled to vanishing point. There remain, however, two successive later Avignon claimants to consider, of which the first styled himself Clement VIII. Before his death at Peñiscola, Benedict XIII had made his four cardinals promise to elect a successor, and the three available chose Gil Sanchez Muñoz, Provost of Valencia and Archpriest of Teruel. Clement did not enjoy the support of the regent of the absent Alfonso V of Aragón, but kept a miniature court on his impregnable promontory, surrounded by a royal army. He created two cardinals and other dignitaries, and excommunicated Jean Carrier, the cardinal who had been absent at his election and who, considering it invalid on account of simony, had nominated a different successor to Benedict XIII.

Alfonso V used Clement VIII as a threat to Martin V, appointed by the Council of Constance to end the schism. In August 1423 Alfonso suspended the measures taken by his regent against Clement VIII, but then counselled abdication when he had settled his differences with Martin V. Clement acquiesced, revoked on 26 July 1429 the condemnations passed by himself and Benedict XIII on Martin V, renounced his rank, and for form's sake called his cardinals into conclave so that they, too, could elect Martin V as Pope. Formally reconciled by the legate, Clement took an oath of allegiance to Martin V and, on 26 August 1429, was made Bishop of Majorca. He held this position until the time of his death.

BENEDICT XIV
(elected 12 November 1425)

When Jean Carrier, the cardinal of Benedict XIII absent from the election of his successor, Clement VIII, returned to his colleagues, he decided on the invalidity of the election of Clement VIII and proceeded to consecrate an alternative Avignon successor to him, who took the title Benedict XIV. His name was Bernard Garnier from Rodez, but that is virtually all that is known of him. A faction appears still to have been loyal to him forty years after his elevation.

INNOCENT VII
(Born c.1336; elected 17 October 1404; died 6 November 1406)

Born at Sulmona in the Abruzzi, Cosimo Gentile de' Migliorati became a professor of law at Perugia and Padua, was appointed to the Curia by Urban VI, and became papal collector of tithes in England for ten years. After being made Archbishop of Ravenna and Bologna, he was made Cardinal Priest by Boniface IX and sent as legate to restore peace between the Visconti family at Milan and the cities of Florence and Bologna. The eight cardinals available for a conclave elected him in spite of pleas from the Avignon claimant, Benedict XIII, to postpone an action which could only aggravate the schism.

Innocent's election met with resistance at Rome, and Innocent had to call on the assistance of Ladislas, King of Naples, to suppress the uprising

Above: The Life of St John *is depicted in frescoes in the saint's chapel at Avignon. Although the schism was ended by the deposal of Benedict XIII in 1417, Clement VIII and Benedict XIV continued the Avignon succession.*

Below: Innocent VII. *Opposed by Roman rebels, Innocent called on King Ladislas of Naples for protection. Ladislas's intransigence hindered his efforts towards a rapprochement with the Avignon claimant Benedict XIII.*

Above: The Castel Sant'Angelo.
When rebellion forced Innocent VII to flee Rome, Ladislas of Naples seized this stronghold. He did not withdraw until Innocent threatened excommunication.

and negotiate a settlement with the Roman people. In return he had had to guarantee to enter into no arrangement with the Avignon court which did not recognize Ladislas's title to Naples. Innocent, who had to swear to abdicate if that was necessary to end the schism, refused Benedict XIII's proposals for a meeting, no doubt partly on account of Ladislas's stipulation. Late in 1404, however, he yielded to Rupert, elected King of Germany, and convened a council of his own obedience to meet on 1 November 1405. The council was twice postponed and then abandoned, presumably because, contrary to Ladislas's conditions, he would have had to accord the safe passage requested by Benedict XIII for his envoys.

During further unrest at Rome, Innocent's nephew, in an attempt to help his uncle, instigated the murder of eleven leading citizens. The Vatican was stormed by an enraged mob, and Innocent was lucky to escape with his court to Viterbo. Ladislas consolidated his grasp on Rome and its surroundings, seizing Castel Sant'Angelo. The Romans then discovered that they preferred Innocent's rule to that of Ladislas, and called him back in March 1406. He had to excommunicate his nephew to get him to withdraw his troops, but then made him lord of Ancona and Fermo.

He reorganized the university of Rome, instituting a chair of Greek.

GREGORY XII
(Born c.1325; elected 30 November 1406; resigned 4 July 1415; died 18 October 1417)

Angelo Correr came from a noble Venetian family and had a distinguished career as Bishop of Costello, Latin Patriarch of Constantinople, Cardinal Priest of San Marco and papal secretary. Learned, austere, and octogenarian, he was elected at the conclave of fourteen cardinals because of his enthusiasm for ending the schism. All the cardinals swore, if elected, to abdicate if Benedict XIII abdicated or died, to create new cardinals only to keep numerical parity with the Avignon Curia, and within three months, to enter into negotiations with the Avignon claimant.

Gregory sent a nephew to Benedict XIII at Marseilles, and a meeting was arranged with difficulty to be held at Savona, of Avignon obedience, before 1 November 1407. Gregory now hesitated, perhaps afraid of a trap, perhaps on account of pressures from his nephews, or from Ladislas of Naples, or the Kings of Bohemia and Hungary. He did not leave Rome until August, and stayed with his Curia at Siena until January 1408, when he moved to Lucca. Ladislas was marching on Rome. The Romans appealed for aid to Benedict XIII, who had, for his part, been at Savona by the appointed date, leaving half the city for Gregory. Then France withdrew its allegiance from Benedict, and all but three of Gregory's cardinals, who were tired of delays and equivocations and angered by Gregory's appointment of four new cardinals, including two nephews, abandoned him and gathered together at Pisa in May 1408.

Gregory returned to Siena, and Benedict, fulminating against the French withdrawal of obedience, made his way to Perpignan. The cardinals joined with four Avignon cardinals at Livorno. Having decided to convene a council, they agreed on Pisa as its location only after Florence had withdrawn obedience from Gregory. The council was solemnly opened on 25 March 1409. Both claimants rejected invitations to attend, and held councils of their own. Gregory now declared that abdication involved heresy and imprisoned those who advocated it, just as Benedict had done. He enjoyed the support of Rupert of Germany and of Carlo Malatesta, lord of Rimini, but they could not influence the council, which virtually resolved itself into a trial of both claimants.

Both were deposed on 5 June and excommunicated as notorious schismatics, promoters of schism, and notorious and obdurate heretics and perjurors. Obedience was withdrawn from both, and the papacy was declared vacant. Sentence was pronounced by the Patriarch of Alexandria in the presence of the Patriarchs of Antioch and Jerusalem, and signed by almost all members of the council, including twenty-four cardinals. A new conclave opened on 15 June, agreeing on the need for a two-third majority from cardinals of each obedience. On 26 June Alexander V was unanimously elected.

Gregory opened his council at Cividale on 6 June 1409. He excommunicated Benedict XIII and Alexander, but sparse attendance forced him to abandon his council on 6 September. He fled in disguise to Gaeta, still supported by Ladislas of Naples, Hungary, Bavaria, and the German king. When Ladislas entered into a treaty with John XXIII Gregory was banished from Naples, and fled to the protection of Carlo Malatesta in Rimini.

The Council of Constance allowed Gregory to convene it, which gave it full ecumenical authority, and allowed the possibility of retrospectively reconstituting the unbroken apostolic succession on which papal jurisdiction was considered to depend. Gregory abdicated, and the council retrospectively ratified the acts of his pontificate, appointing him Cardinal Bishop of Porto and legate for life of the March of Ancona. He was to rank second in precedence after the new pontiff.

Not only the conferment of benefices during the schism, but also, and more importantly, the unbroken transmission of orders and of the episcopal jurisdiction necessary for the valid dispensation of the sacraments had been safeguarded. If the cardinals were the successors of the apostles, as was widely held in the late middle ages, there was no problem of continuity. Cardinals, who did not need to be sacramentally ordained, could be created, if necessary by a council of the Christian community powerful or universal enough to impose its will, even after a break in continuity. As successors of the apostles, they would still have the power of order, that is the ability to create priests, and all necessary jurisdiction.

But if, as modern theologians invariably argue, it is the bishops who are the successors of the apostles, then they alone can validly bestow the sacrament of order, and they must themselves have received the episcopal grade of the sacrament. In modern Catholic theology, the validity of sacerdotal orders, and therefore of the mass itself, depends on the unbroken continuity of the episcopacy's power to ordain. If it is the sacramentally ordained bishops who are the successors of apostles, then, once the continuity of validly ordained bishops had been lost, the power instituted by Christ to ordain, and therefore to pass on to successive generations the power to celebrate mass validly, could not be reconstituted.

The way in which the schism was resolved is therefore of huge importance for the theology of the church. Gregory's reservation of the legality of his pontificate implied the synod's acknowledgement that its previous sessions had not had an ecumenical character, and that Gregory's predecessors up to Urban VI had been legitimate Popes. Had Gregory not been recognized as the legitimate Pope, and not given the council ecumenical status, the council would have to be regarded as schismatic, and, according to late medieval canon law, its acts would have been simply invalid. The apostolic succession necessary for the transmission of sacerdotal powers would have been broken.

Below: Gregory XII, *an aged and austere scholar, owed his election – and subsequently his resignation – to his efforts towards resolving the schism.*

Above: Alexander V. *His election by the council of Pisa in 1409 raised the number of papal claimants to three. He was supported by France, England, Bohemia, Prussia, and most of Italy.*

Right: John Wyclif *reads the first English translation of the Bible to John of Gaunt, Duke of Lancaster, his great patron. A papal bull of 1413 again condemned Wyclif's heresies.*

Once Gregory, as legitimate pope, had conferred legality on the council, he could abdicate, and the council could appoint as pope some other validly ordained bishop. The church's leading canonists were perfectly aware in the fifteenth century that, without the resolution of the matter achieved at Constance, they would have needed to invent an ecclesiology and a sacramental theology quite different from that which actually obtained, and would more closely be defined in the sixteenth century by the Council of Trent.

ALEXANDER V
(Born c.1340; elected 26 June 1409; died 3 May 1410)

Pietro Philarghi, an orphan from northern Crete, had been cared for by the Franciscans, and joined the order. He studied at Padua, Norwich, and Oxford, taught theology in Russia, Bohemia, and Poland, and lectured in Paris, where he received his doctorate in 1381. After teaching at Pavia, he was promoted in succession to the Sees of Piacenza, Vicenza, and Novara. Archbishop of Milan and Cardinal Legate in northern Italy, he had broken with Gregory XII and played a principal role in organizing the Council of Pisa.

His election by the Council of Pisa, which he owed to France, did not end the schism, but only added a third claimant to the papal throne. France,

England, Bohemia, Prussia, and all but the south of the Italian peninsula rallied to him. He freely bestowed benefices on supporters and friends, ratified everything that the cardinals had done since 1408 and re-united the two Colleges of Cardinals. Reforms were deferred to a council to be held three years ahead. Ladislas of Naples, occupying Rome on behalf of Gregory XII, was excommunicated and Naples transferred to Louis II of Anjou, who took it in January 1410. Alexander had settled in Bologna, and delayed when, in February 1410, he was invited by the Romans to come to Rome. He died in May.

He was a scholar and a theologian, author of a commentary on the *Sentences* of Peter the Lombard, who, during his ten-month reign, gave special pastoral powers to the mendicant religious orders which by-passed the ordinary hierarchical diocesan structure of ecclesiastical jurisdiction.

JOHN XXIII
(Born ?1370; elected 17 May 1410; deposed 29 May 1415; died 22 November 1419)

Born in Naples of an impoverished noble family, Baldassare Cossa became a corsair in the war between Louis II of Anjou and Ladislas of Naples. He studied law at Bologna and was appointed archdeacon there by Boniface IX, who later made him papal treasurer, and then in 1402 Cardinal

Deacon of San Eustachio and legate to Romagna and Bologna. He is reputed to have been flagrantly libertine, seducing two hundred women during his legation, as well as being devious, grasping and unscrupulous. But he was successful as well as ruthless in raising money for the Pope and in restoring Bologna to the Papal State.

Cossa was one of the eight cardinals to break away from Gregory XII in May 1408, and with Pietro Philarghi led the movement to hold the council at Pisa with cardinals seceding from Benedict XIII. He then master-minded the proceedings there which culminated with the appointment of Philarghi as Alexander V, whom he was wrongly accused of having poisoned. He was then himself unanimously elected by the seventeen Pisan cardinals out of a mixture of simony, fear, awe, the support of Florence and Louis II of Anjou, and the need for a leader with military qualifications to wrest Rome back from Ladislas of Naples. He was recognized by France, England, and parts of Germany and the Italian peninsula.

Ladislas was defeated by Louis at Rocasecca on 19 May 1411, and John XXIII re-established himself triumphantly in Rome, dragging the standards of Ladislas and Gregory through the streets. In conformity with his election promise he summoned a reform council to meet at Rome on 1 April 1412, but it was poorly attended and its only solemn session was devoted to the condemnation of Wyclif in a bull of 2 February 1413. The council was abandoned in March 1413. John had already had the Bohemian John Hus banned in 1411, and then excommunicated in August 1412 for condemning his crusade against Ladislas.

John had however in the summer of 1412 persuaded Ladislas to withdraw support for Gregory XII, and in exchange recognized Ladislas's claim to Naples. Ladislas nonetheless forced John XXIII to abandon Rome, which he entered on 8 June 1413 and sacked. The Florentines were too frightened to admit John personally, although they gave refuge to his Curia. John was obliged to appeal for help to Sigismund, former King of Hungary and unanimously elected Emperor in June 1411. Sigismund, convinced of the need for all three claimants to withdraw, made John's agreement to a council and a hefty contribution to his purse the condition of his support, and was able on 30 October 1413 to announce a council to meet on 1 November 1414 at Constance. On 9 December John issued the bull

convoking the council. In spite of the urgent need to end the schism, the convocation of the council was a remarkable political feat achieved primarily by Sigismund. He had to juggle the situation in the camp backing Benedict XIII, in which Ferdinand of Aragón wanted to marry his second son, John, to the heiress of Naples, Joanna, sister of Ladislas, with the hostile relationships of England and France, and the uncertainties of the position of Burgundy. Ladislas suddenly died on 6 August 1414. John XXIII, who at first wanted to reconquer Rome, was persuaded to open the council on 5 November, and numbers attending quickly swelled. With no Spanish presence until 1417, the council at Constance voted by "nations", French, English, German, and the college of Cardinals. The Emperor paid homage to John on Christmas Day. John intended to have the Pisan decrees against Gregory XII and Benedict XIII enforced, and then to dissolve the council.

Forced to consent to abdicate if his rivals also did so, John fled from Constance in disguise on 20 March with a single servant, making his way to Schaffhausen, Freiburg, and the Rhine, where Burgundian knights were waiting for him. He intended his flight to disrupt the council, but Sigismund held it together, and the council passed its celebrated decrees declaring its superiority over the pope. It held its power "immediately from Christ". John was surrendered by the Burgundians at Freiburg on 27 April. Twenty out of seventy-four charges against him were dropped by the council, but he was suspended from his functions as Pope on 14 May 1415 and deposed on 29th.

He now acquiesced in the council's judgement, declared it infallible, ratified the sentence, and resigned, thereby making it difficult for subsequent generations to claim a precedent for the deposition of a Pope. Cossa was held for three years imprisoned by the elector Ludwig III of Bavaria, until he bought his freedom in 1419, when he went to Florence to make his submission to the recently appointed Martin V, who made him Cardinal Bishop of Frascati.

MARTIN V
(Born 1368; elected 11 November 1417; died 20 February 1431)

Oddo Colonna was elected at Constance under an ad hoc system demanding a two-thirds majority not

Above: Martin V *presides at an early session of the Council of Basle (Basel), 1431. He had long avoided attending such a council – and died suddenly within a few weeks of this one's prorogation.*

Above: Eugene IV *opposed the efforts of the Council of Basle to limit papal power. His bull of 18 December 1431, proclaiming its dissolution, threatened to cause a new schism.*

Right: Ranuccio il Vecchio, *a member of the Farnese family of Italian nobility, receives honors from Eugene V. Ranuccio was a military leader of the pro-papal Guelph faction.*

only of the twenty-two cardinals, but also of each of the five nations, each represented at the conclave by six elected members. Balloting was therefore not secret. The first one was held on 10 November and Colonna was elected on the next day, taking the name of the saint whose feast it was.

Colonna belonged to one of the greatest of all Roman families. His father had become a bishop and cardinal, and he had himself been chosen by Urban VI for a curial career after legal studies at Perugia. Innocent VII had made him a cardinal, and he had seceded from Gregory with the others in May 1408. He was gentle, without guile, although authoritarian in augmenting papal authority, forbidding appeals from his judgement in matters of faith. He relinquished claims to the revenues from vacant sees, and concluded concordats with Germany, France, Italy, Spain, and England. Except in England, where the statutes of Provisors checked papal nomination to vacant benefices, curtailment of papal prerogatives was restricted to five years, after which annates, the revenue from the first year of a benefice, and other dues were again called in.

Martin reconstructed the Curia with cardinals from both obediences, but undertook only a series of minor reforms. His great ambition was to return to Rome and avoid excessive dependence on Sigismund, but central Italy had passed from the control of Ladislas to that of the condottiere, or mercenary chieftain, Braccione di Montone. Martin nonetheless succeeded in leaving Constance on 16 May 1418 and in making his way through Geneva, Turin, Pavia, and Milan to Mantua. Bologna, which rose up in 1420, refused to receive him, so the route had to pass either through Pisa or Florence, which was eventually chosen, and reached through Ferrara, Ravenna, and Forlì. Martin remained in Florence for nearly a year and a half before reaching Rome on 28 September 1420.

Concessions to Joanna II of Naples, including her coronation, had secured the withdrawal of Neapolitan troops, but the control of Naples remained fragile, and Martin still had to suppress uprisings at Bologna by force in 1429. Two thirds of papal revenue came from the Papal State, and the final defeat of Braccione, who was diverting to himself revenue from the Papal State, did not occur until the Battle of l'Aquila on 2 June 1424. Martin had also to negotiate with remaining pockets of schism, to restore the city of Rome, to reconstitute

the Papal State, to organize the struggle to reimpose ecclesiastical discipline in Bohemia, and to mediate between France and England. He tried and failed to bring about a rapprochement with the Greek church, but did succeed in reestablishing order in the Papal State and vastly increasing his family's wealth by the grant of large estates. He moderated anti-Jewish feelings and activities, regulated the calendar, and held a successful jubilee year in 1423.

In accordance with Constance's decree, Martin called a council to meet at Pavia in 1423 after five years, but he did not attend, and plague forced a removal to Siena. Since pro-conciliar and anti-papal voices were prominent, the council was prorogued on grounds of scanty attendance. Martin was obliged to yield to pressure to call a council at Basle in 1431, but died suddenly of apoplexy three weeks after appointing Cardinal Cesarini its president.

EUGENE IV
(Born c.1383; elected 3 March 1341; died 23 February 1447)

Gabriele Condulmaro was elected at Rome on a wave of reaction to his predecessor's hostility to a collegiate church government. He was a nephew of Gregory XII from a Venetian bourgeois family and a canon regular who had been Bishop of Siena before being created cardinal in the controversial creation of May 1408. All the cardinals agreed to a participation of the College of Cardinals in church government, as envisaged by Constance, and also in income from the Papal State. The new Pope was to undertake the reform of the curia in head and members, to hold a general council, and not to proceed against any cardinal without the consent of the majority. The number of cardinals should not exceed twenty-four, and they should be doctors of theology or law. Creations were to require the written consent of a majority of the College.

Eugene's vindictive measures forcing the Colonna family to return former papal territories caused serious unrest in the Papal State and the Pope was forced to flee to Florence and Bologna in May 1434. Rome was restored to obedience that December, but the Pope remained mostly at Florence, the nursery of renaissance humanism, and did no return to Rome until 1443.

The council was opened at Basle on 23 July 1431, but from the beginning Eugene opposed it. On 18 December 1431, he promulgated his bull

dissolving it, calling on a new council to meet in eighteen months at Bologna. The council, appealing on 15 February 1432 to its superiority over the Pope as laid down at Constance, refused to dissolve, and, with fifteen out of twenty-one cardinals opposing the pope, issued an ultimatum on 18 December, citing Eugene to appear. At first the King of the Romans, France, England, Scotland, Castile, Burgundy, and Milan backed the council, and only Florence and Venice the Pope. Largely through the renewed intervention of the German King Sigismund, whom Eugene crowned Emperor at Rome in May 1433, a new schism was averted, and the dissolution was rescinded in humiliating terms on 15 December 1433.

The council passed measures annulling various papal dues, although only the French and the Germans were unprotected by civil authority against the levying of annates. The decisive clash came over proposals for union with the eastern church. A meeting had been agreed by Martin V, but the location caused a protracted wrangle. The council insisted on Basle, Avignon, or Savoy, while the Pope and most Greeks favored an Italian city. The council had a two-thirds majority, and, although both decisions were promulgated in Basle cathedral on 7 May 1437, only that of the majority was sealed. On 30 May Eugene nonetheless confirmed the minority decision, for which he also won the approval of the Greeks, and on 18 September transferred the council to Ferrara, where it was opened on 8 January 1438, but moved to Florence for financial reasons in January 1439. There were now two rival synods, Basle and Florence. Eugene IV excommunicated the Basle prelates, who went on to depose him.

A decree of union with the Greeks, by-passing the essential difficulty caused by the medieval insertion into the Nicene creed of the "Filioque" clause, stipulating the generation of the Holy Spirit from the Son as well as the Father, was signed on 6 July 1439. Though the decree, needed by the Greeks seeking western help against a threatened Turkish invasion, went virtually unnoticed in the east, the visit of so many Greeks to the Italian peninsula in connection with the projected agreement had a profound effect on the shape that would be taken by the western European cultural movement we call the "renaissance". The French had mostly remained at Basle, but it was Aragónese who led the movement by which Eugene was suspended on 24

· LES GRANDS PONTIFES ·

SOUMISSION de L'ANTIPAPE AMÉDÉE de SAVOIE.

Edition de la CHOCOLATERIE d'AIGUEBELLE (DRÔME)

NICOLAS V.

January 1438 and deposed for heresy on 25 June 1439. Felix V was elected there on 5 November. There had even been a rapprochement between France and the papacy, helped by the twenty-three articles of the Pragmatic Sanction of Bourges on 7 July 1438, which went far towards giving the French church autonomous administrative and financial powers. Eugene recognized the claim to Naples of Alfonso V of Aragón in 1443, thereby depriving the Basle council of its strongest support. Felix's principal advizer, Enea Silvio Piccolimini, had made his peace with Eugene in 1442 and in 1445 mediated an arrangement between him and the German King, Frederick III, which led to a concordat with the German electors in 1447, reinforcing the Mainz agreement of 1439 modelled on that with France in the preceding year. The Curia had unsuccessfully attempted in 1446 to depose the electors of Mainz and Cologne.

NICHOLAS V
(Born 15 November 1397; elected 6 March 1447; died 24 March 1455)

Orsini opposition prevented the election of another Colonna Pope by two votes, and the conclave in Rome chose Tommaso Parentucelli, Cardinal of Bologna and a physician's son, who had joined the Curia in 1426 with the Bishop of Bologna, whose oficial he was. He had recently been elevated to the sacred College because, as legate, he had helped swing the 1446 diet of Frankfurt behind Eugene IV.

He restored order in Rome and the Papal State, conquering, buying back cities, or recognising subordinate princes. The accession of the condottiore

Above: Nicholas V *receives the submission of the antipope Felix V (Amadeus VIII of Savoy), who had been elected in 1449 by the Council of Basle in opposition to Eugene IV.*

Francesco Sforza to Milan and the virtual grant of independence to Bologna left Nicholas with the Papal State restored and unharassed. He ratified Eugene's German arrangement and, in the concordat of Vienna of February 1448, wound up peacefully the now schismatic council at Basle, which went through the motions of electing him Pope, and procured the abdication of Felix V. Censures were annulled, benefices confirmed, and some of Felix's cardinals were admitted to the Roman college. In the year 1450 a successful jubilee restored the papal finances, and Nicholas sent reforming prelates to Germany and France. He crowned Frederick III Emperor in Rome.

Nicholas is best remembered for his patronage of artists, including Fra Angelico and Benozzo Gozzoli, of architects, and of scholars, and for his promotion of translations from Greek He planned to rebuild Constantine's ancient basilica, began to re-design the medieval portion of Rome, and left some 1,200 manuscripts to the Vatican library, of which he was the virtual founder. In January 1453 he had conspirators executed for planning his assassination, and, after the sack of Constantinople by the Turks on 29 May that year, vainly tried to organise a crusade against them. He unsuccessfully attempted to unify Italy, but eventually joined in the Treaty of Lodi of 9 April 1454, arranging for defense of the peninsula and establishing peace for twenty-five years between Venice, Milan, Florence, and the King of Naples and Sicily.

CALLISTUS III
(Born 31 December 1378; elected 8 April 1455; died 6 August 1458)

The election of the seventy-seven-year-old Catalan Alfonso Borgia was another result of a clash between Colonna and Orsini families. One of the candidates was the important protagonist of renaissance Platonism, Cardinal Bessarion. Borgia was a canonist whose role in settling the schism had brought him the wealthy See of Valencia, and he later brought about the reconciliation of Alfonso V with Eugene IV which caused the collapse of the Basle council. He was made a cardinal in 1444.

The whole of his brief reign was directed unsuccessfully to mounting a crusade against the Turks, for whom the Western powers were supplying armaments, and with whom the Italian city states were intriguing. He sent preachers everywhere, laid down galley keels in the Tiber, offered indulgences, and melted down silver and gold for sale. His single successes were the relief of Belgrade, under siege

*Above: **The Journey of the Magi**; a detail from a fresco cycle commissioned by Nicholas V for his private chapel in the Vatican. Among the major artists patronized by Nicholas were Fra Angelico and Benozzo Gozzoli.*

*Below: **Callistus III** devoted the whole of his brief reign to attempts to mount a crusade against the Turks. His only successes were the relief of Belgrade in 1456 and a naval victory in 1457.*

from Muhammad II in July 1456, and the defeat of the Turkish fleet in August 1457. Relations with Alfonso, who was disinclined to fight in the east, deteriorated, and the Pope refused to recognize Ferdinand I, Alfonso's illegitimate son, while bestowing on his own nephew the fiefs of Benevento and Terracina, and putting him in charge of the defense of Rome. He elevated two other nephews in their twenties to the cardinalate, in 1456 reopened the trial of Joan of Arc, who was posthumously pardoned, and again tightened measures against the Jews.

PIUS II
(Born 18 October 1405; elected 19 August 1458; died 15 August 1464)

Born at Siena of a noble, impoverished family, Enea (Aeneas) Silvio Piccolomini was a papal diplomat,

Right: Pius II, *a diplomat and scholar, poet and novelist, led a somewhat profligate life until his ordination at the age of around forty. Like Callistus III, he gave himself to fruitless attempts to organize a crusade against the Turks.*

Above: The poetic Pope. *Enea Silvio Piccolomini, the future Pope Pius II, then secretary to Felix V, is crowned poet laureate by Frederick III of Germany at Aachen cathedral. The scene is depicted in a painting by Pinturicchio.*

Above: Paul II, *nephew of Eugene IV, preferred sports and festivals to intellectual pursuits. He suspected paganism in the cult of classical authors and suppressed several educational foundations.*

who knew Europe well. He was known for his devotion to the new neo-classical learning and the brilliance of his oratory. As secretary to Felix V he wrote dialogues defending the council, and was noticed at the 1442 Diet of Frankfurt by Frederick III, King of Germany, who crowned him poet laureate. He had several illegitimate children and wrote a novel about a love affair of Frederick's chancellor and an erotic comedy, before reforming his way of life, breaking with Felix, and being reconciled with Eugene IV.

He accepted ordination only in 1446, and was made Bishop of Trieste and then Siena. When Callistus made him a cardinal in 1456, he was able considerably to augment his collection of benefices. Elected Pope at fifty-three, when he was already an invalid, he chose the name Pius after the adjective used by Virgil to describe the Aeneas of the poem. He was a prolific poet, and author also of histories, commentaries, memoirs, and discourses, but his overriding purpose was to defeat the Turks. His decision to recognize Ferdinand of Naples and to marry one of his nephews to his illegitimate daughter, brought him the support of Francesco Sforza of Milan, but alienated the French. The discovery of the alum mines at Tolfa brought him renewed financial resources.

The crusade was to be organized from Mantua, for which Pius left Rome in January 1459, stopping at Siena, Florence, and Bologna, but the congress attracted scant support. Venice, without whose help a crusade was unthinkable, had just made peace with the sultan. On his return to Rome, Pius faced strong hostility from France. On his accession in 1461 Louis XI kept a promise to annul the Pragmatic Sanction, but required the creation of two French cardinals. In practice the Sanction was reimposed by decree. A further attempt at gathering a crusading force at Ancona failed when the sick Pope died there, awaiting the arrival of the reluctantly assembled Venetian galleys. A famous, but unsent, letter to Muhammad II suggests that Pius seriously envisaged his conversion. His reign is marked by the obvious growth throughout Europe of anti-curial feeling and its spilling over into open opposition, the Pope's defensive reaction in the appointment of relatives and Sienese associates, and by a failure to implement the spirit, or even the letter of the Council of Basle in the inchoate quarrel with the new King of Bohemia in 1458, George of Podiebrad, suspected of Hussite sympathies.

PAUL II
(Born 23 February 1417; elected 30 August 1464; died 26 July 1471)

The conclave met in Rome and on the first ballot elected Peter Barbo, nephew of Eugene IV. The eighteen-point "capitulation" agreed by all the cardinals included the prosecution of the Turkish war, using the wealth provided by the alum mines, the reform of the Curia within three months, respect for decrees of Constance, and the summoning of a council within three years. The tight supervision of and participation in the government of the church by the College of Cardinals was provided for. After his election Paul II declined to be bound by the capitulation to which he had sworn to adhere.

He took orders when his uncle became Eugene IV and was promoted to cardinal at twenty-three. Of no great intellectual ability, Paul enjoyed sports, carnivals and sumptuous splendour. Although an aesthete rather than a philistine, he suspected the cult of antique authors as pagan, and distrusted the new learning, abolishing the seventy marketable posts of abbreviator created by his predecessor. The historian Bartolomeo Platina, who threatened to appeal to a council, was imprisoned and tortured. In 1468 Paul II suppressed the Roman academy.

Paul did not make crusades a priority, but provided financial support to eastern European powers. A reconciliation with the Russian church was planned, and an alliance with the Iranians against the Turks concluded. On the death of the Duke of Milan, Venice confronted a coalition of Milan, Naples and Florence, and which had been concluded at Rome in January 1467, but there followed a series of realignments of power on the peninsula, in which the authority of the papacy receded. The dispute with the King of Bohemia flared up again when Podiebrad quarrelled with his protector and the Pope's ally, the Emperor Frederick III, and with Matthias Corvinus of Hungary. The Pope excommunicated Podiebrad and pronounced his deposition in December 1466, although Podiebrad managed to maintain himself until his death in March 1471. Paul himself died unexpectedly of a stroke that July.

SIXTUS IV
(Born 21 July 1414; elected 9 August 1471; died 12 August 1484)

Grancesco della Rovere joined the Franciscans when young, studied at Bologna and Padua, was a cele-

TEMPLA DOMVM EXPOSITIS:VICOS FORA MOENIA PONTES:
VIRGINEAM TRIVII QVOD REPARARIS AQVAM.
PRISCA LICET NAVTIS STATVAS DARE COMMODA PORTVS:
ET VATICANVM CINGERE SIXTE IVGVM:
PLVS TAMEN VRBS DEBET:NAM QVAE SQVALORE LATEBAT:
CERNITVR IN CELEBRI BIBLIOTHECA LOCO.

brated preacher and theologian and was from May 1464 General of his order. He was made a cardinal on 18 September 1467. Lavish gifts and promises made him the favorite candidate of the electoral conclave. Personally ascetic, he was also determined and ruthless.

In defiance of the election capitulation, he unscrupulously advanced his relatives, sought to turn the Papal State into a secular principality, and raised two Franciscan nephews to the cardinalate within a fortnight of his election. When one of them died from his dissipations, a third nephew, Girolamo Riario, married to the illegitimate daughter of the Duke of Milan, was made a count and given the territories of Imola and Forlì. It was Girolamo who persuaded the Pope to back the 1478 Pazzi insurrection against the Medici in Florence in which Giuliano de' Medici was killed, and for which the Medici took cruel revenge. The Pope excommunicated the Medici and later laid an interdict on Florence.

Politically, the result was a confrontation between Florence, Naples, Milan, and Ferrara on one side, and the Papacy, Venice, and France on the other. Girolamo wanted a state for himself, and war broke out with complex changes of alignment in which Sixtus turned against Venice and invoked spiritual penalties against it. Papal expenditure, some incurred by the lavishness of presents to the Pope's family, increased exponentially, and the efforts used to raise money, including the reckless multiplication of curial posts, reached unprecedented levels of unscrupulousness and dubious legality. The granting of indulgences touched hitherto unknown dimensions.

The 1484 peace of Bagnolo brought an uneasy return to the status quo, and a vain attempt was made to reconvene the Council of Basle, which had never formally been closed, and to suspend the Pope until judgement could be passed on him. Sixtus found a simple and high-handed way of dealing with this problem: he renewed the ban on any appeals to a council.

Sixtus had initially been enthusiastic for a crusade, and himself equipped a fleet which had modest success. The European powers hung back. When in 1480 the Turks took Otranto on the Italian mainland, its recovery in 1482 was due more to the sultan's death than to the crusade proclaimed in 1481. In France, Louis XI continued to uphold the Pragmatic Sanction and refused to allow publi-

cation of papal decrees without royal approval. True to his Franciscan allegiance, Sixtus increased the privileges of the mendicant orders, approved the feast of the Immaculate Conception, and canonized Bonaventure, the Franciscan contemporary of Aquinas. On 1 November 1478 he authorized the Spanish monarchs to impose credal conformity in the interests of national identity by founding the inquisition, from the beginning a secular instititution. In that year he also annulled the decrees of Constance. He created thirty-four cardinals in all, of whom six were nephews, and continued to replan and rebuild Rome, building the Sistine Chapel, opening, widening, and paving streets, and building a new bridge, palaces, and churches among other public works.

INNOCENT VIII
(Born 1432; elected 29 August 1484; died 25 July 1492)

The election of Giovanni Battista Cibò, son of a Roman senator, at a three-day conclave of twenty-five cardinals, was due partly to blatantly simoniacal signed promises on the eve of his election, and partly to the management skills of his nephew, Giuliano della Rovere, on whom he was totally dependent. He had been brought up at the Neapolitan court, had several illegitimate children, now to be provided for through suitable marriages, and, after studying and taking orders, had been made successively Bishop of Savona, Bishop of Molfetta, and, in 1473, cardinal.

Ill and irresolute, Innocent kept a court of princely magnificence and laxity, deepening an insolvency only partly palliated by the creation for sale of innumerable unnecessary offices. The traditional six posts of apostolic secretary became thirty. Friendly with Venice and the Colonna, but hostile to Naples, Milan, Florence, Siena, Lucca, Spain, and the Orsini, Innocent sided with the baronial opposition to Ferdinand of Naples, who refused to pay the papal dues, threatened appeal to a council, and stirred up trouble both in the Papal State and in Hungary. Innocent had to accept an unfavorable peace in 1486. Peace with Florence was bought by the marriage of the Pope's son with the daughter of Lorenzo de' Medici, whose thirteen-year-old son was made a cardinal. Ferdinand still failed to pay dues, and in 1489 Innocent excommunicated and deposed him. There was reconciliation in 1492.

Money was so short that in 1489 Innocent agreed to keep the Ottoman sultan's fugitive son and potential rival in close captivity in the Vatican for 40,000 ducats a year, and the gift of the lance that had pierced the side of Jesus. The sultan's brother had fled to Rhodes, and the Grand Master of the knights of St John handed him over to the pope in return for elevation to the cardinalate. Innocent's death left anarchy in Rome and the Papal State.

ALEXANDER VI
(Born 1 January 1431; elected 11 August 1492; died 18 August 1503)

The voting lists in the three ballots of the conclave of twenty-five cardinals leave no doubt that the sur-prising election of the Spaniard, Rodrigo Borgia, was achieved by prodigal simony. He was the nephew of Callistus III, who piled benefices on him and in 1456 made him a cardinal. From 1457 he held the lucrative post of vice-chancellor. He led an openly scandalous life, fathering seven children whose names we know, including four by Vannozza de Cattaneis, mother of Cesare and Lucretia. It is probable that, after becoming Pope, he had two more children by the sister of the future Paul III. Lavish provision for his relatives, and especially Vannozza's children, became the Pope's principal aim in life.

France and Spain both disputed both Naples and Milan, so that political hegemony within continental Western Europe was being fought out on the Italian peninsula. Alexander, a shrewd tactician, switched allegiance to Ferdinand of Naples, and then to his son Alfonso II, whom he crowned, since the greater danger to the peninsula came from France. Giuliano della Rovere, taking refuge in France after the death of Innocent VIII, incited Charles VIII of France to invade Italy, inaugurating France's Italian wars. Alexander even sought Turkish aid. Charles travelled through France and took Naples, although Alexander, refusing to invest him with it and aiming to free the peninsula from all foreign occupation, sent Cesare as legate to crown Frederick of Aragón King of Naples in 1497.

Charles was eventually forced to retreat to France by the holy league alliance of the Pope, Venice, Milan, the Emperor, and Spain. Alexander's policy now veered against Venice, and in 1501 he agreed to a partition of Naples between French and Spanish. With French aid Cesare now proceded to subdue the largest province of the Papal State. Alexander, now totally dominated by Cesare, was envisaging the appropriation of the whole Papal State and of central Italy in the interests of the Borgia family. The most unscrupulous means were used to raise money. The cost of membership of the sacred College escalated, assassinations multiplied, and property was simply seized.

It was Alexander who, at the request of the Iberian monarchs, in 1493 created the line of demarcation between Spanish and Portuguese areas of exploration giving them control of the church in the countries they colonized. Savonarola's opposition to Alexander's anti-French policy irked the Pope as much as the puritanical denunciations of his preaching and, at first patient, Alexander finally

Below: Alexander VI *(Rodrigo Borgia), elected as a result of blatant simony, led an openly scandalous life. His many children included the notorious Cesare Borgia and his sister Lucretia.*

Above: Girolamo Savonarola,
a Dominican reformer, attacked
Alexander VI's anti-French policy and
denounced his court's debauchery.
Alexander had him executed for
heresy in 1498.

ereignty in Naples. Although Cesare Borgia, the son of Alexander VI, had re-conquered the Romagna, the territory between Venetia and Tuscany, and the papacy had recently re-emerged as an independent temporal power, Alexander, had he lived, would have had to align with either France or Spain.

Cesare Borgia had resigned the cardinalate and become a secular prince and military leader in 1497, on the death of his elder brother, John. Seriously ill at the moment of his father's death, he was persuaded to leave Rome, but the threat deriving from his power and ambition was still felt at the conclave of 16-21 September. On this occasion the form of the capitulation was solemnly modified.

The new Pope was to summon a general council within two years, and thereafter a council was to be convened at five-yearly intervals. The maximum number of cardinals was confirmed at twenty-four. Neither Julian della Rovere nor the French Archbishop of Rouen, George d'Amboise, could achieve a real majority. Francesco Todeschini-Piccolomini, the seriously gout-ridden nephew of the sister of Pius II, a professional papal diplomat whose life expectancy was not great, was elected instead.

His uncle had taken him into his household, allowed him to use the Piccolimini name and arms, arranged for his studies at Perugia, and made him Archbishop of Siena while he was still a twenty-one-year-old deacon. A few weeks later he was made a cardinal. He had been legate to the March of Ancona, been left in charge of the Papal States when the Pope went to Ancona in 1464 to lead the crusade, and had been Cardinal Protector of Engand and Germany. Paul II sent him as legate to Germany. In 1502 he founded the Libreria Piccolomini at Siena for his uncle's books, and commissioned Pinturicchio to decorate it.

Piccolomini had refused to be bribed to vote for Alexander VI and had protested at that Pope's proposed transfer of papal territories to his son. His health deteriorated after his election, and the ceremonial of his coronation on 8 October had to be curtailed. He died ten days later.

excommunicated him, and had him examined under torture and executed for heresy in 1498. He held a spectacular and profitable holy year in 1500, richly restored Castel Sant'Angelo, commissioned Michelangelo's plans for rebuilding St Peter's, and created the Borgia apartments in the Vatican. His sudden death, and the simultaneous illness of Cesare, is decreasingly often attributed to poison intended for someone else. In spite of his criminality, dissoluteness, and corruption, Alexander VI was genuinely devout.

PIUS III
(Born 1439; elected 22 September 1503; died 18 October 1503)

At the death of Alexander VI, the French, in possession of Milan, were intent on re-establishing sovereignty in Naples.

JULIUS II
(Born 5 December 1443; elected 1 November 1503; died 21 February 1513)

The reign of Julius II is controversial. Once hailed as the restorer of papal glories, and still often

Right: Pope Julius II *was largely instrumental in developing the Vatican complex into what we see today. Here he is shown discussing plans for St Peter's with Michelangelo. Much of the most powerful imagery throughout the Sistine Chapel and elsewhere is down to the patronage of Julius II who saw himself as a keen art critic, although later commentators have seen his pontificate as rather brash and self-aggrandizing.*

regarded as an early promoter of a unified Italy, the ruthless bellicosity of this Vicar of Christ elicited from the peace-loving Erasmus some of his sharpest satire, and from Guicciardini the remark that he had nothing of the priest but the dress and the name. He was certainly a wilful, coarse, and bad-tempered man.

In 1503, just as Europe's agglomerations of feudal units were coalescing into large nation states, the survival of an independent Church could seem assured only by a powerful and independent territorial base. That view was potentially capable of engendering obvious tensions with the moral values of Jesus, and is at the root of the conflicting judgements of the reign of Julius II. Nobody disputes that Julius II aimed not at the aggrandizement of himself or his family, but at the consolidation and extension of the Papal States, and nobody argues that his patronage of Michelangelo, Raphael, and Bramante failed in its attempt to reflect in outer display the dignity of the papal office. But whereas von Pastor's forty-volume history of the post-medieval papacy (English edition 1891-1953) hails Julius as its savior, modern church historians generally regard him as an embarrassment.

The Genoese Giuliano della Rovere was born near Savona to parents of modest means. His uncle, who later became Sixtus IV, had him educated by the Perugia Franciscans. On ascending the papal throne, Sixtus IV made Giuliano Bishop of Carpentras and, in the same year, a cardinal. Other benefices were amassed, and Giuliano, who, while a cardinal, had three daughters, served as legate in France, successfully mediating between the French king, Louis XI, and the Emperor Maximilian over Maximilian's Burgundian inheritance. When, in 1492, Rodrigo Borgia's bribes after the third ballot ensured his election to the papal throne, Giuliano, who had been his rival, fled to Ostia and in 1494 to France, where he advized Charles VIII, accompanied him on his campaign to conquer Naples in 1495-95, and tried in vain to get his support for a council to depose Alexander VI on grounds of the simonaical election.

He failed again to get elected in the first conclave of 1503, but with the help of prodigal bribes ensured his unanimous election at a one-day conclave on the death of Pius III. He was subsequently able to make it impossible for Cesare Borgia to stay in Rome. Within a year Julius II, having reconciled the Orsini and Colonna families and restored to

Above: King Henry VIII of England. *In 1503, Pope Julius II granted a dispensation that allowed the then Prince Henry to marry his brother's widow, Catherine of Aragón.*

empty treasuries and no doubt self-aggrandizing wars to fight, were also taking over from the church the administration of the vast feudal estates of its land-owning institutions.

Having gained his objective, Julius, still needing Venice as a bulwark against the Turks, absolved the Venetians early in 1510 and turned against the French, whom he rightly perceived to be the real danger to Italian unity. He bought Spanish support by making Naples a fiefdom of Ferdinand II of Aragón in the teeth of the French claims, and joined the Holy League with Venice and Spain. Henry VIII joined it late in 1511. In 1510-11 Julius's troops seized Modena and Mirandola, but failed to capture Ferrara and momentarily lost Bologna. Julius was nearly taken prisoner. The League's armies were severely defeated at Ravenna on Easter Sunday, 11 April 1512, but, with the help of the Swiss, had driven the French out of the peninsula by the end of that year. Parma, Piacenza, and Reggio Emilia were now absorbed into the Papal State.

Louis XII had initially retaliated by renewing the 1438 Pragmatic Sanction of Bourges, with the quasi-autonomy it gave to the French Church, and by calling on friendly cardinals to convoke a council at Pisa. Supported by Maximilian, the council met on 1 October 1511 and suspended the Pope. Pope Julius, however, had countered the French move by calling the fifth Lateran Council in July 1511 to meet at Rome on 3 May 1512. Its agenda was to deal with France, reform, and war against the Turks. This council lasted until 1517, ratifying Julius's bull of 14 January 1505, which, probably out of genuine compunction, nullified papal elections achieved by simony.

Europe was seriously fighting for its future. The Pope wanted to keep the great powers out of the Italian peninsula, whose control was now desired by each of France, Spain, and the Emperor. In 1508 Maximilian had himself designated "Roman Emperor-elect". He wanted to unite the ecclesiastical income from the German-speaking empire with sovereignty over the Italian provinces, and appears in 1511 to have contemplated a German church, either on the French model or, if necessary, by schism. When Julius became seriously ill in that year, Maximilian considered having himself made a papal coadjutor, whether of the Pope or of an antipope, or even of having himself elected to the papacy. After Julius's recovery it was Spanish diplo-

them their castles, had allied with France, the Swiss, and the Emperor Maximilian, and had won back from Venice all of the Romagna occupied in 1503 except Rimini and Faenza. In 1506, leading his army in full armour, he won back from their tyrant occupiers Perugia and Bologna.

Then in 1509 he joined the League of Cambrai formed by France, the Emperor, and Spain, and put Venice under interdict on 27 April. French troops defeated Venice so badly at the battle of Agnadello on 14 May, that she was forced to return Rimini and Faenza to the Pope. She also had to surrender taxation rights over the clergy and the lucrative control over ecclesiastical appointments, for centuries still to be the subject of negotiations between the papacy, which conferred the necessary spiritual authority, and the new nation states, which, with

macy which made him switch allegiance to the Lateran Council at its third session.

Julius was conscientious in carrying out his administrative duties. He established the first south American bishoprics, and sent missionaries to the colonized parts of Africa and India. In 1503 he issued the dispensation for the future Henry VIII to marry his brother's widow, Catherine of Aragón. The dispensation was certainly valid although it was later argued, when Henry wanted to marry Anne Boleyn, that such a dispensation infringed divine law laid down in the Old Testament. Canon law faculties later split over the issue precisely in accordance with their nation's political allegiances.

Julius also aspired virtually to rebuild Rome, replacing the old St Peter's, reconstructing the congested business quarter over the river, the Banchi, building a new bridge just downstream from the Ponte Sant' Angelo to be continued by a straight Via Giulia running south, parallel to the river, with another road on the other side of the river linking the two medieval quarters of Trastevere and Borgo. The design was Bramante's, and was part of the Pope's plan to take over what had been the functions of the city commune.

Julius II commissioned Bramante to do much else for him, including the rebuilding of St Peter's, a scheme quickly reduced to an adaptation of the Constantinian basilica. The Pope attended the laying of the foundation stone on 28 April 1506. He also commissioned Raphael to paint mural frescoes in the Vatican, and Michelangelo to decorate the ceiling of the Sistine Chapel and to create forty figures intended to decorate the Pope's tomb. The money for the new St Peter's was raised from indulgences, and Julius, having inherited an empty treasury, left it overflowing. He died of fever in February 1513.

LEO X

(Born 11 December 1475; elected 11 March 1513; died 1 December 1521)

As a result of Pope Julius II's determination to stamp out simony, the election of his successor – the thirty-seven-year-old Giovanni de' Medici – was a straightforward contest between older and younger generations. The Pisan cardinals, who had been deposed by Julius, had been excluded, and the conclave lasted eight days. The new Pope was ordained priest on 15 March, consecrated bishop

two days later, and was enthroned as Pope, only two days after that.

Giovanni was the second son of Lorenzo and head of the family which was allowed in 1512 to return to Florence, of which he then became effective ruler, governing vicariously through his younger brother even during his pontificate. He had been destined for the church, was tonsured at seven, and made a cardinal deacon *in petto* at thirteen. After studying theology and canon law, he returned to Florence, was exiled with his brother as a result of the French campaign in 1494, visited France, the Low Countries, and the empire, and returned to Rome until sent as legate to Bologna in 1511. He led a papal army against Florence when his native city declared itself for the Pisan cardinals, was cap-

Below: **Leo X,** *the first Medici Pope, as portrayed by Raphael in 1517-18. The attendant cardinals are his cousins Luigi de' Rosso and Giulio de' Medici (later Pope Clement VII).*

tured at Ravenna in April 1512, escaped, and finally regained control of Florence in a bloodless coup on 14 September 1512.

His policy largely concerned the protection of Florentine interests and the advancement of his family. In 1513 he reluctantly allied with Maximilian, Spain, and England, in an attempt to keep the French, allied to Venice, out of Lombardy. After defeat at Novara, Louis XII withdrew support from the cardinals at Pisa, but when his successor, François I, reconquered Milan at Marignano in September 1515, Leo met him at Bologna, agreeing a settlement by which the papacy gave up Parma and Piacenza, but the Medici retained Florence.

Both Pope and king had great difficulty in getting the Bologna concordat accepted by their own sides, but in return for abrogation of the Pragmatic Sanction, the French king received the revenue-generating right to nominate to all major French benefices. It was part of the inevitable process by which ecclesiastical revenue was necessarily channelled to the new nation states, all of which were hovering on the brink of the schisms which they threatened in an effort to restrict the outflow of revenue to Rome.

Leo closed the fifth Lateran Council on 16 March 1517, after it had ended the Pisan schism, ratified the concordat with France, confirmed the censorship of books introduced by Alexander VI, defined the individuality of the human soul, and imposed a tithe for war against the Turks. In France, the tithe was used to fund the Italian wars. Leo also continued to promote family interests, by making his cousin, later Clement VII, Archbishop of Florence, and by attempting to carve a kingdom out of central Italy for his younger brother, Giuliano. When Giuliano died in 1516, Leo, in a financially and politically disastrous war which left the Florentine historian Guiccardini aghast, imposed his nephew, Lorenzo, to whom Machiavelli dedicated *The Prince*, as Duke of Urbino. Lorenzo's daughter was the Catherine de' Medici who was to be married to Henry II of France. Then in 1517 Leo uncovered a conspiracy among disaffected cardinals to poison him. He had their leader executed, had several others imprisoned and heavily fined, and created thirty-one new cardinals on 1 July 1517.

The future of Europe was again in balance on the death of Maximilian. Prodigious sums were spent on bribing and then threatening the seven electors, although Maximilian's wealth and determination were always likely to ensure the election of his grandson, already King Charles I of Spain and ruler of the Low Countries, Franche-Comté, and Naples. The election of the Spanish king threatened total domination of Europe by the Habsburgs, and, when Frederick of Saxony would not stand, Leo at first backed the French king, although also treating with Charles I of Spain. Once he was elected Emperor as Charles V on 28 June 1519, Leo concluded an anti-French alliance with him, leaving Wolsey's England to balance French power against the Habsburgs.

Leo had repurchased expropriated Medici property with papal funds and expended huge amounts on the Urbino war, the papal court, and the Pope's artistic patronage. He immensely increased the sale of offices, pawned furniture and plate, and renewed the indulgence decreed by Julius II for the new St Peter's, not daring to send commissioners to France, Spain, or England, but supporting the Fugger loan with which Albert of Mainz bought himself into the archbishopric and electorship. The Pope allowed the Fugger agents to recoup the loan by retaining at the back of the church half the revenue from preaching the indulgence. There was strong German feeling against the collection for Rome of German money, and it was the preaching of this indulgence which moved Luther to contest the doctrinal justification for it, offering in 1517 to dispute his famous list of ninety-five theses.

Leo had been alerted to the danger of heresy when the Cologne scholastics had denounced the teaching of Reuchlin, a leading advocate of Greek and especially Hebrew studies. On hearing the gist of Luther's theses he instructed his order to silence him. Luther offered an explanation, was cited to Rome, and finally met the papal legate, Cardinal Cajetan at Augsburg in October 1518. Leo tried to enlist support from Frederick of Saxony, and a debate took place at Leipzig in the summer of 1519 between Johannes Eck, a professor of theology at Ingolstadt, and Luther, in which Luther contested both the divine institution of the papacy, considered offensive but not necessarily heretical, and the infallibility of general councils, which enabled Eck to claim victory.

Leo published the bull *Exsurge Domine* on 15 June 1520, condemning Luther on forty-one counts, but not as a heretic. Luther's works became more radical that autumn, and on 10 December 1520 he tossed a copy of the bull into a bonfire of papal documents. Leo reacted by excommunicating him on 3

Above: Martin Luther. *Leo X's attempt to raise revenue in Germany by the preaching of an indulgence called forth a determined attack by Luther on its doctrinal justification.*

Above: Frontispiece of Exsurge Domine, *Leo X's bull against Luther published on 15 June 1520. It condemned him on forty-one counts, but did not declare him to be a heretic.*

Above: A bonfire at Wittenberg.

Luther's public response to Leo's bull against him was to burn a copy of it on a bonfire fueled by other papal documents, on 10 December 1520.

January 1521. On 11 October of that year he bestowed on Henry VIII the title of "Defender of the Faith" for his book on the seven sacraments against Luther. Luther retired to the Wartburg, and the schism itself started in Denmark, where Leo had been using the rich benefices to reward members of his curia, and where Christian II now founded a state church, maintained even after his absolution by a new nuncio.

Leo undoubtedly misjudged the seriousness of what was happening, and was preoccupied by Medici concerns. The deaths of his nephew Lorenzo and of his French wife facilitated the alliance with Charles V of 1521. The French were to be driven from the peninsula, Parma and Piacenza were to be restored to papal control, and the Emperor was to protect both Florence and the Church in exchange for being crowned, being invested with Naples, and being supported against Venice. Pope Leo lived to

see the French driven from Milan on 19 November 1521, but was to die suddenly of malaria on 1 December. He had been a serious patron of learning, had established the first Greek printing press in Rome, had surrounded himself with scholars in the new learning, had vastly augmented the size and brilliance of the University of Romes, and had been patron to Raphael, whom he made custodian of classical antiquities.

ADRIAN VI
(Born 2 March 1459; elected 9 January 1522; died 14 September 1523)

The conclave, in which thirty-six Italian and three other cardinals took part and in which Wolsey was a candidate, unexpectedly elected the absent Adrian Florensz Dedal on 9 January 1522. Born in Utrecht and son of a carpenter, he had been raised by his

Above: Adrian VI, *pious and ascetic, had two principal aims: to reform the administration of the Church; and to unite Europe in resistance to the expanding Turkish empire.*

Left: The Siege of Rhodes. *The city's Christian defenders, the Knights Hospitalers of St John, battle to repel a Turkish assault. Rhodes fell in December 1522, following a six-month siege.*

widowed mother with the Brethren of the Common Life, rising to become a Professor of Theology at Louvain. After being chancellor, he was appointed tutor to the seven-year-old future Charles V in 1507. From 1515 counsellor of Margaret, the regent, Dedal was sent to Spain to ensure the succession of his charge. On the death, in 1516, of Ferdinand the Catholic, King of Spain (also known as Ferdinand II of Aragón; Ferdinand V of Castile and Ferdinand II of Naples), Dedal had been co-regent with Cardinal Ximénes until Charles could take over in 1517, when he was seventeen. Dedal had thereupon become Bishop of Tortosa, inquisitor for Aragón and Navarre, then also for Castile and León, having in in 1517 been made Cardinal of Utrecht at the request of Charles.

Dedal was unacceptable to the Castilians, who rebelled in 1520 when Charles returned to the empire. The rebellion was contained, and in late August 1522 Adrian sailed for Rome, attempting to emphasize his independence of both France and the empire. He was ascetic, pious, and regarded the developing schisms as the result of a failure to reform the church's administration. His other principal aim was to unite Europe against the Turks, who had taken Belgrade, were threatening Hungary, and were besieging Rhodes. The Curia did not take well to the change in papal style deriving from Adrian's devout asceticism, his abolition of offices, and his withdrawal of patronage. Rome, in addition, was enduring a visitation of the plague, so that few senior administrators remained in the city.

Adrian did stop the haemorrhage of money from Germany, allowing it to be retained for defense against the Turks. Represented by Francesco Chieregati at the Diet of Nürnberg in November 1522, the Pope insisted on banning Luther's teachings, but achieved very little except a call for a council backed by Pope and Emperor, which should be held in a German city. He failed to lure Erasmus to Rome, disappointed the Emperor by refusing to ally with him against France, and failed, in spite of conniving at an uprising against the Emperor in Sicily, to gain the trust of the French. Francis I staunched the flow of money still going to Rome and prepared to invade Lombardy, and Adrian entered on 3 August 1523 into a defensive alliance with the Emperor, Henry VIII, Ferdinand, Archduke of Austria, and with Milan, Genoa, Florence, Siena, and Lucca. He died six weeks later, on 14 September.

CLEMENT VII
(Born 26 May 1479; elected 19 November 1523; died 25 September 1534)

Giulio de' Medici was the candidate favored by Charles V, who emerged successful after a fifty-day conclave. The illegitimate son of Giuliano, he was brought up by his uncle, Lorenzo. In 1517 his cousin, Leo X, made him Archbishop of Florence and cardinal, ignoring the impediment of illegitimacy. From 1519 he governed Florence, and was a principal papal diplomat under both Leo X and Adrian VI. Hardworking but indecisive, he remained first of all a Medici. He worked to

Above: **Clement VII** *was more successful as a patron of the arts, in the Medici tradition, than as a statesman. His political ineptitude led to the sack of Rome by imperial forces in 1527.*

secure Florence and the Papal State, and to defend Europe against the Turks, but he did not understand how deep-seated was the feeling that underpinned the schisms.

He repudiated the final defensive alliance of Adrian VI, and allied first with France and Venice. The rout of the French at Pavia in 1525 forced him to switch sides, but in May 1526 he changed again, joining the league of Cognac with France, Milan, Florence, and Venice to prevent the Habsburg hegemony from developing further. The result was the imperial attack on the peninsula and the sack of Rome in May 1527 by the unpaid imperial soldiers. Clement locked himself into the Castel Sant'Angelo, but was forced to surrender and for six months was imprisoned. His release in December 1527 cost a huge indemnity and the surrender of important Italian cities, and for a period after his release Clement lived away from the ruined city, first at Orvieto, and then at Viterbo.

In 1529 Clement made common cause with the Emperor to act against schism in the empire and against the Turks, now threatening Vienna, and to restore Medici rule in Florence. In return Clement crowned Charles V at Bologna. It was the last time a Pope was to crown an Emperor. He also covered his position by marrying his twelve-year-old grandniece Catherine to the fifteen-year-old second son of Francis I of France in October 1533, arriving in Marseilles harbour with sixty ships and entering the city accompanied by fourteen cardinals on mules.

Clement presided over the spread of Catholicism in Mexico and South America, but politically he had dithered with regard to the schisms on imperial territory, in Scandinavia, and in the Swiss Stände, fail-

ing to call the council that was needed, and unnecessarily about ratifying the dispensation Julius II had given Henry VIII to marry Catherine of Aragón, niece of Charles V, causing Henry to lose patience and take England into schism. Clement excommunicated him on 11 July 1533, although the sentence was suspended. He was a Medici, a patron of scholars and artists, of Guicciardini and Macchiavelli, of Cellini, Raphael, and Michelangelo, from whom he commissioned *The Last Judgement* in the Sistine Chapel.

PAUL III

(Born 29 February 1468; elected 13 October 1534; died 10 November 1549)

Alessandro Farnese, brother of the mistress of Alexander VI, came from a condottiere family in the

Right: The Council of Trent.
*Stemming from a commission set up by
Paul III in 1536 to investigate the
Church's problems, the great reforming
council sat for eighteen years
(1545-63).*

Below: King Francis I of France
*meets with Emperor Charles V. The two
had been rivals for the imperial throne,
and Paul III failed to persuade them to
act together against the Turkish threat.*

Viterbo region, and was educated at Rome,
Florence, and Pisa. Alexander VI made him treasurer in 1492 and cardinal deacon in 1493. He took
seriously his duties as bishop when given the See of
Parma in 1509, and to implement the new reform
decrees of the Lateran Council in 1513 broke with
the mistress who had borne him three sons and a
daughter. Ordained priest in June 1519, he was
unanimously elected Pope on 13 October 1534 after
a conclave lasting two days.

He is known for his patronage of writers, scholars, and artists, for the beginning of the Palazzo
Farnese to run along one side of Rome's first perfect
renaissance square, for the nepotism which made
two grandsons cardinals at the age of fourteen and
sixteen, for the promotion above all of his family
interests, and for the restoration of the carnival and
high living in Rome. More historically important
are the appointments to the College of Cardinals,
like those of Contarini, Caraffa, and Pole, which
might have healed the schism, and the reduction in
expenditure on the College.

In 1536 Paul appointed the commission to
report on existing ills within the church which produced in March 1537 the important report which
was to be the basis for the reformatory plans of the
Council of Trent. He also sought to convoke a
general council, first at Mantua in May 1537 and
then at Vicenza in 1538, but was foiled by Francis
I and then Charles V. He approved the constitutions
of the Jesuits in 1540, encouraged the reform and
foundation of other religious orders, and instituted
the censorship of books, and the Holy Office for the
repression of heresy.

The political situation finally made possible the
convocation of the Council at Trent on 13
December 1545. It was not the general council of
Christians desired by the Protestants, and it did
not confine itself to matters of reform and discipline, as the Emperor wanted. Its doctrinal decrees
were not to settle all the outstanding major issues,
but were intransigently anti-Protestant. The
Council had to be suspended when the Emperor,
whose relationship with Paul had become tense,
refused consent for its transfer in March 1547 to
Bologna, where the Pope could better control its
proceedings. The Council split, and was suspended
in 1549. In August 1535 the Pope formally
imposed the suspended excommunication of Henry
VIII, putting England under interdict.

He had failed to unite Charles V and François I
against the Turkish threat, and, although he supported anti-Protestant measures in France and the
Catholic league's war against Protestants in the

Right: Emperor Charles V *(also, as Charles I, King of Spain) (1500-58). From the time of his accession to the imperial throne in 1520, Charles was a major factor in the affairs of the papacy. His support ensured the election of Clement VII in 1523. His strained relations with Paul III contributed to the rift in and temporary suspension of the council of Trent in 1549, but he failed in his opposition to the election of the council's co-president, the jurist Giovanni Maria Ciocchi del Monte, as Pope Julius III in 1550.*

Below: Julius III. *Although inclined to idleness and luxurious living, Julius made serious attempts to regain the allegiance of the German Church, following England's return to the fold in 1553.*

empire, his relationship with the Emperor precluded the achievement of any permanent political or religious success. In 1545 he gave Parma and Piacenza, belonging to the church, to his son Pier Luigi, but when his subjects assassinated Pier Luigi in 1549, the Emperor claimed the duchies for his own son-in-law, Ottavio, the Pope's grandson. Paul finally ceded Parma to him.

JULIUS III
(Born 10 September 1487; elected 8 February 1550; died 23 March 1555)

Deadlock between pro-French and pro-imperial factions resulted in a ten-week conclave in which the English Reginald Pole missed election by a single vote. Finally, in spite of the hostility of Charles V to the co-president of the Council of Trent responsible for the transfer to Bologna, the jurist Giovanni Maria Ciocchi del Monte was chosen. He had been taken hostage during the sack of Rome, been chamberlain to Julius II whose name he took, had succeeded his uncle as Archbishop of Siponto, been Bishop of Pavia, twice governor of Rome, and Vice-Legate at Bologna before becoming a cardinal priest in December 1536, and Cardinal Bishop of Palestrina in 1543.

Disinclined to the imperial side, Julius none the less restored the full Council to Trent in 1551. German Protestant estates were admitted to some of the sessions. Having originally deferred to his predecessor's dying wish to cede Parma to his grandson, Julius finally also took the imperial side against Ottavio Farnese, who was supported by the French in refusing to restore Parma to the empire. When the papal and imperial armies failed to defeat the French, and the German princes revolted against the Emperor in 1552, Julius was obliged to suspend the council again, and to restore Parma to Ottavio.

From this point Julius gave up serious management of affairs, and instead built himself the luxurious villa Giulio outside Rome's Porta del Popolo, where he turned to entertainments and banquets, and indulged generally in a grand style of living. The papal finances were in a ruinous condition, and the naturally indolent Pope had scandalously adopted as his brother a fifteen-year-old boy, Innocenzo, whom he made a cardinal. He did sporadically attempt to mediate between Charles V and Henry II of France and carry through piecemeal reforms to control pluralism and restore monastic discipline, and encouraged the Jesuits to found the Germanicum for training secular priests to work in their own countries. He also had serious missionary interests, and saw England return to Roman allegiance on the accession of Mary on 6 July 1553. At the request of Charles V, he sent Cardinal Morone to the Diet of Augsburg in 1555 in the hope of inducing the German Church to follow the English example. He appointed Palestrina choirmaster of his Capella Giulia and Michelangelo as chief architect of St Peter's.

MARCELLUS II
(Born 6 May 1501; elected 9 April 1555; died 1 May 1555)

Marcello Cervini emerged as a reforming Pope from a conclave in which French and imperialist factions were equally matched. Son of a curial official, mathematician and Greek scholar, he completed the reform of the calendar begun by his father. Paul III made him a protonotary apostolic and tutor to his nephew. He was appointed successively to a number of Sees, became a cardinal priest on 10 December 1539, and was used as a papal diplomat, becoming legate to the imperial court and a co-president of the Council of Trent. In 1548 Marcellus was entrusted with the reorganization of the Vatican library, but his outspoken criticisms of Pope Julius III made it necessary for him to retire to his See at Gubbio.

On his election, he threw himself into a radical program of administrative reform and economy, but died of a stroke after twenty-two days. Palestrina's *Missa Papae Marcelli* was written in response to his complaints about the Good Friday chants.

PAUL IV
(Born 28 June 1476; elected 23 May 1555; died 18 August 1559)

The conclave, which lasted nine days, worked under similar constraints to its immediate predecessor, and produced a result similarly displeasing to the Emperor. Giampietro Caraffa came from a noble Neapolitan family, learnt Greek and Hebrew, and was quickly advanced by his uncle Oliviero, on whom Alexander VI had relied. He was Legate of Leo X to Henry VIII, Nuncio in Flanders and Spain, and Archbishop of Brindisi. He was ascetic, devout, rigorous, bad-tempered, and reform-minded, with a deep distrust of Spain, an illiberal disposition, and a repressive attitude towards heterodoxy. As Pope he was to be an autocratic believer in papal supremacy, narrow-minded, harsh, and intolerant as a reformer. He did, however, institute a reform of the divine office, the prayers said by priests and religious orders, and root out some of the grosser abuses in ecclesiastical life.

On returning to Rome, he renounced his bishoprics in 1524 and, with Cajetan, founded the Theatines, a religious order dedicated to poverty and the apostolic way of life. Both at Venice from 1527 and at Rome after his cardinalate in December 1536, he led the reform party. Archbishop of Naples from 1549, Dean of the College of Cardinals from 1553, and Head of the reactivated Inquisition from 1553, he was seventy-nine when elected Pope. He immediately allied with the French to make war on Spain and was defeated in 1557. He denounced the 1555 peace of Augsburg as a pact with heresy, refused to acknowledge the 1555 abdication of Charles V or the 1558 election of Ferdinand, and sought to impose terms on Elizabeth of England which were bound to drive England into schism again.

He was also a nepotist, who made his worthless nephew Carlo a cardinal and invested other relatives with the duchies of Paliano and Montebello, and others with Roman offices of which he later also deprived them when disappointed by their behavior. He preferred to work without the constraints of conciliar decision, and attempted to replace the sus-

pended Council of Trent with a reform commission. He had the innocent Cardinal Morone imprisoned on suspicion of heresy, removed his legatine powers in England from Reginald Pole whom he wanted to try in Rome for heresy, and used the Inquisition, whose sessions he attended, to promulgate the index of forbidden books in 1557 (revised 1559). Jews were for the first time confined to ghettos and forced to wear distinctive headgear.

On his death, the Romans toppled his statue and opened the Inquisition's prisons.

Above: Paul IV *delivers a statute. This elderly ascetic was far from liberal, as may be judged from his use of the Inquisition to promulgate the index of forbidden books in 1557.*

PIUS IV
(Born 31 March 1499; elected 25 December 1559; died 9 December 1565)

Giovanni Angelo Medici, unrelated to the Florentine family, was elected after a conclave of nearly four months, when a third faction led by

Above: Pius IV *canceled a number of the more illiberal measures of Paul IV. The greatest achievement of his papacy was the reconvening of the council of Trent in January 1562.*

Right: St Carlo Borromeo *(1538-84) was the nephew of Pius IV, who appointed him Archbishop of Milan. His work for the reformation of the Church earned him canonization in 1610.*

Cardinal Caraffa broke the deadlock between France and the empire. He came from Milan, studied medicine, then law, and became an administrator in the Papal State, in 1542-43 commissioner with the papal forces in Hungary and Transylvania, and Vice-Legate to Bologna. He had three illegitimate children, and an elder brother who married into the Pope's family. In 1545 he was made Archbishop of Ragusa, and, in 1549, a cardinal. He had no sympathy for Paul IV's hatred of Spain, and in 1558 withdrew from Rome.

Affable and convivial, Pius canceled some of his predecessor's repressive measures, releasing Cardinal Morone, restricting the Inquisition's powers and revising the index of prohibited books. Relations with Philip II of Spain and the new Emperor became cordial, although Philip's arrogance later drove Pius closer to the French, and vacant nunciatures were filled in Vienna, Venice, and Florence. In response to popular animosity, Pius had two nephews of Paul IV, Cardinal Carlo Caraffa and Giovanni, Duke of Palino, tried on nebulous evidence and executed on political grounds in 1561. He was himself a nepotist, but the appointment to the archbishopric of Milan of his young nephew, Carlo Borromeo, later canonized, provided the Church with a leader of its internal reformation.

The great achievement of the pontificate was the reconvening of the council, which decided to continue with the agenda of the Council of Trent, as Philip II wished, rather than to begin again, as France and Ferdinand wanted. Ferdinand still hoped to reconcile the Lutheran communities, and France hoped for a settlement with the Huguenots. The political obstacles were overcome and the council met on 18 January 1562. It faltered on several issues, of which the first was whether the obligation of benefice holders to reside in them was of divine law, and hence not dispensable. Morone was made president in the spring of 1563, and the council was dissolved on 4 December that year. The Pope immediately promulgated its decrees. Primarily intended to devote itself to matters of discipline and reform, the council had also passed the strongly anti-Lutheran decrees referred to in its profession of faith promulgated on 13 November 1564 on the sacraments, the mass, indulgences, prayers for the dead, the church's teaching authority, and the papal exercise of the magisterium.

It is arguable that the anti-Protestant stance, itself incomplete because it failed to define papal

primacy and the nature of the Church, left the most important theological and spiritual issues, like the reconciliation of free will with the gratuity of grace, untouched. They were to surface noisily during the centuries to come.

Pius reserved to himself the interpretation of the decrees, enforced episcopal residence, published the new index, conceded communion in both kinds to the discretion of German, Austrian, and Hungarian bishops, but deferred a decision on married priests. He had already on his own authority reformed the administrative procedures of the Curia, but he did not live to see the completion of the new catechism and the reformed missal and breviary. The need to raise taxes had prompted an attempt on his life in 1565, but Pius IV died with the council as his great accomplishment, and with a record as a patron of learning and with considerable responsibility for the embellishment of Rome.

St PIUS V
(Born 17 January 1504; elected 7 January 1566; died 1 May 1572)

The candidate of Carlo Borromeo's rigorist party, Michele Ghislieri, from a poor Milanese family, was elected after a nineteen-day conclave. A shepherd until at fourteen he became a Dominican and studied and lectured at Pavia, his austerity, vigor in combating heresy, and the discipline he imposed on houses of which he was prior occasioned his

Above: Emperor Maximilian II
was one of the many European potentates irritated by Pius V's less than successful foreign policies.

Right: Queen Elizabeth I of England. *Her excommunication and declared deposition by Pius V, on 25 February 1570, served to make life more difficult for the English Catholics.*

Below: Pius V. *One of his major achievements was the formation, with Venice and Spain, of a holy league against the Turks, who were crushed in the naval battle of Lepanto, 1571.*

appointment as inquisitor in Como. There his zeal was noticed by the future Paul IV, on whose recommendation Ghislieri was made head of the Holy Office in 1551. Paul IV named him Bishop of Nepi and Sutri in 1556, a cardinal in 1557, and Inquisitor General in 1558. Pius IV allowed him to continue, although he was personally repelled by his severity, obstinacy, and censoriousness.

In his allocution to the sacred College on election, Pius pledged himself to maintain peace in christendom, to extirpate heresy, and to fight the Turks. With an old-fashioned crusade in mind, he formed with Venice and Spain, whose commercial interests were at stake, a holy league against the Turks. When the Turks took Cyprus, the league crushed their power in the Mediterranean at the battle of Lepanto on 7 October 1571. It was the last great naval battle to be fought between fleets of galleys, two or three hundred to a side, with the lighter Turkish craft relying on rams, cannons and Greek fire. The Pope declared the 7 October the feast of our Lady of Victory, to be changed by Gregory XIII to our Lady of the Rosary. As Pope, he continued his austere personal life, cut back his court, and sternly introduced the Tridentine reforms in the Papal State. He immediately issued edicts against the profanation of the Sabbath, simony, blasphemy, sodomy, and concubinage. He enforced clerical residence and the rules of monastic enclosure, banned vagrants in Rome and Jews not engaged in trade and resident in ghettos from all papal territory except Ancona. He built a new palace for the Inquisition. Death sentences were executed, the city's pagan antiquities were returned to the people of Rome, and the powers of the congregation of the index of prohibited books were extended. Pius also curtailed venality by reducing the powers of the sacred Penitentiary to grant private absolutions, attacked nepotism by establishing a commission to examine candidates for the episcopacy, refused to advance his own relatives, and banned the alienation of ecclesiastical land within the Papal State.

The results of these measures were not totally happy. Printers fled. The rehabilitation of the Caraffa family was resented, and the secular powers disliked his denunciation of state control of the Church. The excommunication and deposition of Elizabeth I of England on 25 February 1570 made life more difficult for English Catholics and further endangered the life of Mary, Queen of Scots, while also irritating Spain, France, and the Emperor.

Maximilian II was also exacerbated at the infringement of his prerogative when Pius nominated Cosimo I as Grand Duke of Tuscany, and Spain was repeatedly driven to the edge of schism by the Pope's hostility to the state's control of the Church.

But by 1568 Pius had instituted a congregation of cardinals "for the conversion of infidels". He published the new catechism, missal, and breviary, and in 1569 he set up a commission to revize the Vulgate, the Latin translation of the Bible. In 1576 he condemned Baius, whose doctrine that human nature had to have had an aspiration to supernatural felicity had as its consequence that, after the fall, nature could of itself produce no act that was not sinful, and in the same year he declared Thomas Aquinas a Doctor of the Church. He was beatified in 1672 and canonized in 1712.

GREGORY XIII
(Born 1 January 1502; elected 14 May 1572; died 10 April 1585)

Ugo Boncompagni was the fourth son of a Bolognese merchant. He taught law at Bologna, where he had an illegitimate son, whom he later made governor of Sant'Angelo. Boncompagni was ordained some three years after arriving in 1539 at Rome, where he became a papal diplomat and administrator in 1539. After missions to France and Brussels he was in 1558 made Bishop of Vieste, and from 1561 attended the Council of Trent.

Above: The St Bartholomew's Day Massacre. *It is not to the credit of Gregory XIII that he publicly rejoiced after hearing of the massacre of the Huguenots on 23 August 1572.*

Below: Gregory XIII *is widely remembered for his completion of reform of the calendar. Introduction of the Gregorian calendar necessitated the dropping of ten days in October 1582.*

Made a cardinal in 1565, he was sent to Spain, and his election after an unusually brief conclave was due to the support of Philip II.

Although easy-going, there is no hint of scandal in his life after election, and he determinedly set about implementing the Tridentine reforms, instituting a commission of cardinals for the purpose, and turning into instruments of reform the nunciatures, of which he also established new ones at Lucerne, Graz, and Cologne. He vigorously promoted missionary activity in the New World, and in India, China, and Japan, relying heavily on the Jesuits, whose privileges he extended, and whose principal Roman church, Il Gesù, he completed. He called on the Jesuits not only for missionary work, but also to staff the Roman colleges he founded for the education of the clergy from schismatic homelands unlikely to provide the seminaries demanded by Trent. Gregory founded the Roman college, later the Gregorian university, the English college, and secured the future of the German college. He also founded Hungarian, Greek, Maronite, and Armenian colleges, approved Philip Neri's Congregation of the Oratory for diocesan priests and the reform by Teresa of Ávila of the Carmelites. His

best-remembered achievement was the completion of the reform of the calendar, synchronizing the ecclesiastical calendar with the astronomical year by dropping ten days in October 1582. It was under Gregory that the Corpus of canon law was published in 1580-82, codifying its innumerable decisions for the first time. He built the Gregorian chapel in St Peter's and put fountains into the Piazza Navona.

Less happy were his public rejoicing on hearing of the St Bartholomew Day massacre of Huguenots on the night of the 23 August 1572, his subsidies for the French pro-Spanish league, his support for Spanish action in the Low Countries, his support for plans to assassinate Elizabeth of England, and his negotiations with Russia, which failed, and with John III of Sweden, who demanded clerical marriage and the suppression of invocation to the saints. Gregory had greater success in Poland and in parts of the empire, although he had to allow Ernst of Bavaria to accumulate five bishoprics in order to secure Catholic property rights in the northwest. The Pope's need for money led to the dispossession of many occupiers of lands which could be made to revert to papal ownership, so that by the end of the reign there was widespread banditry in the Papal State, and even within Rome.

SIXTUS V
(Born 13 December 1520; elected 24 April 1585; died 27 August 1590)

Felice Peretti was a farmer's son from the March of Ancona who joined the Franciscans at twelve, became a theologian and noted preacher, and achieved renown when taken to Rome by the cardinal protector of the Franciscans in 1552. Nominated Inquisitor to Venice in 1556, excessive severity led to his recall, but Pius IV reappointed him. On a mission to Spain in 1565 he quarrelled with the future Gregory XIII, and returned to Rome, where Pius V made him Vicar-General of the Franciscans, Bishop of Sant'Agata dei Goti, and in 1570, cardinal.

On election he vigorously restored order in the Papal State with huge numbers of public executions. The lesser punishments were still ruthlessly severe, and Sixtus used the same blinkered ferocity to restore the papal finances, taking so much money out of the economy as to cause a severe recession and his own universal execration. The Roman people tore down his statue when he died. He became rich enough to embark on the enormous programme of public expenditure intended to make Rome the world's outstanding city. His intention was to drain the Pontine marshes where the ancient aqueducts had decayed, to lay out great avenues linking the seven pilgrimage churches, and to build up the city towards the east where the ancient villas had been. He incidentally hugely raised the value of his family's property near S. Maria Maggiore.

His designer and architect was Domenico Fontana who, with Giacomo della Porta, completed the cupola of St Peter's. Sixtus added the loggia to the Lateran palace, continued work on the Quirinal, made major additions to the Vatican, built a new Vatican library, established the Vatican press, erected four obelisks, including that of Fontana in front of St Peter's and the Egyptian obelisk of Augustus in the Piazza del Popolo, opened up half a dozen long, straight boulevards, rebuilt aqueducts and bridges, and much encouraged agriculture and industry.

He also reorganized the church's administration, instituting fifteen permanent congregations of cardinals, of which six were concerned simply with the Papal State, limited in 1586 the number of cardi-

nals to seventy (six cardinal bishops, fifty cardinal priests, and fourteen cardinal deacons), designating their titular churches and deaconries. Among his own thirty-three creations was his fifteen-year-old nephew. He enforced the obligatory visits of bishops to Rome to account for their administration, and published too hastily a revision of the Vulgate so full of mistakes that it later had to be withdrawn. He made St Bonaventure, the Franciscan rival to St Thomas Aquinas, a Doctor of the Church.

He dreamt of annihilating the Turks, conquering Egypt, and bringing the Holy Sepulchre to Italy. He also declared Henry of Navarre and Condé incapable of succeeding to the French throne, and excommunicated Henry III for the murder of the Cardinal de Guise, although not for that of his brother, the Duke. Sixtus's vast energy was joined to a fierce determination and a naive sense of political realities.

URBAN VII
(Born 4 August 1521; elected 15 September 1590; died 27 September 1590)

Giambattista Castagna was son of a Genoese father and a Roman mother. A papal administrator, he took part in the final year of the Council of Trent, accompanied the future Gregory XIII to Spain, and remained there as Nuncio. He had been governor of the Papal State, and became Nuncio to Venice and then Governor of Bologna. He was made Cardinal Priest on 12 December 1583. Moderate and serious, Urban VII fell ill with malaria on the night following his election.

GREGORY XIV
(Born 11 February 1535; elected 5 December 1590; died 16 October 1591).

Niccolò Sfondrati was born at Milan, and was friendly with Carlo Borromeo. Named Bishop of Cremona at twenty-five, he attended the final year of the Council of Trent. He was raised to the cardinalate on the same day as his predecessor. Pious, but inexperienced, he entrusted the conduct of affairs to his twenty-nine-year-old nephew, a cardinal from 1590, who supported Spain, and sent aid to Paris when that city was holding out for the league against Henry of Navarre. He renewed the ban against Henry's accession to the crown, and ineffectively sent an army against him. He forbade betting

Above: Sixtus V. *His imposition of discipline in the Papal State was so severe, involving a huge number of executions, that the Roman people tore down his statue after his death.*

Below: Gregory XIV. *His reign, like that of his predecessor Urban VII (who died after only twelve days in office) was short, but he found time to forbid wagering on ecclesiastical events.*

GREGORIVS XIV. Nicola° Sfond-
ratus Mediolanen. creat° die 5.Decemb.
an.1590. Sedit men. io.dies 10. Obijt
die 15.Octobr.an. 1591 Vac.Sed.d.13.

Above: **Innocent IX** *continued the unfortunate run of short-lived Popes. After two months in office, he died as a result of a chill caught whilst visiting seven pilgrimage churches.*

Below: **Clement VIII.** *Although a self-proclaimed ascetic, Clement kept such an extravagant household and lavished so many gifts on his nephews that he reduced papal finances to ruin.*

on the outcome of papal elections, the length of pontificates, and the creation of cardinals.

INNOCENT IX
(Born 20 July 1519; elected 29 October 1591; died 30 December 1591)

Giovanni Antonio Fachinetti was born at Bologna, served Alessandro Farnese, and was made Bishop of Nicastro in 1560. He attended the final phase of the Council, was Nuncio in Venice, but resigned his see and returned to Rome for reasons of health in 1575. He was made a cardinal on the same day as his two predecessors. He followed a pro-Spanish policy with less liberal subsidies. He fell ill on 18 December, and then caught a chill visiting the seven pilgrimage churches.

CLEMENT VIII
(Born 24 February 1536; elected 30 January 1592; died 5 March 1605)

Ippolito Aldobrandini came from a family driven from Florence by hostility to the Medici. Educated by Alessandro Farnese and taken up by Pius V, he was not ordained priest until 1580, was made cardinal in 1585, and became Legate to Poland. He had been seriously considered at three conclaves before he was elected.

Ostentatious in his austerity, piety, and devotion to his humbler duties, he was an intimate of Philip Neri. He suffered much from gout and moved his residence constantly, had household expenses four times greater than Sixtus V, raised three nephews to the cardinalate, one at the age of fourteen, and ruined the papal finances by the extravagance of the gifts that he bestowed on them.

He published the corrected version of the Sixtine Vulgate, new revisions of the liturgical texts, and a stricter index, which included a ban on Jewish books, and he made the Inquisition more severe. During his reign it put more than thirty heretics to death, including the ex-Dominican and mystically inclined syncretist philosopher Giordano Bruno as a relapsed heretic: his view was at least close to pantheism, since he held that individual things were only manifestations of an infinite universe of which God was the soul.

Clement was unable to resolve the conflict between the Jesuit explanation for the individual's power of moral self-determination in the order of grace, and the Dominican inclination to see the human will as subject to physical premotion in the acceptance or refusal of justifying grace. Although technical, the matter was of the deepest religious concern, and centred on the individual's ability in any way to change a pre-ordained eternal destiny to heaven or hell. In 1594, Clement convoked the dispute to Rome, where it was debated before him in sixty-eight sessions between 1602 and 1605. The Jesuit theologian, Molina, came very near condemnation when the Alcalà Jesuits debated whether it was a truth of faith that the reigning Pope was the legitimate successor of St Peter, but in the end Clement could only impose silence on both sides in the theological dispute.

Clement finally recognized Henry of Navarre as King of France, absolved him in 1595, and in 1598 mediated a peace between France and Spain. With the help of Henry, he also secured the reversion of Ferrara to the papacy on the failure of the Este dynasty, in spite of the opposition of Spain and the empire. He allowed the Orthodox Christians of Poland to retain their liturgy on joining the Roman communion, and in spite of political setbacks in England and Sweden, Clement had the credit of appointing Francis of Sales as co-adjutor bishop of Geneva, much strengthening the Church's position in Savoy. He was able to diminish the papacy's reliance on Spain, and the great success of the jubilee of 1600, when an estimated 1.2 million pilgrims visited Rome, allowed him to feel that the church was reaping the fruits of the continuing efforts at renewal.

LEO XI

(Born 2 June 1535; elected 1 April 1605; died 27 April 1605)

Alessandro Ottaviano de' Medici was through his mother a nephew of Leo X. As ambassador of Grand Duke Cosimo I in Rome, he became a disciple of Philip Neri and in 1573 was made Bishop of Pistoia, then Archbishop of Florence, and in 1583, cardinal. He had assisted in the reconciliation of Henry of Navarre with Rome, remaining two years in France from 1596. His candidacy was strongly opposed by Spain, but supported by France.

PAUL V

(Born 17 September 1552; elected 16 May 1605; died 28 January 1681)

Camillo Borghese came from Siena, held a succession of curial posts, and was made a cardinal in 1596 after a successful mission to Spain. He became Vicar of Rome and Inquisitor in 1603, but was little known.

He was a strong upholder of outmoded papal prerogative and, while Savoy, Genoa, Tuscany, and Naples allowed it to prevail, it was bitterly contested by Venice, where the acquisition of land by the Church required permission, and where two clerics were being brought before the secular courts. Paul ineffectively excommunicated the senate and imposed an interdict on the city, ignored by the senate and most of the clergy except the Jesuits, who were expelled. The Servite theologian, Paolo Sarpi, defending the senate, accused the Pope of abuse of power, declared obedience to him sinful, and enlisted the schismatic powers in Venice's support. The European war along sectarian lines which was clearly brewing was only narrowly averted when Spain declined to offer the Pope military support. The Pope was obliged to give in to a face-saving compromise mediated by the French, and Cardinal Joyeuse absolved the Venetian senate on 21 April 1607. The interdict was never used against a state again.

By the time Sarpi issued his anti-papal *History of the Council of Trent* in 1619, The Thirty Years' War had been ignited by the Bohemian revolution. The Catholic alliance under Maximilian I of Bavaria had been formed in response to the Protestant union, allied with England and Holland and led by the Calvinist Elector Palatine. From 1620 onwards, the Pope made substantial contributions to the Emperor Ferdinand II and the Catholic alliance.

In the wake of the Gunpowder Plot of 1605 Paul had forbidden English Catholics to take the oath of allegiance denying the Pope's right to depose the king, and his 1613 condemnation of Gallicanism led in France to the declaration of the Estates in 1614, later withdrawn, that the king held his office by divine right, independently of papal jurisdiction. Nepotism is estimated to have cost about four per cent of the papal income during the pontificate of Paul V, but he did at least continue to promote reform, renew the episcopal obligation of residence and approve the institution of the Italian and French Congregations of the Oratory. He completed the nave, façade, and portico of St Peter's. On the question of grace, predestination, and free will, the Pope could no more achieve a resolution of the problem than his predecessor, and ended up merely ordering silence on the matter. During his pontificate Galileo Galilei was censured and condemned to house arrest for teaching the Copernican theory of the solar system, which appeared to contradict the revelation of Genesis.

GREGORY XV

(Born 9 January 1554; elected 9 February 1621; died 8 July 1623)

Alessandro Ludovisi was born and studied in Bologna and quickly became a trusted curial administrator and diplomat, accomplishing missions to Poland and Benevento before becoming Archbishop of Bologna in 1612, then cardinal in 1616 after reconciling Spain and Savoy. Elected by acclaim, but frail and aged sixty-seven, he delegated the administrative burden to a twenty-five-year-old nephew, whom he made a cardinal. He reorganized the papal balloting system, but his great achievement was the 1622 institution of the Congregation for the Propagation of the Faith, coordinating the missionary activity of the Church all over the globe. He canonized Ignatius Loyola, founder of the Jesuits, Philip Neri, Teresa of Ávila, and Francis Xavier, most important of the early Jesuit missionaries. He deployed determined political effort and provided massive subsidies for the restoration of Catholicism wherever that might be achieved, as in Bohemia. Paris was made into a metropolitan See, and papal troops occupied the Valtellina, the French valley separating the imperial troops north of the Alps from those in Lombardy.

Above: **Paul V** *is shown sharing the Church's treasure with his Borghese relatives. It is estimated that nepotism accounted for about four per cent of papal expenditure during his pontificate.*

Below: **Gregory XV**. *His major achievement was the institution of the Congregation of the Faith, with the aim of coordinating the worldwide missionary activity of the Church, in 1622.*

Above: **Urban VIII** *was the patron of the artist Gian Lorenzo Bernini, whose works in the baroque style remain among the glories of Rome. Urban sought to strengthen the papacy's temporal power.*

Right: Cardinal Richelieu *of France was Europe's pre-eminent statesman during Urban VIII's reign, and proved always able to out-maneuver the Pope.*

Above: *Galileo Galilei (1564-1642), astronomer and philosopher, had been censured by Paul V and – despite their personal friendship – suffered further condemnation from Urban VIII.*

URBAN VIII
(Born early 1568; elected 6 August 1623; died 29 July 1644)

Maffeo Barberini was elected after a three-week conclave by fifty votes out of fifty-five. Born in Florence, he had swiftly ascended the diplomatic ranks, had been twice on missions to France, and had been created cardinal in 1606. In 1608 he was made Bishop of Spoleto, in 1611 Legate of Bologna, and in 1617, secretary of the Curia's central administrative department, the Signatura.

Urban was elected at fifty-five. Authoritarian, and highly conscious of his position, he dealt with all important business himself, and without consultation. He regarded the papacy as a temporal principality, building Castelfranco to the north, fortifying Civita Vecchia, and strengthening the Castel Sant'Angelo, whose cannon were cast, to the scandal of the Romans, from bronze taken from the Pantheon. He established his summer residence at Castel Gandolfo and formed a twenty-year partnership with the architect, designer, sculptor, and painter, Giovanni Bernini. He was himself a scholar, a connoisseur, and a somewhat oratical composer of Latin verse. He raised his brother and two nephews to the cardinalate, advanced other brothers, and treated them so profligately that he doubled the papal debt. He took Urbino into the Papal State.

His reign coincided with the thirty years' war and with Richelieu's ascendancy in France. His political activity strove for neutrality but was effectively pro-French, although Richelieu, who was perfectly willing to ally against the Habsburgs with the northern Protestant powers, and especially with King Gustavus Adolphus of Sweden, always outwitted him.. He withheld until too late further subsidies to the Habsburg Ferdinand II which might have brought relief to the Catholic side, supported the French candidate, the Duc de Nevers, in the 1628 war of the Mantuan succession, and allowed the Swiss in French pay to occupy the Valtellina fortresses, so continuing to cut the Habsburg communication lines through the Alps. Spain called for a general council, while Richelieu threatened schism. When France openly entered the war in 1635, Ferdinand II was compelled to make concessions to the Protestants in the peace agreed at Prague on 30 May 1635, and Richelieu was allowed to subvert the peace agreement made at Cologne in 1638. In any territorial sense, the counterreformation had come to an end.

He played a personal role in the 1631 reform of the breviary, reserved to the papacy canonization, beatification and the authorization of any new saint's cult, and gave strong support to the missions. He also authorized the institution of new religious orders, like the Visitation and the Lazarists (also called the "Congregation of Priests of the Mission".)

Urban acquiesced in the second trial of Galileo Galilei, a personal friend, and condemned in 1653 a series of propositions textually contained in, or associated with, Jansen's 1640 *Augustinus*. Jansen, starting from an attempt to bring the Church back to its fifth-century condition, had discovered the theological importance of defining what had belonged to Adam by nature, but in consequence had gone on to deny that the chance of salvation was actually available to all rational human beings.

The partnership with Bernini, formerly a sculptor in marble, resulted in a commission for him to articulate the crossing under the dome of Sant Peter's, to design the great bronze baldachino with its mock tassels, and to design the Four Rivers fountain in the Piazza Navona. In 1657 Alexander VII would commission him to design the piazza in front of St Peter's with its spectacular colonnade, but it is to Urban's commissions that we must look for the source of the high baroque which Bernini imposed not only on Rome, but throughout the peninsula.

Urban himself spent so prodigally and so unwisely that news of his death was greeted with riotous joy in the streets of Rome.

INNOCENT X
(Born 7 May 1574; elected 15 September 1644; died 1 January 1655)

Giambattista Pamfili was born and studied in Rome, where he became a judge of the Rota and Nuncio in Naples before accompanying the nephew of Urban VIII to France and Spain, where he was appointed Nuncio in 1626 and cardinal in 1627. The conclave lasted 37 days and was dominated by the desire to reverse the pro-French policies of Urban VIII. Mazarin's veto of Pamfili arrived too late to take effect.

Innocent immediately instituted an inquiry into the riches acquired by the beneficiaries of his predecessor's nepotism and sequestered their posses-

Left: Innocent X *as portrayed by the Spanish artist Diego Velázquez in 1650. Innocent favored Spain against France, but took no action when Portugal separated from Spain in 1640.*

sions. They were saved by Mazarin's intervention. Innocent himself indulged in widespread nepotism, but entrusted affairs to his sister-in-law, the rapacious Donna Olimpia Maidalchini, although her son was a cardinal. Innocent was the first Pope to use a Secretary of State, who signed important letters in his own right.

Innocent naturally disliked the concessions made to Protestants by the Emperor Ferdinand III and the Elector Ernst of Bavaria which were included in the 1648 Peace of Westphalia at the end of The Thirty Years' War, and he favored Spain in the continuing hostilities with France. He supported Venice and Poland financially against the Turks, but had no funds to help Ferdinand III. He also took no action when in 1640 Portugal broke away from Spain. He backed the Church's missionary activity, condemned the practice of allowing Chinese Christians to retain their Confucian rites, and had to condemn Jansenism again. Dogmatically, it was being kept alive by Antoine Arnauld virtually alone, although the rigorist spirituality associated with his dogmatic position, and which was never condemned, had gained a considerable hold among members of the richer bourgeoisie and the lesser nobility in France. The central question was reducible to human nature's actual ability or inability to influence personal salvation. The spirituality is most clearly set forth in Blaise Pascal's posthumous *Writings on Grace*.

ALEXANDER VII
(Born 13 February 1599; elected 7 April 1655; died 22 May 1667)

Fabio Chigi, born at Siena, was a career diplomat who entered the papal service in 1628. Appointed Vice-Legate in Ferrara from 1629 to 1634, he was not ordained until 1634, and became successively Bishop of Nardò, Inquisitor and apostolic delegate in Malta, and Nuncio from 1639 to 1651 in Cologne, where he represented the Pope at the negotiations for the Peace of Westphalia. Secretary of State in 1651 and cardinal in 1652, Chigi was elected Pope after an eighty-day conclave in spite of the only slowly relaxed opposition of Mazarin.

Relations with France worsened steadily, chiefly because Rome was sheltering Mazarin's arch-enemy, the cardinal de Retz. Mazarin therefore supported claims to papal territories by Farnese and Este families, and after Mazarin's death in 1661 Colbert

demanded large reparations after an incident in which the papal guard had fired on the carriage of the French ambassador. Alexander kept the new Bishop of Paris waiting two years for his bulls of appointment, while Colbert withdrew the ambassador and expelled the papal nuncio in Paris. Alexander was obliged to accept the humiliating 1664 Treaty of Pisa, although he haughtily, if only implicitly, rebuked the French king for using his own jurisdiction, rather than the Pope's, for the final requirement for the French clergy and academics to sign the formulary crushing Jansenism. For Louis XIV Jansenism represented more a danger to the state than a religious heterodoxy.

Alexander's refusal to acknowledge John IV of Portugal, or to fill his episcopal vacancies, nearly led to a schism. Alexander was a friend of the Jesuits, the firm opponents of the Jansenists. The 1665 canonization of Francis of Sales, who shared the Jesuit view on the human power of self-determination, was partly a political act in their favor. Alexander disliked administration, and preferred his literary interests, his private devotional life, and the patronage and company of scholars and artists.

CLEMENT IX
(Born 27 January 1600; elected 20 June 1667; died 9 December 1669)

Giulio Rospigliosi came from a noble Pistoia family and, patronized by the Barberini, steadily ascended the ladder of curial appointments. In 1644 he was appointed titular Archbishop of Tarsus and Nuncio to Spain. In 1653 he became Governor of Rome, and in 1657 Secretary of State and cardinal. He contrived to retain the support of both France and Spain, and benefited from the desire of the sacred college to see the breach between Paris and Rome healed. Clement IX was known for his literary talent, and the conclave which elected him, partly because of the frailty of his health, lasted only eighteen days.

The brief pontificate was dominated by the Jansenist controversy and the Turkish danger. In France, a movement among the episcopacy to sign the anti-Jansenist formulary only in such a way as not to admit that the five condemned Jansenist propositions had been held by Jansen led to a tacit papal surrender on the issue. The dioceses involved would be allowed to sign with a private reservation on what was known as the point of fact. The fragile

Above: Alexander VII. *His papacy saw continuing friction with France. He rebuked the French monarch, Louis XIV, for using his own jurisdiction, rather than the Pope's, to curb the Jansenists.*

Below: Clement X. *His brief pontificate saw some improvement in relations with France – although this success was overshadowed by the threat of Turkish advances in the Mediterranean.*

CLEMENS X. Æmilius Bonauen
tura de Alterijs, Romanus, creatus
die 29.Aprilis an. 1670.Sedit an.6.mẽ.
2.d.24.Ob.22 Iul an. 1676.V.S.m.j.d.29.

Above: Clement X *took action against the Turkish threat to Poland. He gave financial support to Jan Sobieski, who defeated the Turks at the Dniester in 1673 and became King of Poland.*

Below: King Louis XIV of France, *"the Sun King," devoted his long reign (1643-1715) to the expansion of his realm. This frequently brought him into conflict with the temporal power of the papacy.*

"Clementine peace" was given sanction by a brief of 14 January 1669.

The invasion of the Low Countries by France in May 1667 was ended not so much by papal intervention as by the alliance of Holland, England, and Sweden, which forced the French to withdraw from Franche-Comté in return for keeping their conquests in the Low Countries. The Turks had occupied most of Crete, and Venice wished to recover it. Expeditions of 1668 and 1669 failed, and the Venetians had to withdraw on 6 September 1669.

The stroke which ended Clement's life was no doubt hastened by the sad news of the reversal inflicted upon the Christian cause in Crete (which was to remain a Turkish possession until the early years of the twentieth century).

CLEMENT X
(Born 12 July 1590; elected 29 April 1670; died 22 July 1676)

With vetoes from France and Spain, none of the factions could muster a majority at the conclave, which took nearly five months to elect, with Venetian mediation, the seventy-nine-year-old Emilio Altieri. An ecclesiastical lawyer, Altieri was ordained at thirty-three, was made an auditor at the Polish nunciature and then Bishop of Camerino. As Nuncio in Naples in 1644, he did not satisfy Innocent X, who recalled him in 1652. He was promoted by Alexander VII, and made a cardinal a month before the death of Clement IX.

Clement relied heavily on his "cardinal-nephew" Paluzzi degli Albertoni, whose nephew had married Clement's niece and the sole heir of his family. Paluzzi was authoritarian, and he accumulated riches for his family, much extending his palazzo, and tactlessly offending the diplomatic corps in Rome.

Politically, the danger came from the Turks, now threatening Poland. The Pope and Cardinal Odescalchi personally gave financial support to Jan Sobieski, who defeated the Turks at the Dniester on 11 November 1673 and was elected King against strong opposition on 20 May 1674. In addition to fifteen Italian cardinals, Clement elevated only two French and one each of German, Spanish, and English. Louis XIV in particular sought more, but César d'Estrées used physical force to prevent the Pope from ending an audience, and as a result there were no French names among the last promotion of cardinals of the pontificate.

B1 INNOCENT XI
(Born 19 May 1611; elected 21 September 1676; died 12 August 1689)

A saintly Pope beatified in 1956, Benedetto Odescalchi had polled only eight votes the day before France withdrew its opposition to his appointment. He was then unanimously elected after a two-month conclave. He accepted only when the cardinals agreed to a fourteen-point reform programme. He came of a rich Como merchant family, to whose bank he was apprenticed before studying law and entering the papal service. His posts included President of the Apostolic chamber, Governor of Macerata, Financial Commissary in the Marches, Legate of Ferrara during the 1648 famine, Bishop of Novara, and, in 1645, cardinal.

Innocent was frugal and deeply opposed to nepotism. His measures to enforce public decency were largely ineffectual, but he set the tone for tighter discipline, called for evangelical preaching, and restored the papal finances through his economies. He also condemned a further series of laxist propositions in moral theology associated with the Jesuits, but reluctantly under Jesuit pressure condemned the doctrine of complete passivity in prayer known as quietism.

The major concerns of his pontificate included diffidence about the means employed by James II to reconvert England to Catholicism, and a serious quarrel with France about French pretensions to extend the king's right to the revenues from vacant sees. French decrees of 1673 and 1675 had led to the 1682 assembly of the clergy master-minded by Bossuet which, in four "Gallican" articles, denied any papal rights over secular sovereigns. Innocent refused to ratify the appointments of bishops who had subscribed to the articles.

Tensions were made worse by the flouting in 1687 by a new French ambassador of Innocent's withdrawal of the heavily abused quartering privileges accorded to foreign embassies in Rome. Innocent refused to receive him on account of his subscription to the articles. Matters became worse again when Innocent refused to endorse the French King's candidate for the See of Cologne in 1688, and Innocent informed the King that he and his ministers were excommunicated. The French then in September 1688 occupied the papal enclaves of the comtat Venaissin and Avignon. Schism was avoided by Fénelon's mediation and the effects of the 1689 accession of William of Orange in England.

ALEXANDER VIII OTTOBONVS VENETVS
PONTIFEX MAXIMVS
Creatus die VI Octobris MDCLXXXIX.

Above: Alexander VIII. *Although elected as a result of concessions to the French, Alexander refused to recognize France's campaign in the Low Countries as a religious war, and approved nullification of the "Gallican articles" that denied papal authority over secular sovereigns.*

In spite of France's expansionist ambitions and obstructionist tactics, an imperial and Polish army subsidized by the Pope managed to save Vienna from the Turks in 1683. Venice and Russia joined an anti-Turkish holy league, and the Turks were driven from Hungary and Belgrade.

ALEXANDER VIII
(Born 22 April 1610; elected 6 October 1689; died 1 February 1691)

Europe was at war, allied against France, during the conclave. Louis XIV and the Emperor sent ambassadors, but the cardinals had already agreed on Pietro Ottoboni, nearly eighty, with a career as a curial lawyer behind him. Made a cardinal in 1652, he had been Grand Inquisitor. The French acquiesced in the appointment on condition that the appointments of the bishops who had voted for the Gallican articles would be ratified. Alexander accepted the ambassador whom Innocent XI had refused to receive. Avignon and the comtat Venaissin were handed back, and the abolition of quartering privileges accepted.

Alexander appointed a papal "nephew", in fact a twenty-year-old grandnephew, whom he raised to

the cardinalate and invested with large benefices. He also advantaged other members of his family. Doctrinally important is his condemnation of the view that those ignorant of God are not thereby deprived of justifying grace. He also condemned more Jansenist propositions and further punished followers of Molinos.

Relations with the Emperor cooled when Alexander's third consistory failed to elevate any of the Emperor's nominees, and Vienna withdrew its ambassador. But Alexander also refused to recognize the French campaign in the Low Countries as a religious war, and, since France held firm on the Gallican articles, Alexander issued on 30 January 1691 in the presence of ten cardinals the nullification of them which his predecessor had prepared. Two days later, he died.

INNOCENT XII
(Born 13 March 1615; elected 12 July 1691; died 27 September 1700)

The five-month conclave was the result of internal dissensions among the old power groupings, French and Spanish. Disturbances in the city and the summer heat finally brought matters to a conclusion

Right: The capture of Buda *on 2 September 1686. Charles of Lorraine, a leader of the anti-Turkish holy league formed with the moral and financial support of Popes Clement X and Innocent XI, enters the castle of Buda, capital of Turkish-occupied Hungary, after a nine-week siege of the city.*

when the Neapolitan aristocrat and papal diplomat Antonio Pignatelli was elected. He had been Governor of Viterbo, Nuncio to Tuscany, Poland, and Vienna. Innocent XI made him a cardinal and gave him other high offices.

He economized ruthlessly, reformed the system of justice, hugely reduced the sale of offices, and enlarged the harbours of Civita Vecchia and Nettuno to promote trade. He forced through a decree to crush nepotism. A rapprochement with France was achieved, with the ratification of post-1682 bishops who had not taken part in the assembly, and a diminution in the status of the Gallican articles. By the end of 1693, the French hierarchy was restored. Relations with the empire cooled, and, when a demand was made that all in Italy who owed feudal allegiance to the Emperor should produce proof of tenure, the Pope annulled the decrees. He also reduced his support for imperial forces fighting against the Turks.

Although obliged formally to censure Fénelon, whose condemnation Bossuet demanded, the matter was handled by brief, not bull, and in such a way as virtually to support Fénelon and rebuke Louis XIV. Bossuet never got the expected cardinal's hat nor the desired Sees of either Paris or Lyons. In the matter of the Spanish succession when the designated heir to the king, the Bavarian electoral prince, Joseph Ferdinand, suddenly died in February 1699, Innocent decided to support the fragile claims of Philip of Anjou, grandson of Louis XIV, to the succession. Philip was supported by the Spanish council of state and a commission of cardinals. In the end the Spanish king willed him his throne.

CLEMENT XI

(Born 23 July 1649; elected 23 November 1700; died 19 March 1721)

The fifty-one-year-old Gian Francesco Albani was the nominee of the Zelanti cardinals who tried to remain free of French or imperial pressures. A curial administrator, made cardinal in 1690, he was ordained priest in the September preceding the forty-six-day October to November conclave. He was to issue the celebrated constitution *Unigenitus* finally condemning Jansenism in a series of propositions taken from the works of Pasquier Quesnel. He also ruled against the continued use by Christians of Chinese rites sanctioned in 1656.

Leopold I contested the will of the Spanish king,

recognized the Brandenburg Elector Frederick III as King of Prussia to gain his support, and was backed by Holland and England. Papal neutrality was challenged when both Philip V and Leopold I demanded to be invested with Naples. Tensions with the empire worsened when in 1705 the Emperor Leopold I was succeeded by his son Joseph I. Papal territory was violated by both sides, and the peninsula was occupied by imperial troops, against whom an excommunicatory decree of July 1707 achieved nothing except the freezing of ecclesiastical revenue by the Emperor. Clement XI then attacked the imperial troops, lost, and in 1709 had to recognize Charles III, the imperial candidate for the throne of Spain, in order to re-establish peace. He nearly forced Spain into schism by refusing canonical investiture to bishops appointed by Philip V after he had closed the Madrid nunciature.

Both the Emperor and the French Dauphin died in April 1711. Logic demanded the politically impossible union of the imperial and Spanish thrones under Charles III as single monarch. No notice was taken of the Pope at the subsequent 1713 Treaty of Utrecht, and the Spanish fleet which he had subsidized to ward off a new Turkish threat was finally used against him, to attack imperial possessions on the Italian peninsula. Sardinia, Sicily, Parma, and Piacenza were disposed of without reference to papal claims. Spiritual and temporal jurisdictions were finally being forced to confine themselves to their own areas of competence.

Left: Clement XI. *Although he had a doctrinal triumph with his constitution* Unigenitus, *condemning Jansenism, Clement faced insoluble political problems. French, Spanish and imperial forces violated his territory; his army was defeated by imperial troops; and a Spanish fleet he had subsidized to fight the Turks was used against him.*

INNOCENT XIII
(Born 1655; elected 8 May 1721; died 15 October 1724)

His short pontificate was dogged throughout by illness. He had been elected after a long, disputatious conclave in which the most favored candidate, Clement XI's secretary of state, Paolucci, had been vetoed by the Emperor, who blamed him for Clement's allegedly pro-French policies. Innocent XIII, it was hoped, would be more co-operative with the Emperor, while remaining on good terms with France.

His career had largely been in papal government and diplomacy (in Switzerland and Portugal) and he favored a quiet life. Not surprisingly, therefore, he aimed at detente with the great Catholic powers, which had not always appreciated Clement XI. He pleased the French Regent, Orléans, by giving his powerful and corrupt minister, Dubois, a red hat and invested the Emperor Charles VI with Naples and Sicily.

His predecessor had refused to do this because of the transference of these territories to the Empire in 1720 without consultation with the Pope, a fate which was increasingly to overtake the papacy in the eighteenth century. Indeed, Innocent XIII could not prevent Charles VI from claiming supreme authority over the Sicilian Church or from investing the Spanish prince, Charles, with the traditional papal fiefs of Parma and Piacenza.

Less diplomatically, as regards the Hanoverian dynasty of the new and Protestant state of Great Britain, he continued recognition of the "Old Pretender" as "James III", King of England and Scotland, to whom he paid an income and promised 10,000 ducats if he reclaimed Britain for the Catholic Church.

Within the Church the fact that he had protested Clement XI's publication of the bull *Unigenitus* without consulting the Sacred College, and disliked the Jesuits, aroused hopes of papal favor among French Jansenists. Instead Innocent confirmed *Unigenitus* and censured French bishops who asked for its withdrawal.

The Jesuit issue, so characteristic of the eighteenth century, also arose during his pontificate. He had disliked the Jesuits intensely since his time in Portugal and he was irritated to hear that Jesuit missionaries were not observing Clement XI's ban on "Chinese rites". He would have liked to suppress the order but contented himself with a ban on their receiving novices until they complied.

He was concerned for the economic and cultural development of the Papal States but his reign was too short for much progress. Creditably, however, he did not practise nepotism and, with the exception of Pius VI, this was the pattern of the eighteenth century Popes.

BENEDICT XIII
(Born 1649; elected 21 May 1724; died 21 February 1730)

A Dominican, of the noble family of Orsini (which had already produced two Popes), he was elected as a neutral after another disputatious conclave and had to be ordered to accept his election by the general of his order. He had been an academic and Archbishop of Benevento but essentially he was a simple, zealous friar without political experience who preferred an ascetic life. He was happiest in a pastoral role and as Pope avoided the splendid apartments of the Vatican. He remained an active Archbishop of Benevento. His asceticism led him to condemn the luxurious life of the cardinals and fashionable wigs and beards. He supressed the popular and profitable lottery of the Papal States, a policy more creditable than politic, given the parlous state of papal finances.

It was the glory of the Church to have so holy a man at its head, but someone had to attend to Church and government business, and this Pope was more than usually in need of trustworthy advizers and executives. The estimable Paolucci, his secretary of state, soon died and the Pope gave his complete trust to Niccolo Coscia, an unscrupulous adventurer from Benevento who was made cardinal over the protests of the Sacred College. He assembled a like-minded group of rapacious careerists from Benevento who set about enriching themselves by selling offices and taking bribes, even from foreign ambassadors. In time the Pope was isolated from all other influences and ignored all accusations against the Beneventans despite incontrovertible evidence of their avarice and incompetence. Not surprisingly the finances of the Papal States became even shakier and the reign saw a further weakening in the international standing of the papacy. Victor Amadeus of Savoy by bribery obtained papal recogbition of his royal title (assumed in 1713 without papal sanction) and the right to appoint Sardinian bishops.

Above: Benedict XIII, *an ascetic Dominican, left secular administration to his advizers. Unhappily, the chief among these, the unscrupulous Cardinal Niccolo Coscia, assembled a gang of rapacious careerists whose wholesale simony and taking of bribes discredited the papacy.*

The French Jansenists were less successful. The Dominican Pope did not show the expected favor. Benedict XIII (characterististically) canonized many saints but he provoked a crisis in the papacy's international relations by trying to extend the feast of St Gregory VII, one of his most powerful, illustrious and pretentious predecessors, to the whole Church. Liturgical references to the deposition of the Emperor Henry VI in the 11th century displeased many governments, which banned the texts. The contrast between the position of the papacy in the late 11th century and the eighteenth century was thus painfully emphasized.

The depredations of Coscia and his associates made the Pope unpopular by the time of his death. The fury of the Romans was such that Coscia and his friends were lucky to excape with their lives.

CLEMENT XII
(Born 1652; elected 12 June 1730; died 6 February 1740)

The eldest son of a rich and noble family, Clement XII was elected at the age of seventy-nine. Gout frequently kept him to his bed and from 1732 he was blind, though not to the depredations of Coscia and his friends, whom he brought to justice. He relied greatly on his nephew, Neri Corsini, who unfortunately, however, had no grasp of state business. Nevertheless the new Pope had a certain financial acumen and re-introduced some order into the papal finances by resurrecting the state lottery, issuing paper money and taxing imports. He tried to stimulate trade but corrupt administration, foreign invasions and dwindling revenue from Catholic countries often frustrated his efforts.

He was the first Pope to condemn Freemasonry, a characteristic eighteenth century movement. His decision may have been based on imperfect knowledge of what Freemasonry was, but he denounced its naturalism, religious indifferentism and its demand for secret oaths. He saw it as a possible threat to Church and state.

His keen interest in the missions led him to renew Clement XI's prohibition of "Chinese rites" and he made contact with the Uniate Maronite Christians of the Lebanon. Jansenists were discouraged by his canonization of one of their most uncompromising opponents, Vincent de Paul.

Perhaps the most significant feature of his reign, however, was a further decline in the papacy's inter-

national standing. The Catholic powers increasingly either ignored the Pope or forced him to accept what he was powerless to refuse. When Charles, the son of Elizabeth Farnese, Queen of Spain, inherited Parma and Piacenza, the issue of feudal rights rose again. Spain wanted the Pope to invest him but the Emperor Charles VI also claimed the right to invest and had the two duchies occupied for Charles. The Pope's protests were ignored. Equally, when under the cover of the War of the Polish Succession, Spain, France and Piedmont agreed to dispossess the Emperor of his Italian dominions and a war resulted

Above: Clement XII *is portrayed with his nephew, and closest adviser, Cardinal Neri Corsini. Although blind, he clearly discerned the peculation of Coscia and his associates, and suppressed them. He was the first Pope to condemn Freemasonry, then a growing cult.*

in Italy, which lead to a considerable shift in the balance of power there. The Pope was ignored, and his territories were crossed by foreign armies, who freely recruited among the Pope's subjects. In 1736 Spain and Naples broke off diplomatic relations and the Pope could restore them only by making large concessions.

More happily, in Rome the Pope used his family's wealth and lottery money to embellish the city. Major works included the Museum of Antique Sculptures, the main facade of St John Lateran and the Andrea Corsini Chapel within it. The Piazza Di Trevi was laid out and, to the continuing joy of tourists, the Trevi Fountain constructed.

Below: The Piazza di Trevi, with its famous fountain designed by Nicola Salvi, is one of several magnificent baroque monuments endowed for the embellishment of Rome by Clement XII. It has become a tradition for visitors to the city to throw a coin into the Trevi fountain and make a wish.

BENEDICT XIV

(Born 1675; elected 17 August 1740; died May 1758)

His surprize election was a last-minute compromise after the longest conclave of modern times (six months, during which four cardinals died). He had previously been noted as a canon lawyer and the author of a classic treatise on canonizations.

He was the only Pope of real intellectual distinction in the eighteenth century and the most attractive personality among them, noted for his urbanity, sympathy and wit. He had outstanding literary and conversational skills and he was very approachable, a virtue sometimes exploited as he was not always a good judge of character.

He was interested in literature and history, encouraged education and research in the arts, sciences and medicine, preserved the artistic treasures of Rome, inaugurated the catalog of the manuscripts in the Vatican Library, acquired the largest private collection of books in Rome (the Ottoboniana), published an improved edition of the Index (based on more enlightened criteria), encouraged agriculture and trade, improved the papal finances, and tried strenuously to improve the quality of the clergy. In the age of the Enlightenment he was that rarity among Popes, a seemingly "enlightened" ruler. Although he too denounced Freemasonry and condemned some "enlightened" works (e.g. Montesquieu's *Esprit des Lois*), he was respected by such diverse figures as Frederick the Great, Hume, Horace Walpole (who described him as "a priest without insolence or interest, a prince without favorites, a Pope without nephews") and Voltaire, who corresponded with Benedict, accepted two gold medals and dedicated his drama *Mahomet* to him. A remarkable feat for a Pope! Perhaps his reputed coolness toward the Jesuits helped him gain popularity.

In his international dealings he was inclined by preference and conviction to be conciliatory, recognizing realistically that the decline of the papacy's already weak authority would only be accelerated by intransigence ("I prefer to let the thunders of the Vatican rest"). Yet conciliation merely masked further loss of power. Thus he surrendered practically all Spanish church appointments to the Crown and met John V of Portugal's demands for control of the Portuguese Church. During the war of the Austrian succession (1740-48) the papacy was helpless. All benefices in Austria were sequestered after

Above: Benedict XIV, *generally thought to be the most intelligent and sympathetic of eighteenth century Popes, is seen here with one of his cardinals.*

Right: The Vatican Library. *Benedict XIV inaugurated the catalog of its manuscript collection. He also revized the Index of forbidden books.*

Benedict annoyed Maria Theresa by only belatedly recognizing her hereditary right and then recognizing Charles Albert of Bavaria as Emperor. Spanish and Austrian troops turned the Papal States into a battleground, ignoring papal protests. At the Peace of Aix La Chapelle (1748) Parma and Piacenza were again disposed of without reference to the Pope, his protest being merely noted. By the end of Benedict XIV's reign, despite his personal reputation, the papacy's authority and power had fallen yet lower and under his successors, notably Clement XIV and Pius VI, worse was to come.

CLEMENT XIII
(Born 1693; elected 6 July 1758; died 2 February 1769)

The most favored candidate in 1758, Cavalchini, was vetoed by France and the cardinals opted for a pro-Jesuit candidate who was not in the mold of Benedict XIV.

The new Pope had been a strict and devoted bishop and his concern for public morality continued in Rome. He ordered nude statues and paintings, including Michelangelo's fresco of the Last Judgement in the Sistine Chapel, to be strategically covered. Yet he was a patron of learning and the arts and the Villa Albani and the Trevi fountain were completed in his reign.

Below: Clement XIII, *a stern moralist, resisted pressure from the Catholic powers to suppress the Jesuits, whom they considered over-powerful.*

He was not a friend of the "Enlightenment" and put some key works on the Index. Though his temper was mild, he felt obliged to uphold papal rights uncompromisingly and condemned Febronianism in Germany, a movement which asserted that the Pope was fallible, subordinate to the whole Church and susceptible to appeals to a general council against his decisions; furthermore, that the authority of the Church should be exercized in each nation by its own bishops.

During this pontificate and the next the Jesuits came under a concerted attack by the Catholic monarchs. Attacks on the Jesuits were nothing new; their very success had made them enemies. They had been the shock troops of the papacy since the Counter-Reformation, had helped win back whole regions for the Church, had run successful missions in many lands and achieved great prestige through their schools and colleges. They had become the confessors, educators and advizers of the mighty and won thereby great influence and power, which had been placed at the disposal of Rome. However, they had overreached themselves and won a reputation for intrigue and even dubious moral teaching, such as the rightness in some circumstances of regicide. What was new about the attack in the eighteenth century was its concerted and widespread nature and its persistence. The so-called "enlightened despots", who were intent on consolidating their own authority, did not favor so papal an order as the Jesuits. The men who ruled most Catholic countries regarded papal authority with disfavor and the prevailing intellectual climate of the "Age of Enlightenment" was as hostile to the Jesuits as they to it. In France the *Philosophes* were hostile and Jansenists and the *Parlementaires* awaited an opportunity for revenge. All over Catholic Europe events were moving toward a crisis.

The first blow came in Portugal, where Pombal blamed the Jesuits for Portugal's decline. Only state absolutism could restore the position and the Jesuits stood in the way. Hence they were accused of crimes ranging from illegal trading, usurpation of the royal prerogative and incitement to revolt in Paraguay to the attempted murder of the king. In 1759 the Jesuits were expelled and their property seized. In 1764 they were expelled from France, where the financial embarrassment of Fr. Lavalette, who had become involved in a failed commercial venture in Martinique, led to an investigation. In Spain the chief minister, Aranda, who disliked the Jesuits intensely, persuaded the pious King Charles III, that they were disloyal and had plotted his assasination. In February 1767 with great secrecy and dramatic speed the order was suppressed throughout the Spanish Empire. In Italy, Naples and Parma-Piacenza followed suit in November 1767 and February 1768 respectively.

Clement XIII reaffirmed support for the Jesuits in the bull *Apostolicum Pascendi* in 1765 but to no effect. In Parma he annulled decrees which violated Church rights and imposed the censures of the Maundy Thursday bull *In Coena Domini* on those responsible. All the Bourbon courts protested and when the Pope refused to cancel the brief, France and Naples occupied the papal enclaves of Avignon, Venaissin, Benevento and Pontecorvo. In January 1769 the Catholic powers requested the total suppression of the Jesuits. Clement had no intention of doing this but died on 2 February.

One of this Pope's acts is of specifically British interest. He created Henry, Duke of York, the last male heir of the house of Stuart and in the eyes of his supporters *de jure* king of Great Britain ("Henry IX"), a cardinal.

CLEMENT XIV
(Born 1705; elected 19 May 1769; died 22nd September 1774)

The conclave was dominated by the Jesuit issue and was a contentious affair determined by the manoevring of the Catholic, especially the Bourbon, powers to obtain a Pope who would meet their demand for suppression of the Jesuits. The successful candidacy of Cardinal Ganganelli was promoted by the Spanish Ambassador. Clement XIV had not promised before the elections to abolish the Jesuits but had indicated that he regarded suppression as canonically possible.

He was a Franciscan who had twice declined the generalship of his order, which had led to not unfounded suggestions that he was a calculating and ambitious man. Previously a friend of the Jesuits, he now distanced himself from them and developed ties with the Bourbon ambassadors.

He was scholarly and cultivated but reserved, suggesting a lack of confidence. He liked to work alone and resisted those who sought influence. He conciliated the Catholic powers by making concessions but they still pressed for abolition of the Jesuits. On Maundy Thursday 1770 he pleased

"enlightened" circles by omitting the usual reading of *In Coena Domini* with its controversial anathemas. Because of his implied promise before election and fearing Jesuit poison, he felt unsure about his position and promised the French and Spanish kings that he would abolish the Jesuits but set no date. He manoevred for three years to gain time, suggesting all sorts of concessions that fell short of abolition, but the powers were adamant and threatened a complete break with Rome. In 1773 the Spanish Ambassador submitted a draft bull of abolition and the last obstacle disappeared when Maria Theresa declared her neutrality in the matter. The Pope gave way and in June 1773 signed the abolition document, *Dominus ac Redemptor Noster*.

The "Enlighted" everywhere rejoiced and applauded the Pope, but papal prestige had suffered its most shattering blow since the time of the Protestant Reformation.

Above: The Sistine Chapel, *where nude figures in the frescoes by Michelangelo and other artists aroused the censure of Clement XIV, who ordered them to be covered.*

Right: Emperor Joseph II of
Germany *sought to limit papal
jurisdiction, control seminaries,
secularize education, abolish censorship,
suppress contemplative orders, and
extend toleration to non-Catholics. Pius
VI traveled to Vienna in a vain
attempt to change his mind.*

Above: Pius VI. *In the earlier part
of his long pontificate, Pius seemed
intent on reviving the style of the
Renaissance Popes. He patronized the
arts, spent lavishly on building projects,
and undertook ambitious economic
programs that bankrupted the Treasury.*

**Right: Napoleon Bonaparte
crossing the Alps;** *an event
stirringly recorded by the Neo-classical
master Jacques Louis David (1748-
1825). Bonaparte forced Pius VI to
cede territory to him, and finally made
him a prisoner.*

The suppression proceeded with varying degrees
of unpleasantness, but ironically the Jesuits managed
to survive in Protestant Prussia and Orthodox Russia
where publication and implementation of the Pope's
decision were forbidden. The motive of Frederick the
Great and Catherine the Great was the maintenance
of the school system in the Catholic parts of their
dominions. Elsewhere Catholic education and missionary work were severely damaged.

France and Naples returned the occupied papal
territories but on humiliating terms. The Pope's
fear of being poisoned by Jesuits increased and he
fell into a depression and soon died. The rapid
decaying of his body suggested poison to the suspicious, but modern research does not support the
thesis. Papal prestige was at its lowest for centuries.

PIUS VI
*(Born 1717; elected 15 February 1775; died
21 August 1799)*

Originally regarded as pro-Jesuit, he had avoided
involvement in recent controversies and after a four-
month conclave he was elected unanimously, beginning one of the longest pontificates.

Because of his later sufferings Pius VI has been
seen as a martyr-Pope, but, although pious and
strong in adversity, he was also rather worldly, vain,
self-consciously handsome, ostentatious and concerned with the minutiae of protocol. He resembled
a Renaissance Pope, a new Leo X, patron of the arts
and lavish builder. He also revived nepotism.

His motives, the welfare of his subjects and
reform and economic improvement were good, but
his schemes of road improvement, port moderniza-
tion and the draining of the Pontine marshes were
often badly conceived and, together with his archi-
tectural program, bankrupted the Treasury and
increased the public debt.

With the powers he tried to be moderate and
flexible, but the age was increasingly secular and
even atheistic; governments in Catholic countries
sought ever greater control of national churches.
The new rulers of Spain, France and Portugal were
more favorably disposed to the papacy, but in
Germany Febronianism flourished and when the
Pope tried to establish a nunciature in Munich, the
German bishops rebuffed him.

In Austria and Tuscany Pius VI was faced by the
archetypal "enlightened despots", Joseph II and his
brother Leopold, who sought to limit papal jurisdiction, control seminaries, secularize education,
abolish censorship, suppress contemplative orders
and tolerate non-Catholics. In 1782 the Pope made
an unprecedented journey to Vienna to dissuade the
Emperor, but failed. To placate the Bourbons, he
tried to persuade Prussia and Russia to suppress the
Jesuits. After 1783-4, however, he gave tacit
approval to Jesuit survival in Eastern Europe.

The greatest challenge faced by this Pope was the
French Revolution. At first he cautiously ignored
the Civil Constitution of the Clergy (1790), which
turned them into civil servants, but when an oath
of loyalty to the new arrangements was demanded,
he condemned them and suspended juring clergy.
He also condemned the "Declaration of the Rights
of Man". The French church split, diplomatic relations were broken and papal enclaves in France
occupied. War broke out and Pius VI supported the
First Coalition against France and sheltered royalist
refugees. By 1796 Bonaparte was in Italy and the
Papal States invaded. A large indemnity was imposed
and the Pope forced to recognize the French Republic.

In 1798 the Papal States were reoccupied, the
Roman Republic proclaimed, and the Pope forced
into exile, eventually in France. At Valence in 1799
he died a prisoner. The eighteenth century papacy
had reached its lowest ebb and many assumed that
it could not survive.

PIUS VII

(Born 14 April 1742; elected 14 March 1800; died 20 July 1823)

Brought up at Cesena, in Emilia, Luigi Barnaba Chiaramonte entered the Benedictine monastery of Santa Maria del Monte in his home town, where he pronounced his vows in 1758. After ordination he was Professor of Theology at Parma, and then from 1775-1781 at San Anselmo in Rome. Consecrated Bishop of Tivoli in 1783, he was translated to Imola and created a cardinal in 1785. His rise through the hierarchy was in part facilitated by the fact that his predecessor as Pope, Pius VI, was also a native of Cesena and a family friend.

Given the circumstances of the Napoleonic wars, the conclave which elected Pius VII was held in Venice. One of the chief organizers of that gathering was Henry, Cardinal Duke of York and the expenses were met by the last Holy Roman Emperor, Francis II. In all thirty-five cardinals attend the conclave which lasted three and a half months. Chiaramonte was a compromise candidate who, upon his election, appointed the brilliant thirty-four-year-old diplomat Ercole Consalvi as Cardinal Secretary of State.

The concordat between Napoleon and the Pope, signed on 16 July 1801, was destined to remain in force for more than a hundred years, despite France's unilateral amendments of 1802, the so-called Organic Articles, which were nothing short of pure Gallicanism. Further amendments followed in 1817, as did concordats with other powers, such as Russia and Prussia, whose articles were almost always to the disadvantage of the Church.

Against the advice of his cardinals, Pius attended Napoleon's coronation as Emperor in Paris, 2 December 1804, where his role was reduced to that of little more than a spectator. The French invasion and annexation of the Papal States in 1808 was yet another humiliation, as was Napoleon's insistence, in 1806, that Consalvi be dismissed from his post. The ineffectiveness of the papal excommunication of the French invaders (Quum memoranda 10 June 1809), was underlined by the Pope's arrest the following month. He was to remain a prisoner for the next five years.

Once finally free of Napoleon, Pius re-appointed Consalvi who, at the Congress of Vienna in 1814, managed to secure the restoration of the Papal States except Avignon and the Comtat Venaissim. In an age dominated by politics, the Pope's religious policy was obscured by the turmoil of war and revolution. He did, however, despite political opposition and a personal background of Jansenism and anti-Jesuit influence, restore the Society of Jesus on 7 August 1814. Henceforth the Jesuits were to become an important influence in the growth of Ultramontanism in the nineteenth century.

A patron of the arts and sciences, Pius's desire to reconcile Catholicism with democracy was inhibited by the restorationist conservative impulses which dominated the closing years of his papacy. However, his desire to grapple with the problems of the Church in the aftermath of the collapse of the ancien regime, and his courage and forbearance in the face of the hardship and humiliations he suffered leave the impression of a great man and a constructive pontificate.

Below: Pius VII. *Pius was elected by a conclave held at Venice. His reign was dominated by the demands of Napoleon Bonaparte, who forced a concordat (later amended, not to the advantage of the papacy) on him in 1801 and held him prisoner from 1809 to 1814.*

LEO XII

(Born 22 August 1760; elected 28 September 1823; died 10 February 1829)

A pious man more interested in religion than politics, Annibale della Genga was, nevertheless, widely

experienced in the diplomatic world before assuming the papal tiara. Though in later life he was deeply ascetic and had a horror of nepotism, it was said of him whilst he was Nuncio in Germany, 1794-1805, that he had no morals, and that he was hopeless in money matters. His family, from the Spoleto region, had been raised to the nobility by Leo XI in 1605, and it was from pietas for that favor that he took the name Leo.

Ordained in 1783 he became a private secretary to Pius VI and was made titular Archbishop of Tyre ten years later. Following a period as Nuncio in Paris in 1814 he was successively Bishop of Sinigaglia and Spoleto and was raised to membership of the College of Cardinals in 1816.

In the 1823 conclave the choice of the conservative cardinals for Pope, Cardinal Severoli, was vetoed by Austria, leaving the way open for Leo's election. He was somewhat reluctant to accept the office because of ill health, and told fellow cardinals that they were electing a corpse.

An instinctive conservative, many of his policies would in subsequent years lead to revolution in the States of the Church. His legate to Bologna,

Cardinal Rivarolo, on a single day, 31 August 1825, condemned some five hundred people to various punishments including imprisonment and death. Leo restored the ghetto for Jews and deprived them of some of their civil rights: even as Vicar of Rome he had compelled Jews to listen to sermons on Saturdays. He further enraged the populace of Rome by restrictions of the sale of wine in taverns as a means of curbing drunkenness.

Although it is often said that he abolished vaccination in the Papal States, his action in this matter was determined by the fact that the previous government had made vaccination a condition for poor relief. Many peasants, distrustful of the procedure, simply did not have their children vaccinated and were denied financial help. Leo, accepting the lesser of two evils, made vaccination optional.

His real contribution as Pope was to encourage a great missionary expansion and to recognize that in South America the old political order could not be restored. He therefore paved the way for the recognition of the emergent Latin American republics and hence from 1827 onwards the regularization of the Church in those lands. In this he

Above: The Coronation of Napoleon in 1804. *Pius VII is no more than a bystander as the French Emperor prepares to assume the crown.*

Below: Leo XII. *Conservative and in poor health, Leo undertook repressive measures which earned him hatred in the Papal State and ridicule elsewhere.*

incurred the wrath of Spain and Portugal. He also set about reorganizing and amalgamating bishoprics in Italy.

Leo was eventually reconciled with his great rival from the previous reign, Cardinal Consalvi, making him Prefect of Propaganda. It was Consalvi's suggestion that the Jubilee of 1825 be summoned, an event which that year attracted ninety-five thousand pilgrims to Rome.

Although well disposed to the French radical Catholic thinker Felicité de Lamennais, he showed no such breadth of vision in his Italian policies. The Papal States under his government became a byword in England and France for oppression and tyranny. He died as one of the most hated Popes in modern history.

PIUS VIII

(Born 20 November 1761; elected 31 March 1829; died 30 November 1830)

Francesco Saverio Castiglioni of Cingoli (Ancona), a canon lawyer, was educated at Osimo, Bologna and Rome and was ordained in 1785. Having been Vicar-General of Anagni and Cingoli he was made Bishop of Montalto in 1800. Imprisoned by Napoleon at Pavia and Mantua from 1808-14 for his refusal to take the oath of loyalty to the Emperor, he became Bishop of Cesena and Cardinal in 1816. By 1821 Pius VII had summoned him to Rome as Grand Penitentiary and made him Cardinal-Bishop of Frascati.

Cingoli, by the standards of the nineteenth century papacy, was a liberal who set about undoing some of the more repressive aspects of his predecessor's regime, such as abolishing the elaborate spy network in the Papal States. He continued to oppose secret societies, freemasonry, religious indifference and condemned Protestant Bible societies. Surprizingly, in one so relatively untainted with corruption, he permitted, for financial considerations, the Duke of Modena to resume the practice of appointing bishops and canons in his territory. His foreign policy was largely determined by his Secretary of State Cardinal Giuseppe Albani, whom he had appointed to propitiate Austria. Albani, a man of little religious interests and never ordained priest, conducted a reactionary policy towards popular democratic movements in Poland and Ireland.

Though Pius VIII was less accommodating to the emergent Latin American republics than Leo

XII, he quickly recognized the new political order in France, established as a result of the July Revolution of 1830 which brought Louis-Philippe to the throne. In doing so he showed that he refused to tie the fortunes of the Church to those of the Bourbon monarchy. He issued a brief on 29 September 1830 commanding the French clergy to obey the new king. His actions incurred the anger of the legitimists among the French bishops, and the hostility of his own Nuncio to Paris Cardinal Aloisio Lambruschini.

The Belgian revolution of August 1830, which separated that country from the Netherlands, was not to his liking. His opposition was partly because of the relatively favorable concordat existing between the Holy See and the Netherlands which had been negotiated with the Dutch Protestant king, William I, and signed in June 1827.

Above: Pius VIII, *a liberal for his time, undid some of the more oppressive measures of Leo XII. To avoid any taint of nepotism, he made all his relatives in the papal government resign their posts.*

Difficulties with Prussia over mixed marriages remained unresolved by the end of Pius's brief reign, but he did manage to secure religious liberties for Armenian Catholics living under the rule of the Sultan of Turkey. He established an Armenian rite archbishopric at Constantinople.

Urbane and clever, widely read in biblical studies, his hobby was the study of numismatics. As Pope he forced all his relatives in the papal government to resign their posts. He initially scrupled to appoint Bernard of Clairvaux a Doctor of the Church because St Bernard was a member of the Chatillion family, a French branch of the Castiglioni clan. Overcoming his qualm of conscience he nominated the saint to the title in 1830.

GREGORY XVI
(Born 18 September 1765; elected 2 February 1831; died 1 June 1864)

The son of a lawyer from Belluno, Bartolomeo Alberto Cappellari entered the Camaldolese monastery of St Michael at Murano, near Venice in 1765, against his parents' wishes. In religious life he took the name Mauro. A man of autocratic temper he had little sympathy for the world around him, and, in time, would demonstrate a hatred of all modernity from railways and gas lighting on the one hand to democratic freedoms on the other.

Following his ordination in 1787 he taught both science and philosophy, and published a book in 1799 upholding papal infallibilty and the need for the independence of the Papal States. He became Abbot of the Monastery of St Gregory in Monte Celio in Rome and was subsequently Procurator-General and Vicar-General of his order. He was an adviser to both Pius VII and Leo XII and consultor to several Roman Congregations including the Holy Office. Having refused a bishopric on two occassions he was nominated a cardinal *in petto* by Leo XII in 1825, who proclaimed the fact on 13 March 1826 and made him Prefect of Propaganda.

Cappellari was elected Pope, whilst still only a priest, in a conclave which lasted fifty days, after the veto had been introduced against Cardinal Giustiniani on behalf of Queen Maria Christina of Spain. As the conclave ended, a revolt in Bologna spread throughout the States of the Church; order was restored only after the intervention of Austria. Further trouble in 1831 once again necessitated Austrian help. France also intervened, occupying

Ancona from 1832-38. By 1836 the Austrian Chancellor, Clemens von Metternich, had forced the Pope to appoint the reactionary Cardinal Lambruschini as Secretary of State, hoping for a stronger line against disorder in the papal territories.

Despite pressure from the powers, Gregory resisted various suggestions for reform of the government of the Papal States, although he did allow greater lay participation at the lower levels of the civil service.

In the papal constitution *Solicitudo Ecclesiarum* (7 August 1831), Gregory outlined the position that the Holy See would recognize *de facto* governments without entering into the question of how such governments came about. Nonetheless, he personally remained a legitimist fearful of the consequences in the Papal States of being seen to give succor to revolutionary governments in foreign lands. Indeed, in the encyclical *Cum Primum* (9 June 1832) he castigated Polish attempts at revolution against Russia. This did not prevent him from rebuking Tsar Nicholas I, when the latter visited Rome in 1845, for Russia's brutality in its government of Poland.

He demonstrated his hostility to Catholic liberals by condemning the idea of civil and political liberty in the bull *Mirari vos* (15 August 1832). When de Lamennais responded with his *Paroles d'un croyant* Gregory retaliated with *Singulari nos* (1834), condeming de Lammenais by name and singling out his support of popular revolution for special opprobrium.

Left: Gregory XVI *was an extreme conservative, professing hatred of material and political innovations. He nevertheless showed sensitivity in his approach to foreign missions, and condemned slavery and the slave trade in an Apostolic letter of December 1839.*

Pope Gregory's government was further disturbed by continuing difficulties in Germany and Switzerland over the question of mixed marriages. There was, however, considerable missionary expansion during his pontificate and he rapidly increased the number of bishops in Latin America. In all he named 195 bishops in missionary lands, showing considerable sensitivity to local conditions. He permitted Catholics in Thailand to participate in public ceremonials which he deemed to be civil rather than religious and hence not incompatible with Christianity. He also condemned slavery and the slave trade which still flourished in many parts of the world, in the Apostolic letter *In Supremo* (3 December 1839).

By the time of his death there were some 2000 political activists either in prison in, or in exile from, the Papal States, and the national debt had risen to in excess of 60,000,000 scudi.

PIUS IX
(Born 13 May 1792; elected 16 June 1846; died 7 February 1878)

Giovanni Maria Mastai-Ferretti – Pio Nono as he was known even in England – reigned longer than any Pope in history and witnessed some of the papacy's greatest triumphs and some of its most devastating set backs. Born in Sinigaglia, on the Adriatic coast, Pius suffered from epilepsy as a child, a condition which prevented him from following his first choice of career: the army. It is said

Left: Pius IX, *universally known as Pio Nono, had the longest reign of any Pope (1846-78). His pontificate saw the eclipse of the papacy's temporal power – but also an astonishing growth in the importance of the papacy in the life of the Church at large.*

that he became a priest at the suggestion of Pius VII who ordained him in 1819. His rudimentary education in Viterbo and Rome scarcely exposed him to the world of arts and sciences beyond normal clerical studies.

Immediately after ordination he was sent to accompany Mgr Muzi on a diplomatic mission to Peru and Chile. His rise through the hierarchy was rapid without being meteoric; he was successively appointed Archbishop of Spoleto (1827), Bishop of Imola (1832), and Cardinal in 1840. By the time he was elected Pope, at the age of fifty-three and after a conclave of only two days, he was a well-known liberal. He had sympathized with the aspirations of Italian nationalists whilst maintaining traditional views on the Papal States.

A month after his election the Pope declared an amnesty for political prisoners and exiles from the papal territories, a move which provoked criticism from the Austrian Chancellor, Metternich. Pius basked in the popularity of his political and social reforms over the next two years which included a consultative assembly, a council of ministers and a full municipal government for Rome. By March 1848 Pius had conceded a full civic constitution for the Papal States for the first time in history.

His reforms were aided by his first secretary of state, the liberal Cardinal Pasquale Gizzi. Freedom of the press was established to a limited extent, rail-ways and gas-lighting were introduced, agricultural and educational reforms were set in place, all of which gave the impression that Pope Pius was among the most forward thinking and innovative rulers in Europe.

By the end of 1848 the situation had completely changed. Pius had refused to support Charles Albert of Savoy's war with Austria, a refusal which enraged Italian nationalist opinion, the papal Prime Minister, Pellergrino Rossi, had been assassinated, the Pope himself was in exile in Gaeta as a result of the revolution in the papal territory and the foundation of the Roman Republic, and he had begun resolutely to set his face against liberalism in any form. In this he was encouraged by yet another Secretary of State, the ultra conservative, and somewhat sinister, Cardinal Giacomo Antonelli.

Restored to Rome, with the aid of the French and Austrians, by April 1850 the Pope's political troubles were far from over. There followed the secularization of Italian life, monasteries and convents were closed and divorce laws were enacted. By 1860 despite the great exertions of the papal Minister for War, Mgr Xavier deMerode, most of the Papal States had been lost to the Italians. Anti-clericalism now became a feature of life in those regions previously under papal government. A further attempt by the Italian army to take the Patrimony of Peter, Rome and its environs, was rebuffed by papal and French troops at

Above: Giuseppe Garibaldi and Victor Emmanuel II of Sardinia *meet in 1860 to discuss the unification of Italy. Victor Emmanuel became the nation's first king in 1861 – and the incorporation of Rome into Italy by the referendum of 1870 ended its papal rule forever.*

· LES GRANDS PONTIFES ·

CRUX DE CRUCE

PIE IX.

PIE IX OUVRE LE CONCILE DU VATICAN.

Édition de la CHOCOLATERIE d'AIGUEBELLE (DRÔME)

Above: The first Vatican Council, 1869-70, is opened by Pius IX. *Here papal authority reached its zenith: a declaration of papal infallibility was carried by 533 votes to 2; 55 bishops absented themselves, but most later acceded to the declaration.*

Mantua in November 1866. France was by this stage the sole guarantor of papal political independence. A substantial body of Italian clerical opinion pleaded with the Pope to recognize the new political realities but Pius responded by issuing the decree *Non expedit* in February 1868 forbidding Catholics from participating in Italian political affairs.

In September 1870, upon the defeat of France in the Franco-Prussian war, the Italian army occupied Rome. The city was incorporated into Italy by referendum thus ending forever papal rule. In the following year the Italian government enacted the Law of Guarantees granting the Pope a pension of 3,255,000 per year and complete freedom as a religious leader. Pius, however, refused such overtures and retreated to a self-imposed "imprisonment" in the Vatican.

Alongside this diminution of secular power must be set the astonishing growth in importance of the papacy in the life of the Church at large. Pius's promulgation of the doctrine of the Immaculate Conception as an article of faith in 1854 was a staging post on the road to Vatican I and the Declaration of Papal Infallibility. The Pope invited the bishops of the world to attend upon him at the canonization of the Japanese martyrs in 1863 and again in 1867 for the eighteenth centenary of the deaths of Saints Peter and Paul. In doing so Pius emphasized the papacy's central role in the spiritual life of Catholics and the dependence of bishops upon the papacy as a focus of unity.

His most infamous encyclical *Quanta Cura* (1864), to which was attached the Syllabus of Errors demonstrated Pius's rejection of modern secularist and liberal ideas. The documents represented the Pope's attempt to assert the primacy of the Church's social and spiritual authority in the face of its collapsing political power.

The first Vatican Council, 1869-70, in which Cardinal Cullen of Dublin, and Archbishop Manning of Westminster had prominent roles, witnessed the zenith of papal authority. The Declaration of Papal Infallibility, of 18 July 1870, was carried by an enormous majority of 533 to two, though more than fifty-five bishops absented themselves from the final vote. Nonetheless almost all absentees found it expedient to declare their belief in the doctrine in the following months.

The closing years of Pius IX's reign were overshadowed by the Kulturkampf in Germany. Here Bismarck tried to restrict the Church's freedom by the expulsion of the Jesuits, the imprisonment of priests and bishops and by the introduction of many petty restrictions. Pius condemned the Kulturkampf with the encyclical *Quod nunquam* (5 February 1875), but it had little effect.

Without doubt Pius was the single most important Pope of the nineteenth century and his failures must not overshadow his many achievements. He negotiated many new concordats with countries as diverse as Russia and Spain. An agreement with the Ottoman Empire facilitated the creation of the Latin Patriarchate of Jerusalem in October 1847. Pius also restored the hierarchy in England (1850), and Holland (1853) and presided over an enormous expansion of the Church in the United Sates and the British Empire. In promoting devotion he canonized an unprecedented number of saints and encouraged veneration of the Sacred Heart. He also established both the *Osservatore Romano* and the Jesuit-run *Civiltà Cattolica*, the latter as an instrument of high papal and ultramontane views.

A man of immense charm, Pius also displayed, at times, great emotional immaturity. As a result of his many political set-backs, which were interpreted in the Catholic Church as attacks upon religion, he became very popular in some circles, and after his death there were calls for his canonization.

LEO XIII

(Born 2 March 1810; elected 20 February 1878; died 20 July 1903)

From a family of the minor aristocracy, Vincenzo Gioacchino Pecci was educated by the Jesuits in Viterbo and at the Roman College, before proceeding to the Academia in Rome for training in the papal diplomatic service. Ordained in 1837 he served as Legate in Benevento, south of Rome, 1838-41 and then as Governor of Perugia 1841-3. An exceptionally ambitious young cleric, he was appointed Nuncio to Belgium and titular Archbishop of Damietta in 1843.

Whilst in Brussels he went on diplomatic forays to London, Paris and Rome, but his time in the diplomatic service was cut short by the fact that he interfered in Belgian politics in a dispute between the government and bishops over education, and was recalled to Rome at the express wish of King Leopold I.

In 1846 he was appointed Bishop of Perugia and his nearly thirty-year tenure in that See helped curb him of his ambition. Although appointed cardinal in December 1853 he was never brought into the centre of papal government. He was distrusted by Cardinal Antonelli, Pius IX's Secretary of State, who

Right: Leo XIII *was less avuncular than his photographic image suggests: he was an aloof, humorless individual who inspired little affection. Personally conservative, he was also pragmatic, and was responsible for the "socialistic" encyclical Rerum novarum (1891).*

Above: The Pope on record. *In 1903, only a few months before his death, Leo XIII speaks words of benediction that will be preserved on the cylinders of an Edison-type phonograph.*

Below: The Vatican archives *are opened to historians, one of the measures taken by Leo XIII to enhance Catholic intellectual life and to encourage biblical scholarship.*

thought him suspect on the question of the Papal States. In 1877, the year after Antonelli's death, Pius made him Camerlengo, the official responsible for administering the affairs of the Church on the death of a Pope. Ironically this office holder traditionally is not elected to the papacy.

It was therefore with a great disregard of tradition that Pecci emerged as Pope on the third ballot in February 1878. Given that he was sixty-eight, the cardinals in the conclave may have thought that his would be a short lived papacy: if so it was a massive miscalculation since he survived until he was ninety-three and gave a new feel if not necessarily a new direction to the papal office in the late nineteenth century. In many ways as conservative as his predecessor, he was, nonetheless, more pragmatic, and the fact that in 1879 he made John Henry Newman a cardinal indicates that he was capable of tolerating a diversity of theological views in a way that would have been quite impossible for Pius IX.

A string of encyclicals on social issues culminating in *Rerum Novarum* (1891) – which was in part inspired by Westminster's Cardinal Manning and Archbishop James Gibbons of Baltimore – sought to gain for the Church some of the ground that had been lost to Socialism and Marxism. Leo also made overtures to the Orthodox and Anglican Churches in an effort to promote Christian unity, although this was to some extent undermined by his condemnation of Anglican priestly orders as invalid in the Bull *Apostolicae Curae* (1896).

With *Aeterna Patris* (1879) he revived the study of Thomism and he enhanced Catholic intellectual life in other areas by opening the Vatican archives to historians, and encouraging Catholic biblical scholarship. He founded the biblical commission in 1902 and approved the foundation of the Biblical Institute in Jerusalem. However his refusal to countenance a reconciliation between modern life and traditional Catholic teaching issued in his condemnation of "Americanism", in 1899.

One of his first acts as Pope was to restore the Catholic hierarchy in Scotland He also established a hierarchy in Japan, appointed bishops to work in Scandinavia and reorganised ecclesiastical government in India and Ceylon.

More adroit politically than Pius IX, he helped settle the controversies over the Kulturkampf in Germany although bizarrely he awarded Bismarck, who had persecuted the Church, the Order of Christ. The growing international rehabilitation of the papacy during his pontificate enabled Leo to arbitrate in a dispute between Spain and Germany over the Caroline Islands, and witnessed visits to the Vatican by the German Kaiser and the King of England. His attempt to negotiate a rapprochement between the Church and France was less successful and relations with Italy remained strained if not explicitly hostile over the question of the Papal States. He also antagonised the Triple Alliance, formed in May 1882 between Germany, Austria and Italy, by trying to encourage an alliance between France and Russia.

An aloof and somewhat cold individual, Leo had none of the humor or playfulness of his predecessor and had few redeeming personal qualities. He was perhaps too keenly conscious of the prerogatives of the papal office to inspire much affection.

St PIUS X

(Born 2 June 1835; elected 4 August 1903; died 20 August 1914)

Beatified in 1951 and canonized in 1954, Giuseppe Melchiorre Sarto was the first Pope to be declared a saint since Pius V. The second of ten children, he was born in Riese, Upper Venetia in Treviso. His mother was a dressmaker and his father a postman. Pius was one of several modern Popes to come from peasant stock and his simplicity of life was in sharp contrast to that of his immediate predecessor.

Despite his obvious goodness – and even Pius's contemporaries remarked on his many saintly qualities – he was a man of much obstinacy and inflexibility and given to pessimism. Not one of the most gifted men to have occupied the throne of Peter, he

· LES GRANDS PONTIFES ·

OUVERTURE DES ARCHIVES DU VATICAN.

LÉON XIII.

Edition de la CHOCOLATERIE d'AIGUEBELLE (DRÔME)

Above: St Peter's *sees the coronation of St Pius X. He was the first Pope to be canonized (1954) since St Pius V.*

Below: St Pius X *sternly condemned "modernist" theology in a series of pronouncements in 1907-10.*

by the experience and Sarto emerged as Pope. The following year Pius issued the constitution *Commissum nobis* (20 January 1904), which abolished the veto of Catholic powers in papal elections.

Pius's first act as Pope was to appoint the thirty-eight year old secretary of the conclave, Merry del Val, his Cardinal Secretary of State. Sarto's election was greeted with some enthusiasm by royalists in France who hoped he would set aside Leo XIII's policy of attempting to reconcile the Church with democratic institutions. In this they were to be disappointed.. His relations with the French government were to prove disastrous for the Church in that country, and the responsibility for this state of affairs must be firmly laid at Merry del Val's door.

Diplomatic relations were broken off the year after Pius's election, and in 1905 France unilaterally abrogated the 1801 concordat with the Holy See, removed Church property from ecclesiastical control and separated the Church from the State. This at least had the benefit that the Church could now appoint bishops free from French government interference. On the other hand Pius perhaps showed himself too tolerant of the reactionary views of Action Française. By contrast he severely restricted the socially innovative work of Marc Sanguier and his group, associated with the Sillon newspaper, and by 1910 had effectively brought it to an end.

The Pope's Italian policy was less confrontational. Although careful to maintain the rights of the Holy See on the question of the former papal territories, Pius did allow Catholics in some circumstances to engage in Italian political activity.

Under the Pope's direction, the Vatican negotiated a concordat with Serbia which was signed on 24 June 1914, four days before the assassination of Archduke Franz Ferdinand in Sarajevo.

Even as Patriarch of Venice, Pius had been disturbed by a growing tendency in the Church among thinkers and theologians to apply modern scientific insights, coupled with historical and literary critical techniques, to Catholic doctrine. Whilst not without social and political implications, it was in the realm of dogma that traditional churchmen perceived the threat from "Modernism" most acutely.

In a series of pronouncements: (*Lamentabili* 3 July 1907, *Pascendi* 8 September 1907, and *Sacrorum antitium* 1 September 1910); Pius condemned Modernism as the "synthesis of all heresies" and forced priests to take an oath against it. Even perfectly respectable intellectuals such as the out-

was neither an intellectual nor possessed of sound judgment. Having received his early education in Castlefranco, he proceeded to the local seminary at Padua in 1850.

Ordained in 1858, Pius was to spend the next seventeen years in direct pastoral work as a curate and parish priest. He then served as Vicar-General and Chancellor of Treviso before being appointed Bishop of Mantua in 1884. An effective and committed pastor, it was his devotion to his diocese that brought him to the attention of the Vatican authorities and he was named Patriarch of Venice and Cardinal in 1893.

The conclave of 1903, which lasted five days (31 July to 4 August), saw the veto introduced against Cardinal Rampolla (Leo XIII's Secretary of State), by Cardinal Puzyna of Cracow, on behalf of his Apostolic Majesty, Franz Joseph, the Emperor of Austria. Despite the protests of many cardinals, including Rampolla himself who was ahead in the voting, the conclave seems to have been unsteadied standing French ecclesiastical historian Louis Duchesne had their writings placed on the Index of forbidden books. From 1907 until the time of Pius's death there was what amounted to a witch-hunt against suspected modernists, which was conducted by the Vatican Undersecretary of State, Mgr Umberto Benigni.

In other areas of the Church's life, however, Pius had more conspicuous success. He urged more frequent reception of Holy Communion, and daily Bible reading, established the commission for the codification of canon law, reformed the Roman Curia, set up the Biblical Institute in Rome and founded the Academy of Church Music. His saintly qualities were not always applied to his government of affairs and his papacy is perhaps one of the most ambivalent of the twentieth century.

Below: Benedict XV. *Although his attempts at mediation in World War I were unsuccessful, Benedict opened a relief office in the Vatican to aid the victims of the conflict.*

BENEDICT XV

(Born 21 November 1854; elected 3 September 1914; died 22 January 1922)

A native of Genoa and an aristocrat, Giacomo della Chiesa had several minor birth defects and walked with a limp all his life. Among the most intelligent of Vatican officials in his day, he was ordained on 21 December 1878. His education was completed at the papal Academy of Diplomacy in Rome where he obtained doctorates in canon law and theology. He had already received a doctorate in civil law from the University of Genoa in 1875.

Following two diplomatic missions to Vienna, he was sent to Spain in 1882 as the secretary to the Nuncio, Mariano Rampolla, whose friendship and patronage were to remain important factors in his future career. When Rampolla was made Secretary of State in 1887, della Chiesa returned with him to Rome where he eventually became Undersecretary of State in 1901.

When Rampolla fell from favor under Pius X, della Chiesa's position at the Vatican became somewhat delicate. His great rival Cardinal Merry del Val became Secretary of State and the hostility between them led to della Chiesa's removal to Bologna as Archbishop in 1907, a move not to his liking as he had hoped to be sent as Nuncio to Spain.

Appointed Cardinal only three months before Pius's death, Benedict was elected on the tenth ballot and, owing to the conditions of war, was crowned without too much pomp three days later in the Sistine Chapel.

His attempts at mediation in World War I came to nothing as he was largely distrusted by all sides, who each in their turn regarded him as partisan. He opened a relief office in the Vatican which aimed to give material assistance to the victims of the war and to reunite separated families. Italian intrigue ensured that the Vatican would not be represented at Versailles, whose Treaty the Pope regarded as a recipe for the perpetuation of war and as a "consecration of hatred".

A man of short temper, who was perhaps too closely associated with Rampolla's cast of mind, Benedict's achievements were, nevertheless, impressive. Reversing the policies of his predecessors, he encouraged Catholic participation in Italian elections, re-established diplomatic relations with France, discouraged right-wing political extremism and took a less strident attitude to modernism. His many reforms included the promulgation of the

Code of Canon Law in 1917, the foundation of the Oriental Institute in Rome and the Congregation for the Oriental Churches. He also insisted on the need for the building up of native clergy in missionary lands. It was Benedict's work which largely paved the way for the regulation of the relationship between the Holy See and the Italian State. He died of an influenza-induced pneumonia following an illness which lasted only three days.

PIUS XI

(Born 31 May 1875; elected 6 February 1922; died 10 February 1939)

Of middle class background from Desio near Milan, Ambrogio Damiano Achille Ratti was an able student who eventually held doctorates in philosophy, theology and canon law from the Gregorian University, Rome. He was ordained in 1879 and appointed to the staff of the Ambrosian Library, Milan and professor at the local diocesan seminary. By 1914 he was prefect of the Vatican library. A noted palaeographer, he was also a keen mountaineer and was the first person to climb the Dufour and Zumstein peaks of Monte Rosa in the Italian Alps.

Possibly because of his linguist abilities, Benedict XV consecrated Ratti as titular Archbishop of Lepanto and sent him on a diplomatic mission to Poland, first as apostolic visitor and then Nuncio, in 1919. It was in Warsaw in 1920 that the future Pope had his first brush with communist insurgents, an episode which was to mark him deeply for the rest of his life. His diplomatic activity was not blessed with success and he was recalled to Italy in 1921 to become Cardinal Archbishop of Milan.

A compromise candidate at the conclave of February 1922 in a strong field which included Cardinals Gasparri, Merry del Val, and La Fontaine, he was elected on the fourteenth ballot. Pius XI immediately signalled a change of approach by giving the *Urbi et Orbi* blessing from the balcony of St Peter's. This was the first time the loggia had been used since Rome fell to the Italians in 1870.

His papacy had in many respects an openness not often seen in papal government. The first Pope to broadcast on radio, he founded the papal Academy of Sciences in 1936, membership of which was open to scientists of all religious persuasions. He sincerely hoped for the reunion of Christendom, but very much on Roman terms. Pius made overtures to the

Eastern Churches as well as encouraging the Malines conversations between Anglicans and Catholics, 1921-6. By 1927 he had condemned Charles Maurras, Leon Daudat and the Action Française movement, which espoused extreme conservative political and religious views in addition to being anti-semitic.

Clear-sightedness about the Church's missionary activity in the underdeveloped world led him, in the face of opposition from Vatican officials, to appoint by 1939 forty indigenous bishops: the number of indigenous clergy had risen to more than 7000 by the end of his reign. He founded Catholic Action in 1922 to strengthen the sense of mission among laypeople.

As might be expected, he upheld traditional Catholic views on abortion, and condemned divorce, mixed marriages and artificial contraception (*Casti connubii*, 1930). On the other hand he emphasized the Church's commitment to a just social order with the encyclical *Quadragesimo anno* (1931). Building as he did on Leo XIII *Rerum novarum*, Pius developed the concept of "subsidiarity", concerning the relationship between the state and individuals, an idea which was subsequently to become important for the European Union.

Some fifteen concordats were negotiated during Pius's papacy, and a more conciliatory approach to the relationship with France helped bridge the estrangement between the Vatican and "the eldest daughter of the Church". The most important agreements were, however, with Mussolini's Italy (1929) and Hitler's Germany (1933). Under the terms of the Lateran Treaty, the Roman Question was finally settled. The Vatican City was founded

Above: Pius XI *regarded atheistic communism as the major threat to the Church. His concordat with Nazi Germany, made in 1933, has been widely and not unfairly criticized as lending respectability to a despicable regime. However, in 1933-36 the Vatican made thirty-four protests against violations of the concordat, and Pius condemned Nazi racial theories in an encyclical in 1937.*

Below: Benito Mussolini *(1883-1945), "Il Duce", the fascist dictator of Italy from 1922. In the Lateran Treaty of 1929, he and Pius XI agreed that the Vatican should become a sovereign state.*

as a sovereign state and the Italian government paid the Holy See 1,750,000,000 lire as compensation for the loss of the States of the Church. In addition, Catholicism was confirmed as the state religion in Italy.

There is no doubt that the concordat with Hitler helped give the Nazi regime a certain respectability in international affairs, and quelled Catholic resistance in Germany to National Socialism. It very quickly became clear that Germany had no intention of abiding by the agreement and between 1933 and 1936 the Vatican sent thirty-four notes of protest against violations of the concordat. Finally, on 14 March 1937, Pius issued the encyclical *Mit brennender Sorge* condemning various aspects of Nazism and in particular its racial theories: the following year he was to declare that "Spiritually, we are all Semites". When Hitler visited Rome in May 1938 Pius snubbed him by going to stay at Castel Gandolfo, the papal summer palace in the Alban hills south of Rome.

None of this is to imply that Pius XI was opposed to Fascism in principle since, for example, he supported Franco in Spain. Undoubtedly he regarded the main threat to the Church as coming from atheistic communism.

A man of simple personal life, he was a strict authoritarian who demanded instant obedience, and found it almost impossible to entrust responsibilities to others.

PIUS XII
(Born 2 March 1876; elected 2 March 1939; died 9 October 1958)

Eugene Pacelli's family had for three generations been members of the Roman "black nobility". His grandfather worked in the secretariat of state under Pius IX, and his father was a well connected Vatican lawyer. Pacelli was the first Roman to be elected Pope since Benedict XIII.

Ordained in 1899, after studies at the Gregorian University and the Sant' Appollinare (now the Lateran University), he joined the secretariat of state in 1901. From 1909-14 he taught ecclesiastical diplomacy at the Vatican Diplomatic Academy. His rise in the hierarchy was rapid. Appointed Assistant Secretary of State in 1911, the following year he was named Pro-secretary and by 1914 was the Secretary of the Congregation for Extraordinary Ecclesiastical Affairs, in effect the unofficial foreign minister.

Consecrated titular Archbishop of Sardes by Benedict XV in 1917, he was sent as Nuncio to Bavaria. In 1920 he was accredited to the German Republic. His years in Germany inspired in him a deep love of all things Teutonic. Recalled to Rome, he was made a cardinal in December 1929 and Secretary of State, in succession to his mentor Cardinal Pietro Gaspari, in February 1930. From that time until 1938 he travelled extensively in the Catholic world and was one of the few Roman cardinals well known outside Italy.

A gifted and intelligent man, the quintessential Vatican diplomat, he was the obvious successor to Pius XI. Elected on his sixty-third birthday in a conclave which lasted a single day, he was the first Secretary of State to succeed to the papacy since Clement XI.

In the months before the war he did all things within his power to avert the cataclysm. With the inevitability of the conflict he secured agreement that Rome should be an open city free from troops and the machinations of war, an agreement that was respected until the German occupation of the city in September 1943.

Despite a declared neutrality, Pope Pius XII was a go-between for the Allies and anti-Hitler elements in Germany from November 1939 until February 1940. Distrusted by the Allies because of his perceived German and Italian sympathies, he was very much opposed to the Casablanca demand (1943) for unconditional German surrender. Many commentators have been severely critical of his failure to condemn unambiguously the Nazi treatment of the Jews. Nonetheless his statements of 24 December 1942 and 2 June 1943 were some sort of an attempt, however feeble, to address the issue of the Holocaust.

The fact that, with the Pope's concurrence, many thousands of Jews were given refuge in convents and monasteries in Rome and that some four million dollars were spent in aiding Jews, does not in itself answer Pius's critics. Pressure from such detractors has forced the Vatican to publish eleven volumes of documents relating to the Holy See's wartime operations in an attempt to exonerate the Pope in his handling of the Jewish question.

Much as in the First World War, the Vatican set up a missing persons office, which dealt with more than ten million enquiries. During the war Pius XII issued two documents that were to have important repercussions in the Catholic theological

Above: Pius XII, *believed by Allied leaders to be sympathetic to the Axis, made great efforts to maintain a neutral attitude during World War II. He has since been fiercely criticized for failing to speak out over the Holocaust.*

world. *Mystic corporis Christi* on the nature of the Church and *Divino afflante Spiritu* (both 1943), which gave recognition to modern exegetical techniques in Scripture studies, held out the possibility of a slightly more liberalized approach to theology than otherwise obtained.

In 1951 the Holy Week liturgy was reformed; this followed *Mediator Dei* (1947) which encouraged greater lay participation in the Mass. In 1957 Pius reduced the length of time required for fasting before reception of Holy Communion, paving the way for the celebration of evening masses.

Always a devotee of the Blessed Virgin, Pius declared 1954 as a Marian year. Four years earlier he exercized papal infallible teaching authority to declare the Assumption of the Virgin an article of faith. In 1950 he also reined in the beginnings of theological liberalism with the encyclical *Humani generis* and set in train a process of silencing some of the Church's foremost theologians.

Something of a conservative reformer, he promoted many non-Italians to the College of Cardinals, and appointed the first non-European as prefect of the Vatican Congregation Propaganda Fide. At a political level he was vehemently anti-communist and in 1949 threatened to excommunicate any Catholic who joined the communist party – a pronouncement afterwards modified. Fear of communism also led to severe restrictions being placed on the Worker Priests movement in France, and to agreements being made with right wing governments in Spain and Portugal.

In poor health for the last four years of his papacy, it is said that he was graced with various mystical experiences. More accessible as Pope than many of his predecessors, Pacelli managed to inspire great warmth and affection on the part of ordinary Catholics who streamed to Rome for his general audiences. Nevertheless he remained an austere and aloof figure with an autocratic disposition. He developed a growing distrust for his subordinates, and for the last fourteen years of his life he was his own Secretary of State.

JOHN XXIII

(Born 25 November 1881; elected 28 October 1958; died 3 June 1963)

The third of thirteen children of peasant farmers, Angelo Giuseppe Roncalli was a native of Sotto il Monte, near Bergamo. Having completed his early

education in Celana, he entered the minor seminary at Bergamo when he was twelve. In 1901 he went to the Roman Seminary, where he was taught Church history by Umberto Benigni, the scourge of Modernists under Pius X. Awarded a doctorate in theology, he was ordained in August 1904.

He began a doctorate in canon law but was summoned back to Bergamo to serve as secretary to the newly appointed Bishop, Giacomo Radini-Tedeschi, a post he was to hold for nine years. During this time he also taught Church history in the diocesan seminary and published several volumes on local history. He also began editing a collection of documents, five volumes in all, relating to St Carlo Borromeo, the sixteenth-century Archbishop of Milan. Work on this project brought him into contact with Achile Ratti, the future Pius XI.

After war service in the medical corps and as a chaplain, he was appointed, in 1921, national director of the Italian branch of the Congretation for the

Above: John XXIII *was so obviously a man of simple and holy goodwill that he was respected worldwide by followers of many religions. His impact on the Church, by his convocation of the Second Vatican Council (1962-63), was great and long-lasting.*

Propagation of the Faith. In 1925 Pius XI co-opted Roncalli into the Vatican diplomatic service, consecrating him Archbishop of Areopolis and dispatching him to Bulgaria as apostolic visitor. By 1934 he had become apostolic delegate to Greece and Turkey. These missions not only gave him wide experience of the Church as a minority in a hostile environment, but also brought him into contact with the Orthodox Churches and the non-Christian world.

During World War II he assisted many refugees from the relative security of his residence in Istanbul, where among his friends he numbered the German ambassador to Turkey, Franz von Papen. His work in Greece was less productive, partly because at times he ministered to the Italian army of occupation, which seemed to the Greeks to confirm his partisanship as a national of one of the Axis powers.

In December 1944 Roncalli was appointed Nuncio to Paris. Of the many problems that initially confronted him none was more fraught than the demand by General de Gaulle that up to thirty-three bishops be sacked because they had collaborated with Marshall Pétain's Vichy regime. As a result of Roncalli's efforts at mediation all but three bishops were permitted to keep their jobs. His position brought him into contact with a large cross-section of French society, and by 1951 he had also been appointed as the Vatican's representative to the UNESCO headquarters in Paris.

His personal charms helped avert several major clashes between Church and state in France, including an argument over state support for Catholic schools. He had a slightly more liberal attitude towards Worker Priests than then prevailed in Rome, but the movement was finally suppressed when Roncalli was Pope, by a decree of 3 July 1959. Nominated a cardinal 12 January 1953, he received the red biretta, and the Legion of Honour, at the Elysée Palace from President Auriol on 15 January. Although expected to take up a job at the Roman Curia he was, in fact, appointed on the same day Patriarch of Venice.

In Venice, Roncalli was a popular and dedicated pastor who responded imaginatively to the growth of the Catholic population of the ancient city. His views were not universally liberal, however, and he was especially suspicious of the more radical tendency within the left-wing of the Italian Christian Democratic party.

A compromise candidate in the conclave of October 1958, following the death of Pius XII, Roncalli was elected on the twelfth ballot, at seventy-seven the oldest man elected to the papal office since Clement XII. He was clearly not intended to be more than a stop gap. It was therefore with astonishment that cardinals listened to a speech he gave on 25 January 1959 in which he announced his intention of convoking an ecumenical council, the aim of which was to renew the Church as it faced the problems of the modern age. He lived to oversee only the first session of the Second Vatican Council, 11 October to 8 December 1962. Much resentment was displayed towards the Roman Curia in that session, since the Curia had tried to guide the Council in a conservative direction. A decisive intervention by John on 21 November steered it in an altogether different course.

In his short pontificate Roncalli also abandoned the sixteenth-century regulation that the College of Cardinals could not number more than seventy: on his death there were ninety cardinals. He approved new regulations for the missal and breviary, and added the name of St Joseph to the canon of the Mass, for some a startling innovation.

His encyclicals and public pronouncements were an odd mixture. They ranged from instructions on the need to retain Latin in schools and seminaries to contributions to the development of Catholic social teaching, *Mater et magistra* (1961), and the famous *Pacem in terris* (1963), addressed to all men of good will on the need for peace, justice and liberty as the aim of society. A committed ecumenist, he established the Vatican secretariat for promoting Christian unity, headed by the Jesuit Cardinal Augustin Bea.

A man of obvious goodness, his simplicity and holiness were an inspiration to a whole generation. It is doubtful that he fully understood the implications for the Church of calling the Council. His characteristic radiant joy and optimism were in enormous contrast to his predecessor. The cause for his canonization, and indeed that of Pius XII, were introduced by Pope Paul VI.

PAUL VI

(Born 26 September 1897; elected 21 June 1963; died 6 August 1978)

Giovanni Battista Montini received his early education from the Jesuits in his native Brescia, in

Above: Paul VI, *enthroned in state, makes a pronouncement. He once refused a cardinal's hat – but now is seen in the papal tiara.*

Right: A blessing from Paul VI *is given to those at a public audience. John XXIII lived to preside only over the opening sessions of Vatican II; it was Paul's task to guide the Council's deliberations on the life and development of the Church.*

Lombardy. One of three children, all boys, his father was a wealthy landowner, with journalistic and political interests, who was a member of the Italian Chamber of Deputies from 1919-26. His mother was a member of the minor nobility.

Owing to ill health, and the circumstances of World War I, Montini was permitted to be an external student at the local diocesan seminary whilst continuing to lodge at home. Ordained in 1920, he went to Rome for further studies at the University of Rome and the Gregorian University. He entered the papal Academy of Diplomacy in 1922 and the following year was sent as an attaché to the nunciature in Warsaw. Recalled because of ill health, he completed his studies and began work in the secretariat of state in 1924.

Intelligent, shrewd and immensely cultured, he was appointed to work with the Catholic student movement, which tried to offer an anti-fascist alternative to Italian youth. His activity for students was carried on in addition to his other responsibilities, which included teaching history to future Vatican diplomats.

In 1937 he was promoted to the post of assistant for the ordinary affairs of the Church and thereby a chief assistant to the Secretary of State, Cardinal Eugene Pacelli, the future Pius XII. He was to retain this position until 1953 when he, along with Mgr Dominic Tardini, was named Pro-secretary of State. It was at this time that both he and Tardini refused the cardinatial red hat. Since it was clear that Pius XII would continue as his own Secretary of State, it is suggested that the two officials chose to remain in place and continue to assist the Pope, rather than become cardinals and move to responsibilities in other Vatican departments.

During the Second World War Montini directed the Vatican's relief effort. In particular he ran the missing persons office, which attempted to reunite families separated by the consequences of war. In 1950 he supervized the Holy Year events in Rome and was largely responsible for the organization of the Marian Year of 1954.

Owing to various complaints about his supposedly liberal theological tendencies, Pius removed Montini from his duties in Rome and in November 1954 dispatched him to Milan as Archbishop. Despite protests from the Milanese, Montini had to wait until 1959 to receive the cardinal's biretta, by then from the hand of Pope John XXIII. His time in Milan was a period of intense pastoral activity, during which he revived the religious life of the diocese and tried to wean workers from communism by promoting Catholic trades union organizations.

He closely collaborated with Pope John on the preparatory work for Vatican II (1962-5), although he spoke only twice in the first session of the Council on the documents concerning the Liturgy and the Church.

Much talked of as the next Pope he was duly elected on the second day of the conclave following John's death. His first task was to confirm the importance of Vatican II in the life and development of the Church. He guided the remaining sessions of the Council with skill and determination. At the same time he showed himself capable of disregarding the Council's judgement, proclaiming the Blessed Virgin as Mother of the Church, a title the fathers of Vatican II had declined to bestow on her. Paul's wide-ranging reforms of the Roman Curia included establishing secretariats for Non-Christians (May 1964) and Non-believers (April 1965). He stipulated that cardinals over eighty would no longer have a role in the government of the Church or in the election of a Pope, and that bishops and priests must retire at seventy-five. This prompted speculation that he might himself abdicate in advanced age, but this was not to be.

Until the advent of John Paul II he was the most widely travelled Pope in history. He made apostolic journeys to the Holy Land (January 1964), during which he had an historic meeting with Patriarch Athenagoras of Constantinople, India (December 1964), the United Nations and New York (October 1965), Fatima (May 1967) Istanbul (July 1967), Geneva and Uganda (1969) and the Far East and Australia (November – December 1970) in the course of which an attempt was made on his life in Manila.

Keenly concerned for Christian unity, he received many Orthodox and Anglican Churchmen at the Vatican and left them with the impression that he regarded them as equals in the sacred ministry. Anxious to advance the status of women in the Church and the world, he also proclaimed St Teresa of Ávila and St Catherine of Siena Doctors of the Church, the first women to be so honored.

His official pronouncements included the acclaimed encyclical on social justice *Populorum progressio* (1967). However, his encyclical *Humanae vitae* (1968), which condemned artificial birth control,

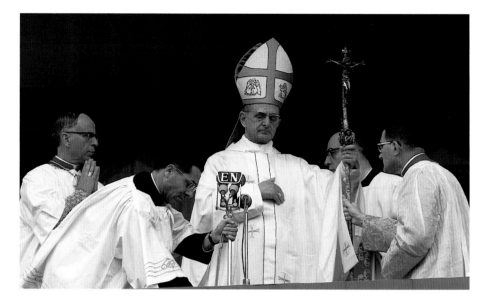

came under sustained and virulent criticism from liberal Catholics. In the face of such hostile reaction Paul lost confidence in his papacy. He never wrote another encyclical.

Temperamentally indecisive, the final years of his reign were filled with much vacillation and anguish. He struggled to keep a sense of his mission as the Catholic Church became increasingly faction torn. His pessimism was compounded by the growth of international terrorism which touched his own life when his friend, and former Italian Prime Minister, Aldo Moro was murdered by the Red Brigade in May 1978.

JOHN PAUL I
(Born 17 October 1912; elected 26 August 1978; died 28 September 1978)

The first Pope to be born in the twentieth century, Albino Luciani was a native of Forno di Canale, renamed Canale d'Agordo in 1964, near Belluno south west of Venice. From a decidedly working class family, his father, Giovanni, whose first wife died leaving him with two young daughters, was a frequent migrant worker in Switzerland and Germany and had something of a reputation as a socialist in his native village.

Luciani attended the local junior and major seminaries, and completed his military service, before his ordination on 7 July 1935. There followed a period of study at the Gregorian University in Rome, where he was eventually awarded a doctorate for his thesis "The Problem of the Origin of the Soul in Rosmini". The intellec-

Above: **Fatima, Portugal,** *where miraculous visions of the Blessed Virgin were seen between 13 May and 13 October 1917, is visited by the future Pope John Paul I. Tradition has it that a prophecy concerning the end of the world, made at that time, may only be communicated to the reigning Pope.*

Below: **John Paul I,** *the first Pope to be born in the twentieth century, came from a humble background. His pastorate as Bishop of Vittorio Veneto was marked by his devotion to the poor, whom he described as the true riches of the Church. His imaginative book* Illustrissimi *became an international bestseller.*

tual influence of Rosmini was pivotal in Luciani's pastoral life. He was especially impressed with *The Five Wounds of the Church* (Rome, 1848) which, among other things, condemned the Church's obsession with material wealth.

After a brief period as a curate Luciani was appointed vice-rector of the seminary in Belluno in 1937, where for the next ten years he taught a variety of subjects including moral theology, canon law and art history. He was steadily promoted through the diocesan hierarchy and by 1948 he became Vicar-General of Belluno. In preparation for a diocesan eucharistic congress in 1949 he organized a series of catechetical courses which resulted in his first book *Crumbs from the Catechism* which went through seven editions. His appointment as Bishop of Vittorio Veneto occurred only fifteen days after the death of his predecessor. The future Pope was personally consecrated by Pope John XXIII on 27 December 1958. His pastorate was marked by devotion to the poor whom he claimed were the true riches of the Church, and by an ability to get on well with everyone in his diocese, including the Communists. During Vatican II he made no direct interventions but is reputed to have read all the preparatory documents. His theological conservatism was manifest in his initial opposition to the draft Declaration on Religious Liberty, but after further consideration of the question he became an enthusiastic supporter.

On 15 December 1969 he was made Patriarch of Venice and five years later, on 5 March 1973, a cardinal. From 1972 until 1975 he was vice-president of the Italian bishops conference. During his time in Venice a more politically conservative approach emerged and he condemned attempts at Catholic-Communist rapprochement. At the same time, he suggested to parish priests that they sell church ornaments and jewels for the benefit of the poor. At the 1971 Synod of Bishops in Rome, which he attended as a nominee of Pope Paul VI, he suggested that the richer churches should give one percent of their annual income to the poor churches of the third world.

During his Patriarchate he hosted two meetings of the Anglican Roman Catholic International Commission and several gatherings of Catholic and Orthodox theologians. It was also during this time that he penned a series of letters on a variety of themes to fictional characters, such as Pinocchio, and authors like Charles Dickens, which issued in the book *Illustrissimi*. The work was later to become an international best seller.

Following the death of Paul VI, Luciani was elected on the first day of the conclave, on the third or fourth ballot, with what seems to have been an overwhelming majority, and amid talk that he was "God's candidate". He immediately dispensed with some of the formalities of the papal office and was inaugurated with the investiture of the pallium rather than being crowned with the traditional tiara. His death, after just thirty-three days in office, marked the shortest reign in the papal office since that of Leo XI in 1605 which had lasted twenty-six days. The failure by Vatican officials initially to give a full account of the circumstance of John Paul's death occasioned accusations that he been murdered, charges which are wholly unsubstantiated.

Above: The inauguration of John Paul I. *His death after only thirty-three days in office, the shortest reign since Leo XI's twenty-six days in 1605, was unexpected. The Vatican's initial failure to give a full account of its circumstances gave rise to wholly unsubstantiated rumors that he had been murdered.*

JOHN PAUL II
(Born 18 May 1920; elected 16 October (1978 -)

From Wadowice, south-west of Krakow, Karol Wojtyla's early life was marked by tragedy. His mother Emilia died when he was seven and his elder brother, Edmund a doctor, died when Karol was thirteen. Brought up by his father, a retired military officer, they moved to Krakow in 1938.

An exceptionally gifted student and a keen sportsman, he began to read Polish language and literature at Jagiellonian University in 1938. During this time he gave free reign to his creative abilities, writing poetry and taking part in amateur dramatics. The German invasion of Poland in 1939 cut short his academic career: the university was forcibly closed by the Nazis, although he continued to study secretly. Forced to engage in manual work from 1940, his life took a different turn following his father's death in 1942.

Entering the clandestine seminary at Cardinal Sapieha's residence in Krakow, he studied for the priesthood and was ordained in 1946. There followed a period of post-graduate study in Rome on St John of the Cross, his thesis being directed by the renowned, and conservative, Dominican Fr Reginald Garrigou-Lagrange. Back in Poland in 1948 he served for a time as a curate and studied for a second doctorate, this time in existentialist philosophy at the Jagiellonian.

For six years he taught ethics at the diocesan seminary in Krakow and at Lublin University, as well as engaging in a full round of direct pastoral activities with students and intellectuals. He was consecrated an auxiliary bishop in 1958, became Archbishop of Krakow in 1963 and then a cardinal in 1967.

From the time of the second Vatican Council (1962-5) he became an important figure in the Church at large. He made several important interventions in the Council debates, particularly on the question of religious liberty, rejecting the notion that "error has no rights" and insisting upon the fundamental liberty of conscience in religious belief. His many travels outside Poland, to the United States, Africa and Australia, brought him face to face with Western materialism which he regarded as being as dangerous to the human spirit as the atheistic communism of the Eastern bloc.

Elected by an overwhelming majority in the second conclave of 1978, he took the name of his pre-decessor with its resonance of continuing the polices of John XXIII and Paul VI. He immediately pledged himself to implement fully the reforms of Vatican II, as properly understood.

The enormous interest aroused in the election of the first non-Italian Pope since Adrian VI, and the first Slav, ensured that his pre-papal works were now translated into numerous languages. In 1994 he published *Crossing the threshold of hope*, which became an international best seller despite its assertion that he saw his role as "convicting the world of sin", a message for the most part unpalatable to contemporary humanity.

His many encyclicals and other writings reflect his concerns for a more just social order, condemning both communism and liberal capitalism, and his hostility to relativist moral and doctrinal opinions within the Catholic Church. In particular he has strongly condemned abortion, homosexual practices, and contraception. In 1995 he issued *Ordinatio Sacerdotalis* making it clear that women could not be ordained to the priesthood. There was some attempt to suggest that this document had about it an "irreformable" character, a code for infallibility, and foreclosing further discussion of the issue.

In the conservative theological ambience which has marked his papacy, some of the better known Catholic theologians have been silenced and one has

Above: Two John Pauls *meet in the Vatican during the brief reign of John Paul I, seen here with Cardinal Karol Wojtyla, an eminent figure in the Church following his contributions to the debates of Vatican II. On John Paul I's sudden death, Cardinal Wojtyla was elected his successor by an overwhelming majority, taking the name John Paul II to signify that he intended, like his immediate predecessor, to continue the policies of John XXIII and Paul VI.*

Left: John Paul II, *the first non-Italian Pope since Adrian VI in 1522, has sternly defended traditional doctrines, but has also placed great emphasis on his relations with other faiths. Here, he is seen addressing a congregation in the Anglican Cathedral of Southwark, London, in May 1982. In 1986 he gathered together representatives of both Christian and non-Christian religions at Assisi to pray for world peace.*

Above: Kissing the tarmac. *This gesture of greeting, suggestive of both thankfulness and humility, has been made by Pope John Paul II on his first arrival in many countries.*

Below: A "People's Pope" *is warmly greeted in St Peter's Square. John Paul II has made the papacy more accessible than at any other time – but his conservative pronouncements on birth control and other aspects of the faith have provoked criticism.*

His many travels as Pope, some seventy journeys to more than 112 countries, have made the papacy more accessible than at any time in history. John Paul has also placed great emphasis on his relations with other religious leaders, summoning both Christians and non-Christians to Assisi in 1986 to pray for world peace. His style is informal, even in encyclicals he uses the first person, and he continues, despite negative publicity, to attract vast crowds to his public celebration of the sacraments both in Rome and abroad. He has done more than any other Pope to expand and internationalize the college of cardinals. The collapse of communism in Eastern Europe during the later 1980s has been credited to his efforts by no less a person than the former leader of the USSR – its executive president from 1990 – Mikhail Gorbachev.

After the attempt on his life on 13 May 1981 by the Turkish gunman Mehmet Ali Agca which left him severely wounded, he attributed his deliverance from death to the intervention of Our Lady of Fatima. The experience confirmed in him a certain apocalyptic disposition in which he sees himself at the vanguard of the battle against the forces of evil, as the Church approaches the dawn of the third millennium. Dogged by ill health in more recent years, he is widely believed to suffer from Parkinson's disease, yet continues to exercize his ministry with enormous assurance and astonishing energy.

been excommunicated. The Jesuit order was taken to task for its overt liberalism, the Pope at one point taking over the government of the Society, and the whole approach of South American "Liberation theology", which attempted to marry Catholic thinking with Marxism, has been undermined. John Paul has also shown himself well disposed to the more right-wing organizations within the Church, such as Opus Dei and Communione e Liberazione. Under his direction the revized code of canon law was promulgated (1983) and a new catechism for the Catholic Church was issued in 1992. He has canonized more saints than any Pope before him.

INDEX

PICTURE CREDITS

The publisher wishes to thank the following organizations and individuals who have helped to illustrate the book, credited here by page number and position. For reasons of space, some references are abbreviated as follows:

AA&A: Ancient Art and Architecture Collection
BAL: Bridgeman Art Library
ETA: ET Archive
MEPL: Mary Evans Picture Library
VAL: Visual Arts Library

1: Galleria Dell' Accademia/BAL; 2/3: Christie's London/BAL; 5: S. Benedetto Malles/ETA; 6: John Heseltine; 7: Peter Abbey/LNS/Camera Press London; 8: Spectrum Colour Library; 9: VAL/Vatican; 10/11: Massimo Siragusa/Katz Pictures; 11: Peter Abbey/LNS/Camera Press London; 12: James Davis Worldwide Photographic Travel Library; 13: Jean-Francois Pin/Katz Pictures; 14-16: Massimo Siragusa/Katz Pictures; 17: John Heseltine; 18/19: Vatican Museums and Galleries/BAL; 20: (top) Museo Correr/VAL, (bottom) City of Bristol Museum and Art Gallery/BAL; 21: Galleria Dell' Accademia/BAL; 22: (top) MEPL, (bottom) Johnny Van Haeften Gallery/BAL; 23: City of York Art Gallery/BAL; 24: (both) MEPL; 25: Estonian Art Museum/BAL; 26: MEPL; 26/27: Louvre/Peter Willi/BAL; 28: (both) MEPL; 29: Hermitage/BAL; 30/31: Chapel of Nicholas V, Vatican/BAL; 30: (bottom) MEPL; 32/33: Galleria Degli Uffizi/BAL, 32: (middle and bottom) AA&A; 33: (bottom) AA&A; 34: (top and bottom) MEPL, (middle) BAL; 35: (top) Chiesa Di S. Francesco/BAL, (middle) BAL, (bottom) AA&A; 36: (top) Musee Des Beaux-Arts, Rouen/Peter Willi/BAL, (bottom) AA&A; 37: (top and bottom) MEPL, (middle) BAL; 38: MEPL; 39: (top) MEPL, (middle, lower middle, bottom) AA&A; 40: Galleria Dell' Accademia/BAL; 41: (all) MEPL; 42: (top) MEPL, (bottom) Louvre/BAL; 43: Richardson and Kailas Icons/BAL; 44/45: Vatican Museums and Galleries/BAL; 45: MEPL; 46: (left) MEPL, (right) AA&A; 47: (left) AA&A, (right) MEPL; 49: Vatican Museums and Galleries/A. Held/VAL; 50: AA&A; 51: (left) AA&A, (right) MEPL; 52: AA&A; 53: AA&A; 54/55: San Vitale Ravenna/ETA; 56/57: Abbey of Monteoliveto Maggiore Siena/ETA; 57: (right) MEPL; 58: MEPL; 59: (left) AA&A, (right) MEPL; 60: (left) VAL, (right) MEPL; 61: (top) MEPL, (bottom) Musee Conde/BAL; 62: Madrid Palais Du Senat/Oronoz/VAL; 63: Sta Giustina Basilica Padua/ETA; 64: (top) AA&A, (bottom) VAL; 65: Palazzo Barberini, Rome/K & B News Foto, Florence/BAL; 66: (top) MEPL, (bottom) AA&A; 67: (left) MEPL, (right) AA&A; 68: MEPL; 69: (left) AA&A, (right) MEPL; 70: (both) MEPL; 71: (top) MEPL, (bottom) A. Held/VAL; 72/73: MEPL; 74: (top and middle) MEPL, (bottom) AA&A; 75: St Benedict Sacro Speco Subiaco/ETA; 76: (top and middle) MEPL, (bottom) AA&A; 77: Percheron/VAL; 78: J. Pole/VAL; 79: (left) National Library Madrid/ETA, (top and bottom right) MEPL; 80: (top) MEPL, (bottom) AA&A; 81: (left) MEPL, (right) AA&A; 82: (top) MEPL, (bottom) Vatican/A. Held/VAL; 84: Musee Goya, Castres/Giraudon/BAL; 85: Cathedral Treasury, Aachen/ETA; 86: (both) MEPL; 87: Musee Goya/BAL; 88: (top) MEPL, (bottom) AA&A; 89: MEPL; 90: MEPL; 91: Lambeth Palace Library/BAL; 93: (top left) Michael Nicholson, (top right and bottom) MEPL; 94/95: AA&A; 96: (top) VAL, (bottom) MEPL; 97-103: MEPL; 104: Herrenchimsee Castle, Germany/ETA; 105-113: MEPL; 114/115: Haghia Sofia, Istanbul/ETA; 116: Michael Nicholson; 117-121: MEPL; 122: (top) MEPL, (bottom) Snark/VAL; 123: (top) Biblioteque Nationale/VAL, (bottom) MEPL; 124: (top) Biblioteque Nationale/VAL, (bottom) Biblioteque Nationale/BAL; 125: (both) MEPL; 126: Church of the Badia/BAL; 127: (both) MEPL; 128: MEPL; 129: Bibli2teque Nationale/BAL; 130: Biblioteque Nationale/BAL; 131: (top) MEPL, (bottom) Museo Correr/BAL; 132: MEPL; 133: (top) Museo Correr/BAL, (bottom) Stadtmuseum Aachen/ETA; 134/135: Palazzo Ducale/BAL; 135: Vatican/VAL; 136: Victoria & Albert Museum/ETA; 137: (both) MEPL; 138: (both) MEPL; 139: AA&A; 140/141: Nimatallah/VAL; 142: Prado/ETA; 143: San Francesco Assisi/BAL; 144: San Francesco Assisi/ETA; 144/145: Musee Conde, Chantilly/Giraudon/BAL; 146: AA&A; 147: San Francesco Assisi/ETA; 148: Museo Tridentino/ETA; 149: Santa Croce Florence/ETA; 150: AA&A; 151: Rome Museum/VAL; 152: Vatican Museums and Galleries/BAL; 153: (top) AA&A, (bottom) MEPL; 154: Cambridge, Corpus Christi/VAL; 155: Louvre/ETA; 156: Michael Nicholson: 157: (top) MEPL, (bottom) AA&A; 158: (top) MEPL, (bottom) Vatican/J. Martin/VAL; 159: (top) Biblioteque Nationale/ETA, (bottom) MEPL; 160: (top) AA&A, (bottom) MEPL; 161: (top) Michael Nicholson, (bottom) MEPL; 162: (both) MEPL; 163: (top) AA&A, (bottom) MEPL; 164: (both) MEPL; 165: Bologna Museo Civico Medioevale/Nimatallah/VAL; 166: (top) AA&A; (bottom) VAL; 167: Museo E Gallerie Nazionali Di Capodimonte/BAL; 168: (top) AA&A, (bottom) VAL; 169: ETA; 170: Musee Capodimonte/VAL; 171: Sevilla Mus Bellas Artes/VAL; 172: Uffizi/ETA: 173-175: MEPL; 176: Louvre/ETA; 177: (top) Michael Nicholson, (bottom) MEPL; 178: (top) AA&A, (bottom) MEPL; 179: National Gallery of Scotland/BAL; 180: Raccolta Bertarelli/ETA; 181: MEPL; 182: Palais Des Papes/BAL; 183: (top) Palais Des Papes/Giraudon/BAL, (bottom) MEPL; 184: Roy Miles Gallery/BAL; 185: MEPL; 186: (top) MEPL, (bottom) Bradford Art Galleries and Museums/BAL; 187: MEPL; 188: MEPL; 189: Faranesi Palace, Rome/VAL; 190: VAL; 191: (top) Palazzo Medici-Riccardi/BAL, (bottom) MEPL; 192: Piccolomini Library/ETA; 193: (top) Siena Cathedral/VAL, (bottom) MEPL; 194: Vatican Museums and Galleries/BAL; 195: MEPL; 196: Vatican Library/VAL; 197: Civicche Racc Verona Castellvecchio/ETA; 198/199: Louvre/ETA; 200: Windsor Castle/ETA; 201: Galleria Degli Uffizi/BAL; 202: (top) Toledo Museum of Art/VAL, (bottom) Weimar, Staatlische K./VAL; 203: Biblioteque Nationale/VAL; 204: (left) Biblioteque Nationale/VAL, (right) MEPL; 205: Galleria Nazionale De Capodimonte/BAL; 206: (top) VAL, (bottom) Church of the Gesu/ETA; 207: (top) Louvre/Giraudon/BAL, (bottom) Farnese Palace/ETA; 208: (top) Farnese Palace/ETA, (bottom) MEPL; 209: Oratorio Dei Crociferi/BAL; 210: (left) MEPL, (right) Orleans, Musee des B.A./J. Pole/VAL; 211: (top left) Prado/ETA, (bottom left) MEPL, (right) London Tate Gallery/VAL; 212: (top) Musee Des Beaux-Arts, Lausanne/VAL, (bottom) MEPL; 213-215: MEPL; 216: (top left) MEPL, (bottom left) Ufizzi/ETA, (right) Paris Sorbonne/Guillot/VAL; 217: VAL; 218: (top) MEPL, (bottom) ADPC/VAL; 219: (top) MEPL, (bottom) Uffizi/ETA; 220: (top) MEPL, (bottom) National Gallery of Hungarian Art/ETA; 221: Prado/BAL; 222: MEPL; 223: Corsini Palace, Rome/Bapier/VAL; 224: ETA; 225: (top) Mus Breschi, Rome/VAL, (bottom) Spectrum Colour Library; 226: New Orleans Museum/VAL; 227: Vatican Museums and Galleries/BAL; 228: (top) Gripsholm Castle/ETA, (bottom) MEPL; 229: Schloss Charlottenburg/BAL; 230: Louvre/VAL; 231: (top) Louvre/Giraudon/BAL, (bottom) MEPL; 232: Queretaro Museum/ETA; 233: MEPL; 234: Roudnice Lobkowicz Collection/BAL; 235: Palazzo Pubblico Siena/BAL; 236: VAL; 237: Biblioteque Nationale/VAL; 238: (top) ETA, (bottom) VAL; 239: (top) ETA, (bottom) VAL; 240: Prado/BAL; 241: (top) MEPL, (bottom) IWM/ETA; 242: MEPL; 243: MEPL; 244: VAL; 245: Bavaria Verlag/Spectrum Colour Library; 246: (top) Tim Page/Eye Ubiquitous, (bottom) Michelle Noon/Camera Press London; 247: Hecht Photo Features/Camera Press London; 248: (top) Hecht/Roma/Camera Press London, (bottom) VAL/Universal Pictorial Press; 249: (both) Massimo Siragusa/Katz Pictures.